CULTURAL IDENTITY AND EDUCATIONAL POLICY

Cultural Identity & Educational Policy

**Edited by Colin Brock
and Witold Tulasiewicz**

ST. MARTIN'S PRESS
New York

© 1985 Colin Brock and Witold Tulasiewicz
All rights reserved. For information, write:
St. Martin's Press, Inc., 175 Fifth Avenue,
New York, NY 10010
Printed in Great Britain
First published in the United States of America in 1985

Library of Congress Cataloging in Publication Data
Main entry under title:

Cultural identity and educational policy.

Bibliography: p.
Includes index.
1. Education and state–Addresses, essays, lectures.
2. Educational anthropology–Addresses, essays, lectures.
I. Brock, Colin. II. Tulasiewicz, Witold.
LC71.C85   1985   370.19   85-14359
ISBN 0-312-17849-2

Printed and bound in Great Britain

CONTENTS

CONTRIBUTORS TO THIS VOLUME

Colin Brock is Chairman of the International Education Unit, University of Hull Institute of Education.

Witold F Tulasiewicz who lectures in Education at Cambridge University is a Fellow of Wolfson College, and currently Guest Professor at the University of Mainz.

. . . .

Philip R de Lacey is Reader in Education at the University of Wollongong, New South Wales, and Director of the Project Enrichment of Childhood Pre-School at Boarke, New South Wales.

Erwin H Epstein is Professor of Sociology at the University of Missouri-Rolla, and Fulbright Scholar at the Universidad de Monterrey.

Anthony J Fielding is Senior Lecturer in Education at the University of Wollongong, New South Wales, and visiting lecturer at the University of Lancaster.

Paul Hurst is Lecturer in Education in the Department of Education in Developing Countries, University of London Institute of Education.

Yaacov Iram is Chairman, Educational Foundations at Bar Ilan University, Israel.

Gail P. Kelly is Professor of Education in the Department of Educational Organization, Administration and Policy, State University of New York at Buffalo.

Tetsuya Kobayashi is Dean and Professor of Comparative Education at Kyoto University, Japan.

Nathan Kravetz is Director of the West Coast Office of the John Hopkins University Centre for Talented Youth.

Martin McLean is Lecturer in Comparative Education at the University of London Institute of Education.

Wolfgang Mitter is Professor of Education and Director of the Department of General and Comparative Education at the German Institute for International Educational Research in Frankfurt am Main.

Leonid Novikov is Senior Researcher at the Department of General and Comparative Education at the German Institute for International Educational Research in Frankfurt am Main.

William M Rideout Jr is Professor of Education at the University of Southern California and Consultant to a wide variety of international development agencies.

Elizabeth Sherman Swing is Associate Professor of Education at St Joseph's University, Philadelphia.

Norma Bernstein Tarrow is Professor of Education at the California State University Long Beach, and Chairman, Department of Human Development.

ACKNOWLEDGEMENTS

The editors ackowledge with thanks the collaborative effort of all the contributors to this volume, with several of whom it has been their privilege to have had discussions at conferences and lectures about cultural identity problems in a number of countries.

In particular they wish to thank Professor Emeritus William W. (Bill) Brickman of Philadelphia University for his early advice and help with finding two collaborators to this volume. The editors thanks are due to Bobbie Coe, Shirley Brock and Lore Tulasiewicz for professional assistance and advice.

Colin Brock   Witold Tulasiewicz

THE CONCEPT OF IDENTITY: EDITORS' INTRODUCTION

Colin Brock and Witold Tulasiewicz

It would be inappropriate to attempt a rigid
definition of the term cultural identity in the
title of this volume.
Disciplines using the term: philosophy,
psychology, sociology or anthropology agree in
defining identity as a state of distinctiveness
achieved by an act of separation produced either by
external pressures exercised by a group or
individual upon another with the aim of isolating it
or by a group, society or individual using its own
'forces propres' to conceptualize and arrive at some
unique characteristics. Identities are formed in
selective repudiation or assimilation of
identifications; Kashmiri espousal of secular
democracy before the partition of India
distinguished the state from Jinnah's theocracy, and
gave Kashmir an identifiable characteristic - its
own 'religious' or 'secular' identity. Since an act
of separation involves a contest or agreement,
identity can only be formed in a system of relations
which crystallize into a commitment. Politics -
indeed educational policies - can be used to
further, transform, or destroy a social, cultural or
national identity and does affect groups or
individuals in different levels of scale of change,
which is the main theme running through this volume.
In the fourteen cases selected, politics is used to
obtain practical (material) or expressive
(spiritual) gains. A war or a struggle can be used
for the same purpose as politics. A broadly socio-
anthropological definition of identity affected by
educational policies has been adopted in the
contributions to this volume.
An emerging identity can be manifest in at
least two main ways. It can operate as a quality of
maturity. The carriers of the distinctive feature

1

are ready to proclaim their distinctiveness, their identity preserved by conforming to certain expectations: linguistic or religious, or through decisive events such as wars and treaties. Most of the case studies fall into this category. Identity, however, does not have to be the result of a successfully separating identity after a confrontation. It can spring from an accomodating attitude and result in a shared identity, which is bigger than the original separate ones. A good example of this would be the case of Senegal as portrayed and analyzed by Rideout. Here the French culture has been used as a catalyst to bring out modern Senegalese identity: a symbiosis that appears to be successful in coping with the post-colonial context. In such cases some of the individual parts may not endure, because a desire to strengthen links can result in an alliance of identities where one changed part affects the integrity of the the rest. For example, the linguistic identity of individual Soviet Union republics is changed by a common Soviet cultural identity, deliberately encouraged by a collusion between the dominant Soviet partner and the individual republican ones, ultimately resulting in loss of minority language. This theme is examined in depth by Mitter and Novikov in respect of the control of social processes in the USSR. They concur in general with this position but succeed also in producing evidence of increased linguistic and cultural identity in some minorities through resistance to such pressures from the centre.

Collective identity springs from a dialectic between an existing demographic, economic, cultural, or political reality and a separating force. Different media may be used in the formation processes: linguistic for spontaneous contact, religious for ritualizing it, with social forms underlying its structure. The policies examined in the individual contributions to this volume show evidence of all of these, although language is the most frequent example and proves its strength as an identifying element. Yet the relationship between culture and language is not absolute. There are examples included in this volume where, either the distinctive language is not spoken by all who adhere to the culture, such as the Basque region of Spain, where present cultural and political revival has been carefully analyzed by Tarrow or where other cultural identifiers are predominant as in the case of Black Americans, and some of the ethnic

2

minorities in the United Kingdom examined by McLean
in respect of their initiatives in safeguarding
their various identities and interests.

The dialectic process is responsible for
identity being qualified by an adjective, as in this
recent quotation from The Guardian: "Romanian
'national identity' maintains a political
independence vis a vis its communist partners'
Warsaw Pact policies". Political, national identity
signals a country's 'official' or governmental
stance. Geographical identity by contrast
underlines the situational distinctiveness of a
territory, relative to others. This is a
comparative matter, as for example in the case of
minorities as between different countries, or the
geographical and ecological identity of small
tropical island states within groups such as in the
South Pacific, Indian Ocean and Caribbean zones.
The chapter on Grenada is largely concerned with an
attempt to create inter alia a new attitude to
insularity: one that charges a reformed system of
education with the fostering of a new identity both
individually and collectively.

Cultural identity is achieved by access to the
elements of culture of a national or ethnic group.
The cultural identity of the group is kept up by
constant reference to the reservoir of its culture.
The term culture itself, taken to mean more than the
cultivation of the mind, is applied to a system
which informs the whole social activity of a nation,
people or group. In comparative anthropology,
cultural identity is used to designate a distinctive
way of life - a lived culture within political,
economic or more specific educational and social
structures. Culture is thus a major element of
social order itself, it does not derive from it. [1]
The term cultural identity in this volume has been
taken to refer to such a pattern of life. It
pertains to norms, values, attitudes and policies,
rather than to a restricted meaning such as when
applied to certain prestigious artistic,
intellectual activities only. In both cases,
however, it is the material and spiritual
manifestation of a pattern in society. In an
ideational sense, confined to the factors guiding
human efforts rather than the efforts themselves, it
is a way of structuring experience and the
perception of it, a cognitive system of knowledge
and belief which determines the way in which norms
and values are taken up, attitudes and behaviour
exercised. [2] This too has not been restricted to

3

the artistic intellectual segment, and no
contribution in this volume deals exclusively with
the position of the intellectual, the artist or the
production of art, although the chapter on the GDR
interprets a work of fiction.

In abstract terms, cultural identity is the
internalized cultural consciousness - an
identification with a distinct concept of reality,
accepted by virtue of participation in it. [3] Like
national identity, it is born of a common heritage,
a sense of oneselfness condensed in organizational
structures, for example of church and state, the
emergence of an intelligensia, the formation of a
school system or pursuit of cultural activities as
shown by Swing in the case of the Puerto Ricans in
New York and some other major cities in the USA.
Partly through the mechanisms of positive
discrimination operating in the USA there seems to
have been a reaffirmation of identity within this
group, though perhaps distinctive in strict
comparison with Puerto Rico itself. Nonetheless,
within cultural identity, the social structure and
individual relations, art, religion assume
substance, meaning and form, [4] and so cultural
identity can be projected into the political field
or indeed into political identity. This is perhaps
most clearly exhibited in the case of the
Aboriginals of Australia, examined by de Lacey and
Fielding, where the special cultural distinctiveness
is being used as a lever for wringing political and
economic rather than cultural identity concessions.

Cultural identity and nationalism, the reaction
of communities or groups upon each other, with
certain patterns of identity being selected as
criteria for the creation of an independent
existence or distinct political nationhood, are
linked. The elements recognized as entitled to an
independent existence such as language, religion,
history, artefacts or symbols, fields of activity,
each have a distinctive importance for raising a
sense of a particular cultural and national
identity. Selected indicators show up clearly in
the contributions to this volume on the Black
Americans' fields of activity and the Jews of
Israel, by Kravetz and Iram respectively. Why some
elements are chosen in preference to others, as
suitable vehicles for separate political identity
depends on various compounds of factors, such as
successful alliances forged to bring about the
desired result. This is particularly well
illustrated by the case of Israel, where the

Ashkenazim and Sephardim have had to cooperate in developing and maintaining the state despite widely different cultural origins found even within each of these major groups. It is not always the historically given cultural identities which determine the new national political identity but a conscious selection is made of available identifiable realities by those actively promoting an identity as in the choice of Marxism-Leninism in the GDR, albeit in a context of some pressure from the USSR. In this case, various additional selections have been made from the German and Soviet cultural inheritance available to those formulating the identity of this relatively new country, competing with alternative German, European and Anglo-American inheritance.

Political identity is coeval with political organization, while cultural identity may lie athwart political boundaries, although the dominant political organization may help foster or indeed damage it. Both draw on linguistic, religious, 'customs', or an amalgam of these factors but must also include successive layers of common historical and social experiences to reinforce identity. Of the two, cultural identity is more enduring than political, [5] which derives from it, as in the case of newly emerging autonomous regions. In this process however traditional value systems, the relations between people or between them and their environment are shifted, new identities arise in part or in toto, sterile original cultures being renovated, or from among imported values of a dominant alien culture some appropriate ones may be selected and put into circulation. In the Grenadian case, for example, the prime task of the revolutionary regime of 1979-83 was to engender a new national identity based on different assumptions and aspirations in respect of human ecology and economy.

The question of heritage utilization is important, as when the indigenous culture makes a distinct contribution to a new pluralist identity. [6] Here again, Israel is a suitable example, as it is also in respect of the tendency of deliberate attacks on a traditional identity often to strengthen it: striking among the contributions in this respect would be that by Kobayashi on Japan, which shows very clearly how the resilient traditional culture of Japan, while accomodating the demands of modernity has nonetheless emerged from beneath the post war blanket of American tutelage with renewed confidence.

Educational or cultural policies surface when a weaker minority is the upholder of a cultural distinctiveness against the majority. A variant of this is the process of modernization imposed upon an existing traditional identity. It is a feature of both 'progressive' and 'traditional' forces that they can be seen to act to achieve or destroy an identity. Success depends on the strength or existence of a prior identity and a history of maintained unity, for example its coherence, and also its allies in the process of consolidation. The resources available from richer friendly countries may have been crucial in several of the cases treated in this volume, for example, the GDR, Japan and Senegal, among others.

Cultural aggression aims to achieve control of cultural identity. It too can come from within or without; as a consolidating force in economic and political advance. The Eighth Ethnographic Conference [7] in Helsinki used the term cultural imperialism, which it saw as the imposition of a uniform, technologically/economically efficient culture upon a weaker, traditional folkloristic one which in due course it would destroy. In this process it is not the working pattern of lived culture which is being destroyed, new values, religion or even language being imposed – but the pattern for culture, the very code itself, which is being changed. [8] This might be accomplished by friendly missionaries as much as by foreign aggressors or persuasive educationists introducing new ideologies resulting in new patterns for behaviour which in turn produce actual new attitudes and values. New languages, religions or customs may be adopted if they are brought by those economically stronger or more viable, new symbols may be accepted if more effective as for example with the transcription of Polynesian and Soviet languages into the Roman and Cyrillic alphabets respectively. Such changes can result in transforming regionally distinctive identities into common, similar, national ones, individual cultures becoming lost or at least fundamentally changed. Minority regional identities may be seen as threats to the bigger national, 'patriotic' ones; they are then labelled as anti-democratic or non-egalitarian. Missionarism and progressivism, political ideologies, economic efficiency or higher standards are invoked to induce different organizations. Countries achieving a complete change are the best examples of this.

Playing the political realities of the time, invoking any of geographical, linguistic, social historical, legal and religious factors, can effect changes. The distinctive cultural aspect of educational policy effectively consolidates them, such as splitting the Swiss Canton of Jura, with internal 'forces propres'. Resistance to external pressure may be met, however, and the Japanese case after the Second World War, is a most successful example.

Cultural identity is a set of adaptations ranging from ethnicity, through religion, philosophy, social structure, privilege patterns and national consciousness, art and science to domestic practices, myths, games and language patterns acquired in different informal and formal ways, including through educational policies. This diversity makes for the endurance and innovating power of cultural identity. Even in changes affecting an entire nation some cultural areas will be less affected. This is exemplified here by Hurst in respect of the dichotomy of scientific innovation and development and fundamental Islamic movements in a significant number of countries, especially in the Middle East. The author has in this case chosen to take a systematic rather than nationalistic perspective and with reference to the phenomenon in question, clearly illustrates the relative traits of political and cultural identity.

Formal educational policies shift the emphasis away from 'domestic practices identity' to governmental measures; reforms which go to make up a more 'institutionalized cultural identity'. This has been the concern of all the contributions to the present volume. The identities pertaining to traits of language, socio-economic structure, religions and customs are differently affected. They can latch on to existing traditions. For example, the original Basque or German identity can be called upon, or they can combine with new ones, as with the legacy of a former colonial power. They assume a different form again, as illustrated by political moves to secure privilege or advancement. The example here is colonial Vietnam, where as Kelly shows there was a detailed political contest between the French colonial regime and demands from the Vietnamese for certain educational provisions.

The ongoing tensions between forces of change and reaction, or maintenance of the status quo, engendered from both within and without, in respect of the various dimensions of identity, are

7

exemplified in the contributions which interpret
identity in a way typical for their country at the
formative stage in the emergence of social
structures. Language which reflects cultural and
ethnic affiliation and includes values and modes of
perception which are encapsulated within it, is the
most frequently found part of cultural identity and
its maintenance is a political act of supreme
importance. Nonetheless, identity can proceed
without language, as in ethnic music or customs,
also in political and social organizations.
'External' policy pressures such as strong rule from
above and drives for conformity are powerful factors
in making a cultural impact which even a widely
spoken language and customs cannot resist. The case
of the educational policy of Peru in respect of the
substantial minority of Amerindian culture within
that country is taken up by Epstein in his
contribution, and this is in varying degree a
regional phenomenon in Latin America. Yet despite
the overwhelming European and North American
dominance of that region in demographic, political
and linguistic terms, there is a resilience in the
indigenous cultures supported, where available, by
their internal processes of education.

In inviting contributions to this volume and in
arranging the contents for publication, the editors
have had in mind the various facets and dimensions
of the interface between cultural identity and
educational policy that have been outlined in this
introduction. All the contributors have taken the
link between politics and education recently
expounded in a Pergamon publication [9] as firmly
established; in widening the concept of educational
policy they have been able to apply it to a third
constant: that of cultural identity - a
characteristic less strictly 'educational'.

The contributions respectively range across the
spectrum, from the large scale domination of one
culture by another in educational as well as
political terms, to the small but effective
resistance or even emergence of educational
structures supporting the interests of minorities,
whether it be by 'external' policies of positive
discrimination or through minority group
initiatives. The ordering of the contributions in
general ranges across this spectrum, though other
rationales for sequencing have also been involved.
For example, there is an element of chronological
ordering in that we begin with an historic case
study, that of Kelly, where in respect of colonial

Vietnam, the detailed political struggle for educational provision on the part of the indigenous cultural group is examined. We move then to two examples - Senegal (examined by Rideout) and Grenada - where in different ways the attempted transition from colonial to post-colonial is exhibited. The case of Grenada presented by Brock introduces the element of 'new colonialism' that is the involvement of modern world powers in the affairs of emerging nations, and this theme finds some parallel, albeit at a much larger scale in the case of the redevelopment of Japan after 1945 under American auspices and the resilience of the indigenous culture. Superpower influence is also fundamental to the phenomena examined by Mitter, Novikov and Tulasiewicz in respect of aspects of education and identity both within the USSR and in the GDR, the latter much tempered by the original and native Marxist philosophers and a reinterpretation of indigenous heritage not yet complete.

The wider geographical scale continues with Hurst's examination of another major world influence, that of Islam, in respect of the question of identity in a context of tension between socio-economic modernity and technical advance on the one hand, and the rise of fundamentalist Islam on the other. There is in this case a spreading outwards of this trend, from the heart of the Islamic world, whereas in the case of Israel that follows, presented by Iram, we have an example of the creation of a national identity from the coming together of Jewish elements from a wide variety of cultures and former national identities all over the world. So modern Israel is an amalgam of minorities, and this leads us on to a consideration of the issues of cultural identity and education that confront selected minorities elsewhere, whether numerically so or not. The Peruvian Indians, the Basques of Spain and the Aboriginals of Australia presented for this volume by Epstein, Tarrow, de Lacey and Fielding respectively all serve to illustrate the theme in respect of indigenous minorities, as to some extent does the study of Black Americans by Kravetz. For while they identify with external links, the American Blacks are arguably more indigenous than the majority of the white American population. Puerto Ricans in the USA, however, examined by Swing, serve to illustrate the theme from the perspective of more recently settled minorities, and this is also the situation of the minorities in Britain considered by McLean in the final chapter, where he examines the initiatives taken by some of them to establish supplementary schools in British cities and their aims.

Notes and References

1. Williams, Raymond, _Culture_, Fontana, 1981.
2. Keesing, R.M. and F.M., _New perspectives in cultural anthropology_, Holt, Rinehart and Winston, 1971.
3. Kluckhohn, Richard, ed., _Culture and Behaviour_, Collected essays of Clyde Kluckhohn, The Free Press of Glencoe, 1962.
4. Taylor, David and Yapp, Malcolm, eds., _Political Identity in South Asia_, Curzon Press, Humanities Press, 1979.
5. ibid.
6. Sandbacka, Carola, ed., _Cultural imperialism and cultural identity: proceedings of the 8th Conference of Nordic Ethnographers and Anthropologists_. (Transactions of the Finnish Anthropological Society: No 2.) Suomen Antropologinen Seura, 1977.
7. ibid.
8. Keesing, op cit.
9. Murray Thomas, R., ed., _Politics and Education_, Pergamon Press, 1983.

EDUCATIONAL REFORM AND RE-REFORM: POLITICS AND THE
STATE IN COLONIAL VIETNAM*

Gail P. Kelly

Between 1918 and 1926 there were at least three
major educational reforms in colonial Vietnam which
drastically changed the organization, content and
control of schooling. The 1917/1978 Code of Public
Instruction set up a centralized, comprehensive,
unified educational system that taught in French.
By 1926, two reforms later, the schools were
decentralized, the language of instruction changed
to Vietnamese in the first three years of education,
and the school system became class stratified. This
article argues that these educational policy shifts
occurred because, while in colonial Vietnam there
may have been some consensus that educational reform
was desirable, nonetheless consensus broke down once
specific reforms were enacted. Not only did those
who provided the initial consensus for reform reject
the government's educational plans, new oppositional
groups emerged that further eroded the fragile
consensus that had given rise to reform in the first
place. These new oppositional elements, as will be
shown, sprung in some instances from the reform
itself. The erosion of consensus arose not only
from enacted reforms, but also from the social and
political context of Vietnam which was ruled by a
foreign power and was divided by conflicts of region
and class. Throughout the colonial period, power in
the society was bitterly contested. Given the
tensions in the society which could find no
resolution while the French ruled, the colonial

----

* To facilitate printing, the various accents
normally found in the foreign-language terms
utilised here have been omitted. This policy
has been adopted throughout the volume.

11

government had no choice but to reform and re-reform the schools as it sought to consolidate its control over colonial society as French and Vietnamese vied for power and privilege.

In order to illustrate the preceding points, one set of reforms and their reversal in an eight-year period have been selected. The 1917/1918 Code of Public Instruction was the first of the major school reforms of the interwar period; discussion will begin with the political consensus that gave rise to this set of reforms and then turn to details of the reforms and their impact. The development of opposition to the 1917/1918 Code will be traced, as will attempts by the government to control sources of that opposition by re-reforming the schools in 1924 and 1926.

The Fragile Consensus on the Need For School Reform

The colonial government felt a pressing need to bring about school reform in the first decade of the twentieth century, once Vietnam had been fully pacified. It was driven by sets of conflicts between the Vietnamese monarchy and the colonial government; Vietnamese villagers and traditional elites; the newly formed colonial Vietnamese elite; and the French community residing in Vietnam. By 1918 a consensus arose that reform was necessary, but that consensus was fragile. Various constituencies sought reform for divergent reasons. The differences in their motivation account in large part for not only the shape of the 1917/1918 Code of Public Instruction, but also the pressure after 1918 to rescind the newly founded school system.

There is no question that French political authorities perceived the need for educational reform by, if not before, the turn of the twentieth century for the very reason that Vietnam before the French conquest had had a viable national school system. [1] Schooling in the Vietnamese mind was associated with access to power through the mandarinal examination system; it also represented the nation in the village and, through the teachers who were unsuccessful candidates for the Vietnamese civil service, represented the village to the nation. The school, entrenched in rural Vietnam for centuries, had strong associations with national political culture and served also as the locus of oppositional political culture. The backbone of many sectional and class rebellions that characterized Vietnamese history was the village teacher (thay do, giao-su) selected and sustained by

those whom he taught. The armed resistance against
the French was, in large part, mobilized through the
pre-colonial 'Schools of Characters' [2] and that
resistance persisted despite the surrender of the
Monarchy in Hue to the French. [3] The French
significantly labelled Vietnamese warfare against
them in the nineteenth century as the 'scholars'
revolt'. The impetus to found colonial schools
derived from a clear recognition that indigenous
education was a real political threat to French
hegemony. [4]

The Vietnamese monarchy in Hue began to share
France's dim view of traditional schools. The Court
understood full well the scholars' disaffection with
a Vietnamese monarchy that accepted foreign rule and
collaborated with it. The Court wanted to establish
its own control over the schools, thereby
influencing the socialization of future generations
and enabling it to recruit administrators loyal to
the Nguyen dynasty. Yet the Court trod softly
because it feared the support the thay do and giao-
su commanded at the village level. While the Court
wanted to control these teachers, the intention was
not to replace them with individuals who had no
sense of loyalty toward an independent Vietnamese
state. The Co Mat, the Court's high political
council, worked to reform the schools of Annam. [5]
Its efforts, however, were limited. It introduced
instruction in Vietnamese written in Roman script
(traditionally Vietnamese had been written in
Chinese characters) and civic education that
stressed loyalty to the Monarchy. It also
designated some schools by educational levels
(elementary, primary) that seemed logical to the
French. Most of the Court's reforms, however,
centred on elite education that trained the
Monarchy's civil servants, the mandarins. French
language was introduced into the Royal College as
were some notions of modern administrative
techniques.

French political authorities were not
particularly impressed with the Court's efforts at
reform, since village schools were left in most
respects as they always had been, in the hands of
the thay do who, according to French school
inspectors, were dirty, ignorant men, teaching in
unsanitary hovels, hostile to the French, if not to
the Court of Annam. [6]

Before 1918 the French tried to get the
Monarchy to bring about additional reforms. In most
instances the Council of Ministers refused to

discuss French proposals. As a result, the Court was often faced with a fait accompli, as in the case of the abolition of the triennal examinations which ended the rational recruitment of the Court's administrators. [7] Given French pressure, the Court desired some kind of reform, but one that would revive and redevelop a Vietnamese national school system, not one that would extend French hegemony.

The consensus that reform was needed extended beyond political authorities, both French and Vietnamese; it also had its roots in the French community, the colons residing in the colonial territory, and in newly formed Vietnamese elites. In the major administrative centres, particularly in Hanoi and Saigon, two French lycees had been opened to serve the European community. These schools followed metropolitan curricula and were staffed by teachers on loan from schools in metropolitan France. The prestigious college (later lycee) of the Protectorate in Hanoi, like its counterpart in Saigon, the Lycee Chausseloup Laubat, catered for a Vietnamese as well as a French clientele. Vietnamese children were often admitted as repayment to their parents for services rendered to the colonial government. [8] In the first decades of the twentieth century the pressure on these institutions was intense. As late as 1922 an inspector visiting the lycee in Hanoi was horrified to find that the school had been inundated with Vietnamese, especially after Governor General Van Vollenhoven in 1914 had tried to limit Vietnamese entry. Of the 800 or so students in the school as of 1922, 266 were French, another 113 were Eurasian, while 422 were Vietnamese. [9] The result, according to the 1922 report, was a lowering of educational achievement levels, especially of French students. "The result has been not the Frenchification of Annamites, [10] but the Annamitization of Frenchmen." [11]

The French community's concern with Vietnamese flocking to their schools was not rooted entirely in fears that their own children might be Vietnamized, so much as real fears that their own careers in Indochina might be abruptly terminated while Vietnamese who had similar qualifications, were hired by the government at lower salaries. This concern was well founded, as the colonial government sought to cheapen administrative costs by indigenizing the administration. The government had a clear policy to get rid of a 'European proletariat' and limit Frenchmen to a few supervisory positions. [12] The colons, especially those at the lower levels of administration, were organized in unions and resisted such moves tenaciously. They insisted loudly that Vietnamese should not be given French education [13] and challenged the government to create schools for the natives. They were not especially concerned about what these schools might teach, as long as they were not equivalent to French ones and did not prepare Vietnamese for top level administrative positions.

While the French colon community agitated for the development of native schools, new Vietnamese elites - large landowners of the Mekong Delta, Vietnamese urban white-collar workers and employees - complained bitterly about lack of places for their children in French schools and insisted not only that French education in the colony be expanded, but that scholarships be given as freely to Vietnamese to study in France as they were awarded to French nationals residing in Indochina. [14] These elites insisted on nothing less than the same education as well as the same rights as the French colonizer.

The consensus that school reform was pressing did not arise solely from concern about the political ramifications of Vietnamese indigenous education and the friction between colon and Vietnamese over access to French education. Two other groups made it clear that some sort of government intervention in schooling was in order. Resentment against colonial rule ran deep in Vietnamese society and particularly in Tonkin as Vietnamese anti-colonialists, disillusioned with the Vietnamese monarchy and convinced of the need for the modernization of indigenous education freed from the Court of Annam, sought to open their own schools like the short-lived Dong Kinh (Tonkin) Free School. [15] This school taught a curriculum that tried to synthesize Vietnamese culture and traditions with modern science and western liberal thought. It was heavily involved with self-education movements and the diffusion of literacy in Vietnamese to the masses, with an eye to modernizing them so that they could once again be capable of ruling themselves. French political authorities found the school intolerable and closed it. The French accused the Free School of complicity in tax protests as well as in a movement to refuse to accept newly minted French coins as legal tender. Vietnamese, if left on their own to establish schools, might, like many Chinese self-strengtheners and revolutionaries who formed Western style schools, use education as a means of anti-colonial political action.

The Dong Kinh Free School, regardless of French interpretations of its subversive character, did represent a desire for school reform. Many urban intellectuals as well as rural intelligentsia were disenchanted with Vietnamese educational traditions, but they did not see French education as a viable alternative for their children or their nation. [16] They strove instead, as did the suppressed Free School, for change that would bring both a modern and a Vietnamese national education that could be found in neither the French lycees of Indochina nor in the Court of Annam's neo-traditional schools.

Reform of education then, was on everyone's agenda by the first decades of the twentieth century. The French civil administration, French colons, the Vietnamese monarchy and newly emergent Vietnamese elites all disliked the educational diversity in Indochina and the lack of a clear cut policy that would defend their interests, no matter how contradictory those interests turned out to be. Given this context, one would have thought that Albert Sarraut's 1917/1918 educational reform would have been a welcome change. But it was not, for it was far easier to arrive at consensus that change was needed than to agree on the substance of that change.

The Code of Public Instruction

With a great 'fanfare', Albert Sarraut, the Governor General of Indochina, promulgated a Code of Public Instruction in late December 1917 that instituted a new comprehensive school system that traversed the three Vietnamese states of Annam, Cochinchina, and Tonkin within the colonial artefact of Indochina. The schools the 1918 reform established were to serve 'native', or more precisely, Vietnamese youth who up to that point had diverse educational options open to them.

The school system envisioned by the Code of Public Instruction was to consist of five years of primary education, five years of higher primary and three years of secondary education. [17] Crowning the system was the newly resurrected Indochinese University in Hanoi that housed faculties of Indochinese Studies, Medicine, Pedagogy, Public Works, Veterinary Sciences, Posts and Telegraphs and Pharmacy. [18] The school system was to teach an 'adapted' curriculum using French as the exclusive medium of instruction while emphasizing Vietnamese culture and moral traditions. The orientation of the schools was decidedly vocational. The school system was to be staffed by teachers trained in colonial normal schools, certificated by the state and placed in career ladders. The school system was centralized, with a bureaucracy situated in Hanoi — the Office of Public Instruction — that would commission texts, hire and place teachers, administer degree examinations, keep student records and oversee school inspection. Sarraut, who masterminded the reform, heralded it as removing education from the hands of the politicians. [19] He may have done so for a short while, but in reality scarcely removed the schools from the political arena. As surely as the Code of Public Instruction set up a school system, it also gave rise to more intense political debate about education and greater, rather than less, opposition to government educational policies.

Oppositional Politics

Almost no one was uncritical of the Code of Public Instruction. Colons objected to the fact that the schools taught in the French medium and thereby might cause 'deracination and revolt' as well as permit Vietnamese to gain access to French schools and universities. They were also alarmed that the reforms brought a university to Indochina. Cognacq, the Governor General of Cochinchina who doubled as the first Director of Public Instruction, stated their position concisely: "This country needs no intellectuals." [20]

Vietnamese were unhappy with the Code as well and, as will be shown here, their actions helped make political authorities aware that substantial modification of the 1917/1918 reform was necessary if Vietnamese of any social stratum were to support the newly founded schools. While the very groups between which the government had mediated in the process of devising the Code of Public Instruction found fault with it, groups that had hitherto been relatively silent about educational policy began to exert pressure on the government. Two such groups were the Roman Catholic Church which, prior to the 1917/1918 reforms felt that public education was not its concern, and the professional education bureaucrats whose number and influence expanded markedly as a result of the new policies.

The Vietnamese Monarchy: Resistance and Negotiation

The Vietnamese monarchy in Annam, while it may

have favoured reform that would bind rural peasants
to it and bring the thay do under some semblance of
control, was decidedly unenthusiastic about the
1917/1918 reform. The court simply tried to ignore
the Code of Public Instruction. Technically Annam
was an independent nation. While the Governor
General could promulgate laws for Tonkin and
Cochinchina, the Court of Annam, under treaty
obligations that set up the Protectorate, had to
decree the reform before it could be legally
enforced in the state. The Court simply refused to
enact the 1918 Code of Public Instruction and held
out until 1919 in this stance. The Council of
Ministers between 1914 and 1919 avoided putting the
reforms the French Resident Charles had placed on
their agenda. [21] They argued in private that some
elements of the reform were unacceptable and that
the Monarch, Khai Dinh, had repeatedly made this
clear in conversations with the French. The Council
agreed that teachers needed better training and that
school inspection was a good idea. Neither did it
object to introducing Vietnamese written in the
Roman script into the schools. However, as far as
the Court was concerned, in Annam the masses spoke
Vietnamese and had no need to learn French.
Teaching French as the reform required was simply
out of the question. The Court also objected to the
absence of instruction in the Chinese characters.
The Chinese characters, the Court maintained, were
critical to teaching Vietnamese their duties to
their monarch as well as to each other. Without the
characters, mass education would lose its national
essence. The Council of Ministers did not want to
mandate a reform that would mean the schools of
Annam would teach loyalty to France rather than to
the Vietnamese throne. [22]
     In addition, the Monarchy found the entire
direction of Sarraut's reform not to its liking on
other grounds. The 1917/1918 Code stressed
vocationalism. The Court's concern, however, was in
perpetuating itself and training its administrators.
The reforms made no provision for such training in
Annam. Rather, it had proposed a university with a
faculty of Indochinese Law and Administration in
Hanoi. [23] The Monarchy interpreted this to mean
that the Court would lose complete control over the
education of its own administrators, since they
would be sent outside of Annam and trained to become
French petty civil servants, not Vietnamese
mandarins. In its 1919 meetings the Court held out
for the development of a separate administrative

training school in Annam. Failing that, it proposed
that the Faculty of Law and Administration of the
Indochinese University be moved to Hue where the
Court could superintend training. In exchange for
agreement to promulgate the 1917/1918 Code of Public
Instruction for primary education in Annam, the
Resident Superieur in Annam areed to support the
creation of a law school in Hue, much to the chagrin
of the Governor General in Hanoi. The Resident
presented the Court's case for modification in the
Code as well. The Governor General responded
angrily, sensing quite correctly that such a
development would remove higher education "from the
control of the French authorities". As late as
October 16th 1919, the Emperor Khai Dinh refused to
sign papers that would put the new school law into
effect. He insisted on assurances regarding higher
education, which he got from the Secretary to the
Governor, Monguillot, who agreed to locate the law
school in Hue. Sarraut, on his return to Indochina,
reneged on Monguillot's promises.

While the French may have been able to enforce
the reforms in respect of the Vietnamese Court, they
were not able to get them acted upon. The Court
simply went along with French efforts to upgrade
urban primary schools and the elite college, Quoc-
Hoc, so that these schools serving the traditional
elite, could offer the finest in French medium
education. But the Court made no attempt to move
French medium schools into the rural areas and,
having convinced the French Resident in Hue of the
righteousness of their position, the Resident not
only refused to enforce the Code but agitated
actively for its repeal. In 1922 Pasquier, the then
Resident, wrote an eloquently worded note to the
Governor General in which he maintained that the
Code was inapplicable to Annam; since it was an
independent country, not a French colony. It had a
monarch who must rule as he has through the
centuries. Pasquier wrote:

> Every one requests that their children be
> raised to respect the traditions of the past,
> in adoration for their king and in observance
> of rites and customs. [24]

He threatened the government in Hanoi with dire
consequences if the Code were enforced.

> This is above all a political question. If we
> don't watch out, we will soon see our schools

deserted and clandestine schools opening their
doors. The people will go where the mandarins
tell them to go or, otherwise, confusedly, they
will believe themselves to be responding to a
secret desire of a spirit and go
elsewhere. [25]

There was no way, Pasquier maintained, to
enforce the 1917/1918 Code. The French lacked the
power to do so and the Vietnamese monarchy had
enough influence to mobilize the population against
the French. Worse yet, the population would respond
to "a secret desire of a spirit" and do "God knows
what". In short, to oppose the Court meant quite
clearly that other more insidious forces might be
let loose and create worse political problems.
Pasquier suggested that the government could get
around political controversies that might arise from
revoking the Code in Tonkin and Cochinchina if it
decentralized education. The message from Annam was
very loud, and it was effective, given the power the
Monarchy still retained.
The Vietnamese new elites in Tonkin and Annam
lacked this kind of power, but their reactions to
the Code of Public Instruction were important to the
French, since the schools the Code had created were
destined to serve this particular stratum of
Vietnamese society.

Urban Vietnamese Elites: The Demand for a Stratified
School System
The Vietnamese urban elites greeted the Code of
Public Instruction with mixed feelings. On the one
hand, there was genuine support for the government's
efforts to build a modern mass educational system
which these elites assumed was the major intent of
the reforms. However, the same elites were
initially puzzled and quickly incensed at two
features of the Code. First, if the system was a
mass school system, why was it providing French
medium education? And, if the school system was a
mass system, why was a university re-established?
These issues were raised repeatedly in the
Cochinchinese Colonial Council by members of the
Vietnamese Constitutionalist Party and in the
Chamber of Native Representatives of Tonkin. [26]
In Cochinchina, Vietnamese, particularly
members of the Constitutionalist Party, were by 1920
mounting overt and well organized attacks on the
university. As far as they were concerned, the
French designed the university to produce only

underling clerks and 'ya-yas', not elites or true
national leaders. They labelled the university a
'school of servitude'. [27] Van-The-Hoi, in the
pages of the Constitutionalist newspaper, Echo
Annamite, complained:

> This institution will be only a nursery for
> petty officials. More or less all that will
> become of it, at the price of so many
> praiseworthy efforts, is to furnish local
> industries with foremen and master labourers.
> But the enterprise founded with Vietnamese or
> French capital will never find there engineers
> capable of building a factory or directing one
> under their own capability. [28]

Others were less kind and saw the university as a
plot to keep the Vietnamese wallowing in ignorance
so that they would be more easy to rule. [29]
    The protest against the university was an
attack on the visions of elite education imbedded in
the 1918 Code. The new elites of Tonkin and
Cochinchina claimed that the effect of the Code
would be to deny the Vietnamese an opportunity for
anything more than rudimentary education. They
interpreted the emphasis to be on primary, not post-
primary education despite the re-institution of the
university in Hanoi. On countless occasions the
representative advisory bodies on which Vietnamese
sat, petitioned the government to pay greater
attention to the development of higher primary, and
secondary schooling. If the government was
unwilling to provide such training, they asked that
public budgets subsidize private efforts, though
this request fell on deaf ears. [30] The issue, as
far as they were concerned, was whether Vietnam
would have an educated elite worthy of the name.
    The anxiety about the kind of education future
Vietnamese elites would receive, pervaded criticism
of primary schooling as well. Vietnamese perceived
new primary schools to be second rate. One
publicist summed it up:

> What kind of education do we have? We have
> 'Franco-native' education. What do we mean by
> the epithet 'Franco-native'? It is not a mixed
> education, simultaneously French and native, it
> is only an education sui generis which gives us
> much good and bad of the French. Generally it
> is more bad than good. [31]

Nothing less than metropolitan French education was appropriate to the training of the elite.

It would be a mistake to assume that the new elites of Tonkin and Cochinchina proposed that all Vietnamese be given a French education. Many of the criticisms of the Code centred on primary education, which was assumed to be mass education. Mass education should be in Vietnamese, not French. It should emphasize useful information and introduce new techniques of farming and production. The 1917/1918 Code provided an education that had no utility, and emphasized moral behaviour rather than the diffusion of new technologies which would improve the existence of the peasantry. In short, it was not "modern" education. [32]

The Vietnamese elites called upon the government to reconsider its approach. Instead of a unitary, comprehensive school system serving all Vietnamese, they demanded that a stratified system be established that clearly differentiated between elite and mass education. While it made much protest in the press and passed a good many resolutions, this elite also had the power to boycott the system the French had proposed under the reform. After 1918, Vietnamese pressure on French lycees increased rather than declined, thereby exacerbating tensions between the French residents of Vietnam, the Vietnamese, and the government. [33] Increasingly the landed gentry of Cochinchina and wealthy businessmen sent their sons to metropolitan France to study. [34] Most of the students were following primary and secondary education; very few were enrolled in tertiary institutions. The 1917/1918 reforms were in large part designed to deflect Vietnamese from French schooling but by 1923 it was clear that the opposite had occurred.

While the Vietnamese for whom the Code of Public Instruction was intended found little that was good in it and proceeded to subvert government policy, the very process of reform introduced new opposition groups that helped impel the government to re-evaluate its educational policy. One of these groups was educational bureaucracy which the 1917/1918 Code had created and empowered.

The Pedagogues and the Code

From the turn of the century, metropolitan educationists had had a hand in education in Indochina. These professionals, however, until the 1917/1918 reforms had little independent power. They were in the service of the Residents of Annam

and Tonkin and the Governor of Cochinchina often as
political appointees with almost no staff or budget.
    The 1917/1918 Code and the enabling legislation
that ensued, created a centralized educational
bureaucracy staffed by inspectors who either were
detached from metropolitan cadres or recruited
through civil service examination. [35] They were
given power to open schools, train teachers, award
teachers' certificates, develop curriculum and
texts, set matriculation examinations, and in
general exert pedagogical control over all schools
in Indochina except those attached to metropolitan
France.
    The first Director of Public Instruction was
Cognacq, the extremely controversial Governor
General of Cochinchina. Cognacq, who was a medical
doctor, came to Indochina in the first decade of the
twentieth century from Martinique to direct the
Medical School in Hanoi. During his stint in
Cochinchina as Governor he was implicated in a
series of land frauds, and was particularly hated by
the Cochinchinese Constitutionalist Party for his
maligning of Vietnamese who received French
education. [36] His successors as Director of Public
Instruction were all former metropolitan school
inspectors or Rectors of an Academie. Under the
Director were tiers of school inspectors who had
made a career as education professionals. Their
concern was not necessarily with politics, but
rather with educational standards and learning.
Their referent groups were metropolitan school
inspectors not colonial politicians. In fact,
several, like Lafferanderie, Thalamas and de la
Brosse were placed in their positions without having
had prior experience in Indochina. [37] By 1921 some
of these inspectors were appalled at the low level
of education given in the new schools, where for
example, teachers who could barely speak French were
teaching in a French incomprehensible even to the
educationists let alone anyone else. [38] The rural
schools lacked materials and furniture. The
teachers not only spoke French badly, but also had
little conception of the task at hand. The reformed
'schools' of Annam and Tonkin barely deserved that
designation. In 1924, Blanchard de la Brosse, a
former Rector of an Academie who became Director of
Public Instruction, pointed out that classes became
vocabulary drills and children learned nothing. [39]
    The school inspectors not only bemoaned the
incompetence of teachers and the deplorable
facilities, they questioned whether financing could

23

be found to rectify the situation. Blanchard de la Brosse pointed out that the solution lay partly in improved teacher training, the production of better school texts, and the development of new facilities. All these took time. In the interim, something had to be done about education.

His views were echoed by Lafferanderie, who spoke for his colleagues when he wrote:

> Taking into account realities in which nine times out of ten, the native child of modest means lives and the fact that he has but a short time to acquire the knowledge indispensible to him, ... the teaching of this knowledge [must] be given in the only language in which he can rapidly acquire it, the mother tongue. [40]

While pedagogues argued for mother tongue instruction on educational grounds, they also warned the government that changes in the Code of Public Instruction had to be made on political grounds as well. Blanchard de la Brosse argued cogently that Vietnamese parents were quite aware of how worthless the schools the reform had established were; for they knew their children learned nothing there. [41] As a result, he claimed, there was slackening of school attendance and the re-emergence of the seditious Schools of Characters. Merlin, Governor General of Indochina, in defending the change in the medium of instruction, from French to Vietnamese in the first three years of schooling, to the Minister of the Colonies, made two charges. First, that the one group of people who wanted the French medium education were profiteers who tried to squeeze money out of the government for textbooks they had written to teach French to Vietnamese. Second, that the only other supporters were French teachers who feared for their jobs in a school system based on Vietnamese, a language they could not speak. Merlin went on to echo de la Brosse's arguments:

> Vietnamese won't learn to be loyal to France unless they understand the benefits of French rule and French ideas, which could only be done on a mass level in the Vietnamese language. [42]

Not only were the educationalists convincing when it came to matters of the medium of instruction, they also expressed concern about the lack of pedagogical control in the educational system. The 1918 reform had established schools, but it had not provided for any real means of ensuring that students were taught the state-prescribed curriculum. There was no way until the end of the five primary grades of exerting such controls, since there were no intermediate level examinations and few resources had been put aside for school inspection. If the government wished to be assured its curriculum was followed, then it could institute a series of examinations administered centrally. The pedagogues proposed that such an examination might be introduced in the form of a grade attainment level diploma at the end of the first three years of schooling. [43]

While the 1918 Code created a centralized bureaucracy of professional educators that exerted power independently and to which the government had to respond, the reform also brought the Catholic Church into deepening conflict with the colonial government.

The Catholic Church: The Challenge to the State's Right to Control Education

The Roman Catholic Diocese of Tonkin had been surprisingly silent about the need to develop an educational policy in a debate that led to the 1917/1918 Code of Public Instruction. It had assumed that whatever the state did was irrelevant to the educational network the Church controlled, which in Vietnam was considerable. It should be noted that only 10 per cent of all Vietnamese were Catholic. However, this Catholic minority was influential inter alia through education. In Tonkin and Cochinchina many Vietnamese civil servants working for the colonial government had been recruited through Catholic schools. [44] By 1920 close to 20,000 students attended Church-run schools. In all, the Church educated at least one-tenth the number of students who went to public schools as late as 1924. [45]

The Roman Catholic Church had been a polarizing force in Vietnamese society for a long time. One excuse for French intervention in Vietnam in the first place was the persecution of Catholics. Many, particularly in Tonkin, lived separately from non-believers in not-so quiet hostility. In several of these villages the Church had opened confessional schools which were greatly resented because priests had tithed villagers for their upkeep. Apparently there was some confusion in Vietnamese minds, which the clergy never sought to clarify, as to whether villagers were being taxed to pay for Catholic schools which were closed to non-Catholics. With the 1917/1918 reforms, villages asked that the government build them secular schools. [46]

In February and March of 1919 the clash between Church and state over the schools became evident. The Bishops of Tonkin and northern Annam lodged an official protest against the Code of Public Instruction. In a letter to the Governor General they claimed the Code undermined Catholic education and intruded upon parents' rights to control their children's religious training. The Code, the Bishops alleged, "contains prescriptions against the Catholic faith," by which they meant that the schools taught Vietnamese moral codes, derived from Confucianism. Most of the school's curriculum, as far as they were concerned, "was irreconcilable with Catholic doctrine." [47] Equally objectionable to them was the fact that priests, unless certificated by the state through secular normal school training, were barred from teaching in public schools, whereas they had been able to do so in the past. Behind the Church's protest was the fear, quite well founded as time would show, that the government would tax villages to construct public schools, thus making it more difficult for the Church to raise funds for their own educational efforts. In 1922 open conflict arose in Ninh-Binh Province where the local clergy enjoined the Catholic residents of three villages not to pay taxes, and by doing so to stop the construction of government schools. They even threatened to excommunicate any Vietnamese who obeyed the civil authorities. Monseigneur Marcou, the Apostolic Vicar of Maritime Tonkin, supported the local clergy. [48] The Church's actions incensed the Governor General as well as education officials and underscored to them the inadequacy of the current school reform to deal with the Church's assertion of authority in matters of education.

Re-Reforming Education

While there may have been some consensus in Vietnam that educational reform was a good idea in 1917, once the reform had been enacted, all consensus broke down, posing in some ways greater challenges to the government than was the case before the Code of Public Instruction had been promulgated. The Code had unexpectedly created new opposition groups and had accomplished little in gaining the support of Vietnamese elites or masses at whom the reforms were directed.

By 1923 it had become apparent that strict enforcement of the Code of Public Instruction would be absolutely disastrous. The Vietnamese monarchy was openly defiant; Vietnamese village 'Schools of Characters' were reopening; new Vietnamese elites were putting additional pressure on French schools in both Europe and Vietnam and colons were becoming angry as their schools became overcrowded; while the Catholic Church was encouraging villagers not to pay taxes. In 1924 the state acted to silence opposition and bring education under its control once again by re-reforming schools. [49] In 1924 the medium of instruction in the first three years of schooling was changed from French to Vietnamese written in the Roman script. This move was meant to placate all but the Catholic Church. The Court was now assured the masses would be educated in their mother tongue; educators that something useful might be learned in the schools; and Vietnamese elites that the government did indeed intend to do something about mass education.

While the 1924 reforms stipulated that the first years of education were to be given in Vietnamese, the rest of schooling, destined for the elites, used French as the language of instruction. The differentiation between Vietnamese medium elementary education as mass schooling and French medium primary education as elite schooling was strengthened in the 1924 reform with the imposition of a diploma examination – the Certificate of Elementary Native Studies (Certificat d'Etudes Elementaires Indigenes) after the third year of schooling, and testing proficiency in Vietnamese administered language and in numeracy. Possession of the diploma was one of the prerequisites for gaining admission to primary education, now the fourth year of schooling.

While the government was willing to distinguish between elite and mass education within a Franco-native system, it was not willing to define French education as appropriate schooling for the Vietnamese elite. In 1924 the government moved to impose restrictions on Vietnamese travel to France for education and, through executive order, encouraged outright discrimination against Vietnamese seeking to attend French lycees in Indochina. In 1924 stiff fees were imposed on Vietnamese in French schools, although these were not levied on French nationals attending the same schools. By 1927 the government directed Vietnamese

to separate institutions, an action which greatly
pleased the French community in Indochina. [50]
     While changes in the language of instruction
and the distinction between mass and elite education
were compromises designed to undercut oppositional
groups, many of the reforms the government
instituted between 1924 and 1926 were directed to
undermine the ability of opposition groups to
challenge the state. The government promulgated a
private school law which outlawed both the 'Schools
of Characters', and Catholic schools which did not
meet government standards and/or did not teach the
state prescribed curriculum. It also imposed
restrictive conditions on private groups wishing to
open new schools. [51] This law effectively
curtailed the Church's interference in education,
for the costs of complying with the private school
code were prohibitive and the Church could not
possibly accommodate the teaching of Confucian moral
doctrines in their schools. The private school law
also gave the state the legal right to close down
the many clandestine schools that had re-emerged in
the countryside. The state may have been willing to
concede the linguistic medium of instruction and the
distinction between mass and elite education, but it
was not likely to relinquish control of education to
the Court of Annam, Vietnamese thay do, or the
Catholic Church.
     The reforms of 1924 and 1926 also reasserted
the primacy of the politicians in educational
matters. While the new laws conceded to
educationists their pedagogical points, they
weakened the professional educators' real power to
make decisions affecting education. The private
school law represented one form of erosion of the
education bureaucracy's power, for only the
political police had the power to decide to shut
down an existing school or to allow a new one to
open. The power of the bureaucracy was undermined
in 1924 as schooling again became decentralized.
Primary and most of post-primary education was taken
out of the hands of the Director of Public
Instruction in Hanoi and dispersed to newly created
Educational Services in each of the states. [52] The
Educational Services were headed by Chiefs appointed
by the Residents of each state; in the case of
Cochinchina by the Governor. Sarraut heralded his
1917/1928 reform as a major step towards taking
education away from the politicians. In the period
1924 and 1926, education was put back in the
politicians' hands if only because political

authorities had learned that professional educators and politicians could not be counted on to see eye to eye. The 1917/1918 reform had created an intolerable situation where the professional educators might have primacy in making decisions that had major political ramifications.

The first re-reforms, those of 1924, were not received with any great enthusiasm. The metropole was taken aback to learn that French had been removed from many of the schools; and the new laws brought much discontent in the countryside as the government finally closed down 1835 clandestine 'Schools of Characters' in Annam and Tonkin. [53] As a result, the thay do began to agitate against the government with the support of irate villagers and the sympathy of some members of the urban elites. By 1926, the government, fearful of the political forces that might be unleashed in the countryside against the state, once again shifted its position relative to indigenous schools. The communal school law enacted in 1926 allowed villages to hire the thay do to teach in locally funded schools; [54] no longer were Vietnamese 'Schools of Characters' considered 'private' schools, instead they were hailed as part of 'native school provision' of the colonial system. As such, they were to teach a state prescribed curriculum to the best of their ability, but not to provide access to the educational system in the colonial federation. Political authorities, over the protests of educational authorities, simply left well enough alone, opting for the principle of state control of education by redefining state control as the absence of overt oppositional political forms located in schools.

The 1926 legislation by no means marked the end of government re-evaluation of its educational policies. Throughout the inter-war years the schools were re-reformed as political authoricies strove to keep the conflicts between politicians and educators, Vietnamese and French, the Vietnamese monarchy and new elites, and elites and peasants under control while keeping power firmly in the hands of the state. The Certificat d'Etudes Elementaires Indigenes of the 1920s was abolished in the 1930s; there was an attempt to transform the communal schools into farm schools in the 1930s; the Chinese characters banned from schools in 1917 were reintroduced in the 1930s; the local control of the 1920s was retracted a decade later in the face of peasant uprisings in Annam and Cochinchina; and the faculties of the Indochinese university rose and fell and were reorganized.

The shifts in educational policy and the seemingly endless chain of revisions, often contradicting one another, reflected not only the many conflicting demands made on the colonial state that lacked any clear resolution under colonial rule, they also mirrored changes in the opposition groups and their power relative to the government and to one another over time. Each time a reform was promulgated, that very reform created its own opposition. This was the case with the 1918 reforms and it remained the case in each subsequent effort as the state strove to maintain its power in a society where the state's legitimacy was deeply contested. [55]

Notes and References

The following abbreviation has been used in the references below:
AOM - Archives National de France, Section Outre Mer
JOIF - Journal Officiel de l'Indochine Francaise

1. Tran-Van-Trai, L'Enseignement traditionnel en An-Nam. Lapagesse, 1942;
Buu Bong, The Confucian Tradition in the History of Vietnamese Education. Unpublished Ph.D. Dissertation, Harvard University, 1958;
Woodside, Alexander, Vietnam and the Chinese Model. Harvard University Press, 1975.
See especially Nguyen Khac Vien, Marxism and Confucianism in Vietnam, in Nyuyen Khac Vien, Tradition and Revolution in Vietnam. Berkeley: Indochina Resource Center, 1974.

2. Schools of Characters, which were widespread in pre-colonial Vietnam, taught Vietnamese written in Chinese characters and stressed Confucian texts and moral precepts. They were the sole route to officialdom, and teachers in these schools were aspirants to the civil service that administered the country before the French conquest.

3. Osborne, Milton, The French Presence in Cochinchina and Cambodia: Rule and Response, 1858-1903. Cornell University Press, 1969.

4. Gourdon a M. le Gouverneur General de l'Indochine, No. 815 G (Confidentiel), Copie No. 888s, 19 Aout, 1908, AOM, Fonds du Gouvernement General 7707;
Note du Gouvernement General de l'Indochine Au Sujet

des Credits Prevus pour l'Enseignement dans le
Projet d'Emprunt, Juin 1911, AOM, Fonds du
Gouvernement General 2579.
   5. Comite de Perfectionnement de
l'Enseignement en Annam. Compte Rendu, Seance du 25
Mai 1907 (Matin). AOM, Fonds du Gouvernement
General 48.091;
Resident Superieur en Annam, Hue, 14 Fevrier 1914 a
M. le Gouverneur General de l'Indochine (Inspection
Conseil de l'Enseignement), Objet: Au Sujet d'un
Projet d'Arrete Portant Reorganisation de
l'Enseignement Franco-Annamite en Annam (Signe
Charles), AOM, Fonds du Gouvernement General 2690;
Conseil du Co Mat, Proces Verbal de la Cinquieme
Seance du Mardi, 12 Aout 1919, AOM, Fonds du
Gouvernement General 51.080.
   6. Gourdon a M. le Gouverneur General de
l'Indochine, No. 815 G, op cit;
Russier, Henri (L'Inspecteur de l'Enseignement en
Indochine), Rapport a M. le Gouverneur General de
l'Indochine, Saigon, 13 Juillet 1915 (Au Sujet d'une
Inspection des Ecoles de l'Annam) No. T. 21, AOM,
Fonds du Gouvernement General 51.079.
   7. No. 243, 1 Mai 1911, Le Resident Superieur
en Annam p. i. a M. le Gouverneur General de
l'Indochine (Saigon) a.s. Institution d'une Ecole
des Hau Bo a Hue, Fonds du Gouvernement General,
51.122;
30 Aout 1917, Le Resident Superieur au Tonkin a M.
le Gouverneur General de l'Indochine, Saigon, No.
448 a.s. Reorganisation de l'Enseignement Indigene,
AOM, Fonds du Gouvernement General 19.091;
No. 580A, Nam-Dinh, le 29 Novembre 1915,
L'Administrateur de 2e Classe, Lt. Tissot, Resident
de France a Nam Dinh a M. le Resident Superieur au
Tonkin, AOM, Fonds du Gouvernement General, 48.043;
Nam Dinh, 1 Octobre 1915, Quelques Apercus sur
l'Enseignement Indigene, Nguyen-Huu Thu, AOM, Fonds
du Gouvernement General 48.043.
   8. 9 Septembre 1914, Van Vollenhoven le
Gouverneur General a M. le Resident Superieur au
Tonkin, No. 1719 a.s. de l'Admission des Eleves
Annamites dans les Ecoles Francaises, AOM, Fonds du
Gouvernement General 51.221.
   9. See especially Rapport a M. le Gouverneur
General de l'Indochine, No. 1.397 G (Inspection
Conseil de l'Enseignement) (24 Octobre 1924), AOM,
Fonds du Gouvernement General 51.221;
Rapport sur l'Enseignement a Distribuer au Lycee de
Hanoi, AOM, Fonds du Resident Superieur du Tonkin, R
24, No. 36.311.

10. The French often referred to Vietnamese as Annamites, which many Vietnamese perceived as insulting, since Annam literally means 'South China'.

11. Rapport sur l'Enseignement a Distribuer au Lycee de Hanoi, AOM, op cit, p 5.

12. No. 804API, Hanoi le 21 Juin 1921, Le Gouverneur General de l'Indochine a M. le Ministre des Colonies a Paris, AOM, Fonds du Gouvernement General, 51.523.

13. See L'Indochine – Le Congres de Perfectionnement de l'Enseignement Indigene. L'Asie Francaise, 10, 115 (Octobre 1910);
Gourdon, H., L'Enseignement des Indigenes en Indochine. Paris: Societe Generale d'Imprimerie et d'Edition Levee, 1910;
Pretre, G., L'Enseignement Indigene en Indochine. L'Asie Francaise, 12, 137 (Aout 1912);
La Session du Conseil de Perfectionnement de l'Enseignement Indigene en Indochine. L'Asie Francaise, 10, 116 (Novembre 1910);
La Ville-Ouverture de la 4e Session du Conseil de Perfectionnement de l'Enseignement Indigene. L'Avenir du Tonkin, 30, 5466 (9 Avril 1913).

14. This kind of demand persisted through the interwar years. For example, see: Voeux concernant l'Enseignement, L'Echo Annamite, 6 (Nouvelle Serie), 421 (30 Octobre 1925);
Quelques-uns des Voeux des Nos Conseillers Coloniaux. L'Echo Annamite, 1, 108 (12 Octobre 1920);
Voeux Formules par la Population Annamite de Vinh Long, 26 Septembre 1931, AOM, Nouveau Fonds, Carton 54, Dossier 632.

15. This discussion of the Tonkin Free School Movement is based on: Vu-Duc-Bang, The Dong Kinh Free School Movement, 1907-1908. In: Vella, Walter ed., Aspects of Vietnamese History. University of Hawaii Press, 1973;
Marr, David, Vietnamese Anticolonialism: 1885-1925. University of California Press, 1971, chapter 4.

16. Marr, David, Vietnamese Tradition on Trial, 1920-1945. University of California Press, 1981.

17. Gouvernement General de l'Indochine Francaise, Code de l'Instruction publique, 21 Decembre 1917 et 1921. Hanoi: Imprimerie D'Extreme Orient, 1921;
Projet de Loi Fixant l'Organisation de l'Instruction Publique aux Colonies, 28 Octobre 1919, AOM, Nouveau Fonds 2259-2223 (1);
Rapport au Gouverneur General Suivi d'Arretes (1)

Portant Modification du Reglement General de l'Instruction Publique, JOIF, 33, 52 (Juin 1921).

18. Legislation concerning higher education: 25 Decembre 1918, Arrete Promulguant le Reglement General de l'Enseignement Superieur en Indochine, JOIF, 31, 5 (1919);
9 Novembre 1921, Arrete Portant Revision du Reglement General de l'Enseignement Superieur, JOIF, 33, 92 (1921).
Among the legislation setting up the faculties are:
15 Octobre 1917, Arrete Creant a Hanoi une Ecole de Droit et d'Administration, JOIF, 30, 25 (1918);
15 Juillet 1918, Arrete Portant Reorganisation de l'Ecole des Travaux Publics, JOIF, 30, 61 (1918).
For greater detail on the history of the University see: Kelly, Gail P., The Myth of Educational Planning: The Case of the Indochinese University. In: Spitzberg, I., Education and the New International Order. Praeger, 1980, pp 93-108.

19. Le Gouverneur General de l'Indochine a Messieurs les Chefs d'Administration Locale, No. 19 bis, Reglementation Generale de l'Instruction Publique en Indochine, Hanoi, 20 Mars 1918 (Signe Albert Sarraut), AOM, Fonds du Gouvernement General, 51.174.

20. Cognacq was quoted repeatedly by southern intellectuals. Nguyen-Phan-Long, L'Instruction de la Jeunesse Annamite. L'Echo Annamite, 3, 362 (1 Aout 1922) p 1;
See also Nguyen-An-Ninh, L'Ideal de la Jeunesse Annamite. La Cloche Felee. 1, 5 (7 Janvier 1924), pp 3,4;
ibid 1, 10 (14 Janvier 1924), p 3.
Hier et Aujourd'hui - Coup d'Oeil sur le Niveau Intellectuel et la Vie Materielle du Peuple Annamite, Avant et Apres la Conquete Francaise. La Cloche Felee, 2 (24 Decembre 1925) p 1;
Nguyen-Phan-Long, Ayons une Veritable Elite. L'Echo Annamite, 5 (Nouvelle Serie); 53 (13 Juin 1924) p 1.

21. No. 280-e, Note Circulaire, Hue, 30 Juillet 1919, Le Resident Superieur, p. i. en Annam a MM. les Residents Chefs de Provence, le Resident Maire de Tourane et les Delegues de Pamrang et Song-Cau, AOM, Fonds du Gouvernement General, 51.080 (This is the final enabling legislation that the Court passed);
Co-Mat-Vien, kinh thu Tru Kinh Kham-su-dai than Tissot dai tien thanh giam, Hue, 14 Juillet 1919, AOM, Fonds du Gouvernement General, 51.080;
No 113. Resident Superieur en Annam, Hue, 14 Fevrier 1914 op cit.

22. No. 1222, Hanoi, le 30 Juin 1919, Le Gouverneur General de l'Indochine, p.i. a M. le Resident Superieur en Annam a.s. d'un Projet d'Ordonnance Royale a l'Enseignement Primaire en Annam, AOM, Fonds du Gouvernement General, 51.080.
23. This dispute is outlined in Transformation de l'Ecole des Hau Bo a Hue en Section de l'Ecole de Droit et d'Administration avec Etude Obligatoire des Caracteres Chinois. 1918/1919, AOM, Fonds du Gouvernement General, 51.122;
See also: Gouverneur General de l'Indochine a M. le Resident Superieur en Annam, Saigon, 12 Avril 1922, No. 35-S a.s. Creation a Hue d'une Ecole des Hautes Etudes en Remplacement de la Section de L'Ecole de Droit et d'Administration de Hanoi, supprimee a Compter de Juillet 1922, AOM, Fonds du Gouvernement General, 51.122;
Saigon, 12 Septembre 1924, Le Resident Superieur, Directeur p.i. de l'Instruction Publique en Indochine a M. le Gouverneur General de l'Indochine, Signe Blanchard de la Brosse a.s. Projet d'Arrete Joint, AOM, Fonds du Gouvernement General, 51.123.
24. No. 2A, Hue, 2 Janvier 1922, Le Resident Superieur en Annam a M. le Gouverneur General de l'Indochine, AOM, Fonds du Gouvernement General, 51.080.
25. ibid.
26. Telegramme Prive, Saigon, 20 Septembre 1928, Signe Bui-Quang-Chieu, Vice President, Conseil Colonial, No. 2988, AOM, Fonds du Gouvernement General, 51.109;
No. 1277, Le Gouverneur de 1ere Classe des Colonies, Gouverneur de la Cochinchine a M. le Recteur d'Academie, Directeur de l'Instruction Publique en Indochine, 3 Mars 1923, AOM, Fonds du Gouvernement General, 51.226;
Voeux No 14, Chambre des Representants du Peuple du Tonkin, 1928, AOM, Fonds du Gouvernement General, 51.257;
Au Conseil Colonial - Seance Plenaire du 20 Novembre 1925. L'Echo Annamite, 6 (Nouvelle Serie), 438 (21 Novembre 1925);
Quelques-Uns des Voeux des Nos Conseillers Coloniaux. L'Echo Annamite, op cit;
Lettre Ouverte a M. le Gouverneur General, le Gouverneur de la Cochinchine, Le Directeur General de l'Instruction Publique en Indochine. La Voix Libre, 3, 251 (24 Septembre 1924).
27. Bui-Qung-Chieu, France d'Asie - L'Indochine Moderne - Ou Ne Pas Etre Vers La Domination. Toulouse Imprimerie du Sud-Ouest, 1925, p 4;

Bui-Quang Chieu, Pour la Domination Indochinoise.
Viet-Nam Hon, 1, 1 (Janvier 1926) p 4;
Nguyen-Phan-Long, Un Danger a Double Face pour les
Francais et les Annamites. L'Echo Annamite, 8
(Nouvelle Serie), 921 (8 Juillet 1927) p 1;
Van-The-Hoi, L'Enseignement Superieur en Indochine.
L'Echo Annamite, 1, 35 (8 Avril 1920) p 1;
L'Enseignement Superieur en Indochine et les Cadres
Lateraux. L'Echo Annamite, 5 (Nouvelle Serie), 11
(27 Fevrier 1924) p 1;
L'Universite Indochinoise. L'Ecolier Annamite, 1, 1
(8 Novembre 1924) p 3.
          28. Van-The-Hoi, L'Enseignement Superieur en
Indochine. L'Echo Annamite, 1, 35, op cit.
Similar charges were made in Van-The-Hoi, Il y a
Elite et Elite. L'Echo Annamite, 1, 106 (7 Octobre
1920), p 1.
          29. Van-The-Hoi, La Grande 'Pitie' de
l'Enseignement en Indochine. L'Echo Annamite, 1,
103 (28 Septembre 1920).
          30. See Lettre No. 16505I du 26 Novembre 1928
du Resident Superieur au Tonkin Portant Envoi de
Deux Voeux de la Chambre des Representants du Peuple
Concernant l'Enseignement Secondaire et
l'Enseignement Superieur a le Directeur General de
l'Instruction Publique, AOM, Fonds du Gouvernement
General, 51.270;
Voeux No 14, Chambre des Representants du Peuple du
Tonkin, 1928, op cit;
Au Conseil Colonial - Seance Plenaire du 20 Novembre
1925. L'Echo Annamite, op cit;
Quelques-uns des Voeux de nos Conseillers Coloniaux.
L'Echo Annamite, op cit.
          31. Phan-Van-Troung, L'Enseignement Indigene -
Attention! Nous Sommes sur le Borde de l'Abime.
L'Annam, 3, 103 (4 Octobre 1926) p 1.
          32. Marr, David, (1981) op cit;
see also, Can, L'Instruction du Peuple Annamite-II.
L'Enseignement Primaire. L'Echo Annamite, 1, 15 (10
Fevrier 1920);
Van-The-Hoi, Instruction du Peuple en Indochine.
L'Echo Annamite, 1, 79 (29 Juillet 1920);
Van-The-Hoi, L'Instruction Populaire en Indochine.
L'Echo Annamite, 1, 34 (1 Avril 1920).
          33. See especially Rapport sur l'Enseignement a
Distribuer au Lycee de Hanoi, AOM op cit;
Rapport a M. Le Gouverneur General de l'Indochine
No. 1397G, op cit;
No 728G 9 Octobre 1924, Le Resident Superieur,
Directeur de l'Instuction Publique en Indochine a M.
le Gouverneur General de l'Indochine a.s. de la

Retribution Scolaire des Classes Primaires du Lycee Albert Sarraut, AOM, Fonds du Gouvernement General, 51.121;
Saigon, 28 Avril 1931 (Le Proviseur Tullie), Lycee Chausseloup-Laubat, Rapport Sommaire sur le Projet de Construction du Nouveau Lycee, AOM, Fonds du Gouvernement General, 51.109.
34. See, for example, Aix, le 15 Janvier 1923, Le Proviseur du Lycee, Mignet, a M. l'Inspecteur d'Academie, Signe A. Berget, Objet: Eleves Indochinois dans nos Lycees, AOM, Fonds du Gouvernement General 51.536;
Liste Nominative des Annamites Ayant Fait ou Faisant Leurs Etudes en France de 1920 a 1931, AOM, Fonds du Gouvernement General 51.532.
35. Projet de la Loi Fixant l'Organisation de l'Instruction Publique aux Colonies, 28 Octobre 1919 et Projet Sommaire de l'Organisation de l'Administration de l'Instruction Publique aux Colonies, 3 Juillet 1919, AOM, Nouveau Fonds 259-2223 (1). A summary of the organization of the Office of Public Instruction and a reprint of the Arrete of May 20, 1920 that established the office appearing in the Journal Officiel de France may be found in La Direction de l'Instruction Publique en Indochine. L'Echo Annamite, 1, 70 (6 Juillet 1920).
36. An exposee of Cognacq's career may be found in Langlois, Walter, Andre Malraux - The Indochine Adventure. Praeger, 1966.
37. See Decret Nominant le Recteur de l'Academie de Lyon Directeur de l'Instruction Publique en Indochine, 28 Octobre 1922, Bulletin General de l'Instruction Publique, Partie Officielle, 2, 6 (Fevrier 1923);
For background on Thalamas see Dandolo, M., A propos de M. Thalamas. L'Avenir du Tonkin, 42, 8772 (27 Juin 1925);
No. 518-IP, Hanoi, 12 Avril 1922, Le Gouverneur General a M. le Ministre des Colonies (Inspection Conseil de l'Instruction Publique), AOM, Fonds de la Residence Superieure du Tonkin, R6, 36.412.
38. See, retrospectively, Brachet, F., Inspecteur de l'Instruction Publique de l'Indochine (Ordre des Sciences) a M. le Recteur d'Academie, Directeur General de l'Instruction Publique en Indochine. Rapport sur Certaines Questions Concernant l'Enseignement Primaire en Cochinchine. AOM, Fonds du Gouvernement General 51.208;
de la Brosse, Blanchard, Une Annee des Reformes dans l'Enseignement Public en Indochine (1924-1925). Hanoi: Imprimerie d'Extreme Orient, 1925;

Hanoi, le 25 Novembre 1921. Rapport sur l'Instruction Publique en Indochine, Execution des Prescriptions de la Circulaire Ministerielle du 10 Octobre 1920, AOM, Fonds du Gouvernement General 2721;
Nguyen-Van-Ngoc, Su Phat o Hoc Duong. Hoc Bao, Luan Thuyet So 26 (27 Fevrier 1922).

39. de la Brosse, op cit, p 7.

40. No. 691-C. Le Chef du Service de l'Enseignement au Tonkin a MM. les Directeurs et Mesdames les Directrices des Ecoles du Tonkin. Objet, L'Instruction Elementaire et l'Enseignement du Francais, 31 Mars 1925, AOM, Fonds de la Residence Superieure du Tonkin, Rl 36.313.

41. de la Brosse, op cit, p 10.

42. See Le Gouverneur General de l'Indochine a M. le Ministre des Colonies, Mars 1926, No. 442-IP a.s. de l'Arrete du 18 Septembre 1924 Reglementant l'Usage de la Langue Indigene dans les Trois Premiers Cours de l'Enseignement Primaire et Consacrant dans Tous les Cours de cet Enseignement les Modalites de l'Enseignement du Francais et de l'Enseignement en Francais (Signe Merlin) AOM, Fonds du Gouvernement General, 51.174.

43. de la Brosse, op cit.
See also No. 739g, Le Recteur d'Academie, Directeur General de l'Instruction Publique en Indochine a M. le Gouverneur General de l'Indochine (Signe Thalamas), 29 Mai 1926, AOM, Fonds du Gouvernement General 51.131.

44. See Nguyen-Huu-Trong, Les Origines du Clerge Vietnamien. Saigon: Imprimerie Paulus Le-Trung-Thinh, 1959;
Osborne, op cit.

45. Gouvernement General de l'Indochine, Rapports au Conseil du Gouvernement. Session Ordinaire, Deuxieme Partie, 1924, Tableau, L'Enseignement Prive. Hanoi: Imprimerie d'Extreme Orient, 1924.

46. See Minute No. 1712sa, Hanoi, le 4 Novembre 1924, Le Gouverneur General de l'Indochine a M. le Ministre des Colonies, Objet: Missions Catholiques du Tonkin, AOM, Fonds du Gouvernement General 51.566.

47. Protestations des Eveques du Tonkin et du Nord Annam contre le Reglement General de l'Instruction Publique, 10 Mars 1919 et 20 Fevrier 1919, AOM, Fonds du Gouvernement General 51.222.

48. Phat-Diem, le 8 Decembre 1923, Marcou, Vicariat Apostolique du Tonkin Maritime a M. le Resident Superieur, AOM, Fonds du Gouvernement

General 51.566.

49. 18 Septembre 1924, Arrete Relatif a
l'Enseignement en Langue Indigene au Cycle Primaire
Franco-Indigene. Art. 134, JOIF, 4, 3 (Novembre
1924);
Le Gouverneur General de l'Indochine a M. le
Ministrè des Colonies, Mars 1926. No. 442-IP a.s.
de l'Arrete du 18 Septembre 1924 Reglementant
l'Usage de la Langue Indigene, op cit.

50. See Gouvernement General de l'Indochine
Francaise, Rapports au Conseil du Gouvernement,
Session Ordinaire, Deuxieme Partie, 1923, 1924,
1925. These policies were made into law by 1927.
See 15 Juillet 1927, Arrete Portant Reorganisation
de l'Enseignement Secondaire Franco-Indigene.
Bulletin General de l'Instruction Publique, Partie
Officielle, 7, 1 (1 Septembre 1927);
N. 728G, 9 Octobre 1924. Le Resident Superieur,
Directeur p.i. de l'Instruction Publique en
Indochine a M. le Gouverneur General de l'Indonchine
a.s. de la Retribution Scolaire, op cit.

51. See Decret Reglementant l'Ouverture et le
Fonctionnement de l'Enseignement Prive en Indochine
(Promulge le 18 Septembre 1924), JOIF, 36, 79
(Octobre 1924).

52. 15 Avril 1924, Arrete Portant Creation dans
Chaque Pays de l'Union d'un Poste de Chef Local du
Service de l'Enseignement. Bulletin General de
l'Instruction Publique, Partie Officielle, 3, 10
(Juin-Aout 1924).

53. Gouvernement General de l'Indochine,
Rapports au Grand Conseil des Interets Economiques
et Financiers et au Conseil de Gouvernement.
Deuxieme Partie: Fonctionnement des Divers Services
Indochinois. Hanoi: Imprimerie d'Extreme Orient,
1925, Table entitled: Enseignement Prive en
Indochine, no page number given.

54. Circulaire - Le Resident Superieur au
Tonkin a MM. les Administrateurs, Maires, Residents,
Chefs de Province et Commandants des Territoires
Militaires, 2 Decembre 1926 (Signe Robin) a.s.
Creation et Organisation des Ecoles Communales du
Tonkin, Hoc Bao, Cong Van, So 19 (10 Janvier 1926);
Arrete No 4146 Autorisant les Communes du Tonkin ne
Disposant d'Aucune Ecole Officielle a Ouvrir des
Ecoloc Elementaires Publiques Confiees a des Maitres
n'Appartenant pas aux Cadres Reguliers de
l'Enseignement (du 26 Decembre 1926). Bulletin de
l'Amicale du Personnel Indigene de l'Enseignement au
Tonkin, 17, 14 (Juillet 1926 - Juin 1927);
Annam, 16 Septembre 1927, Circulaire Relative aux

Ecoles Elementaires Communales. <u>Bulletin General de
l'Instruction Publique, Partie Officielle</u>, <u>7</u>, 6
(Fevrier 1928).
    55. For a fuller discussion of the many reforms
of the interwar period see Kelly, Gail P., <u>Franco-
Vietnamese Schools, 1918 to 1938</u>, Unpublished Ph.D.
Dissertation, University of Wisconsin, 1975.

EDUCATION IN SENEGAL: TWO PROMISING REFORMS

William M. Rideout, Jr.

Introduction
    Senegal provides a rather intriguing case study
opportunity.   Among the sub-Saharan African states,
it has had the longest, most intensive contacts with
Western Europe. The Portuguese reached the region
in 1444 but after 1638 France, with only brief
interruptions, became the dominant foreign presence.
Dakar, the capital of Senegal since its independence
in 1960, had previously served as the capital of
French   West   Africa.   Understandably,   this
relationship with France over a period exceeding 400
years profoundly influenced Senegal; as a colony
which provided manpower for French military forces
and colonial administrative cadres;   as a trading
partner including the slave trade; and as a staunch
supporter of the international Francophone bloc
since   independence.   In   reviewing the impact of
these historical links on Senegal's contemporary
education and human resources sector a number of
points are noteworthy. First, the country possesses
some excellent schools, the capstone of which is the
University of Dakar, founded in 1956.   There is in
consequence an educated and highly sophisticated
elite, many of whom have received training in
France. Furthermore, founding President of Senegal,
Leopold   Senghor,   was   elected to the Academie
Francaise, the only black African ever to receive
this honour.
    Given such a range of accomplishments, it is
somewhat of a shock to note that Senegal continues
to have a very high illiteracy rate of 85-90 per
cent and that less than 50 per cent of its primary
school-aged children are in fact at school. This is
despite the fact that the total amount of money
spent annually by the Government of Senegal on all
types of education now accounts for about one-third
of national recurrent costs. [1] In a country where
per capita gross national product (GNP) is estimated

40

at US$250 per annum, there is a growing need to increase the internal efficiency of the system since larger budgetary contributions to education are out of the question.

Perhaps even more demanding is the need to resolve the mounting crises in external efficiency. One author has observed that:

> When university students (do) graduate, they don't view themselves as peasants or farmers, but (as) government agents, there (only) to assist the peasants. They are paid whether the crop is good or bad, whether their program is successful or not. [2]

And a study conducted by the Centre de Recherche et de Documentation Pedagogique (Educational Research and Documentation Centre) in 1978 found that in a country where 80 per cent of the population makes its living in the agricultural sector only 2 per cent of high school students sampled, responded that they would choose careers in agriculture. [3]

Given these circumstances, there has, at least since the late 1960s, been increasingly serious attention given to reforming the educational system out of sheer necessity rather than out of any desire, especially on the part of most educated elite, to disestablish the existing system which has nurtured them. French remains the official language and the language of education even though it is estimated that not more than 15 per cent of the population are proficient in it. Meanwhile, the major indigenous groups - the Wolof (41 per cent), Serer (14 per cent), Peulh (13 per cent), Tukulor (11 per cent), Dyolar (7 per cent), Mandingo (5 per cent) and other groups totalling 9 per cent - traditionally learn their respective languages and cultures outside and independent of the formal education system. Continuing with the French-derived colonial model has, however, been more politically expedient than has been tackling the problem of determining what to teach in place of the present language and curriculum.

In a sense the existing model has focussed on acculturation, that is to say the teaching of a second culture and language to Senegalese, namely French. This approach has been preferred to that of enculturation, the process of learning the indigenous culture, language and life style relevant to Senegal. While there has been an expansion in the use of Wolof as an indigenous vehicular

Senegal

Figure 1

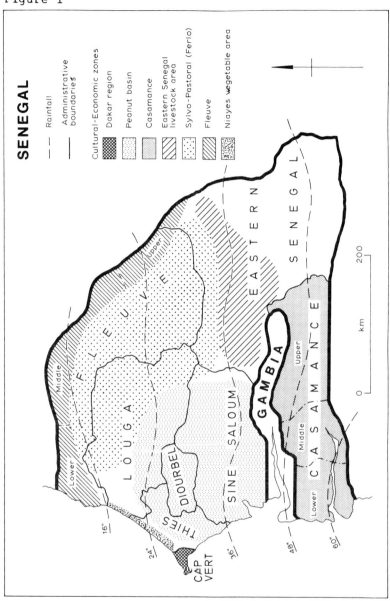

language, the Wolof, as indicated above, constitute
less than half the population, so that Wolof and
Senegalese are not culturally synonymous. As a
result, it has been difficult to 'Senegalize' the
educational system because there is not yet
consensus on what would constitute a national
Senegalese curriculum. The educational system
therefore, continues to serve mostly to acculturate
in schools those who attend long enough to form the
elite and who are or soon become basically urban and
non-agriculturally oriented.

After a quarter of a century of trying to
extend nationwide this modified French colonial
model - French in language of instruction, French in
world view and French in academic content and
elitist orientation - Senegal is now seriously
involved conceptually and practically in a major
educational reform effort in both the formal and
non-formal sectors to make education and training
more directly relevant to the lives of the
Senegalese masses; that is to those who are
overwhelmingly rural and agriculturally based and
who for the foreseeable future will remain so. This
reform effort requires greater participation by the
'average' Senegalese in order to reach a consensus
in planning and implementing revisions. To achieve
these ends calls for extensive decentralization of
the existing highly centralized system in order to
permit, encourage and accomplish broader popular
participation.

This paper will be divided into two sections,
one focussed on formal and the other on non-formal
(systeme extrascolaire) education, in which each
will be surveyed, and a key reform effort in each
sector aimed at promoting decentralization and
popular participation will be analyzed. While
dividing the education system into formal and non-
formal sectors can be logically justified and does
indeed facilitate the study of two complex
structures, it should be kept in mind that they must
be considered together so as to assure maximum
internal and external efficiency in education and
human resources development efforts, the success of
which is ultimately the sine qua non of all
development.

Formal Education

Since its inception the Government of Senegal
has strongly endorsed and supported the formal
education system. National policy has aimed first
to achieve universal and compulsory primary

education, then to expand student recruitment at the secondary and higher educational levels to provide more medium- and high-level professionals, and generally to establish closer correlation between production and manpower needs.

In pursuit of these goals, expenditure on education had increased steadily until 1970 when it began to stabilize at over 25 per cent. Enrolments at the primary level had jumped from 18.5 per cent of the 6-13 year old age group at independence to 35-38 per cent by the early 1970s. Since then progress towards achieving the first goal, universal and compulsory primary education, has ceased. By the time of the Fifth Plan (1977-81), the Government did not even manage to achieve the targeted 3 per cent annual increase necessary to keep up with the population growth rate of school-age children. With an enrolment of 31.5 per cent of the age group in 1979/80, the Government felt it necessary for the proposed Sixth Plan (1981-85) again to limit growth to 3 per cent per annum. This decision was made on the assumption that it would maintain the existing proportion of children in primary school. [4] The first policy remains, therefore, an ideal rather than an active goal.

In addressing the second, the Government of Senegal achieved growth rates substantially higher than those at the primary level. Details are given in Figure 2.

Figure 2: Middle and Secondary School Enrolments 1979/80 [5]

Middle school (grades 7-10)	(1979/80)	Rates of Growth, 1977-78/1979-80 per cent
Total	69,519	5.17*
General	65,348	
Technical	4,171	(Public schools increased by 3.17 per cent while private did by 9.29 per cent)

Secondary school (grades 11-13)	(1979/80)	
Total	18,306	8.24
General	14,798	7.65
Technical	3,508	10.83

* separate figures not available

44

Source: Division de la Planification, Direction de la Recherche et de la Planification, Ministere de l'Education Nationale, Evolution des Effectifs de l'Education Nationale durant les Annees Scolaires 1977/78-1978/79-1979/80. Dakar: Juillet, 1980, MEN/SG/DRP - BA 07/80.

While these increases have been impressive, there has nevertheless been a growing concern that enrolments have been excessively high in the general streams and seriously inadequate in the technical. Consequently, there has been an added emphasis on expanding the technical side which, unfortunately, has continued to be criticized because it is still failing to provide students with the kinds of skills the country requires. On the other hand, the World Bank has also cautioned that any continuation in the expansion of the general secondary streams would be very difficult to justify by manpower data.

The problem related to school output and manpower requirements, the third national goal, is plaguing not only the middle and secondary levels but the primary and university levels as well. As many as 30,000 primary school leavers each year are unable to continue their education and with only general academic education behind them are not qualified for employment. In 1981 400 liberal arts graduates from the University of Dakar were unable to find employment as well as some 80 with engineering degrees. Students graduating from all educational levels are finding it increasingly difficult to find jobs. The government can no longer serve even as an employer of last resort; the problem of educated unemployment has hit Senegal with a vengeance.

Bearing in mind the educational reform goals the Government has established for itself, we now turn to an analysis of the present system.

Primary Education

Since independence, the Government has completely indigenized and significantly improved the quality of primary school teachers, increased the proportion of girls enrolled to 39.7 per cent, one of the highest in Africa, and reduced the rate of students repeating grades 1 to 5. However, although primary education has continued to receive 60 per cent of the nation's education budget, the cost per pupil had, between 1974 and 1979 increased from US$60 per pupil year to US$131.

There are a number of serious problems facing the primary system and it should be stressed that

Senegal

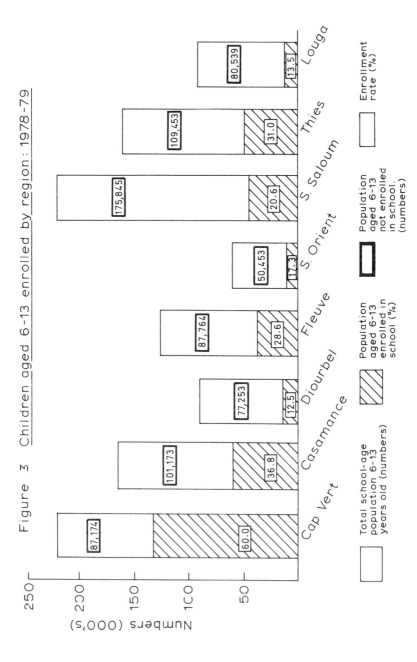

Figure 3 Children aged 6-13 enrolled by region: 1978-79

with few exceptions they are prevalent throughout most of Africa. One of the worst is the persistent imbalance in access to primary education based both on regional and on rural-urban inequalities. The most significant increase since 1960/61 in the percentage of all children enrolled - 3 per cent in fact up to 1978/79 has occurred in the urbanized Cap Vert region. There was only a 1 per cent increase in Thies, and even a decrease in Sine-Saloum, Senegal Oriental and Fleuve. Diourbel has remained unchanged. Figure 3 illustrates the number of children aged 6-13 attending school by region. Cap Vert is again in a highly privileged position with 60 per cent, and only Casamance with 36.8 per cent among the remaining regions is above the national average. Cap Vert and Thies combined, with only 4 per cent of the national territory, have 51 per cent of the total primary school population. Figure 4 gives the enrolment figures by region at the primary and secondary levels.

In spite of the fact that total education costs accounted for 33 per cent of the Government's recurrent costs in the fiscal year 1980, 700,000 children in the 6-13 age group have never had chance to attend school, and these are overwhelmingly in the rural areas. For every 30 persons who live in a village, only one has attended primary school. In contrast, one in every three has attended school in the urban areas. [6] Moreover, outside of the urban areas (hors commune) 84 per cent of the schools have only one to three classes providing an incomplete primary cycle. Consequently the primary education which rural children do receive may well be too short-termed to permit them to achieve literacy which, according to UNESCO estimates, requires the completion of four years of schooling. Therefore, since only 31.5 per cent of children attend school and since some 15 per cent of them drop out before becoming fully literate, the formal school system is failing to increase the national literacy rate, especially in the rural areas.

Another problem which is causing growing concern is the fact that in rural areas, parents are increasingly refusing to send their children to school. As a result, primary schools in some regions of the interior are beginning to close, forcing the Government to alter its strategy of trying to establish schools with an incomplete number of grades (eg, only grades one to three) in every village, to one of locating three or four schools with all six grades (cycle complet) in every

Senegal

Figure 4 Enrolments by Region

Region	Area A/ KM²	Pop. 1976 B/ (000)	School-Age C/ Pop. 6-13	Number in B/ Primary School 6-13	Number in D/ Middle School	Number In D/ General Secondary
Cap-Vert	550	985	218,100	130,926	32,970	9,806
(%)	(28)	(19)		(60.04)	(47.42)	(53.03)
Casamance	28,350	736	160,037	58,864	9,257	1,593
(%)	(14.4)	(15)		(36.79)	(13.31)	(8.6)
Diourbel	4,359	425	88,318	11,065	1,544	225
(%)	(2.2)	(8)		(12.53)	(2.22)	(1.2)
Fleuve	44,127	528	122,880	35,116	5,994	3,784
(%)	(22.4)	(10)		(28.58)	(8.62)	(20.47)
Louga	29,188	418	93,108	12,539	1,737	
(%)	(14.8)	(8)		(13.47)	(2.5)	
Senegal O.	59,602	286	60,978	10,525	1,090	
(%)	(30.3)	(6)		(17.27)	(1.56)	
Sine-Saloum	23,945	1,008	221,359	45,514	7,432	1,767
(%)	(12.2)	(20)		(20.57)	(10.69)	(9.56)
Thies	6,601	669	108,714	49,261	9,495	1,313
(%)	(3.35)	(14)		(31.04)	(13.66)	(7.1)
Senegal	196,722	5,055	1,073,494	353,810	69,519	18,488
(% of Total)	(100)	(100)	(100)	(31.50)	(12%) E/	(5.55) E/

Senegal

Figure 4 (continued)

Notes:

A. Ministere du Plan et de la Cooperation, Republique du Senegal, VI° Plan Quadriennal de Developpement Economique et Social. Mimeo, (ler Juillet 1981-30 Juin 1985), p. 59.

B. World Bank, The Economic Trends And Prospects of Senegal, vol V, Human Resources. Report No. 1720 a-SE, Dec. 1979, p. 43.

C. Direction de la Recherche et de la Planification, Ministere de l'Education Nationale, Republique du Senegal l'Exercise du Droit A l'Education Au Senegal, Bilan et Perspectives. Mimeo. Avril, 1980, Tableau No. 3.

D. Division de la Planification, Direction de la Recherche et de la Planification, Ministere de l'Education Nationale, Evolution des Effectifs de l'Education Nationale durant les Annees Scolaires 1977/78-1978/79-1979/80. Mimeo, Juillet 1980, MEN/SG/DRP-BA 07/80.

E. Age group population figures 13 through 16 (579,036) and 17 through 19 (329,814) derived from A.K. Diop, Projections demographique de la population du Senegal. Direction de la Statistique, 1976.

49

one of the 92 <u>arrondissements</u> instead. [7] The lack
of relevance between what the schools teach and what
the children need to know to improve their lives is
stark: the national primary school curriculum makes
no allowance either for language and cultural
diversity or the significant climatic and
agricultural differences within the country.
Parents are disenchanted with educated unemployment,
with losing their children to urban areas and with
having the schools contribute to what they feel is
the moral deterioriation of their children. A
comment often heard in the countryside is "all they
learn is to become thieves and prostitutes".

Another development is that while Government
primary schools have been losing students, Arab or
Koranic schools located in the same regions have
experienced a dramatic increase in their enrolments:
in 1979 they reported 49,291 students of whom 27,647
were boys and 21,644 girls. This total represented
an increase of 40 per cent over the previous
year. [8] These schools are supported by
contributions from parents of up to 1000 CFA
units [9] (approximately 20 French Francs), per
month, if they can afford it; from local religious
leaders (<u>marabouts</u>); and from Arab states.
Therefore, even though the Government indicates an
interest in introducing elements of the national
curriculum within these schools, and worries about
their relevance to national development, it would,
in fact, probably be politically difficult to impose
modifications which would ensure inclusion of key
components of the national curriculum in them.
Koranic schools outnumber traditional schools by as
much as ten to one in much of the countryside.

Yet another problem related to the internal
efficiency of the primary system is the wastage
rate. While this is not excessive in comparison
with other Francophone African countries for grades
one to five (see Figure 5), at the sixth grade the
picture changes for the worse. This is the final
year of primary schooling, and the promotion rate to
secondary (middle) school is 19.4 per cent; the
repeater rate is 33.5 per cent; and the dropout rate
is 47.1 per cent. If primary education were
acknowledged as being basically a self-contained,
complete programme with a curriculum relevant to
such a policy, it would not be necessary to deny
primary school students the right to satisfactory
primary school leaving certificates. At present,
being awarded the <u>Certificat d'Etudes Primaires
Elementaires</u> (CEPE) not only signifies successful

Senegal

Figure 5 Primary Education Wastage Rates

Grades	Enrolments 1978	Enrolments 1979	Repeaters 1979	Promotion Rate (Percent)	Repeater Rate (Percent)	Dropout Rate (Percent)
1st-Cl	71 151	75 679	8 788	86.6%	12.4%	1%
2nd-CP	63 093	69 476	7 825	85%	12.4%	2.6%
3rd-CEI	57 616	61 204	7 600	82.1%	13.2%	4.7%
4th-CE2	50 805	54 442	7 115	81.9%	14.0%	4.1%
5th-CM1	50 382	49 129	7 547	84.4%	15.%	.6%
6th-CM2	53 538	60 482	11 952	19.4%	33.5%	47.1%

completion of primary school, but it also entitles
students to admission to the secondary (middle)
level. Therefore, in order to reduce pressure on
the post-primary, and subsequently the post-
secondary institutions, the number of CEPEs awarded
is restricted. The result is that over 30,000
students are thrown out of the system every year
without any useful qualification. Dreams of
pursuing academic secondary education are shattered,
and as this is the only direction in which the style
of primary school is leading, the basic educational
experience of most Senegalese is extraordinarily
dysfunctional.

In an attempt to compensate the 38-50 per cent
of children who do complete primary school, but are
not admitted to regular middle level schools, the
Government of Senegal proposed a middle level
practical teaching programme Enseignement Moyen
Pratique, (EMP), which was to have eventually
enrolled 81 per cent of them in a four year 'non-
formal' programme. The EMP, however, which was to
have 800 centres (foyers) completed by 1982,
presently has but 15 functioning. The programme was
poorly conceived and it has been under-financed,
under-staffed and clustered in the most heavily
populated areas. Since it was to be opened only to
those who successfully completed their primary
school, it ignored the thousands who were unable to
receive even these certificates. Moreover, the
programme fails to serve rural needs since it
actually provides pre-vocational, rather than
specific skills training. A national educational
reform conference the Etats Generaux has already
recommended that, given the cost and lack of
relevance of the middle level practical teaching
programme it should be terminated. Government
officials have confirmed the likelihood of the
demise of the EMP scheme.

Middle Level Education
As previously stated there are two streams of
middle level formal education, technical and
general, and during 1979, 6 per cent of students
were enrolled in the former and 94 per cent in the
latter. It is interesting to note that 33 per cent
of the students at this level are enrolled in
private schools and that 47 per cent are in the Cap
Vert region. Both streams totalled 8,873 students
in 1961 and increased to 69,519 by 1979, an 11.9 per
cent annual growth rate. The proportion of girls
enrolled increased from 25.4 per cent in 1961 to

33.7 per cent in 1979. Middle level education
terminates at the end of the tenth grade with an
examination for the leaving certificate (DFEM), [10]
which students must pass to continue up the academic
ladder either in the regular secondary stream or to
enter professional training schools, like the Ecole
Normale which has a four year programme for training
primary school teachers. Only 20 per cent of all
students attempting the DFEM passed in 1979. The
remainder must seek employment with few marketable
skills in an economy suffering acute unemployment
problems.

Secondary Education

The general and technical streams found in
middle level education are continued at the
secondary level with 80.8 per cent in the general
stream and the rest in the technical. General
secondary streams enrolled 14,798 in 1978/79 which
means secondary education had achieved a 14.2 per
cent annual rate of growth since 1961. The
technical secondary programme totalled 3,508
equalling a 28.9 per cent growth rate during the
same period. Beginning in 1979/80, students who had
been admitted to the secondary level were required
to take an additional examination to determine if
they would be permitted to continue on to the final
year, the classe terminale and thus the
baccalaureat. Only half of the students passed.

A third option at the secondary level is
provided through the professional training schools.
There are some 34 centres for training, upgrading
and reconversion which are supervised by the
Ministry of Education. The number enrolled in these
centres in 1979 totalled 4,679.

On a regional basis, Cap Vert in 1979/80 had
53.6 per cent of the total secondary enrolment while
20.7 per cent were in the Fleuve - for the most part
in St. Louis, presently the regional capital but
prior to independence the colonial capital of
Senegal. Dakar then served as colonial capital of
the whole of French West Africa. Of the total
national secondary enrolment, 26.8 per cent were
girls.

The lack of concordance between the career
aspirations of some 900 high school students and the
employment opportunities available to them in a
country where 80 per cent of the population makes
its living in the agricultural sector was
illustrated by the responses the students made to a
survey question in 1978 when they were asked what

kind of work they would like to do: 35 per cent
wanted to be teachers, 9 per cent wanted to go into
industry, 6 per cent wanted to go into a liberal
profession, 3 per cent chose the army, 6 per cent
wanted to pursue diverse professional careers such
as salesmen, and only 2 per cent chose agriculture.
The remainder either did not respond or chose a
category which constituted less than one per
cent. [11] The misfit between career goals and
potential employment opportunities was almost
perfect; the external efficiency of the system was
close to zero.

Higher Education
      Founded in 1956 to accommodate 5,000 students,
the University of Dakar dominates the higher
education system in Senegal. By 1978/79 it had a
total of 11,677 students of whom 8,759 were
Senegalese citizens. During the past three years,
there has been an annual increase of 17 per cent in
enrolment. As of 1976 the cost per student year
totalled US$1,573. An annex for the university
being built at St. Louis, Gaston Berger University,
scheduled to open in October 1982, but still
unoccupied in 1983, was to accommodate 4,000 to
5,000 students attending the first two undergraduate
years (lower division) in law, economics and
humanities.
      As in the rest of the educational system one of
the greatest problems of the university is the total
lack of articulation between students' courses of
study, the numbers of graduates with those academic
specializations and the socio-economic needs of the
country. In the Fifth Plan, (1977 - 1981), the
needs in the 'literary disciplines': Law, Economics
and Humanities were as follows:

University Faculty		Law	Economics	Humanities
Needs from	1977-1981	60	130	378
Enrolled:	1979-80	520	696	578
	1978-79	432	531	839
	1977-78	308	331	704

It can be seen that the enrolment in any one year
greatly exceeded the needs for the entire four year
plan period and the excess by field of study was
becoming worse in all disciplines except humanities.
It is not surprising that high level unemployment is
increasingly what is awaiting the university's
graduates. In 1980 it was reported that there were
some 615 law and 658 humanities graduates who were

Senegal

jobless. [12]

Popular Reform: The Etats Generaux

After committing 33 per cent of its annual
recurrent budget to education in 1979/80, it is
tragic that the Government can derive so little
satisfaction from the status and potential future
contribution of that system to national development.
Given the amount allocated to this sector it is
unlikely that there will be any significant change
in the funding level. On the other hand it is
likely that the provision of education will, for the
foreseeable future, be a socio-political as well as
an economic factor and this may well inhibit rather
than promote national development. It is obvious
that further delays in implementing reforms in this
sector would be extremely hazardous to even the
maintenance of present living standards in Senegal,
let alone any prospect of development.

It should be emphasized that the Government of
Senegal is painfully aware of the problems it faces,
and it appears at present that significant, even
dramatic changes in the educational system are
underway. While the national policies listed at the
beginning of this section have not yet officially
changed, the Government's immediate strategy is
first: to serve national manpower needs more
effectively so that "... training, and the sectors
which are immediately productive, will be the
priorities of the Sixth Plan", [13] and second: to
place stress on quality rather than quantity
especially with regard to the output of the primary
system.

The Government's new concerns to promote
quality and relevance have received endorsement with
particular stress on the implementation of long term
national educational reform as a result of a popular
National Education Reform Conference held in
January, 1981. This conference, the Etats Generaux,
the name originally selected by trade union leaders,
was convened by leaders of the different parties
involved, not the Government. It could certainly
claim similarities to its French namesake. It was
revolutionary in terms of the substance of its
recommendations but evolutionary in its proposed
processes of implementation. Furthermore it was
'representative' in its composition, for even though
it too was not popularly elected, its participants
were selected from among the membership of major
trade unions, including those of teachers and
peasants; parents' organizations; political parties;

55

cooperatives; government officials and religious leaders. In spite of its diversity, an impressive degree of consensus emerged in the recommendations proclaimed at its conclusion: 100 per cent primary school enrolment; Islamic education and instruction in national languages within the formal school system; greater interaction between school and community; new teacher training programmes established to accomplish these recommendations; and greater recognition of teachers as active development agents who should be provided with adequate physical and material facilities for their educational tasks.

Even though the Etats Generaux were not convoked by the Government and thus did not have an official national mandate, they have, nevertheless, received increasing governmental endorsement and sanction as they have evolved. It would, after such events be difficult for the Government to attempt to degrade or ignore their workings and recommendations. For example, the Prime Minister himself agreed to deliver the opening address and declared that educational problems were so complex that they could only be successfully addressed if all concerned in the nation participated. Following the conclusion of the Conference, the President approved its recommendations, agreed that the Etats Generaux would in the future meet every four years, and supported the appointment of four standing commissions named to follow-up on Conference recommendations and preparations for the next meeting. These commissions have been submitting reports based on their deliberations and studies. Final recommendations by all four bodies will be completed before the next scheduled meeting of the Etats Generaux in early 1985. Staff and secretarial support for the commissions are being provided by the Government. Even as these reports are being published, they appear to be exerting influence on national plans and policies. [14]

This apparently spontaneous creation of the Etats Generaux, their determination to reform and their commitment to implementation, appear originally to have caused some trepidation within Government circles. However, the degree of consensus achieved, the ability of the Etats Generaux to conduct themselves with dignity and concern for due process of the law, and respect for citizens' rights, won them the Government's respect and then support. Here through this rather amorphous construct was an almost unique instance

among highly centralized Francophone African nations
where there was massive popular support for, and
participation in, educational policy formation with
a commitment to follow-through with implementation.
For a change the central Government was a supporting
partner and it has played this role faithfully,
trying neither to capture nor to subvert, nor to
politicize this popular manifestation.

The results of the 1985 meeting of the Etats
Generaux may not only determine the future
configuration of formal education in Senegal but it
may also influence the future growth of
decentralized democracy there. Meanwhile, the
importance of education in Senegal has been further
underscored by the emergence of the Etats Generaux
phenomenon for it was popular concern for education
which spawned a rare and promising popular response
in Senegal which was, moreover, at the same time,
peaceful. This is remarkable, since the potential
for violence was there, particularly if the mandate
had not been confined to educational change.

Some Conclusions in respect of Formal Education

The educational system in Senegal is probably
the finest model of the traditional French education
system in Africa. It has provided a highly
qualified elite for government and civil service
positions. However, the Government has reached the
point where it can no longer absorb what the
university is producing, and when alternative
occupational opportunities are not available. What
is available, graduates are not trained for. At a
cost of one third of the annual recurrent budget,
one third of the population is provided with some
schooling. However, this opportunity is badly
skewed in favour of Cap Vert and the urban areas.
Such disparities and inequalities have persisted
unrelentingly since independence. Given these
circumstances, it is understandable that graduates,
and especially those at the higher levels, are
overwhelmingly urban oriented:

> Rather than channel Senegal's best human
> resources toward development, the university
> turns them away from it. The university
> channels students' hopes, perceptions and
> thoughts away from the rural world ... and is
> the final stage in a process of alienation
> which begins in the primary school. [15]

The system needed reforming even prior to 1971

when the Government first initiated the educational
reform effort. In fact almost nothing has happened
to correct the problems which had been identified
even then. The system has now reached a point where
there is severe educational unemployment at the top
while at the bottom the rural population has begun
to withdraw voluntarily from schooling. Nationwide
discontent with the system culminated in the
convocation of a popular conference determined to
attack a system which was increasingly viewed as
'the enemy'. The Government acquiesced vis-a-vis
the meeting of the Etats Generaux, and then
increasingly welcomed their deliberations and
recommendations, supporting the follow-up activities
which are directed towards the preparation of
carefully considered and finalized lists of
educational reforms to be presented to the nation by
1985. Based upon interviews with Government
officials, one feels there is a strong consensus
that there will be a profound reform of the
educational system launched by the beginning of the
academic year 1985/86 and smaller reforms will be
initiated as different commissions of the Etats
Generaux complete their preliminary findings in
preparation for the second quadrennial reunion. If
the present reform efforts proceed on schedule, as
they have thus far since the Etats Generaux, then
the education and human resources development sector
which has been worrying the Government at least
since 1971 could receive a powerful stimulation
towards becoming a dynamic force in providing the
kind of trained people Senegal requires most to
support its rural sectors and its mainly
agricultural economy.
    From data provided by the Government and
international organizations, it is readily apparent
that producers in the rural areas are desperately in
need of basic literacy and numeracy training. The
formal education system in Senegal has not seriously
been used as an instrument to attempt to meet those
needs despite the fact that it still remains: a
major consumer of national funds; the most pervasive
national structure which is also readily susceptible
to governmental manipulation; a labour-intensive
institution staffed by well-qualified people trained
to teach others. In a country where illiteracy
exceeds 80 per cent, it is a resource which cannot
be squandered.

Non-Formal Education
    The following Government agencies are actively

involved in promoting human resources development training in the non-formal sector:

(A) The Ministry of Rural Development, (Ministere de Developpement Rural) is overwhelmingly the most important governmental development unit. It includes agriculture, livestock, vegetable production and cooperatives. It also oversees the Rural Development Agencies or ADR's, whose activities are specified by Government mandates which the Ministry is responsible for enforcing.

(B) The Secretariat of State for Human Development, (Secretariat d'Etat de la Promotion Humaine). The Secretariat of State assists with supporting staff functions and includes: the Direction of Rural Animation (Direction de l'Animation Rurale); the Direction of Practical Training (Direction de la Formation Pratique) encompasses Middle Level Practical Training (Enseignement Moyen Pratique - which was previously discussed in the Formal Education section); Literacy (Alphabetisation) and Home Economics (Enseignement Menager Social); and Direction of Family Welfare (Direction du Bien-Etre Familiale), including the activities of Maison Familiale and Family Planning (Espacement de Naissance). Recently the Secretariat of State has been enlarged by the incorporation of the Secretariat of State for Women's Concerns (now the Direction de la Condition Feminine); the Executive Secretariat for the Multipurpose Centre for Rural Expansion (Centre d'Expansion Rurale Polyvalente, or CERP). This is also known as CER - Centre d'Expansion Rurale, the two designations being used interchangeably. Activities were transferred from the Ministry of Rural Development and the National Funds for Community Development (Fonds Nationals pour le Developpement Communautaire - FONADEC), which has been established as a clearing house for soliciting donor funding for community development projects.

However, in the case of the Secretariat of State, perhaps even more than elsewhere in the Government lack of funding has crippled outreach programmes.

(C) The Rural Development Agencies (Agences de Developpement Rural or ADR's). Although the Rural Development Agencies report directly to the Ministry of Rural Development, they are expected to coordinate their activities with lower governmental administrative levels as well. While established as temporary organisms to increase agricultural productivity by focussing on key crops and schemes,

59

the Agencies have, in fact, been functioning
continuously, albeit with changes, since
independence. They are staffed with a mixture of
civil servants and contract personnel and have been
heavily financed by foreign donors. Since they have
been able to secure funding to promote their
programmes even when governmental agencies normally
responsible for complementary and even comparable
types of functions were incapacitated for lack of
funds, Rural Development Agencies have continued to
expand into activities which, while beyond their
original mandates, were in areas in which fully
operational programmes were essential in order to
permit the Agencies to achieve their goals. While
their autonomy has permitted them to attract
disproportionate support, especially from abroad,
they have also come under recurrent criticism
because perpetual programmatic and structural
changes have made it impossible to evaluate their
performance with any exactitude. As a result, the
inability to substantiate their rural development
successes contributed to the Government's acceptance
of a World Bank recommendation in 1982 that
contracts be negotiated between the Ministry of
Rural Development and the Rural Development Agencies
and agreed upon so that ultimately their performance
can be effectively evaluated. Even before the
contract concept was established, the performance of
two of the largest Agencies, ONCAD and SONAFAR, led
to such peasant malaise that the Government
abolished them.

(D) The Ministry of the Interior (Minstere de
l'Interieur). This Ministry has traditionally been
responsible for local government administration.
However, following the Reform of July, 1972 a
council was established at each level of the
administrative hierarchy to assist the
administrator, so that: the Governor at the Regional
level would preside over a Regional Council, the
Prefet at the Departmental level over a Departmental
Council, and the Sous-Prefet at the Arrondissement
level over an Arrondissement Council. The basic
purpose of these councils has been to advise the
responsible administrator by providing a forum for
greater community participation staffed by both
elected and appointed members from different social
and economic groups who convene to debate the
developmental objectives of their respective areas.

In addition to the establishment of these
councils, and this is what makes the Ministry of the
Interior much more involved in the developmental

Senegal

processes, was the 1972 Reform's creation of a new
ground-level administrative component, the Rural
Communes (Communautes Rurales). The Rural Communes
gradually extended nationwide between 1972 and 1978,
and now total 284. They constitute the major reform
to be discussed in this section. With the
establishment of the Rural Communes the
arrondissement ceased being the lowest basic rural
tier of the political and administrative structure.
This was a profound innovation, and since it is at
this level of decision that rural development
ultimately succeeds or fails, the Commune is of
critical importance.

There are usually at least three Rural Communes
per arrondissement, although there may be up to
seven depending upon area size and population
density. The Rural Commune is a legal entity
(personne morale), with legal rights (droits
publics), and has its own financial base. From its
annual budget based on locally levied taxes, it
plans local development efforts and has ultimate
control over the land and its use within the Commune
area. It has a primate village and takes its name
from that village. [16]

In addition to Government agencies, non-
official private voluntary organisations also
participate actively in non-formal educational
activities. Although small by comparison with the
Government organisms in terms of budget, staff and
distribution of programmes, they do, nevertheless,
make an important contribution by expanding sources
of innovation inputs into rural regions. Their role
will not, however, be considered further in this
chapter.

The Ministry of Rural Development, the
Secretariat of State for Human Development and the
Rural Development Agencies are all characterized by
excessive staffs, in part because personnel ceilings
were originally influenced by the numbers who had
been assigned to Dakar before independence when it
was responsible for all of French West Africa, [17]
and in part because the Government of Senegal has
used civil service employment as a means for
reducing educated unemployment.

The result of this excessive bureaucracy, given
the increasing shortages of funding, has meant that
support for rural development has been consumed in
wages, which have been the last item to be cut,
leaving little or nothing to pay for actual project
implementation over and above personnel costs. It
is not uncommon to find qualified officials able to

assist with rural development who are rendered
almost useless for lack of necessary supplies or
materials. This has been complicated by a
preoccupation with a French oriented commitment to
deductive planning which nearly becomes an end in
itself especially since implementation is often
either precluded (or excused) because of the lack of
funds, or rendered impossible to evaluate because of
reforms or reorganizations. Thus planners need not
be seriously burdened or challenged by the inductive
realities of implementation. Furthermore, in the
French structural model the senior civil service,
(cadre de conception or 'A' level planners), are by
definition and role deliberately separated from the
lower level technicians, (Grade 'C' civil servants)
responsible for implementation. In short, the
planning process at the centre is inadequately
connected to the reality of the field where
implementation and production will or will not
occur. There is a need to stress implementation and
output and to inject inputs at the field level so
that they are not diverted by the myriad of
bureaucratic channels through which they must pass
before reaching the goals for which, at least
ostensibly, they were originally intended.

The Rural Communes and Rural Development
Article 1 of Law No. 72-25 defines a Rural
Commmune as

.... a certain number of villages constituting
one common territory; unified by ties of
neighbourly solidarity and common interests;
capable of finding the resources needed for its
own development. [18]

The Commune elects a Rural Council once every five
years with a President and Vice-President and,
depending upon the Commune's population from 12 to
21 council members who are called rural councillors,
none of whom are civil servants. Voting is based on
universal suffrage.
The Rural Council meets at the 'primate
village' as often as its President deems necessary.
The Council is, however, obliged to meet: for the
budgetary session between December 1 and January 31
of each year; when the Sous-Prefet (the ranking
official at the arrondissement level) deems it
necessary; and when one-third of the members deem it
necessary. [19]
Application of the reform was gradually phased

in region by region and there is consensus among the evaluations of Rural Commune activities that those which have been in operation longest are, understandably, the most effective. The Rural Commune's own budget is based upon receipts from a 'rural tax.' The rural tax rate is decided upon in October by the Departmental Council - it cannot be more than 1,000 CFA nor less than 500 CFA per taxable inhabitant in the Commune. This rural tax accounts for anywhere from 75 per cent to 100 per cent of the Rural Commune's total budget. For example, a Commune of some 15,000 inhabitants, of whom 10,000 were taxable, which had a tax set at 1,000 CFA would obtain 10,000,000 CFA for the year. However, there would be an obligatory deduction of 25 per cent (2,500,000 CFA) for the 'Solidarity Funds' which are redistributed to the poorer rural communes. In this hypothetical case other minor sources of income might provide an additional 500,000 CFA so that the Commune would end up with 9,000,000 CFA, approximately US$32,150 at its disposal. [20]

The Sous-Prefet plays a key role in estimating Commune revenues over the projected budget year and in making recommendations about expenditures. Income and expenditures must balance and the 'ordinary expenditure', recurrent costs, must be paid before funds are allocated to developmental projects. Once the budget has been voted by the rural councillors it is sent to the councils at the arrondissement, departmental and regional levels and is also reviewed by the Prefet and the Governor. Thereafter, it returns to the Sous-Prefet who is responsible for its execution.

Obviously, there have been problems with this budgetary process, with control of expenditures, with projects being funded which never existed, with rural councillors trying to perform their duties despite their own illiteracy and other handicaps. [21] In spite of its problems during the first years of the reform, an evaluation concludes,

> The rural councillors are becoming ... more aware of their rights. More importantly, the rural populace now has an institution which it can use to solve its own problems ... In spite of the problems, the reformed system is a significant improvement over what previously existed. [22]

Promising reports of Commune achievements are

beginning to surface such as the account of the activities of the Communaute Rurale de Taiba Ndiaye in the Thies Region where from 1978 until 1982, the Commune's accomplishments included 15 new wells, repairs to 23 existing wells, opening up a village market place, a school, including necessary desks and furniture, a village pharmacy and the construction of a 2 kilometre feeder road to connect the village to a secondary route. [23] In the light of case studies such as this one, it is difficult not to become perhaps overly enthusiastic about the Rural Commune's potential contributions to rural development.

Multipurpose Centres for Rural Expansion, Technical Assistance and Training

Government technicians available to assist the Communes in planning their development activities are stationed at the Multipurpose Centres located at the arrondissement level. The Multipurpose Centre is usually directed by a Chef and staffed by a group of technicians at the 'C' grade level in the civil service. The composition of the Multipurpose Centres for Rural Expansion group can vary according to projects within the arrondissement or the needs of the people. Depending upon these considerations, the standard Multipurpose Centre cadre usually includes specialist agents from agriculture, livestock, water and forestry, cooperatives and public health; in addition there might also be others from youth and sports organizations, environmental development, fishing and fish farming, national education or technical education and monitrices for rural home economics.

The Chef of the Multipurpose Centre for Rural Expansion and his team must know the arrondissement thoroughly and be able to provide the Rural Communes in the arrondissement with the expert advice they require to plan their development projects. The Centre, in fact, has the only development agents available at the arrondissement level to serve the Rural Communes unless one of the Rural Development Agency is involved with a programme in the area. If such programmes are functioning in the arrondissement the Rural Development Agency might have technicians available to advise the Centre and the Rural Communes in technical matters related to the Rural Development Agency programme. Unfortunately, the effectiveness of the Multipurpose Centres has been seriously eroded by the fact that they have been receiving only about 2,500,000 CFA

every six months, and based upon a recent study, it
is estimated that more than double that amount, or
at least 6,000,000 CFA is required every six months
for the Multipurpose Centre to be minimally
effective. This recommended sum is, incidentally,
the same amount as was provided to comparable rural
development components almost twenty years ago.

Conclusion

For purposes of this analysis, four major
entities have been identified as predominantly
concerned with training human resources to promote
Senegal's rural development efforts. The focus has
not been on the training of Senegalese technicians
because for the most part there are sufficient
existing facilities to satisfy these needs and in
many cases there are already technicians, often too
many at the higher levels, whom the Government can
no longer afford to absorb. The more critical
problem area for the time being is that available
trained personnel are not effectively transmitting
their know-how to the producers. These are the
farmers trying to feed their own families as well as
to produce a surplus which can be exported to
provide Senegal with the income and foreign exchange
it needs to advance economically.

In addition to the Ministry of Rural
Development, the Rural Development Agencies have
been created with specific and limited mandates to
accomplish special rural development goals and
promote special projects. There has been a serious
lack of coordination between The Rural Agencies and
the Ministry of Rural Development and other
ministries active in rural development, and
especially in the training area. Undeniably, the
existing structures, including the cooperatives,
have not provided the training, motivation and
assistance farmers have needed to achieve the
production levels desired by the central Government.
Consequently, major reforms have been initiated by
the Government involving all of these units in an
effort to rectify acknowledged shortcomings.

Still to be tested, also in order to determine
their ultimate impact on rural development efforts,
are the basic components and most pervasive links in
the adminstrative/bureaucratic chain of command: the
Rural Communes which are in fact staffed by the
villagers themselves and the Multipurpose Centres
for Rural Expansion which were added to the
arrondissements to provide technical assistance to
producers in the Communes in their production and

development efforts. The on-the-job and production-
oriented training which can be provided by
Multipurpose Centre staff to meet the Rural
Communes' needs should be studied, evaluated and
assisted. The Centres have often been inoperative
because of budgetary shortages and this needs to be
corrected in order to determine the extent of their
potential contribution if they have the basic
supplies required.

It must be emphasized, however, that it has
been increasingly found that successful development
requires that people who are the target of
development efforts must become participants rather
than objects, or obstacles, in the process. [24] For
farmers to participate in the process requires
decentralization so that they participate in the
planning as well as the implementation and
evaluation and so that the developmental activities
are appropriate and relevent within each
locale. [25] Unique in all of Sahelian Africa, the
Senegalese administrative reform of 1972 has
provided that country with a governmental mechanism
through which the rural population might achieve the
kind of control over their own lives which is often
discussed elsewhere in Africa but which in fact is
almost never transferred from the officials in the
capital city to the farmers in the fields. This
reform constitutes a democratization and
decentralization of the system complete with local
elections to determine local leadership and with
taxation and budgetary powers and other prerogatives
all of which are seldom seen outside of the
developed democracies. It provides an unparalleled
opportunity to determine the extent of impact such a
structural reform can make on rural development in
Africa. Obviously some activities attempted by the
Rural Communes during the past few years, their
first years of existence, have not succeeded. But,
their rate of success must be considered in the
context of very large and significant failures by
well-staffed, well-educated and heavily-financed
governmental structures which have had years of
experience to fall back on and have, nevertheless,
contributed to a state of near national bankruptcy.
It is not suggested that popular government is
infallible - simply that it is better than the
competitive options available; it deserves,
therefore, to be supported and given a chance. A
critical element the local leadership desperately
needs is education and training - beginning with
functional literacy and numeracy - advocated by the

Etats Generaux - as soon as possible.

This unique effort at decentralization at the administrative level together with the Etats Generaux's decentralized structure and mode of operation reminiscent of developed democracies may be presented as the specific cultural identity in matters of education and development of this African country.

Notes and References

1. Carvin, Joseph, Education and Training in Senegal, USAID and The Ministry of Planning and Coordination, Republic of Senegal, Joint Planning of US Assistance Programs in Senegal. Dakar: May 1981, Vol. I, pp 1-18.

2. ibid, p 2.

3. D'hondt, Walter, Ndiaye, Abdoulaye, and Vanewiele, Mackel, Les Lyceens Senegalais: Etudes Psychologiques. Universite de Dakar: Centre de Recherche et de Documentation Pedagogique de l'Ecole Normale Superieure de Dakar, Mars 1980.

4. Direction de la Recherche et de la Planification, Ministere de l'Education Nationale, Republique du Senegal, l'Exercise du Droit a l'Education au Senegal, Bilan et Perspectives. Mimeo., Dakar: Avril, 1980, p 2. (Hereafter referred to as Droit a l'Education).

5. Secondary education in Senegal is divided into middle secondary which includes grades 7, 8, 9 and 10 in general or technical streams and higher secondary. Upon obtaining the leaving certificate, Diplome de Fin d'Etudes Moyennes (DFEM), at the successful completion of grade 10, students can continue in secondary education proper, with grades 11, 12 and 13. The BA (License) requires three additional years - 14, 15 and 16 - at university.

6. Study conducted by the Centre de Recherche et de Documentation Pedagogique in 1978 as quoted by Joseph Carvin, Education and Training in Senegal, op cit.

7. Droit a l'Education, op cit, p 7.

8. ibid.

9. CFA stands for Communaute Financiere Africaine (units of account).

10. See note 5.

11. D'hondt, W., Ndiaye, A., and Vanewiele, M., op cit.

12. Carvin, Joseph, op cit, Vol. I, Summary.

13. Ministere du Plan et de la Cooperation, Republique du Senegal, VIe Plan Quadriennal de

Developpement Economique et Social: Orientations et Programmes d'Action (1981-1985). Dakar: Nouvelles Imprimeries du Senegal, 3e trimestre, 1981, p 17.

14. As preliminary reports by the four major commissions established by the _Etats Generaux_ to make recommendations to the next meeting in 1985 began to circulate in 1981, it was apparent that truly profound recommendations for reform of the primary school were being considered. See _Le Soleil_, a major Dakar newspaper, of the following dates in 1981: February 2, 4 and 5; May 3; August 10, 24 and 25; September 28; October 7 and 12.

15. Carvin, Joseph, op cit, Vol. I.

16. Government of Senegal, Article 1 of Law No. 72-75, dated 19 April, 1972, _Relative aux Communautes Rurales_. Dakar.

17. Colvin, Lucie, Private Initiatives in the Senegalese Economy, Potential Modes of AID Assistance, USAID and The Ministry of Planning and Coordination, Republic of Senegal, _Joint Planning of US Assistance Programs in Senegal_. Dakar: May, 1981, Vol. II. (Hereafter USAID/GOS).

18. Government of Senegal, Article 1 of Law No. 72-75, op cit.

19. ibid, Article 4.

20. Carvin, Joe, Progress Report of the Administrative Reform, 1971, the Rural Communes, _USAID/GOS_, Vol. II, pp 26-31.

21. Ecole Nationale d'Economie Appliquee, _Report de Stage_, conducted in the summer of 1979 at Nguekokh;
Ecole Nationale d'Economie Appliquee, _Report de Stage_, conducted in the summer of 1979 at Noto Tassette;
Ecole Nationale d'Economie Appliquee Report, Les Communautes Rurales Senegalaises et le Developpement a la Base, p 1.

22. Carvin, Joe, op cit, Vol. II, p 39.

23. La reforme administrative regionale et locale. Dakar: _Le Citoyen_, No. 2, Mars-Avril 1982, pp 3-8.

24. Mathieson, John A., _Basic Needs and the New International Economic Order: An Opening for North-South Collaboration in the 1980s_. Washington: Overseas Development Council, 1981, pp 17-27.

25. Schramm, Wilbur and Lerner, Daniel, _Communication and Change: The Last Ten Years - and the Next_. The University Press of Hawaii, 1976; Lele, Uma, _The Design of Rural Development: Lessons from Africa_. The John Hopkins University Press, Published for the World Bank, 1975.

CULTURE AND IDENTITY IN GRENADIAN EDUCATION

Colin Brock

Introduction
       Grenada achieved a brief notoriety in October
1983 with the execution of the Prime Minister,
several of his ministerial colleagues, and the
subsequent invasion of this small island nation by
the world's mightiest power, the United States of
America. Ostensibly, the invasion was to secure the
safety of the students at a private medical school –
an offshoot of the entrepreneurial dimension of
American education, examples of which abound in that
part of the world. It was, however, primarily the
taking of a golden opportunity to put into action a
well rehearsed invasion plan developed to thwart the
socio-political stance of the regime that had ruled
Grenada since the bloodless coup of March 1979. [1]
A prominent feature of that regime was its
educational programme which, though distinctive in
some degree, owed much to the Cuban model and to
practical support from that country.
       In 1984 a full year after the invasion, Grenada
is still under the direct control of the USA, though
with most of the military gone it is not clear what
will be the effect of American tutelage on the
future redevelopment of Grenadian education.
Nonetheless, there has been considerable influence
from that source throughout the Commonwealth
Caribbean for some decades now, and so there is some
basis for speculation as to the possible effects of
what is now inevitably a 'special relationship' with
the USA, in the short-term future. A consideration
of the implications of this phenomenon for the
culture and identity of Grenada, constitutes the
final section of this chapter. The main focus of
this discussion is a comparison between the
educational dimension of the Grenadian revolution of
1979-83 and the British colonial legacy in respect

of education that was manifest so strikingly in this
particular island.

Grenada was the first of the Windward Island
nations, indeed of any of the small islands of the
Eastern Caribbean, to gain full Independence from
the United Kingdom. [2] This occurred in 1974 amid
considerable disquiet expressed within Grenada,
elsewhere in the Commonwealth Caribbean, and in
London. Some of this concern was in respect of the
capacity of such a small political entity to operate
as a truly independent state, but most pertained to
the person of the Grenadian leader Eric Gairy, who
had brought the country to its new status. During
the period of British colonial rule, [3] Grenada had
acquired a degree of status in respect of its
fellows in the Windward quartet [4] by being the
location of the headquarters of the Governor-General
of the group. Indeed, perceptions of status and
scale, together with actual possession and
dependence are part of the colonial legacy
bequeathed to the West Indies by the various
European powers that have had interests there.

> Smallness has condemned the islands to a
> history of tutelage and, in some cases to
> microscopic versions of political dependence.
> A decade and a half ago only the three largest
> units - all in the Greater Antilles - were
> independent, and some of the smallest islands
> were dependencies of dependencies. Carriacou,
> subordinate to Grenada, boasts its own fief,
> Petite Martinique. [5]

Figures 1 and 2 serve to illustrate the situation of
Grenada, and aspects of its internal geography. As
was the experience of many West Indian islands,
Grenada was controlled by different European powers
during the period of so-called 'classical
colonialism'. Despite the name, Spanish contact was
minimal, and the first significant settlement was
carried out by the French in 1650. Between this
date and 1738 when Grenada finally became a British
colony, the basic patterns of land use and
settlement were established, a process which
included the extermination of the indigenous
Amerindian population and the introduction of
African slave labour to the sugar plantations. The
British takeover did not affect the pattern of human
ecology which, as a derivative of the exploitative
economy, was a key factor in the formation of
certain traits of identity, different in detail from

Grenada

Figure 1

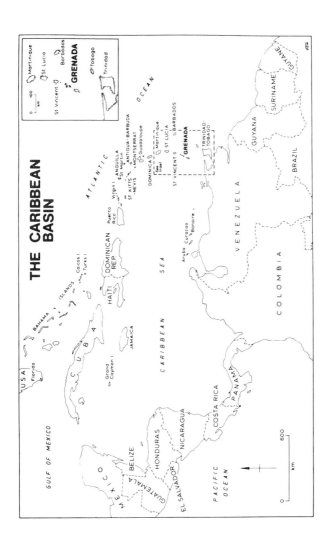

island to island but sharing a collective
dependency. [6] The cultural legacy of the French
period may be seen not only in many of the place-
names of Grenada, but also in the religious
persuasion of the population, which is approximately
two-thirds Roman Catholic and only one-quarter
Anglican.

The abolition of slavery led to the
emancipation of the Grenadians of African origin and
the importation of indentured labour for the
plantations. This began in 1839 with 164 Maltese,
continued with 438 Madeirans in 1846-47, grew in
1849 with 1,055 liberated slaves from Yorubaland and
culminated with 3,000 or so Indians between 1856-
73. [7] This particular selection, and especially
the Yoruba element, together with the freed slaves
and the mixed origins of the plantocracy is the
material from which the Grenadians of today derive.
It is a distinctive mix, as is that of every other
island or territory of the former 'British West
Indies', and in itself makes a contribution to
contemporary Grenadian identity.

The economy of Grenada is still very insecure,
dependent, and in the ACP classification [8] ranks
as being of 'Lower-Middle Income'. Sugar has given
way to bananas as the main plantation crop and
visible export, but the export agriculture of
Grenada is a little more diversified than that of
the other Windward islands. Nutmeg is the most
distinctive of the other crops, giving rise to
Grenada's image as 'the spice island', and so
enhancing the exotic ambiance so much to the fore in
the portrayal of the events of October 1983 from
whichever political slant they are viewed. In fact
the island of Grenada is in many areas immensely
fertile and well capable of supporting the present
population, given some sort of land reform to bring
the plantation lands into the internal economy.
This is a very important factor in relation to the
most central of the educational reforms introduced
by the revolutionary Government of 1979-83. This
internal capacity is also related to the hopes and
plans of that Government in respect of tourism,
which is the only other significant visible export
of Grenada. As with agriculture, so in tourism,
this island has the best natural resource, ie,
beaches, in the Windward group. The stated
objective of the PRG, the People's Revolutionary
Government of 1979-83, in seeking to develop a major
international airport in S.W. Grenada was to
maximize this undoubted tourist potential, an

Figure 2

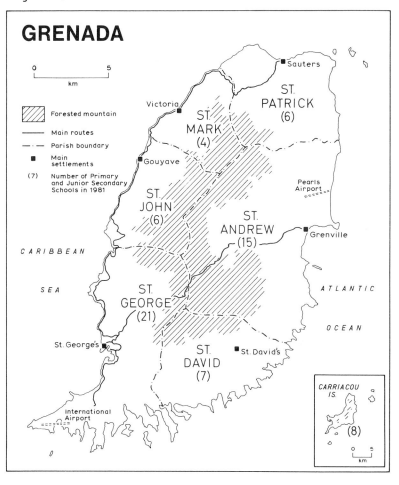

GRENADA

0 — 5
km

Forested mountain

Main routes

Parish boundary

■ Main settlements

(7) Number of Primary and Junior Secondary Schools in 1981

■ Sauters

ST.
PATRICK
(6)

Victoria ■

ST.
MARK
(4)

Gouyave ■

Pearls
Airport
=======

ST.
JOHN
(6)

ST.
ANDREW
(15)

■ Grenville

C A R I B B E A N

S E A

A T L A N T I C

O C E A N

ST.
GEORGE
(21)

St. George's ■

ST.
DAVID
(7)

■ St. David's

International
Airport
========

*CARRIACOU
IS.*

(8)

0   5
km

explanation that was never accepted by the USA. Grenada, from 1979-83 was seeking a new identity, one which would enable this small country to break away from the plantation syndrome on which the whole rationale of the British West Indies had been based in colonial times, and which had not been challenged after Independence in 1974.

The core of this chapter will seek to analyze the contribution of educational policy and provision to the identity bequeathed to Grenada by colonialism, and to compare with this the educational dimension of the thrust towards a new identity from 1979-83. This will be followed by a brief comment on the educational aftermath of the 1983 invasion, and an attempt to provide a synopsis of the culture - education - identity relationship in respect of Grenada.

Colonial Education and Derived Identity

Grenada shares with the rest of the Commonwealth Caribbean the educational legacy of colonialism, [9] for the most part that of British colonialism. As Beckford has neatly pointed out:

> ... the most intractable problem of dependent societies is the colonised condition of the minds of the people [10]

Beckford, a leading West Indian scholar, made this point in the context of plantation economies, which was of course the only economic rationale of the colonial West Indies. Slavery may have been abolished, but plantations were not, and the social structures emerging in the post-emancipation 'British West Indies' dominated the form taken by educational provision at that time, and in general have continued to do so. The sentiments of the Sterling Report of 1835 graphically illustrate the paternalism of the formative period of public educational provision in islands like Grenada:

> For although the negroes are now under a system of limited control, which secures to a certain extent their orderly and industrious conduct, in the short space of five years from the first of next August their performance of the functions of a labouring class in a civilised community will depend entirely on the power over their minds of the same prudential and moral motives which govern more or less the mass of the people here. [11]

Not surprisingly, the pattern of provision that followed was very much along the lines of that unfolding in England. Much reliance was placed on churches and missions, not only for elementary education, but also for a limited amount of selective secondary schooling and teacher training. The selective dimension obviously favoured the emerging, often creole, middle class, but expert opinion seems divided as to what extent Grenada could by the mid-twentieth century be truly classified as a plural society in the terms outlined by Farrell. [12] Smith's book of 1965, based on data collected in 1952-53 favoured a plural definition and perceived a sharply divided society as between an underprivileged, predominantly black rural mass, and a small white and creole urban elite, with only the latter benefiting from the selective education system. [13] Steele on the other hand, using information of some twenty years later, perceived Grenada as a rapidly unifying society, with educational provision being very much in the vanguard of such a trend. [14] The latter was writing in the aftermath of the relatively affluent decade of the 1960s and immediately after the flurry of educational aid programmes in the Commonwealth Caribbean in the early 1970s. As in many countries, considerable quantitative development in provision took place at this time, but first hand experience of the qualitative dimension of Grenadian education during that period would tend to confirm Smith's position.

The two dominant characteristics emerging from such a highly selective and elitist model in the small island context were: the 'West Indian intellectual', and 'education for migration'. These were of course often the same thing, and in general concerned only the elite, though many poor rural families made great sacrifices in the hope of a child, usually then a boy, breaking into the system.

> Despite the odds, however, the elitism enshrined in that greatest of glittering prizes, the island scholarship, concentrated the efforts of urban and rural pupils alike in intense competition. They 'played' the curricular system, selecting a field more susceptible to cramming which on the whole meant a furthering of the status of classics and literature. [15]

The export of talent thus engendered was in effect a

parallel of, indeed perhaps even part of the exploitative economy to which the West Indian islands remain 'enslaved' more than a hundred years after the abolition of individual slavery. In Grenada, this phenomenon seems to have been more highly developed than in most other islands of the Commonwealth Caribbean. This may have something to do with the idiosyncratic nature of educational investment in the various islands under the Crown Colony system, which operated for about 100 years in this region. Whatever the reason, it was certainly the case that Grenadian professionals were, at the height of the opportunities for migration in the 1960s and early 1970s, disproportionately over represented in other West Indian countries and metropolitan locations alike. Pride in their achievements was tempered by realization at home that their talents were sorely needed there. Derogatory terms such as 'white nigger' and 'mimic men' were coined to describe the attachment of West Indian intellectuals not only to the international system that still tended to exploit and disadvantage their countries, but also to the life-styles and cultural traits of the white middle classes.

Much depended of course on the political standpoint of the observer. To the conservative, it was merely a proper and logical use of talent and opportunity to further the fortunes of one's family, which in the Grenadian middle classes was becoming increasingly nuclear. To those taking a more socialistic or collective view it was more a question of dereliction of duty, even of exploiting the masses, most of whom had contributed indirectly to the support of island scholars. This is a matter of personal persuasion, and in Grenada the division was by no means along class lines. Many of the rural people supported the selective system because they identified with it, perhaps because it fitted the overall pattern of things, or perhaps because of the occasional success in the locality and the family, and village pride engendered thereby. A significant section of the educated minority, especially teachers, perhaps because of their involvement in the machinery of selection and certification, and despite their personal success, recognized its profligacy and dysfunctionality in terms of the needs of a small island nation.

So there developed a cleavage in the Grenadian elite due at least in part to the obsession of Gairy to encourage the 'exportation' of professionals. He became the archetypal 'mimic man' with little regard for the manpower needs of the country.

> The onset of Gairyism only intensified these tendencies. Education became an almost magical concept, associated with going away, becoming a 'big man', identifying even more closely with the eurocentric and metropolitan vision and creating a dream of alienation from work, production and the people. [16]

It must also be remembered that from the early 1970s, if not before, the emigration of educated and professional manpower was becoming increasingly difficult. This was not only due to tighter controls in Britain and North America in respect of immigration and work, but also similar restrictions in the various members of the Commonwealth Caribbean as they reached Independence. This in itself created an intensified insularity and forced greater attention on the problems of survival and related economic adjustments in the context of a small and very finite territory.

As the opposition of the teachers and some other professionals began to develop into a well organized set of opposition groupings, so the reaction of Gairy and his henchmen became ever more extreme and oppressive, until in March 1979 he was ousted while on a visit to North America. What then was the detailed legacy of Gairy and the whole accumulation of metropolitan influences, in terms of the Grenadian system of education as it stood in 1979? How can this be interpreted in respect of Grenadian culture and identity?

Despite an enrolment figure of 60 per cent, the pre-school sector did not really exist in any genuine or significant sense. The primary education stage, however, has been universal for generations - one of the advantages of smallness of national scale. But little had been done during the Gairy years to cope with decaying facilities, or to improve significantly on the low proportion of suitably trained teachers in this sector. In any case, the small teachers' college approached its task in an academic manner, and was treated at least by a proportion of its intake as a stepping stone out of the occupation of teaching and into higher education or more prestigious professional fields. In fact only about 40 per cent of primary teachers were trained by 1979. Of the remainder, many were young and lacking both knowledge and expertise. A special aspect of primary enrolment was in the form of 'all-age' classes. For various reasons of difficulty these pupils may have begun their primary schooling late or have missed or repeated years. Many were rural, and most from poorer families, and the fact that a strict age limit on entering for the "common entrance" examination to secondary school was applied, gave further advantage to the urban middle classes. identification with the selective and competitive mode of education was manifested in an almost complete lack of relationship between school and community.

In purely quantitative terms, the figure of more than 10,000 secondary sector pupils in 1979 seems impressive, but in fact nearly half of these were in the aforementioned 'all-age' classes of primary schools. As Davis points out:

> It is merely a remedial form of education and some schools add into that a little bit more of technical subjects. They do a little more Agriculture, a little more Home Economics and Woodwork etc. I think the general idea is, well, since these children are "not any use" in the academic thing, well they might see what they can do with their hands. [17]

Here is a very striking example of the cultural trait derived from Britain of the low esteem afforded to the technical aspects of education. Add to this the association contrived between low achievement and additional agriculture in the curriculum in a society based on the legacy of plantation slavery, and the formula for nemesis is complete. One can hardly, therefore, regard this part of so-called secondary schooling to have been worthy of that designation. A somewhat different problem existed with the relatively new sub-sector of junior secondary schools, an innovation derived from Jamaica and possibly influenced in turn by the "junior high" and "middle school" models of the USA and UK respectively. In the context of the flow of educational aid in the early 1970s, an incomplete sub-sector of this sort appeared in several of the Eastern Caribbean nations. In Grenada, as elsewhere, there was no clear rationale for the innovation, and the schools became idiosyncratic: some sought to become mini grammar schools preparing for the British General Certificate of Education (GCE), others worked towards the Grenada School Leaving Certificate, which is what the primary schools were doing anyway!

All that really mattered at that time in the
secondary sector was the 50 per cent of it that
comprised the traditionally selective academic
secondary schools, entered through competing in the
"common entrance" examination, a culturally
revealing term if ever there was one. [18] In
Grenada, some of these schools had their own private
examination for entry, accounting for about one-
third of their intake - a suitable vehicle for
nepotism. Despite their prestige, the academic
record of these selective schools was extremely
poor, as were the staff profiles, with only about
one in ten of their teachers a fully trained
graduate.
Beyond the secondary sector in its normal sense
lay only miniscule institutions for technical and
teacher education, both with high unit costs, and
inadequate curricula. At the genuine tertiary level
there existed the gratuitous extra-mural annexe of
the Kingston based University of the West Indies
found on all non-campus members of that
institution's constituency, and the aforementioned
and totally extraneous St George's University: "Set
up for American students who were unsuccessful in
their attempts to enrol in mainland US medical
schools ..." [19]
Clearly by 1979, after more than a century of
colonially derived educational structures and
provision, Grenada exhibited more than most of her
Caribbean neighbours those traits of cultural
dependence associated with such a particular
tradition, and especially the spurious
intellectualism contracted from the 'diploma
disease'. That is not to say of course that
individual Grenadians of genuine intellectual
distinction did not come up through this system.
Indeed, they did, as revealed by the high figures of
talented emigrants from the island. Rather it is to
say that the collective culture suffered from the
regular export of the only type of product the
colonial education system was designed to produce.
C.L.R. James, that doyen of West Indian
intellectuals is well entitled in one and the same
statement both to praise the capacity of the West
Indian populations to succeed in this form of
education, and also to recognize that the rationale
for the colonial system of education no longer
applies to the realities of the region. Speaking at
a congress of intellectuals gathered together by
Fidel Castro in Cuba, he included the following
comments:

> .... the mass base which the West Indian
> intellectual needed to find in Africa and in
> the literatures of Europe must now be sought
> for in the population of the West Indies
> itself. This population is unique in that it
> is the population of an underdeveloped country
> where the language of the great mass is an
> advanced European language.

and, after complaints that the Congress did not
include the main embodiment of local culture, that
is to say, the mass of the population or
representatives thereof:

> The function of this Congress is that
> intellectuals should prepare the way for the
> abolition of the intellectuals as an embodiment
> of culture. [20]

The young Grenadian intellectuals who recognized the
cultural inability of the colonial inheritance to
further local development, in particular the
inappropriate educational legacy, and who succeeded
in ousting the corrupt Gairy regime, had then to set
themselves the task of cultural regeneration. Like
C.L.R. James, they were impressed with the
educational achievements of the Cuban Revolution,
and no doubt agreed with Fidel Castro that
"Revolution and education are the same thing". [21]
They realized that the focus must be on Grenada
itself and understood the different ecological
imperatives, human and otherwise, of an independent
small island state. Unlike James - a Trinidadian -
they did not share his reduced perception of Grenada
either in physical terms or in respect of its
capacity for meaningful independence.

> I believe Grenada has about 20,000 people and
> is 10 miles long by 5 miles broad, or some such
> figures: absurd when you think of independence.
> What kind on independence? [22]

They had taken control of an independent Grenada,
and were set on an education-led revolution, and the
formulation of a new identity.

Revolutionary Education and Contrived Identity

Whereas the received educational system had
served to replicate and reinforce a derived social
class structure, the main thrust of the PRG policy
in this field was directed towards mass involvement

in shifting the balance of education towards an
internal rather than an external model. Central to
this scheme was a profound reform in the training
and education of teachers, not least due to the
involvement of radical teachers in the New Jewel
Movement. [23]

One of the earliest decisions of the PRG was in
effect to convert the Teachers' College into a
Curriculum Development Unit (CDU) and to abolish the
existing pattern of teacher training. The CDU was
established in 1979, and the year 1980 designated as
"the Year of Education and Production", no doubt
inspired by the Cuban precedent which had of course
been demonstrably successful at least in the
educational dimension. In January of 1980 a
"National Training Seminar" of two weeks duration
was convened in St George's for all of Grenada's
primary school teachers, many of whom were young and
untrained. The theme was "A New Kind of Teacher for
a New Society". In his opening address, the Prime
Minister, Maurice Bishop analyzed the deficiencies
of the inherited system of education, outlined what
he saw as the main elements for a "revolutionary
education system", and in particular alluded to a
new role and attitude for the Grenadian teacher:

> Your single most urgent task will probably be
> to assist in the process of wiping out the
> colonial prejudices and beliefs associated with
> the nature of education: the task of creating a
> curriculum relevant to the lives and
> experiences of our people, the task of raising
> hiher and higher our organizational capacity to
> handle our school systems.
>
> Today marks another important and historic
> step in the development of education within the
> Revolution. Because with this seminar, we are
> beginning the process in which the rigid
> distinction between teacher and student will be
> changed. For we believe and recognize that the
> teacher too is a learner and has the sacred
> responsibility to the students and to himself
> and to the Revolution to further develop
> himself as he goes along. [24]

During that seminar, the various local communities
set about the repairing of the delapidated primary
school buildings and equipment, and from then
onwards, until the tragic events of October 1983,
strong emphasis was placed on community cooperation
in respect of formal education provision. Such

cooperation was formalized in October 1980 with the joint creation of the National In-Service Teacher Education Programme (NISTEP), and the Community School Day Programme (CSDP). This was a scheme whereby the initial and in-service strands of teacher education and training were interwoven. Teachers spent four days per week in school, and one at the Teachers' College - or Curriculum Development Unit. This way many of them could be involved in the production of new programmes and materials in a very direct and practical way. Likewise the various members of local communities, from pupils to senior citizens, made not only a practical but also an intellectual contribution to their primary schools. So generations of accumulated local knowledge became acceptable, and some of this was translated by primary school teachers into new curriculum materials.

Not only was this reform of teacher training ecologically based and locally relevant, it was extremely economic:

> whereas the linear costing of the traditional college based method over time amounted to some $17.5 million (EC), the NISTEP method required only $3.7 million (EC). There was also a considerable saving in time. Under the traditional method it would have taken between 20 and 35 years, but through the in-service route barely a quarter of that time was envisaged. [25]

As well as acquiring local knowledge for curriculum renewal, NISTEP was also a process through which a "national standardized curriculum" could be achieved, and consequently a means of networking and diffusing the new ideology. Furthermore, there was the financial incentive whereby teachers were awarded differential pay increases in respect of their level of attainment in the certification arising from completion of the programme. [26] In such quaint ways do local cultures infuse their own individuality into received ideologies! On the issue of certification of NISTEP candidates, it should also be recognized that an important factor in the acceptance and support of the scheme was the speedy cooperation of the University of the West Indies, normally - and often with good reason - regarded as one of the most conservative and constraining of colonial legacies in respect of educational reform in the region.

Primary teachers attended the NISTEP programme for three years and, if successful with their certification they received qualified teacher status. This certainly proved an incentive, but in the area of involvement in curriculum reform and materials production, many were demonstrably less well motivated. This was quite likely a cultural constraint, whereby teachers had been used to following curricula, even syllabuses laid down for them by the Ministry or by the headteacher, and were uncertain about their own new role. Also, many headteachers were uncooperative in respect of supporting the involvement of staff in this way. Nonetheless the Curriculum Development Unit did produce a large amount of well organized material, largely due to the work of returned Grenadian intellectuals and other professionals who came to Grenada to support the educational revolution. A major cultural breakthrough was achieved in the field of primary Language Arts, with the production of the "Marryshow Readers", [27] which aimed to develop language skills by taking account of Grenadian 'creole' English and utilizing genuine everyday situations. In cultural terms and in respect of identity, these readers presented a direct challenge to the "Royal Readers", the series developed in the colonial context and still used at the time of the Revolution in 1979. It was not only, of course, in the formal system and with children that the PRG saw the need for radical changes in education. Indeed, the adult education programme, known as the "Centre for Popular Education" (CPE), was probably the most significant element in the process of ideological dissemination. While mindful of and inspired by the pioneer work of radical schemes in the field of adult literacy such as the "Cultural Missions" in post-revolutionary Mexico, and the impessive literacy campaigns in Cuba and Nicaragua, the smallness of Grenada and the concomitant proximity of urban and rural life was a distinct advantage. [28] With the practical backing of Cuba, simple but good quality materials were produced for 'Phase One' of CPE which had the aim of providing a literate base for subsequent phases. [29] In the event 'Phase Two' was rather slow in getting off the ground, and had been only seven months in operation before the invasion of October 1983 brought it to a premature end. But in that short time there was already evidence that the radicalism of the original approach was being clawed back by the residual influence of the formal academic legacy, for CPE was attempting in this second phase to use the newly acquired literacy of the population to put them through a relatively academic exercise, that of the formal study of subjects. It failed.

> The learners themselves might have been more motivated if the link between work and study had been more direct at this stage. A related point was that many of the potential learners had already gone through some form of schooling and had been declared failures. As adult literacy workers in this country will testify, this is the greatest barrier to entering adult education. Something tried and failed is much harder to attack than something never tried. Perhaps incentives were also not immediate enough to help them overcome this obstacle. [30]

The plan was that following a phase of literacy acquisition and a phase of formal study, a third phase of linking education with production would be able to operate. [31] This was not to be, and the reason was cultural not military. The leaders of PRG and CPE exhibited their own intellectual servitude, the sort attacked by James, in ascribing a role in the process to the very mode of provision that had already shown itself to be relevant to Grenada only in the 'emigration model'.

This was a pity, because in addition to the successful community involvement in CSDP there were also imaginative and energetic schemes of community education under way. These were designed to promote a confident national image. In addition to community meetings at various levels, there were 'workplace classes' based on Russian, Chinese and Tanzanian models, and a number of organizations including the National Women's Organization and the National Youth Organization, Trades Unions and the People's Militia. Despite the sterling work of inspired individuals in such organizations, it is readily apparent that they, like the old colonial model, are culturally alien. The really innovative and genuinely local curricular reforms and adult literacy drives should have been allowed perhaps to go more steadily and thoroughly on their own and to go on for longer.

Thus it would seem that the initial radicalism, genuine local focus, and perception of the ecological implications of a new Grenadian identity suffered not only from the residual strength of the colonial cultural legacy in educational terms, but also from the application, on ideological grounds, of radical models from other cultures. Of particular note is the fact that significant sections of the old formal system remained unchanged after 1979. The teacher education and curriculum development thrust was limited to the primary stage, while for example the traditional academic approach of the most prestigious secondary schools, especially Grenada Boys' Secondary School, was if anything boosted by the PRG.

Nonetheless, while noting such professional anomalies and misjudgements, one must recognize the release of popular cultural energy engendered by the revolution. In his examination of West Indian education, John Figueroa [32] recognizes the need for these island nations to reconsider their priorities in respect of development:

> From this inward examination and outward look we must come to decide whether the present values of the developed countries are necessarily those which we in the West Indies wish to adopt.

Being more aware and knowledgeable than most of the important place of poetry especially in West Indian culture, he also argues for the recognition of the distinctive contribution that the creative arts have to make in the whole idea of 'development'.

> The role of imaginative language, of poetry, in short of all kinds of fiction, in the development of human values is central; it needs a study in itself. And formal education in the West Indies does not seem to be aware enough of the centrality of fiction and other works of the imagination. [33]

The Grenadian Revolution certainly recognized and released this important human dimension. Through the regular work of the CPE, other aspects of community education, and especially 'Festivals of the Revolution', poetic output was encouraged. The belief in education often surfaces in these popular works whether in respect of 'production' or 'freedom' or both:

> Tis Education's Potent Arm
> That shields us from oppression's harm.

That guides our feet in freedom's way.
. . . . [34]

Conclusion

Sadly, the internal and external forces unleashed in October 1983 have halted the tremendous potential of the revolutionary drive of the previous four years to tackle the considerable legacy of cultural dependency with which Grenada is still faced. Indeed this could well be reinforced by decisions taken since the US invasion. Of the various educational innovations promoted by the PRG, only the NISTEP programme has survived, and the CSDP element of this remains as the only 'community' project. At the primary level, the "Marryshow Readers" have been discontinued and the comments of a 'high-level' official as reported by Lesser are culturally revealing:

> He said that although the family structure in the Caribbean tends toward large, extended families, and illegitimacy is widespread, he thought schoolbooks should promote "the ideal family". The Marryshow Readers, he insisted, "encourage promiscuity". [35]

The momentum of the adult literacy programme, already slowed by inappropriate curriculum design has been halted pending 'depoliticization'; the schools named after 'martyrs of the revolution' have been renamed yet again; and US cultural propaganda has been strong:

> Obliteration of the PRG is also a priority at the US Information Service's seafront office, where schoolchildren troop in to watch a short propaganda film, Grenada: return to Freedom. [36]

Yet perhaps the most damaging reverse has been in economic perceptions. The PRG, while encouraging certain external elements, such as tourism did see the implications for Grenada of the virtual closing down of emigration outlets. They focussed their attention on the upgrading of agriculture to improve and promote internal consumption, though the choice of the culturally derived 'state-farm model' was unfortunate. Some Grenadians seem to have assumed that the 'US rescue mission' will lead further to the reopening of migration opportunities to the US

itself, and the popularity of the 'mission' may be
partly ascribed to that. This seems unlikely to
happen, though the so-called 'screwdriver' assembly
industries might well come to the island to take
advantage of cheap labour.

There are many small island nations throughout
the Caribbean, Indian Ocean and Pacific regions,
like Grenada, created as pawns of European empires,
for whom the efforts of the PRG to come to terms
with the educational implications of enforced
insularity were a very meaningful experiment,
whether they shared the ideological stance or not.
There is an increasingly urgent need for this issue
to be confronted, but the replacement of old
colonial dependencies by creating new ones is not
the answer. A more thorough-going consideration of
island ecology, human and environmental; of regional
cooperation between groups of small islands; and the
implications of both for identity and education, is
required. [37] For as Lowenthal commented in respect
of processes of emigration and external dependence
in Caribbean societies:

> ... they lend credence to the local prejudice
> that things West Indian are second-rate,
> impotent, not worth having. Extreme episodes
> may subvert society altogether: a mass exodus
> of young adults or a sudden takeover by a
> foreign power can be catastrophic. But
> emigration and dependency are so endemic in the
> Caribbean that West Indian society now largely
> accomodates them. [38]

In recognizing the ecological implications of a
post-emigration society the PRG in Grenada were
inevitably faced with the need to challenge existing
concepts of identity, individual and national.
Irrational and emotive hostility to the PNG on the
part of the United States and the United Kingdom,
leading to a lack of practical support engendered
closer links between Grenada and Cuba and the Soviet
Union. This in turn appropriated the drive towards
a new identity for Grenada and introduced certain
ideological rigidities that led to the conflict
within the ruling elite and the murder of Maurice
Bishop and several of his supportive ministerial
colleagues.

Lowenthal's prediction of the catastrophic
nature of the takeover of any Caribbean society,
such as Grenada, by a foreign power is well
illustrated in the case of that particular island,

but should be limited to neither the 'American' military invasion, nor to physical conquest and control per se. We are talking about a generic cultural dependency that will tend to operate in relation to any external connections. Genuine Grenadian identity will only become a reality if and when it grows and operates on the basis of the ecological imperatives of a truly independent small island nation. The colonial legacy in educational terms would, and does act against such a development; the reforms of the PRG in this field began well in this respect, but were partial; the post-invasion educational policy has to be approved by the USA and therefore acquires an additional strand of dependency. Educational policy in Grenada may be said therefore to have been an important component of, respectively and successively, 'derived', 'contrived' and 'imposed' forms of national culture and identity.

Notes and References

1. There has been a plethora of publications since the 1983 invasion, each attempting an analysis of the recent history of Grenada. See, for example: Ambursley F. and Dunkerley J., Grenada: Whose Freedom? Latin America Bureau, London, 1984; O'Shaughnessy H., Grenada: Revolution, Invasion and Aftermath. Sphere Books, 1984; Payne A., Sutton P. and Thorndike T., Grenada: Revolution and Invasion. Croom Helm, 1984; US Department of State and Department of Defense, Grenada: a Preliminary Report. Washington, 1983.

2. Although Barbados achieved Independence in 1966 and is small in surface area, it has more than double the population of Grenada, is officially designated as one the MDC's (More Developed Countries) of the Commonwealth Caribbean, and although only 200 kilometres from Grenada is not strictly speaking in the Eastern Caribbean.

3. Grenada achieved Independence in 1974; however it had in fact been independent once before, as part of the ill-fated Federation of the West Indies (1958-62). From 1962 the various individual components of the Federation reverted to colonial status, and most have moved from there through 'Associated Statehood' (Grenada in 1967) to full Independence.

4. The term 'Windward Islands' is here used in the sense of the political geography of the former British West Indies. Within that operational

definition, the group comprized: Dominica, Grenada, Saint Lucia and Saint Vincent. The archipelago of smaller islands between Grenada and Saint Vincent is divided politically between those two states. Most of these, known collectively as the Grenadines, are part of Saint Vincent, the southernmost two are part of Grenada.

5. Clarke C.G., Insularity and Identity in the Caribbean. Geography, 1976, 61, 1.

6. Brock C., Education and the Multicultural Caribbean. In: Corner T., ed., Education in Multicultural Societies. Croom Helm, 1984.

7. The term 'Indians' was used at that time to designate people from the Indian Sub-Continent, nowadays sub-divided into Bangladesh, India and Pakistan. Since it has become customary in contemporary West Indian classifications to term this section of the population 'East Indian', the matter has become even more confusing, especially in areas such as Guyana where descendants of true East Indians are found, deriving from the indentured labour brought into their Caribbean colonies by the Dutch from what is nowadays Indonesia.

8. The 'ACP' countries are those of African, Caribbean and Pacific location linked to the European Community through the Lome Convention. 'Lower-Middle Income' is designated as being a per capita GNP of between US$300 and 699.

9. Brock C., The Legacy of Colonialism in West Indian Education. In: Watson J.K.P., ed., Education in the Third World. Croom Helm, 1982.

10. Beckford G.L., Persistent Poverty: Underdevelopment in Plantation Economies of the Third World. Oxford University Press, 1972.

11. Report of the Rev. J. Sterling to the British Government, May 11 1835. As quoted in: Gordon S.C., A Century of West Indian Education. Longmans, 1963.

12. Farrell J., Education and Pluralism in Selected Caribbean Societies. Comparative Education Review, 1967, 11, 2.

13. Smith M.G., Stratification in Grenada. University of California Press, 1965.

14. Steele B., Social Stratification in Grenada. Independence for Grenada - Myth or Reality? London Institute for International Relations, 1974.

15. Brock C., op cit (1982).

16. Bishop M. and Searle C., Grenada: Education is a Must. The British-Grenadian Friendship Society, London, 1981.

17. Davis C., A Critical Examination of Grenada's Education System. Paper presented to the National Teachers' Seminar, St George's, January 16, 1980.

18. "Common entrance" is the name of the entrance examination to British independent (public) schools.

19. Payne A. et al., op cit.

20. James C.L.R., The Revolutionary ... In: Singham A.W., ed., The Commonwealth Caribbean into the Seventies. Centre for Developing-Area Studies, McGill University, Montreal, 1975.

21. Castro F., Educacion y Revolucion. Universidad Popular, 6th Series, 1961.

22. James C.L.R., op cit. Grenada is in fact more than 15 miles by 10 along its main axes, and more significantly, at the time James was writing had a population of about 90,000.

23. The New Jewel Movement was established in 1973, following the merger of two opposition parties, the Joint Endeavour for Welfare, Education and Liberation and the Movement for the Assemblies of the People. NJM became the Opposition Party in 1976 and the PRG in 1979.

24. Bishop M., Feature Address delivered at the Opening of the National Training Seminar at St George's on Friday January 4, 1980.

25. Brock C. and Parker R., School and Community in Situations of Close Proximity: the Question of Small States. In: Lillis K., ed., School and Community in Developing Countries. Croom Helm, 1985. (EC) designates Eastern Caribbean Dollars.

26. Lesser L., Education in Grenada: Before, During and After the Revolution. Internal UNESCO paper, 1984.

27. Named after Albert Marryshow, one of Grenada's greatest sons who in 1915 founded the forerunner of the present national newspaper The Free West Indian. A lifelong supporter of a Federation of Caribbean States, he became one of the first senators in the West Indian Federation in 1958, but died that very year at the age of 81. Always mindful of the African dimension of West Indian heritage, he was clearly the sort of Grenadian figure about whose activities contemporary Grenadians could profitably be informed.

28. The most direct link with this tradition of radical approaches to adult literacy objectives was the active support of the Brazilian educator, Paulo Freire. See for example: Report of the Paulo Freire

Grenada

Workshop, February 20-28, 1980;
Work Study Approach for Community Education.
Curriculum Development Unit, Ministry of Education,
St George's, Grenada, 1980.
   29. Phase One materials of the CPE programme
comprised a reader, Let us Learn Together, and a
teacher's guide, Foreward Ever, both published in
1980. They were enthusiastically received and
certainly successful.
   30. de Block L., Lessons from Grenada. Paper
presented to the Universtiy of Bristol School of
Education Conference: Learning from the South -
What, Why and How? January 1984.
   31. Plan for Development of Adult Education in
Grenada, Centre for Popular Education, Grenada,
March 30, 1981.
   32. Figueroa J.J., Society Schools and Progress
in the West Indies. Pergamon Press, 1971.
   33. ibid.
   34. CPE Brigade, Carriacou, Tis Education's
Potent Arm. In: Tongues of the New Dawn: An
Anthology of Poems, Festival of the Revolution,
March 10-13, 1981.
   35. Lesser L., op cit.
   36. Chamberlain G., Grenada's love-hate affair
with the US. The Guardian, June 12, 1984.
   37. See for example: Brock C., Education,
Economy and Employment in Small Commonwealth
Countries. In: Watson J.K.P., ed., Youth, Education
and Employment. Croom Helm, 1983;
Brock C., Scale, Isolation and Dependence:
Educational Development in Island Developing and
Other Specially Disadvantaged States. Commonwealth
Secretariat, London, 1984.
   38. Lowenthal D., West Indian Societies.
Oxford University Press, 1972.

FROM EDUCATIONAL BORROWING TO EDUCATIONAL SHARING: THE JAPANESE EXPERIENCE

Tetsuya Kobayashi

Japan, which accomplished her modernization in education by 'educational borrowing', the transmission that is of foreign educational experience in the later nineteenth century, had to undergo the experience of a second educational borrowing under the occupation of the UN-American Force as a result of her defeat in 1945. The development of Japanese education since then has been in several stages, generally identified as:
  a) the period of educational reform under the occupation (1945 to 1951),
  b) the period of the 'reversed course', or the re-examination of occupation policies after independence (1952 to 1960),
  c) the period of economic growth and educational expansion (the 1960s to the first half of the 1970s),
  d) the period of educational re-orientation (the second half of the 1970s to the present).
The "post Second World War educational reform", unlike the one of a hundred years ago, took place under occupation and was modelled on the educational patterns of the occupying country. This fact accounts for much in the development of the educational policies and politics of Japan during the subsequent forty years, since any argument inevitably has to take a stand for or against the American inspired reform. While the post-war reform held up an ideal of democratic education which was universalistic in nature, and to this extent might be acceptable to any nation including the occupied Japanese, the fact that the reform was carried out under the direction of the foreign power made it difficult for Japanese sentiment to conceive of the reform as genuinely national. Furthermore, the

post-war reform, modelled on a foreign system rooted in different historical and cultural traditions, was adopted under conditions of severe economic and social constraint. Though reform plans were duly discussed by the Japanese themselves before being put into practice, these discussions were carried on within the framework set by the occupation authority; any criticism of the framework was likely to be taken by the occupying power as a sign of non-cooperation.

Thus the post-war reform under the occupation contained problems from the outset which would come to the fore with the restoration of Japan's political independence. Indeed, a re-assessment of the American-styled educational reform was taking place already towards the end of the occupation period, and since then in the course of educational development over the next forty years, criticism of this reform has been repeatedly voiced by responsible political authorities. As recently as March 27, 1984, the government presented to the National Diet a bill for setting up an "Extraordinary Council on Education to consider reforms necessary to accommodate education to changes in society and the development of Japanese culture". [1] Not content with the present condition of the nation's education, Premier Nakasone himself initiated this proposal. According to him, the post-war reform had planted alien ideas and systems under the guidance of the occupying power and this must change.

This reaction towards reform could be interpreted as reactionary. Indeed it is. The author of this chapter however, takes the view that this critical movement may be considered in the long run as part of a re-adjustment process related to the post-war experience of educational borrowing. As was the case with the first educational borrowing of a hundred years ago, it takes time for any foreign-born ideas and systems to take root in Japanese practice. There seems to be no doubt that the Japanese on the whole have accepted the consequences of the second educational borrowing, though with a few important modifications. For roots to take hold, however, the Japanese would have to overcome their resistance to the 'enforced' educational borrowing and to re-adjust this borrowing to their own contemporary national situation. This chapter will attempt first to examine the nature of this enforced educational borrowing and then to inquire how this borrowing has been adjusted to Japanese tradition.

Post-War Educational Reform: 'Enforced Educational Borrowing'

The UN-American occupation policies in the period 1945-51 brought tremendous changes in the political, economic, social and cultural life of the Japanese. It was a great educational process through which the Japanese were trained to become citizens of a democracy. Occupation policies in education, as in other areas, were pursued with two main objectives in mind: de-militarization and democratization. The former sought to expel wartime educational leaders from positions in education, to abolish thought control by the government, and to prohibit militarist-nationalistic propaganda. It also suspended the teaching of Shushin, [2] History and Geography which were regarded as effective tools for spreading military attitudes, and excluded militarist-nationalistic elements from textbooks of other school subjects.

These policies for de-militarization were accepted by the Japanese as punishment for defeat with almost no resistance. Japanese pride was hurt but a war-weary people, placing the blame on their war-time leaders, bore this national disgrace with equanimity. The reaction of the Japanese became more hostile, however, once the matter affected the fundamental identity or culture of the nation. When the occupation authority went beyond the eradication of militarism and ultra-nationalism and in the Report of the US Commission on Education in 1945 criticized the national character and traditional culture of the nation as legacies of 'feudalism', it bewildered the Japanese and left deep scars. These scars would cause emotional reaction later, but for the time being the Japanese who had not yet recovered from the shock of defeat and, seeking survival under substandard economic conditions, accepted the entire de-militarization process.

The democratization policies of the occupation authority consisted on the one hand of presenting the American model of democracy as one to follow and, on the other, of encouraging democratic elements among the Japanese themselves, elements which had been much weakened by the militarism of the 1930s. To formulate a model for democratic education, a US Education Mission was dispatched to Japan in February, 1946, and after a month's study made its recommendations for educational reform. Together with its interpretations and suggestions for implementation by the occupation authority, these formed the democratic model for Japan. A committee of Japanese Educators consisting of liberals was set up to cooperate with the American Mission, [3] and later, under its new title of Education Reform Council, it formulated detailed reform plans under close supervision of the US authority. The main proposals were enacted by the National Diet into a number of educational laws, and the Ministry of Education duly issued appropriate regulations and circulars. In adapting these laws and regulations, local government authorities were also under the close supervision of the local military government officers of the occupation army.

Democratization under the occupation was carried out under the forceful direction of the US authority, as was the imposition of the American model, but it included at least a semblance of reform proposed by the Japanese themselves. In the field of education, as seen above, while the intention of the occupation authority – the imposition of American ideas and systems – was clear, it expected voluntary cooperation of the Japanese. In its turn then the occupation authority was more flexible in striking a compromise with traditional Japanese practices. Later when the dual nature of educational reform under the occupation came to be analyzed, controversy developed as to whether or not the reform was simply forced upon the Japanese. [4]

In the civil occupation policies, 'New Deal' influences were apparent, most typically in agrarian reform, the unionization of labour and the emancipation of women. In education, John Dewey's New Education movement was strongly reflected in the American model presented. While democratization policies extended to almost all areas of education, certain major points deserve examination here. The first is related to the educational objectives of post-war Japanese education which were set in accordance with the recommendations of the US Education Mission – specifically: to recognize the worth and dignity of the individual; to provide educational opportunity matching the abilities and aptitudes of each person; to foster freedom of inquiry and training in ability to analyze critically; to prepare the individual to become a responsible and cooperating member of society. [5]

These aims which were to guide the people forward through a new democratic education were apparently opposed to those which had been dominant

in pre-war Japanese education, namely: the training
of loyal subjects; narrow nationalistic
perspectives; blind obedience to authority. The
American objectives were, however, not necessarily
entirely new in Japanese education, since they had
been advocated by Japanese liberal educators in the
1920s as part of a world-wide New Education
movement. Some commentators therefore justly
interpreted the post-war reform as a revival of the
pre-war Japanese liberal education movement. [6]

In setting up these educational objectives,
Japan adopted its own method of implementation.
This was to pass legislation in the form of the
"Fundamental Law of Education" in 1947. [7] This Law
consists of a preamble and eleven articles each
dealing with specific areas of public education: its
general objectives; the equality of educational
opportunity; the length of compulsory schooling; the
principle of co-education; the school system and the
preparation of teachers; the teaching of social
education; political education; religious education;
the administration of education; and educational
legislation. The Law was prepared in accordance
with the adoption of the new Japanese Constitution
of 1947, which was itself to nullify the old
Imperial Constitution and at the same time the old
Imperial Prescript on Education. The latter was
promulgated by the Emperor Meiji in 1880, it stated
the aims of education and had been observed with
veneration ever since. Establishing the new
principles of education in the Fundamental Law of
Education passed by the National Diet as the supreme
authority of democratic Japan, instead of by the
Emperor, the supreme authority of Imperial Japan,
was in itself a genuinely radical act.

The practice of defining educational objectives
by legislation is not uncommon in a country which
has experienced a big political change, and
certainly it was necessary and practical for post-
war Japan which had to be transformed from an
imperial to a democratic nation in a short period of
time. The Fundamental Law which had constitutional
authority would thus guide the course of the
development of the nation's education in the years
to follow. On the other hand educational objectives
cannot be achieved only through constitutional
authority, however democratic it and the law-making
processes may be. They must be put into practice at
the popular level in an atmosphere of free self-
criticism. Unfortunately, in the initial stage of
democratization, the Fundamental Law of Education

became a new authority in itself, and its application in practice tended to be uniform and standardized. This left little opportunity for local and individual interpretation.

Another important area to consider is that of the School and College systems. Following the principle of equal opportunity in education, the School Education Law of 1947 established a single track school system. The six-year universal free education at primary school was basic as it had been in the pre-war system, but in place of pre-war selective secondary education with several parallel tracks, a six year course of secondary education, with a compulsory common lower secondary school of three-years followed by an optional three-year comprehensive upper secondary school, was to be set up. All kinds of pre-war tertiary education institutions were to be developed into four-year colleges or universities. This so-called 6-3-3-4 system was proposed by the US Education Commission as a model and adopted uniformly throughout Japan. It is noteworthy that despite the fact that many and varied school systems besides the 6-3-3-4 variant were in existence in the United States, the US authority recommended a unitary model for Japan.

The school leaving age was raised from 12 to 15. The extension of the period of compulsory schooling from six years to nine was well received and soon put into practice by the Japanese, despite the severe financial and material conditions in the immediate post-war period. This ready acceptance of the extension of the period of compulsory schooling was partly due to the fact that it followed the line of a decision which had already been made in 1941 by the Japanese themselves, and which had been suspended during the war. While all pupils automatically moved from the elementary to the lower secondary school at the age of 12, the move from the lower to the upper secondary school at the age of 15 was made on the basis of a selection examination. The comprehensive upper secondary school thus established did not follow the American pattern in which students went on to high and senior high school without taking an examination and were free to choose their courses or school subjects. On the contrary, it rather resembled the European pattern in which students were allocated to different courses within the school or to different schools according to their ability and aptitude. Indeed the upper secondary school was more in accord with the traditional structure of Japanese secondary education, and served to maintain the hierarchical order as between the more prestigious academic courses and the less honoured vocational courses, though both were now available within the new comprehensive school system.

Pre-war higher education institutions of all kinds were transferred to the new four-year colleges or universities, in which a new 'general education' component was introduced as an integral part of undergraduate courses of study. However, the traditional hierarchy among the higher education institutions remained and the former Imperial Universities continued to dominate all others. In such circumstances, the newly introduced general education courses were unable to develop from a supplementary and inferior position in relation to professional education. Little development was observed among liberal arts colleges, while most undergraduate courses showed a marked trend towards specialization. The traditional autonomy of the faculty within the administration of state universities remained unchanged, and the proposed American-modelled system of administration, including lay members, met with strong opposition and was never taken up.

In pre-war Japan, teachers had not necessarily been in a low social position, and the training of primary school teachers had already been raised to the level of the junior college. In the post-war reform the training of both primary and secondary teachers, in order to improve their qualifications, was raised to the level of college education. Economic difficulties in the immediate post-war period prompted the unionization of teachers. The Japan Teachers Union, contributed to the improvement of the teachers' economic status and, through its activities, expanded its political influence over educational administration at both central and local levels.

As far as educational administration in general is concerned, the post-war reform intended to decentralize the system. The traditional pattern of administration had been highly centralized. According to the recommendations of the US Education Commission, new boards of education were to be created at both prefecture and municipal levels. [8] The members of these boards were to be elected from among the lay people by popular vote. This was to ensure greater participation by non-professionals and to remove the schools from the bureaucratic control of the central government. As it turned out in the elections of 1948 and after, the majority of board members were either ex-principals or teachers who often represented professional circles or unions. For a while their expertise was a great asset in placing new education on the right track. Soon after however, the Japan Teachers Union became involved in politics at the national level, [9] while the local boards of education also became politicized. This led to the introduction of a system of nominated board members in place of elected ones. [10]

Local administration in education, achieved a great measure of autonomy from central authority in becoming responsible for establishing and maintaining schools, employing teachers and designing school curricula. The formerly dominant central Ministry of Education was nearly abolished during the planning of the reform, but succeeded in remaining as a coordinating, advising and assisting organ to the local authorities, although ministerial bureaucracy was to be checked by councils consisting of laymen and education specialists. Despite its weakened statutory position, however, it continued to exercize control, since post-war educational reform 'from above' required an office at the central level to receive and interpret the directives of the occupation authority. Central expertise was also needed to implement the education reform nationwide. In any case, financial support by central government was urgently called for by local authorities at this time of extreme financial difficulty, immediately following the economic and physical ravages of war. Thus contrary to intentions the advice of the Ministry was in practice taken as mandatory, and the regulations and standards set by it controlled almost every aspect of local educational administration.

In summary it may be noted that while there were indeed some significant changes as a result of occupation policies, there were also important examples of Japanese inspired reforms as well as some manifestations of inertia.

The Promotion of the Post-war Reform and its Revision

The occupation ended in April 1952, with the activation of the Peace Treaty which had been concluded in San Francisco the previous September. A democratized Japan which had been under the patronage of the occupation authority for nearly seven years now made a new start for herself. As a

first step, the Japanese government undertook a
review of various cabinet orders which had been
issued during the occupation period. The Ordinance
Review Committee thus established, [11] dealt not
only with the legality of the ordinances but also
with the content of any which might be 'against the
actual condition of Japan'. [12] As to education,
the Committee in its report of October 1951, held
that while the post-war reform contributed to
correct the faults in the pre-war system and to
establish a democratic educational structure in the
country it nonetheless had significant shortcomings.
It had adopted foreign models in many respects of a
different national tradition and impetuously pursued
alien educational ideals. [13] This resulted in the
system's disharmony with the actuality of Japan.
Such alien aspects, the Committee recommended,
should be carefully examined to ensure the new
educational system related more closely to native
conditions and thus be made more effective in actual
practice. In other words, the Committee expressed
its discontent with the inefficiency of the new
American style educational system.

A particularly strong feature of this criticism
was a widespread dissatisfaction with the quality of
the newly established 6-3-3-4 pattern, which had had
in any case to start under severe financial and
material difficulties. Another strong reaction
reflected the discontent of industrial circles with
the insufficiency of vocational education,
considered by them as essential for industrial and
economic reconstruction. They considered this
aspect to have been neglected in comparison with
general education, which had been given priority as
part of the American emphasis on citizenship
training. While a minority report of the Committee
advocated return to the pre-war school system, the
majority accepted the post-war 6-3-3-4 model in
general but recommended some modifications or
'flexible applications' of it. These
recommendations included the strengthening of
vocational education in middle and high schools, and
the establishment of separate vocational high
schools and colleges. The Committee also suggested
more efficient teaching at school level by re-
emphasizing specific subject-matter oriented
curricula in languages, mathematics and science.

The Committee's criticism was only one example
of the prevailing discontent with the quality of
teaching, which was focussed on child-centred
teaching methods and on 'social studies' in

particular. This area of study was introduced in place of pre-war Shushin, History and Geography, and with the intention of imparting the knowledge, attitudes and skills considered necessary for future citizens. For the teaching of this and other study areas, the so-called experimental method was introduced to promote children's initiatives in the teaching-learning process. After some years of practice, 'social studies' was said to have failed in keeping up both the academic standards which would have been assured by the teaching of traditional History and Geography syllabuses and the moral standards of children which had been the objective of pre-war Shushin education. Controversy over social studies and moral education continued in the 1950s, until finally the curriculum revision of 1958 decided that Moral Education (Shushin) was to be taught for one hour per week in elementary and middle schools. At the same time, within the 'social studies' area the systematic teaching of History and Geography was re-introduced. In high schools, a further curriculum revision of 1960 subdivided Social Studies into four separate school subjects: History, Geography, Political Science-Economics and Ethics-Civics. [14]

As far as vocational education was concerned, legislation over the following years included the "Vocational Education Promotion Law" in 1951, [15] the "Science Education Promotion Law" of 1953, [16] and measures for expanding science and engineering education in colleges and universities in 1959-1961. These no doubt contributed to the economic development of Japan which would make its full impact in the 1960s. It should be noted that these measures for vocational education were given much stimulus from similar policies in the United States and Great Britain in the post-Sputnik era.

On the administrative front, according to the recommendation of the Ordinance Review Committee of 1951, the Board of Education Law was amended in 1956 which introduced the system of appointed school board members in place of elected ones. As mentioned earlier, this revision was a conservative reaction to what was believed was an increasing politicization of local educational administration. The introduction of the appointive system lost the boards of education their independence so that they became an office of the head of local government. This new system, however, was considered to be more in keeping with the traditional Japanese pattern of local educational administration.

Within a decade or so of regaining
independence, some major changes occurred in the
Japanese educational system. Political opponents
often labelled the changes or revisions as a
'reverse course', thereby implying that these
changes would abandon the ideals of the post-war
democratic reform and take Japanese education back
to its pre-war problems and status. [17] It cannot
be denied that a nostalgic sentiment for pre-war
education existed among proponents of these
revisions, nevertheless their efforts should also be
understood as a conservative readjustment of the
post-war reform. Such readjustments, as has been
noted above had already been made to some extent
during the occupation, but at this later stage
particular effort was made to establish specific
educational conditions that were reckoned to be
essential for the economic development planned for
the 1960s and beyond. Nationalistic reaction
against the foreign-modelled educational system,
already observable at this stage of readjustment,
would become more apparent in the later stages when
Japan buoyed by her economic success would regain
her full self-confidence.

After passing through the period of revision of
the 1950s, Japanese education entered into the
period of expansion of the 1960s and the 1970s.
While the enrolment rate of compulsory middle
schools had been almost 100 per cent since their
inception, that of non-compulsory high schools had
increased from 42.5 per cent in 1950 to 57.5 per
cent in 1960, 82.1 per cent in 1970 and 94.2 per
cent in 1980. The enrolment rate for higher
education had also increased from 10.3 per cent in
1960 to 23.6 per cent in 1970 and 37.4 per cent in
1980. [18] This educational expansion was made
possible by the recovery and growth of the Japanese
economy, which had by the late 1950s already
overtaken its pre-war level. While economic
conditions contributed to educational expansion it
can also be argued that the rapid economic
development owed much to the well-educated labour
force, and in particular to the young workers who
benefited from the expanded general and vocational
education opportunities after the war. This close
relationship between education and the economy was
well appreciated by the policy makers of that time,
so that during the period of the 1960s and after,
utilitarian and economic motivations were dominant
in Japanese educational philosophy and practice.

The enormous expansion of educational provision

did not however take place without problems. The popularization of schooling inevitably brought a greater number of pupils and students with different abilities and aspirations into schools, and this caused such problems as drop-outs, truants, maladjusted and alienated students, and other manifestations of anomie. Educational institutions moreover often failed to adjust their curricula and organization to cope with this changing nature of the student body. Educational administrators and policy makers were preoccupied with the re-examination of the post-war educational system which had to accommodate such change and expansion. Thus it is not surprising that the first report of the Central Council for Education published in the 1960s was on higher education. [19] As a result of the output of the expanded school system the tertiary sector was to experience rapid transition from an elitist to a mass provision while the traditional administrative and educational patterns remained strong within it. Recommendations of the Report covered almost all aspects of higher education. Some of them, such as the diversification of higher education institutions according to their educational and research functions, and the improvement of the system of student selection, were put into effect by the government. Several experimental types of institutions were set up in the following years. The recommendations which clarified the roles and responsibilities of the state and the university in the settlement of campus disputes were effectively applied in the nationwide disorders of the 1970s.

In the greatly expanded and popular high school education sector too, the Central Council in this period recommended in its report of 1966 a greater degree of diversification in courses and curricula. The object of this was to meet the different abilities and aspirations of students and also to satisfy the diversified vocational needs of society. Various means of integrating opportunities of vocational training into the school system were proposed and adapted in the following years.

While readjustments in the school and university systems were going on, general reconsiderations of educational objectives were also being discussed. In 1966, the Central Council for Education published the paper: "On the Image of the Ideal Japanese", which clarified the ideal moral and ethical qualities of the national culture. [20] This was the first official and open criticism of the universalistic Fundamental Law of Education of 1947. Whereas, according to Masaaki Kosaka, [21] an eminent philosopher and chairman of the subcommittee which drafted the statement, the 1947 Law was too abstract to apply to Japan's particular situation, the 1966 paper specified in detail the qualities desirable in a Japanese national. They ranged from the necessary personal qualities and abilities to each individual's sense of membership of his family and of society at large, and dealt with his possession of the proper form of patriotism, respect and love for the symbols of the state, and the promotion of excellent national characteristics. [22]

One may be struck by the strident nationalistic tone of the statement, which is but a reflection of the heightened national sentiment released after independence and further reinforced by the economic successes of the 1960s. Notably, however, the Report just as emphatically mentions "the Japanese opening to the world", implying that the Japanese people could no more live alone in the world and that they should seek the peace and welfare of mankind in cooperation with other nations. This point of internationalism was further stressed in the Central Council's report of 1974: "On the International Exchanges in Education, Science and Culture". [23] It stated the objectives of international exchanges to be: to educate the Japanese people for international responsibility; to deepen foreigners' understanding of Japan and that of the Japanese of other nations; to develop education, science and culture through mutual respect and stimulation; and to participate in international undertakings for the solution of problems common to the human race. To achieve these objectives, the Report recommended various measures, most of which were put into practice in the following years.

These two reports, above all the earlier one, provoked much controversy among those concerned with the nation's education. Some critics notably the Japan Socialist and Communist Parties were reminded by the strident tone struck in the 1966 Report of pre-war nationalistic education. Others, like the philosophers Kosaka and Teiyu Anano, accepted the statements as an expression of genuine nationalism which, suppressed during the occupation, now began to regain its due place in the nation's education. The support of internationalism in the 1974 Report as an essential element of education for living in cooperation with others in an internationalized world was less contentious but still difficult in some aspects to build onto Japanese traditions.

Even today, the controversy continues, provoked by Premier Nakasone who holds a nationalistic view of education and who urges a further re-examination of the nation's education system including its objectives. It will take time to see any kind of resolution of the various arguments pertaining to the aims of Japanese education. However it should be noted that this ongoing debate is part of the process of transformation of educational ideas and practices introduced to occupied Japan by the UN-American authorities some forty years ago.

From Educational Borrowing to Educational Sharing

From the above observations it may be concluded that the development of Japanese education for the past forty years has been a process of revision of what was reformed under the occupation. This process seems to be activated by three motivations:

a) nationalistic reaction against forced reform under the occupation.
b) adaptation of the adopted foreign (American) model to indigenous (Japanese) cultural and social conditions.
c) adaptation to the changing social, economic and educational needs of the late twentieth century.

Of these three, the first became actualized towards the end of the occupation and since then has been a *leitmotiv* of the reform movement, varying its tones from expressions of nationalistic sentiment to the firm ideological commitment to nationalism. The second was already observed at the time of the introduction of the American model during the occupation, thus qualifying the educational borrowing of the post-war reform as selective borrowing, though the choice lay within certain limits. After independence it continued to exist, and more recently the claim for adapting a foreign system to the Japanese culture has been intermingled with the nationalistic reaction. The third motivation has been underlying the contemporary reform movement of the 1970s and 1980s and, building on the others, has worked towards a truly Japanese model of educational development.

The Report of the Central Council for Education proposed that the recommendations of 1966 be carried out with the status of the "Third Educational Reform". [24] The first great reform had been the

time of the Meiji Restoration in the late nineteenth
century, and the second immediately after the Second
World War. Despite attempts to provide a
significant image and thrust, only ad hoc reforms
took place in the following years and the radical
"Tnird Educational Reform" did not occur. In
analyzing the reasons for this, Shogo Ichikawa
pointed out among others the following:
  a) non-existence of awareness of national
     crises which may call for total reform such
     as occurred in the first and second reforms.
  b) non-existence of a central authority for
     enforcing total reform, an existence instead
     of varied and conflicting values and
     ideologies among the people, which makes any
     consensus on a total reform difficult to
     achieve.
  c) non-existence of foreign models for a third
     reform to follow: the first followed the
     emerging systems of the advanced Western
     nations; the second followed the American
     model. [25]
    The third reason quoted by Ichikawa is now
widely accepted by the Japanese. During a hundred
years of her modern history, Japan strove to 'catch
up' with the advanced nations, not only in
education, but in all aspects of the nation's life,
following models borrowed from these countries. [26]
Now after passing the half way mark of the twentieth
century, Japan suddenly finds herself among the
advanced nations and does not see any more models
worthy of borrowing from others. Complacent as it
may sound, this statement satisfies the
nationalistic sentiment of the Japanese who once
totally lost their self-confidence through the
defeat in the Second World War. On the other hand
it implies that Japan now has to create her own
model to follow. Thus the Japanese people are
confronted with the problem of how such a model can
be created and, also in relation to this problem,
what should be the role of educational borrowing
from which Japan profited so much in the past. Will
there be no need for such borrowing in the future?
    It may appear that the emergence of the three
motivations listed at the beginning of this section
has diminished the importance of educational
borrowing from the United States. For example, the
nationalistic reaction against the imposed foreign
model may alienate people from the American model.
Similar effects may be observable in the other two.
In reality, however, the United States has continued

to supply models for Japan to copy but with an obviously lighter impact than during the occupation itself. [27]

In the first instance, the United States no longer monopolizes a role-model for Japan; it has become only one of several which Japan examines. In the early 1950s when she sought to improve vocational education, Japan sought models from the United Kingdom as well as the United States. In the 1960s when reform of local educational administration was stressed, it was the British system that was referred to. Similar examples can be shown for other cases of borrowing in which not only the United States and the United Kingdom but almost all other major industrial nations have been referred to in some way.

Second, the American model has come to be viewed by Japan with greater objectivity. After independence Japan saw the United States as a source for models not only in the positive sense but also in the negative sense. While various educational experiments in the United States have been viewed as 'good examples' or models to be followed, other more negative features of the American experience such as school vandalism, low attainment and high drop-out rates of pupils, to quote just a few examples, serve as warning signals from which Japan may have still to learn. The question of 'educational standards' is always an important consideration here, given the origins and traditions of the system. [28]

This relative attitude in looking for models is, in a way, in accord with the traditional pattern of Japanese borrowing, which may be called 'selective borrowing'. However, while in the past Japan weighed only the value, real and potential, of foreign models for her use, now she includes the Japanese model itself on an equal footing with other models to be exploited. Behind this change in attitude is the increasing self-confidence of the Japanese in their own education. Though this self-confidence has grown as Japan's international status has increased, it has risen also as observers of Japanese education from outside the country have increasingly come to appreciate the efficiency of Japanese education. Such appraisals usually see education as a key factor contributing to the high economic growth and political stability of Japan. The high scores obtained by Japanese pupils in the surveys conducted by International Educational Achievement (IEA) have been quoted as proof of the high academic standards of Japanese schools. [29]

The well-disciplined cooperative school climate has also been quoted to explain the excellent labour relations and high productivity of Japanese industry.

Thus what may be called "Japanese models" were first created outside the country. Such models were not always· fully accepted by the Japanese themselves, but they provided an. impetus for them to see their own educational provision from a different perspective. Above all, they have given encouragement to those Japanese who value the traditional patterns of Japanese education, since "Japanese models" now emphasize those very characteristics of Japanese education which owe much to the cultural tradition of the nation: service, hard-work and loyalty.

Nonetheless there is a potential pitfall in the recognition of a definitive Japanese model of the traditional type which some have begun to claim, and that is complacency. In the past it was educational borrowing that enabled Japan to avoid this pitfall. Looking to other nations certainly brought improvement in Japan. Now the country is in a position in which it does not have to follow a model from any single nation, indeed, it can serve as a model to others. On the other hand there are a number of signs that Japanese education also faces the crises already recognized by the reports of the Central Council in the later 1960s and the early 1970s. [30] These crises were reported in such a way as if they were peculiar to Japan, but in fact they are common to all industrialized nations and to some extent to other nations as well. Thus the Japanese may be wise to continue educational borrowing, or at least keep track, through comparative educational study, of the policies of other nations to combat these crises.

As the report of the OECD on Japanese education rightly pointed out in 1971, there is "a need for new attitudes" in Japan. [31] The report stated that Japan should no longer look at the world as a market in which skills and raw materials can be acquired and products sold, but should play "a major role in creating more universal science and technology for world needs, not only for domestic needs". In short it recognized the imperative of interdependent development.

This point was indeed recognized by the Central Council in its reports, [32] which inter alia stressed the importance of educating the Japanese for "openness to the world", and the necessity of

international exchanges in education as well as in
other fields. Internationalism has now become an
important element of Japanese education, [33] though
as mentioned above this standpoint can also bring
problems. For example, in respect to the increasing
number of Japanese being found in contact with other
peoples in the fields of politics, economics,
cultural exchange and even in ordinary daily life,
the question has been raised whether they are
sufficiently equipped with qualities equivalent to
those of other peoples to enable them to work well
together. The issue of overseas students can be
considered in this context; as the number of
overseas students studying in Japanese universities
has increased, questions have been raised as to
whether these overseas students are being trained as
well as their Japanese fellow students, or indeed as
well as their friends studying in other countries.
So as the contact of Japan with other nations
rapidly develops, Japanese education is being
increasingly scrutinized and subjected to
international comparison. The results of such
scrutinies have not always been satisfactory, and
many Japanese have now begun to realize that there
is no room for complacency but only for improvement
in Japanese education. [34]

Japan must recognize that education is a
humanistic endeavour, in which all the human race
participates on an equal footing. Thus borrowing is
as mutual as sharing. In education, any nation may
borrow from other nations who in turn may borrow
from it. The result should be a mutual improvement
of education, and ultimately of human kind. Japan
may be saved from falling into the pitfall of self-
complacency by changing her traditional pattern of
borrowing for her own benefit to educational sharing
for the sake of humanity. It is to be hoped that
the Japanese-American relationship will develop in
this direction.

Notes and References

1. The Extra-ordinary Council on Education is
now officially called the Provisional Council on
Educational Reform. The bill was enacted on August
8th, 1984, as Law for the Establishment of a
Provisional Council on Educational Reform.
Accordingly on August 21st the 25 council members
were appointed by Prime Minister Nakasone. They
included three university presidents (one former),
five professors, four former governmental high

officials, four business men, three school administrators, one school teacher, two labour union leaders, one journalist, and one novelist. Dr. Michio Okamoto, former President of Kyoto University and Professor of Medical Science, was appointed as Chairman of the Council. They held their first meeting on the 5th September 1984 and are expected to submit their recommendations to the Prime Minister within three years. The Japan Teachers Union opposes the Council.

2. Shushin is a school subject in elementary and secondary schools which was regarded as the most important subject to cultivate children's moral character till 1945. The teaching of Shushin was based on nationalism, Confucianism and Shintoism, and included elements equivalent to Civic Education and Religious Instruction in Western schools. During war-time, Shushin became a tool for military and ultra-nationalistic propagation, and was considered by the national government at that time to be the most important subject of the curriculum.

3. The title of the committee was, Committee of Japanese Educators, which was formed by the Memorundum of the General Headquarters of the Supreme Commander for the Allied Powers for Imperial Japanese Government dated January 9th, 1946.

4. The arguments have been made over the whole post-war period since 1945. As an earlier example at the political level, see the speeches and discussions between the Government and the ruling party, the Liberal Democratic Party, and the opposition parties during the 42nd Session of the House of Representatives in March and April, 1956. Sengo Kyoiku Shiryo Shusei (Source Books on the Post-war Japanese History of Education), vol. 5, Sanichi Shobo, 1983, pp 44–77.

5. Report of the US Education Mission to Japan. US Department of Education Publication 2579, Far Eastern Series II. Washington, US Government Printing Office, 1946; Ministry of Education, Science and Culture, Course of Studies. Governmental Documents Publishing Centre, Tokyo, 1947.

6. Kaigo Tokiomi and Murakami Shunryo eds., Kindai Kyoikushi (History of Modern Education), Seishin Shobo, 1959, p 258.

7. Ministry of Education, Science and Culture, Education in Japan 1982 – A Graphic Presentation. Governmental Documents Publishing Centre, Tokyo, 1982, p 9.

8. Administratively Japan is divided into 47

prefectures and 3,255 municipalities, each of which has its own local government elected by popular votes. The national government, however, has certain power over the local governments, the power of which is stipulated by the laws and regulations. Among the local governments, the prefectural government is given certain power over the municipal governments within the prefecture.

9. After World War Two, the pre-war union movement of school teachers which had been oppressed in war-time was revived, and in 1947 the Japan Teachers Union (Nikkyoso) was set up. Presently a little over half of the teachers belong to the Union, which is the largest national union in Japan. The previous president of JTU was once the chairman of Sohyo, (a Japanese equivalent of the British Trades Union Congress). Politically it has been one of the strongest supporting organizations for the Japan Socialist Party, although it includes an equally influential Communist element. (See Duke C. Benjamin, Japan's Militant Teachers. The University Press of Hawaii, 1973.)

10. Kobayashi Tetsuya, Society, Schools and Progress in Japan. Pergamon, 1976, p 81.

11. The Ordinance Review Committee (or the Committee for Reviewing Ordinances), was created on May 1, 1951, at the suggestion of the Supreme Commander for the Allied Powers by the Cabinet of the Japanese Government as an informal advisory committee which was to review the Ordinances that had been issued by the Japanese Government under occupation, and to recommend to the Prime Minister the policies and means for enactment necessary after the abolition of the Ordinances. The Committee held its first meeting on May 14, 1951 and completed its work by the end of that same year. It made several sets of recommendations, including those on education. Its eight members included lawyers, economists, journalists, businessmen, and one educator.

12. The guidelines for deliberation set by the Ordinance Review Committee at its first meeting. Asahi Nenkan (Asahi Yearbook), 1952, p 142.

13. The Report of the Ordinance Review Committee on the Reform of the Educational System, July 2, 1956. In: Kindai Kyoiku Seido Shiryo, Vol 1.

14. Ministry of Education, Science and Culture, Education in Japan 1964 A Graphic Presentation. 1964, pp 64-69.

15. Sagara Iichi, Gakko Roppo, (Educational

Laws and Regulations), Kyodo Shuppan, 1984, pp 245-247.

16. ibid, pp 243-244.

17. Gyakumodori Kyoiku wa yurusanai (No reverse course in education shall be approved). Nikkyoso Kyoiku Shinbun (Japan Teachers Union Newspaper), February 24, 1956. Sengo Kyoiku Shiryo Shusei, vol. 5.

18. Monbusho, Monbu Tokei Yoran, (Ministry of Education, Science and Culture, Educational Statistics). Governmental Documents Publishing Centre, Tokyo, 1984, pp 140-141.

19. Ministry of Education, Science and Culture, Central Council for Education, Chuo Kyoiku Shingikai, Daigaku Kyoiku no Kaizen ni tsuite (Central Council for Education, On the Improvement of University Education), Report, Governmental Documents Publishing Centre, Tokyo, 1963.

20. Chuo Kyoiku Shingikai, Risouteki Ningenzo ni tsuite, (Central Council for Education, On the Image of the Ideal Japanese). Report. In: Koki Chuto Kyoiku no Kakuju Kaizen ni tsuite (on the Expansion and Improvement of Later Secondary Education), Governmental Documents Publishing Centre, 1966.

21. Masaaki Kosaka, a Kantian philosopher was formerly Professor of Philosophy of Education, Kyoto University, and then President of Tokyo University of Education.

22. These themes are all headings of chapter 4 of the 1966 Report; see note 20.

23. Monbusho, Kyoiku, Gakujutsu, Bunka niokeru Kokusai Koryu ni tsuite: Chuo Kyoiku Shingikai Toshin (Ministry of Education, Science and Culture, Central Council for Education, On the International Exchanges in Education, Science and Culture) Report, Governmental Documents Publishing Centre, 1974.

24. Ministry of Education, Science and Culture, Central Council for Education, Basic Guidelines for the Reform of Education. Report, Governmental Documents Publishing Centre, 1972. (Japanese Original published by the Ministry of Education in 1971).

25. Ichikawa Shogo, Gendai Nippon no Kyoiku Seisaku (Educational Policies of Contemporary Japan). In: Shinboni Michiya and Aoi Kazuo eds., Nippon Kyoiku no Rikigaku (Dynamics of Japanese Education). Yushindo, 1983.

26. Kobayashi, Tetsuya, op cit.

27. The curriculum reforms and educational innovations in the USA during the 1950s and 1960s

influenced these matters in Japan.

28. Ministry of Education, Science and Culture, Educational Standards in Japan, 1975: Quinquennial Report on Education. Governmental Documents Publishing Centre, Tokyo, 1976 (Japanese).

29. The IEA test in mathematics conducted in 1964 revealed that the Japanese pupils in the 13-year-old age groups ranked highest in mathematical achievement among those of 10 countries. Similar high scores were observed in the science test conducted in 1970. See T. Husen ed., International Study of Achievement in Mathematics. John Wiley and Sons, 1967; IEA, International Studies in Evaluation, I-IX, John Wiley and Sons, 1973-76.

30. For example: the Central Council for Education made such comments in its 1963 Report in the first chapter (note 19), its 1966 Report in the first chapter (note 20) and its 1971 Report in the preface (note 24).

31. OECD, Japan: Reviews of National Policies for Education. Organisation for Economic Cooperation and Development, 1971.

32. Ministry of Education, Science and Culture, Central Council for Education, On the International Exchanges in Education, Science and Culture. op cit.

33. ibid, see note 23.

34. Kobayashi, Tetsuya, Into the 1980s: the Japanese Case. Cooperative Education, 1980, 16, 3.

EDUCATIONAL POLICY AND MINORITY ISSUES IN THE SOVIET
UNION

Wolfgang Mitter and Leonid Novikov

Introductory Remarks on the Theme and the
Terminology Used.
        This chapter is chiefly concerned with the part
which the Soviet education system and its
institutions have played in the implementation of
the present 'national' policy of the Communist Party
of the USSR and of the Soviet state. The
traditional and for Western researchers,
comparatively well documented instrument of this
policy of bilingualism in Soviet education, will be
examined in particular depth. At the same time, the
multidisciplinary nature of the theme will not be
overlooked.
        The point of departure is arrived at from two
directions. On the one hand, educational science,
in discussing the theme, needs to examine the
statements and reflections of adjacent disciplines
like the social sciences. On the other hand, apart
from the more or less pronounced 'strict pedagogic'
perspective of this multidisciplinary problem, in
which the concept 'multicultural education' takes on
a central position, reference to research carried
out into "bilingualism" and "multiculturalism", in
themselves complex and multidisciplinary matters, is
called for. [1] It is beyond the scope of this
chapter fully to apply this two-stage
multidisciplinary approach to the analysis of the
case of the Soviet Union. It is however necessary
to begin by outlining certain significant basic
criteria, in order to help the understanding of the
specifically Soviet brand of educational policy in
general and of bilingual and multicultural education
in particular.
        Conceptual difficulties arise from
discrepancies between the terminology most often
employed by Western and by Soviet authors. Soviet

114

social sciences follow the politically ideological mode of expression in the use of terms like "multinational collective" [2] and "international education" which refer to the basic concepts of 'nation' and 'nationality' or 'ethnic group'. Whereas 'nation' (natsiia) comprises both ethnic-linguistic and socio-political characteristics as the more comprehensive category, 'nationality group' (natsional'nost') is confined as a rule to ethnic and linguistic traits only. [3] A specific connotation is inherent in the concept 'autochthonous nationality' (korennaia natsional'nost') which contrasts with a 'nationality' or 'ethnic group' consisting of immigrants. [4] Western sociologists borrow this terminology in their investigations, which makes sense in so far as the specific factors (both objective and subjective) of the Soviet model of multiculturalism are thereby brought to the focus of attention. [5] This chapter is orientated around the terminology which has become established in the West in comparative sociology and comparative education; in it the concept 'culture' is seen as a fundamental category for the identification of and differentiation between ethnic groups. 'Culture' in this sense comprises origin, language, religion, upbringing and national consciousness, where all these features may occur together or in combinations of single factors (eg, origin and language without religion). It is according to this definition that one may speak of the Soviet Union as a 'multicultural' and not merely 'multinational' country.

The problem of terminology, which can only be summarily defined here, has a practical political side as well as an academic one, as it has formed the rationale for the implementation of administrative measures at various junctures in Soviet history: from the entry in the identity card of every Soviet citizen of membership of a particular nationality or ethnic group to the bestowal of exit permits (to both German states as well as to Poland and Israel) for those affiliated to the corresponding groups.

It should be noted at this point that nationhood is by no means interpreted in the same way by all communist parties and is therefore not a little politically explosive. The use of this term in a recent Soviet study published by S. Brouk referring to the French population provoked a letter of protest from the chairman of the French Communist

Party, Georges Marchais, to the Central Committee of the Communist Party of the Soviet Union. The party newspaper L'Humanite published on February 29th 1984 the exact wording of the protest, expressing the "strong displeasure of the Central Committee of the French Communist Party" despite its habitually close ties with the Soviet Communist Party. The Soviet author's "ethnological classification" and his attempt, based on this assumption, to divide the French population into two groups - ie,

> on the one hand, the 44 million or 82.5 per cent of the population representing the French people, and on the other hand, the Bretons, Basques, Catalans, Corsicans, Jews, Armenians and Gypsies

is criticized as "dangerously close to racism". Marchais adds that it is

> an affront to our national conscience to describe certain members of the French community as not 'pure' French people. [6]

The Soviet concept of "international education" is found to have a dual meaning in Soviet sources. Firstly, it expresses the multinational character of Soviet society and of Soviet education as a whole (the macro-level), as well as of local social units and schools in particular (the micro-level). [7] In addition, "international education" refers to a central aspect of political education, which is reckoned as being complementary to "patriotic education". [8]

Occasionally this concept is understood to signify pedagogical efforts aiming at solidarity between socialist countries. As a rule, however, it is used of intra-Soviet relations, where the participants are individual nations and nationalities of the Soviet Union. In this context the question 'multicultural' or 'intercultural education' remains to be clarified. The term 'intercultural education' has been chosen here because it renders more appropriately the international and purposeful character of this domain of educational theory and practice.

The use of the concept "bilingual education" causes no problems except in that there must be a clear demarcation between it and monolingual and multilingual education, where as a rule monolingual education falls in the same category as instruction

through the medium of the mother tongue. In the
Soviet Union this type of instruction is enjoyed
mainly by the Russians who normally have to learn no
"second mother tongue". In opposition to this,
there exists in the Soviet Union multilingual
education, above all in the form of 'trilingualism'
whereby non-Russian minorities from outside the
RSFSR acquire both the majority language of their
Union Republic and Russian.

Some basic historical and socio-political factors.

The Soviet Union has inherited its
multicultural structure with over a hundred ethnic
groups ("nations and nationalities") from tsardom.
Its policies thus are determined by a centuries old
tradition which, if one disregards the early
subjugation of the Finnish speaking 'original'
inhabitants of the northern areas of European
Russia, stretches through the wars of conquest from
the sixteenth century on into the second half of the
nineteenth century. Soviet expansionist policies
have added only little to this heritage - East
Galicia in 1939, North Bukovina in 1940 and Tuva in
1944. The fact that the three Baltic republics,
east Karelia and Bessarabia as well as western
Belorussia changed hands repeatedly does not belong
in this context as these areas were part of Russian
territory before the October Revolution.

Comparisons with the development of other
European empires spring to mind. Two peculiarities
of the Russian development, however, are worthy of
note, all the more so, as they are not unimportant
for the comprehension of the present situation. One
of these concerns the unity of the whole territory,
while the other refers to the comparatively close
link between ethnic and social factors revealed
during the incorporation of new areas.

Soviet policy has always defined the
integration of its multicultural society as a
central task. To the present day, it has taken the
relevant norms from Marxist-Leninist (and for a time
also Stalinist) ideology. Clearly neither
ideological directives nor political practice
justify the assumption of a linear process; this is
also true of the varying importance of these two
elements. There is a multiplicity and variety of
both Soviet and Western literature on the subject,
which is particularly concerned with whether and to
what extent the current theories, precepts and
directives can be derived from Lenin's maxims and

which is further complicated by the fact that these
themselves are open to controversial
interpretations.

The central question, which is repeatedly
asked, relates to the reconcilability of national
and cultural plurality with the postulated unity of
socialist society, which should be distinguished not
only through the definitive abolition of all class
differences, but also through the "amalgamation"
(sliianie) of nations and nationalities. Indeed,
the use of the term "Soviet people" anticipates this
goal. As against this the Marxist-Leninist ideology
also represents the theory of the "blossoming"
(rascvet) of the socialist nations [9] and of the
"growth of national self-awareness" and which the
former General Secretary of the Communist Party of
the Soviet Union, Iurii V. Andropov, for example,
designated as a "logical and objective process" in
his address of December 23rd 1982 on the occasion of
the sixty-fifth anniversary of the Soviet
Union. [10] The contents and range of the similarly
employed theory of "reconciliation" (sblizhenie)
remain unclarified in so far as in its usage, as
with all general ideological statements, current
analysis is intermingled with future expectations.
As an apt example of recent warnings against an
exaggerated application of the 'reconciliation
theory' to intra-Soviet linguistic and cultural
policy, O.I. Dzhioev's contribution, published in
the journal Voprosy Filosofii may be cited. In his
general reflections on the relations between nation,
culture and personality, he argues that

> with the growth of social homogeneity of the
> nations, with the process of their intellectual
> reconciliation and mutual cultural enrichment
> ... the awareness of their national identity
> (grows) at the same time. Yet, however one
> chooses to solve the problem of the future
> existence of the nations it is vital not to
> confuse the process of their reconciliation –
> in the sense of a consolidation of their social
> homogeneity and their political-moral unity
> with the process of liquidation of every ethnic
> difference between them. [11] (editors'
> translation).

The new Soviet party leader K.U. Chernenko is
clearly aware of the dangers involved in an
undifferentiated confusion of visionary perspectives
and harsh realities. In his first major speech of

118

The Soviet Union

March 2nd 1984 he pleaded expressly for a sober analysis of Soviet society ("without any trace of utopic notions"). His comments contain on the one hand clear hints at a proposed enlargement of the scope of the individual Union Republics in the economic domain by means of some relaxation of the constraints of central planning, on the other hand, he accentuates the "internationalistic nature" of Soviet society and the communist world view and defines the Soviet economy as an "integrated economic complex" [12] (editors' translation).

Multiculturalism has been affected by demographic changes, brought about by the differing birth rates in the European part of the Soviet Union as opposed to those of the Transcaucasian and Central Asian republics. [13] From the point of view of the traditional leadership demands granted to the Russians, this development is of the greatest political significance, as the proportion of non-Russian nationalities has grown between 1970 and 1979 (years of the last two censuses) from 37 to 49 per cent. [14]

Demographic changes tend to encourage internal migration, a fact which is also confirmed by centuries of tradition to which above all the eastward movement of Russians from the central Russian region towards the Pacific bears witness. This development was continued by the industrialization policies pushed through by Stalin, who also continued the particular enforcement measures of tsarist policy characterized by deportations, exile and resettlement. At the present time, migration policy plays upon the spirit of adventure of the young and on the attraction of material incentives. As a result the main direction of internal migration has altered, so that the traditional movement southwards and eastwards has been replaced by a "rush to the north", [15] and indeed away from those areas with a surplus of workforce (eg, the Caucasus and Central Asia) into the urban industrial centres of European and Asian Russia. This basic factor is of great significance to the topic of multicultural education in that the latter is increasingly being confronted with the emergence of "multinational collectives". [16]

The effect of intra-Soviet migrations on the logistical situation in schools may be illustrated by two reports. In the first the principal of a boarding school (classes 1-10) in the Jewish Autonomous Region is reported as saying that the 250 pupils at his school belong to thirteen nationalities: among them Russian, Jewish, Ukrainian, Belorussian, Lithuanian, Uzbek and German. [17] The second announces that in the Novosibirsk region there are no fewer than 75 nationalities and in some families two languages are used in everyday routine, namely the (non-Russian) mother tongue and Russian. Kolesnikov draws attention in particular to the situation, where children attend Russian language schools, speak their mother tongue among each other and at home and retain their 'national identity'. He mentions in this context on the one hand the folklore, on the other, using the Kazaks as an example, the following important national traditions which are transmitted through upbringing in the family and education at school:

> fear of one's elders, respect for one's parents, return to the house of one's parents after obtaining a qualification. [18]

No doubt this trend could be illustrated further if the scanty general information about the multicultural composition of the population of the new industrial centres of Togliatti and Novocheboksary (Chuvash ASSR) could be supplemented by data about the national composition of the local schools. [19]

The Soviet Union is today still characterized by the existence of concentrated cultural ethnic communities, above all in its rural areas, which causes special problems not only in educational policy, but also in matters of public health. Physicians and geneticists have located regions in Central Asia and Azerbaydzhan where hereditary blood diseases occur "all too often". According to reports, these are passed on from one generation to the next and are "rooted" in certain population groups of rural areas, where for centuries marriages have traditionally occurred between the inhabitants of two neighbouring villages or settlements on ethnic or religious grounds. N. Bochkov, a leading Soviet geneticist also expresses concern that some cities are not fulfilling their "melting pot" function and that some nationality groups exist who favour intermarriage. As a result of such notions, he has diagnosed more frequently severe metabolic disturbances and blood diseases, well above the average incidence in the population as a whole, in these voluntarily "ghetto-bound" groups when compared with the urban average. [20]

In addition, the increased mixing of people of various ethnic origins in "multinational collectives" has also attracted the attention of sociological research, where the prime interest is centred around mixed marriages and interpersonal relations at work and in day-to-day situations. As an example the investigation led by Iu.V. Aratiunian of the Institute for Ethnography of the USSR Academy of Sciences, carried out between 1971 and 1976 and between 1973 and 1980 at 35 bases, may be cited. The ongoing results, arrived at by taxonomical analysis, were summarized in the journal Sotsiologicheskie Issledovaniia, namely that the quality of interpersonal relations at work depended upon the level of education of those concerned as well as being generation-linked. Urbanization and social mobility, however, were seen as the most important factor. Alongside this complex of objective factors, subjective elements are not unimportant; they are reflected above all in the private sphere, particularly in family life, which as always is deeply imbued with cultural tradition: mores and customs. The quality of interpersonal relationships is also affected by competition at work (where there is a surplus of qualified workers) and by "bourgeois ideological" influences. [21] In a specific sense, this problem is made politically relevant by the underrepresentation of certain nationality groups in the decision-making bodies of party and state in multicultural regions, as pointed out by Iurii V. Andropov's critique, amongst others. [22]

The fact that mixing of those of differing ethnic origin brings forth tensions in daily life has of late been taken up in almost every article, even official ones, as a current problem. Thus in a resolution issued on January 12th 1983, the presidium of the Supreme Soviet of the USSR stressed the need to

> fight against national pride, presumption and disrespectful behaviour towards other nations and nationality groups. [23]

Intercultural Education.
a) Intercultural Education in the Curriculum.
The esteem, attested by Soviet linguistic and literary didacticians and the universal role ascribed to work on Russian literature in non-

Russian schools leads directly to the theme of intercultural education in the curriculum. N.M. Shanskii and M.V. Cherkezova propose the theory that the practice of teaching Russian literature in school suffers as a result of too little consideration being given to the intellectual and cultural backgrounds of the school child. In this context the "Marxist-Leninist philosophy of the dialectic of the general, particular and individual principle" is quoted. While the principle of the general and of the individual is normally taken into account when teaching Russian literature to non-Russians, the particular national principle has been neglected. [24]

Both authors pay particular attention to the use of illustrations as a means of introducing non-Russian children into the spirit of Russian literature. This procedure should be handled very sensitively, so that the children do not assimilate the visual material through the medium of their mother tongue. This view leads on to the argument that the teaching of Russian literature should be considered in the context of the peculiarities of both the Russian and of the non-Russian literatures. The conclusions inferred from these considerations lead on to the demand that the teaching of Russian literature to non-Russian children should be distinct from the process of teaching Russian literature to Russians, which would involve a direct connection with the objectives of intercultural education.

The contribution of history teaching to intercultural education has been made clear in an article which appeared in the journal Prepodavanie Istorii v Shkole. P.S. Leibengrub begins by stating that it is characteristic of Russian history that members of many nationalities have been involved in "progressive and patriotic movements", examples being the peasant wars in the seventeenth and eighteenth centuries, the first patriotic war of 1812 and the Crimean war of 1853-6. The "common historical fate of the peoples of our country should be demonstrated to the pupils". [25] He attaches significance to the point of view already mentioned in this chapter, namely that in Russian history oppressors and oppressed alike have been spread right across the various nations. He demonstrates, with reference to Lenin, that every ethnic group of the Soviet Union has the right to decide its own destiny but that this basic self determination is by no means identical with complete segregation in particular cases. [26]

Further information on the link between curriculum and intercultural education can be found in several articles on the problems of education in the schools of the far north, in which the children of northern peoples must be given an education and an upbringing which leads them to a mastery of both Russian and the mother tongue (in Russian speaking schools) and which at the same time, does not alienate them from their parents' lifestyle. These children usually live in boarding schools on account of the huge distances involved; despite the transport difficulties, with 120-500 kilometres separating the boarding school and the parental home, the organs of party and state are anxious to facilitate regular contact between children and parents.

A most important role in the children's education relates to their adaptation to the occupations and work forms of their parents, who live above all by hunting, breeding reindeer and catching fish; training in other skills, such as the sewing of clothing and head coverings is also a part of their vocational education. [27] N. Petrachuk points to the danger that traditional professions may die out all the earlier, the more often pupils continue their training in 'modern' technical schools and institutes. [28]

The latter example outlines the collision of two cultural structures in the education process of non-Russian children in which intercultural education should become a means of overcoming the resulting tensions. All too often, however, this unrelieved tension leads to a parallelism in daily life, to which E.G. Lewis, who for many years carried out penetrating comparative studies on multicultural education (particularly in the Soviet Union and in England and Wales) under the special frame of reference "dichotomy between home and work", has drawn attention. [29]

b) Integration through the Educational System.

In its attempt to make living conditions more uniform and to promote the mixing of members of different nations and nationalities, Soviet policy has ascribed a central function to the education system. This policy places greater hopes on the contribution of school and related extra-curricular educational activities than on the experience gained at the place of work, in that intercultural education (in a general sense), in addition to the activation of "multinational collectives", also provides direct access to adolescents through instruction and may thus increase the "subjective factors" of the integration process. [30] In this context Soviet politicians and social scientists like to refer to the notable achievements of Soviet educational policy in the establishment of the ten years of compulsory schooling and of the institutions of further education as well as to the creation of a sizable intelligentsia in certain regions, particularly Central Asia and the far north, where the illiteracy rate before the October Revolution was particularly high.

The specialist literature also devotes particular attention to the exchange of students in higher education and also in the intermediate level professional schools and vocational technical schools. [31] The central authorities also support the education of the future elite of non-Russian Union Republics at the prestigious universities, technological universities and academies of art in Moscow and Leningrad. [32] A similar role is envisaged for the pedagogical institutes of the RSFSR, Belorussia and the Ukraine regarding the training of teachers of Russian for other republics.

Bilingual Education.
It is not surprising that there exists a close correlation between the concepts of intercultural education and of bilingualism, given the significance which language plays in all aspects of human life. The attempt to preserve the inherited cultural identity even after the relinquishment of the language concerned presents a particular problem, as can be observed, for example, in Germans and Jews on the one hand and also in the nationality groups of the far north.
A. The Objectives of Bilingual Education
The definition of the objectives attributed to bilingual education in the Soviet Union relate to a large extent to "Russian national" bilingualism, as this constitutes the focal point of language policy; the acquisition of Russian by non-Russians being the main objective of bilingual education. Without overlooking the other forms of bilingual education, the following comments will concentrate upon this main aspect of bilingualism. Mention will be made of examples of dual bilingualism involving Russian and the respective local tongue, as in Azerbaydzhan. [33] Other examples refer to bilingualism between two non-Russian tongues. [34]

This variety is widespread where minorities acquire the major language of their (non-Russian) republic or region. [35]

The general goal of bilingual education of the "Russian-national" variety is the fluent mastery of Russian by all non-Russians. The scheme developed by E.G. Garunov which takes this as its starting point emphasizes the quantitative aspect of language instruction, which can be assessed by the level of acquisition of passive and active linguistic competence with its particular skills (pronunciation, reading comprehension, listening comprehension, speaking, thinking and writing). [36] As against this differentiation, the aforementioned "dichotomy between home and work" alludes to a linguistic competence which is characterized by two levels of usage, the local language being restricted to the private and intimate spheres. [37] Here Lewis offers convincing examples founded upon an evaluation of studies on the Tartars of Kazan and the Latvians. [38]

B.   Methods of Organization and Legal Definitions

The translation of the goals of bilingual education of the "Russian-national" variety into the organizational and curricular reality of the Soviet education system as a whole is determined by the key question of the relationship between the first language as the primary medium of instruction and the second language. Here the particular nature of this structural relationship within the Soviet linguistic spectrum, as distinct from the position of "foreign languages" such as English and French in the Soviet school time table becomes evident. Under this system of classification, languages which may appear both as (intra-Soviet) "national tongues" and as "foreign languages" are granted special status; this is especially true of German and Polish.

From the point of view of the medium of instruction, one may divide the Soviet education system broadly into "national schools" (schools with a specific nationality profile) which have a non-Russian language as the medium of instruction, Russian speaking schools and two further, special types:

a) In 1979 "national schools" in the whole of the Soviet Union were attended by approximately 33 per cent of the relevant age group, though in some areas as in the Union Republics of Armenia, Azerbaydzhan, Georgia, Lithuania, Tadzhikistan, Turkmenistan and Uzbekistan the corresponding proportion reached over 80 per cent. [39] Hitherto, there has existed in these schools a noteworthy variety of practice as far as the start made with the teaching of Russian and the amount of weekly lesson time available for Russian is concerned. Russian is taught from the first semester of the first school year in the Autonomous Republics of the RSFSR and the Union Republics of Armenia, Georgia and Uzbekistan, and from the second semester of the first school year or from the beginning of the second year in the other Union Republics (eg, the Ukraine and Lithuania). According to the new model syllabus, however, [40] all (three year) elementary schools in the whole country are supposed to teach Russian from the beginning of the first school year. In an attempt to smooth over the opening stages, pre-school education has been drawn into the programme of Russian teaching, including both the traditional nursery schools and the experimental "zero grade" preparatory classes, with children starting school at the age of six, which were introduced for this very purpose throughout the whole Soviet Union in the last decade and which have quickly developed. [41]

The total of weekly lesson time in the "national" general education middle school (classes 1 to 10 or 11) for Russian ranges from 33 periods for the whole of the 10 or 11 years in Estonia, Latvia and Moldavia to up to 40 in Kirghizia. Within this allocation, the different proportion in the various horizontal intermediate stages must also be considered. The following figures for weekly lesson totals in the elementary stages (years 1 – 3) were cited: the Baltic republics 7-8 weekly periods, Georgia 14, Tadzhikistan 12, RSFSR 26. Comparatively low figures prevail in the upper secondary level (years 8/9 and above) of the Central Asian and Transcaucasian republics and in Moldavia. [42]

b) Russian-speaking schools exert a great attraction for non-Russian pupils. Their organizational structure can be classified into three types, that is to say, into schools for:
non-Russian nationalities within the RSFSR (eg, Chuvash, Tartars, Bashkirs), second,
immigrants into the RSFSR from other Union Republics (eg, Armenia, Kirghizia) and third,
Russian and non-Russian pupils in the non-Russian Union Republics. [43]

As far as the growth of Russian speaking schools attended mainly by non-Russians is concerned, the most recent developments show a wide

range of practice: from between 75 and 90 per cent
of pupils attending (eg, in Bashkiria) to low
percentages, the lowest being in the Baltic
republics. Although the "national schools" have
also been incorporated into the current educational
and didactic policy measures for the promotion of
Russian instruction, Russian speaking schools
clearly fulfil higher expectations in this
respect. [44] Furthermore, within this type of
school great significance is ascribed to the "zero
grade" classes, especially for a speedy transition
from the parallel learning of the native and of the
Russian tongues [45] to the exclusive use of Russian
as medium of instruction, with the exception of the
lessons in the non-Russian mother tongue.
c) As an innovative measure for the improvement of
Russian-speaking instruction within the framework of
the "national school", schools have been developed
which provide an intensive programme of Russian
instruction. These are largely boarding schools
with experimental status. Their weekly lesson quota
for Russian has been raised by 8-10 periods; in
addition from year 7, other subjects, particularly
the natural sciences, are being taught in Russian.
Articles used in this chapter include reports on
such schools in Azerbaydzhan, Kirghizia, Latvia and
Uzbekistan. [46] A. Useinov's critique of the (in
his view) inconsistent policies for the development
of this type of school is most revealing; he
indicates that during the past decade three major
changes have been undertaken, although no supporting
scientific evidence for them has been produced. [47]
d) In the reform programmes, schools also appear
which are characterized by a parallel commitment to
both Russian and native instruction. Kirghizia (153
schools with 200.000 pupils) and Lithuania are
mentioned as centres of this development. [48]
Regrettably, no information on the 'bilingual'
character of these schools has yet come to the
knowledge of the authors of this chapter. The term
'parallel' apparently indicates only the existence
of parallel classes with different media of
instruction rather than of a kind of 'true
bilingualism' in each class.
e) This list could be expanded by the incorporation
of optional activities which aim at the
intensification and improvement of the linguistic
competence acquired by students during compulsory
lessons and which are offered both by the schools
themselves and by educational centres outside the
school (such as youth clubs). This chapter will

refrain from the assessment of these methods, nor will it deal with the Russian language instruction offered by the universities and other higher educational establishments of the non-Russian Union Republics. [49]

There is a standardized syllabus for Russian speaking schools in the whole of the Soviet Union, whereas in the non-Russian republics and regions, instruction in the respective mother tongue may be given widely varying status; thus in the Tartar and the Bashkirian Autonomous Republics, pupils receive such instruction until the tenth year, while in the Chuvash and Daghastan Autonomous Republics, for example, it is restricted to classes 2 - 4. [50]

The expansion and improvement of Russian instruction in the "national schools" to which the following remarks are devoted, has been the subject of repeated legislation in the past two decades. The "General Education Middle School Statute" of September 8th 1970 allows for the possibility of the extension of compulsory schooling from ten to eleven years; the three Baltic republics have made general use of this law. [51] The second regulation of relevance contained within the Statute is concerned with the authority granted to Union Republics to rearrange the timetable in favour of Russian lessons. Clearly the two or three additional weekly lessons already assigned everywhere to the timetables of "ntional schools" for the completion of the Russian syllabus are insuffcient; extra time is normally procured at the expense of "foreign languages".

The legal foundation for the current reforms of Russian language instruction was produced by "Ordinance No. 835 of the Council of Ministers of the USSR" of October 13th 1978. [52] It contains regulations on the since implemented introduction of the new "model syllabuses for the Russian language", the division of classes with more than 25 pupils into two groups for Russian lessons, outline regulations concerning Russian instruction in pre-school institutions and in schools with additional Russian instruction, measures for the improvement of teacher training and the provision of teaching materials. The reforms deemed to be necessary for Russian lessons in pre-school establishments are specified in the "Decree of the Minister for Popular Education No. 137" of July 18th 1979. [53] Finally, after prolonged consultations in the Politburo, 1983, the Central Committee of the Soviet Communist Party and the Council of Ministers of the USSR have

The Soviet Union

passed a

> Common Ordinance on additional measures for the
> improvement of Russian language instruction in
> general schools and other educational
> institutions of the Union Republics. [54]

Motivation and Achievement.
What constitutes the motivation causing non-
Russian parents to send their children to Russian
speaking schools? The answer poses no problems for
Soviet authors. Apart from referring to ideological
reasons, they explain the motivation quite simply by
the position of Russian as the lingua franca which
is already familiar to children. As S. Amonashvili
remarks, referring to his researches with Georgian
children, they like to learn Russian because they
want to understand the programmes of All-Union
(central) television, they dream of travelling to
Moscow and want to be able to converse with their
contemporaries in Russian. [55]
Recently, Western educationalists and
sociologists have also been discussing the
motivation question. In the debates, the socio-
economic and socio-political position of Russian as
a lingua franca has also aroused particular
attention. Isabelle Kreindler does not question
"the situation, in which the Russian language
represents a key to economic and social mobility"
and despite her basic adherence to the theory of
Russification, she concedes that "ambitious parents
naturally wish their children to possess this
key." [56]

Indeed, from her considerations she concludes, that
Russian "would in any case have been selected as the
lingua franca". [57] In this particular point
Isabelle Kreindler's line of argument does not
contradict the official Soviet version of the
voluntary nature of Russian lessons for non-
Russians. In Soviet legal documents this principle
is linked to the parental right to choose the
education they consider to be most suitable for
their children. This principle is admittedly
relativized in practice, inasmuch as only the
Russians have the full range of educational and
cultural facilities (including modern mass media)
available in their mother tongue everywhere and are
thus the only nation in the position to make genuine

use of the right guaranteed to their children by the constitution. [58] The comments mentioned above accordingly show a close correlation between motivation to learn Russian and the strength of upward and horizontal mobility in the Soviet population. [59]

Apart from this general correlation, reports on real life situations help the attempt to comprehend the question of motivation. As an example of such data, we can cite S.A. Chekhoeva's most graphic comparison of two general middle schools in the Orenburg region. [60] Complications with regard to Russian language teaching arise among others from geographical factors, such as long distances and adverse climatic conditions. In this context, however, E.G. Lewis's theory that such complications may trigger off counteracting effects is most illuminating:

> Life in isolated farmhouses in the Soviet Union impedes the spread of bilingualism; still more important, however, is the fact that a country upbringing may give rise to a desire for bilingualism as a means of escape. [61]

He refers to the close correlation between attitudes to Russian learning and successful language acquisition.

> It is significant that the Georgians, who are normally seen as a nation apart, who have developed the greatest resistance to Russification and who have a lukewarm attitude to Russian, are constantly being criticized for the low standard of their Russian. [62]

As far as information on the results of attempts to promote the learning of Russian by means of improved organization and curriculum is concerned, unfortunately the available sources are too meagre to permit a representative evaluation. As with other sociological investigations, assessment must depend on the availability of case studies and on quantitative surveys confined to small localities. [63] Conclusions drawn from more expansive surveys, however, are lacking in the necessary supporting technical information, on random samples, test procedure and other. This characterizes, for example, M. Baltabaev's report on surveys in experimental "zero-grade" classes in Kirghizia. [64]

130

Concluding Remarks: Summary and Future Perspectives.

That considerable importance is attached by Soviet policy to the contribution of bilingual and international education to the development of an "All-Union Soviet culture" is indisputable. [65] The data obtainable from the evaluation of the census as well as the information contained in case studies and available primary investigations make it clear however that nothing would be more incorrect than to regard Soviet multiculturalism as a homogenous phenomenon. The available sources indicate a multiplicity of approaches and procedures in the education system, which are part of a specific historical tradition and which must be interpreted within the context of the general considerations outlined in the introductory remarks. The vital part which multicultural education plays in the formation of the Soviet brand of multiculturalism, is an indication of the fact that wider social changes are stimulated by the educational policy and pedagogical developments. Does the identification of this part allow us to draw conclusions as to the objectives of Soviet language policy, which clearly gives priority to the "Russian national" brand of bilingual education and which raises Russian for non-Russians to the rank of second language or even "second mother tongue"? [66] Both the legal and administrative measures taken as well as accounts of local and regional developments evaluated for the present survey show that the expansion of Russian instruction with its various institutional, didactic and material factors has been accelerated. This trend indicates that the party and state leadership do not see the justification to proceed with greater circumspection and caution concerning the spread of the lingua franca. They even reckon with provoking some resistance with their policies, as variously reported by several authors of the collection edited by Isabelle Kreindler. [67]

Nevertheless, the available facts on developments in the education system do not appear to prove conclusively that the theory of a general 'Russification' (as suggested by Isabelle Kreindler) can be inferred from this policy. Above all, a closer examination of the several legal and didactic measures to which Bernard Comrie's aforementioned scheme refers, tends to refute the general validity of this theory. In addition, Alexandre Bennigsen's well supported and illustrated theory of a different susceptibility to such measures - he distinguishes between "historical" and "unhistorical" nations -

points to an interpretation in this direction. [68]
For such a view demonstrates that while intensive
learning of the Russian language may in fact lead to
a 'Russification' (above all in small nationalities
or ethnic groups with a poorly developed 'modern'
vocabulary) given certain historical and socio-
economic conditions; it may, in other cases, even
lead to an increasingly defensive attitude in the
face of a threatening erosion of ethnic
identity. [69] Indeed, the persistence and intensity
with which the criticism brought by Western
sociologists against the Russification policy has
been taken seriously and rejected in the Soviet
Union is motivated not only by a desire to fend off
outside attacks, but clearly by the need to take a
stand against internal controversy and conflict, as
is demonstrated by the party and government
resolutions cited in this chapter, amongst others.
Both motives explain the legitimating character of
the numerous declarations centred around the theory
of the voluntary nature of Russian national
"bilingualism" and the equality of all languages
spoken in the Soviet Union. [70]

A closer appraisal also focusses attention on
developments which run parallel to the promotion of
Russian as illustrated by Bill Fierman in his
thorough evaluation of publications in the Uzbek
language on the current ongoing increase of
"national schools" which is taking place alongside
the expansion of Russian-speaking schools in
Uzbekistan. He arrives at the following conclusion:

> More Uzbeks may voluntarily be reading more
> Russian novels than 30 years ago, but how many
> Uzbeks of earlier generations could read novels
> in any language? Uzbeks today are also reading
> more Uzbek literature. An Uzbek university
> student in Tashkent today who mails a letter to
> his parents in the village may, in fact,
> address an envelope in Russian, but the letter
> is probably in Uzbek. Two generations ago most
> parents of such students, being illiterate,
> could not have read any letters from their sons
> or daughters. [71]

Fierman's general conclusion is substantiated, for
example, by a report by G.D. Kuznetsov and
S.A. Chekhoeva on the growth of "national schools"
in the Tartar Autonomous Republic. [72]

Finally, in the assessment of Soviet
multiculturality, the question of the effect of the

norms set by official policy and its underlying ideology on everyday education must be raised. The current findings of Eastern European educational and sociological research provide ample evidence that the practice of bilingual and indeed intercultural education strongly influences the teachers' everyday work. They also bring to notice 'side effects' which result from the impetus of the processes of industrialization and modernization and, for example, transform the daily lives of Soviet youth and their parents in the "multinational collectives" and give rise to various reactions, determined by the origin and biography of those concerned. The connection between "the control of social processes" and the interest in such side effects whose emergence had long been regarded in official Soviet comments as mere unwanted relics of a pre-socialist past and as a foreign capitalist attempt at disruption, now appear to be receiving more attention, even in the Soviet Union. An article by two members of the respected Institute of Economic Research of the Siberian branch of the Academy of Science of the USSR in Novosibirsk which appeared at the end of 1983 in the journal Voprosy Filosofii is an indication of this. In their critique of the current programmes for the "practice of the control of social processes", they emphasize that

> it has often been forgotten that the development of society is a process determined by history and nature and that an exaggerated view of the possibilities of control (with regard to lifestyle, the personal needs and interests of people as well as the development of personality) brings with it the danger of unwanted results. [73]

An investigation of the 'micro-level' mentioned in this chapter paves the way for intercultural comparisons which can for their part assist in the elucidation of Soviet multiculturality as can the comparison based upon official policy documents undertaken in the Soviet/Canadian example on the 'macro-level'. [74] Intercultural comparison on both levels remains a rewarding task for multidisciplinarily oriented research.

Notes and References

1. Grant, N., Linguistic and Ethnic Minorities in the USSR: Educational Policies and Developments.

In: Tomiak, J.J., ed., <u>Soviet Education in the</u>
<u>1980s</u>. Croom Helm, 1983;
<u>Lewis</u>, E.G., <u>Bilingualism and Bilingual Education</u>.
Pergamon Press, 1981.
2. Multinational collectives are large
settlements of workers made up of members of several
nationalities (and nations) arrived at as a result
of migration in search of work. Language policy is
obviously of crucial importance and the
multinational collectives mentioned on p 8 at
Togliatti and Novocheboksan have become objects of
research (pp 9-10) to monitor its results.
3. The Russian term <u>natsiia</u> is adequately
rendered by English 'nation', <u>natsional'nost'</u> on the
other hand is 'nationality' in the sense of 'ethnic
group', a minority incorporated within a nation,
with no separate political unit such as a republic
in Yugoslavia or republic or ASSR status in USSR.
Scharf, R., Nationalitaetenfragen in der
Sowjetunion. <u>Osteuropa</u>, 1981, <u>31</u>, 6.
4. Karypkulov, A.K., <u>Razvitie</u> sistemy
narodnogo obrazovaniia - vazhnyi faktor ukreplaniia
internatsional'nogo edinstva sovetskogo naroda.
<u>Voprosy Filosofii</u>, 1982, <u>37</u>, 10, p 31.
5. Kreindler, I., ed., The Changing Status of
Russians in the Soviet Union. <u>International Journal</u>
<u>of the Sociology of Language</u>, 1982, <u>33</u>, pp 7-39. A
'focus article' by I. Kreindler and 'comments' by
others followed by the 'integrative reply' by
I. Kreindler;
Anweiler, O. and Kuebart, F., "Internatsional'noe
vospitanie" und "multicultural education". Aspekte
eines Vergleichs zweier politischer Konzepte. In:
Mitter, W. and Swift, J., eds., <u>Education and the</u>
<u>Diversity of Cultures: The Contribution of</u>
<u>Comparative Education</u>. Boehlau 1984 = <u>Bildung und</u>
<u>Erziehung</u>, Beiheft 2.
6. Marchais, Georges, <u>L'Humanite</u>, February 29,
1984. See also <u>International Herald Tribune</u>, March
1, 1984.
7. Arsenov, V.G., Narodnoe obrazovanie v
avtonomnykh okrugakh severa. <u>Sovietskaia</u>
<u>pedagogika</u>, 1980, <u>44</u>, 10, pp 8-16.
8. Prokof'ev, M.A., Sovetskaia shkola-shkola
razvitogo sotsialisticheskogo obshchestva.
<u>Sovietskaia pedagogika</u>, 1978, <u>42</u>, pp 4-12.
9. Rywkin, M., Code words and catchwords of
Brezhnev's nationality policy. <u>Survey</u>, 1979, <u>24</u>, 3,
pp 83-90;
Kocharli, F.K. and Kurbanov, P.O., O reaktsionnoi
sushchnosti kontseptsii 'musul'manskogo

natsional'nogo kommunizma'. <u>Voprosy Filosofii</u>, 1982, <u>37</u>, 12, pp 106-113.

10. Andropov, Iu.V., Shest'desiat' let SSSR. Doklad. <u>Pravda</u>, December 22, 1982, pp 1-2.

11. Dzhioev, O.I., Kul'tura - natsiia - lichnost'. <u>Voprosy Filosofii</u>, 1983, <u>38</u>, 10, pp 76-82.

12. Chernenko, K.U., Rech' tovarishcha K.U. Chernenko. <u>Pravda</u>, March 2, 1984.

13. Di Maio, A.J., Jr., Contemporary Soviet population problems. In: Desfosses, H., ed., <u>Soviet Population Policy. Conflicts and Constraints.</u> Pergamon Press, 1981.

14. Lavrova, A.M., Izuchenie natsional'nykh otnoshenii v teme "Sotsial'no-politicheskii stroi razvitogo sotsialisticheskogo obshchestva". <u>Prepodavanie istorii v shkole</u>, 1983, <u>50</u>, 3.

15. Perevedentsev, V., Die gemischtnationale Familie im Leben der Sowjetunion. <u>Die Sowjetunion Heute</u>, 1982, <u>27</u>, 12, Koeln: Presseabteilung der Botschaft der UdSSR, pp 25 and 28.

16. Tarasenko, N., Osushchestvlenie leninskikh printsipov natsional'noi politiki. <u>Pravda</u>, December 16, 1983.

17. Prishkol'nik, I., Vo mnogonatsional'noi sel'skoi shkole. <u>Narodnoe obrazovanie</u>, 1976, <u>59</u>, 6.

18. Kolesnikov, L., Uroki dukhovnogo obshcheniia. <u>Pravda</u>, October 19, 1983, p 3.

19. Rashidov, Sh.R., Iazyk nashego edinstva i bratstva. <u>Narodnoe obrazovanie</u>, 1979, <u>62</u>, 9, pp 2-4; Prokop'ev, I.P., Problemy sovershenstvovaniia patrioticheskogo i internatsional'nogo vospitaniia podrastaieshchego pokoleniia v svete trebovanii XXVI s'ezda KPSS. <u>Sovietskaia pedagogika</u>, 1981, <u>45</u>, 9.

20. Bochkov, N., Ot iabloni iablochko. <u>Izvestiia</u>, February 29, 1984.

21. Drobizheva, L.M., Mezlichnostnye natsional'nye otnosheniia: Osnovnye cherty i osobennosti. <u>Sotsiologicheskie issledovaniia</u>, 1982, 4.

22. Andropov, Iu.V., op cit; Tadevosian, E.V., Internatsionalizm Sovetskogo mnogonatsional'nogo gosudarstva. <u>Voprosy Filosofii</u>, 1982, <u>37</u>, 11.

23. Zasedanie Prezidiuma Verkhovnogo Soveta SSSR. <u>Pravda</u>, January 13, 1983, pp 1-2.

24. Shanskii, N.M. and Cherkezova, M.V., Russkaia literatura v natsional'nykh sholakh soiuznykh respublik. <u>Sovietskaia pedagogika</u>, 1982, <u>46</u>, 4.

25. Leibengrub, P.S., O natsional'noi politike KPSS v kursakh istorii SSSR. Prepodavanie istorii v shkole, 1983, 50, 3, p 11.
26. ibid p 13.
27. Tret'iakova, I., Est' u severian pogovorka ... Uchitel'skaia gazeta, 1983, 59, October 29, 1983;
Arsenov, V.G., op cit.
28. Petrachuk, N., Deti severa. Izvestiia, November 2, 1976.
29. Lewis, E.G., op cit, p 305.
30. Karypkulov, A.K., op cit.
31. Il'ina, L., Uchilis' userdno. Pravda, January 31, 1984;
Karypkulov, A.K., op cit.
32. Novikov, L., Die Nationalitaetenpolitik der sowjetischen Hochschulen. Osteuropa, 1981, 31, 12.
33. Dzhafarov, J.B., K voprosu o sushchnosti dvuiazychiia v SSSR. Sotsiologicheskie issledovaniia, 1980, 4, pp 42-48;
Chekhoeva, S.A., Nachal'noe obuchenie russkomu iazyku v natsional'nykh shkolakh. Narodnoe obrazovanie, 1982, 65, 2, pp 42-44;
Zdravomyslov, A., Sotsial'naia politika KPSS i natsional'nye otnosheniia. Pravda, August 27, 1982.
34. Comrie, B., The Languages of the Soviet Union. Cambridge University Press, 1981;
Lewis, E.G., op cit;
Desheriev, Iu.D. and Protchenko, I.F., Perspektivy razvitiia dvuiazychiia v natsional'nykh shkolakh SSSR. Sovietskaia pedagogika 1976, 40, 8.
35. Garunov, E.G., Leninskii printsip internatsionalizma v deiatel'nosti shkol s mnogonatsional'nym sostavom uchashchikhsia. Sovietskaia pedagogika, 1980, 44, 2.
36. Garunov, E.G., Nekotorye problemy shkol s mnogonatsional'nym sostavom uchashchikhsia s russkim iazykom obucheniia. Sovietskaia pedagogika, 1975, 39, 11.
37. Simon, G., Russen und Nichtrussen in der sowjetischen Gesellschaft. In: Aus Politik und Zeitgeschichte, Beilage zur Wochenzeitung Das Parlament, B 17-18/1982, in particular p 38;
Lewis, E.G., op cit p 74.
38. ibid.
39. Prokof'ev, M.A., Puti dal'neishego uluchsheniia izucheniia i prepodavaniia russkogo iazyka v soiuznykh respublikakh. Narodnoe obrazovanie, 1979, 62, 9, pp 5-9.
40. Shamsutdinova, S.S., O tipovoi programme po russkomu iazyku. Ruskii iazyk v natsional'noi

shkole, 1980, 24, 3;
Shamsutdinova, S.S., O prepodavanii russkogo iazyka
v natsional'noi shkole. Narodnoe obrazovanie, 1983,
66, 7.
    41. Barannikov, I.V.   and   Uspenskii, M.B.,
Povyshat' kachestvo programm i uchebnikov.   Ruskii
iazyk v natsional'noi shkole, 1981, 25, 5;
Schetchikov, N.G., Russkii iazyk nuzhen chuvasham
kak svet ili vozdukh. Ruskii iazyk v natsional'noi
shkole, 1981, 25, 2;
Baltabaev, M.,   Eksperiment provoditsia v klasse.
Podvodia itogi. Uchitel'skaia gazeta, 1983, 59,
June 23, 1983 .
    42. Shamsutdinova, S.S.,   Russkii   iazyk   v
natsional'noi shkole. Sovietskaia pedagogika, 1979,
43, 4, p 36.
    43. Lewis, E.G., op cit.
    44. Prokop'ev, I.P., op cit.
    45. Arsenov, V.G., op cit.
    46. Shamsutdinova, S.S., (1983) op cit;
Reshenie kollegii Ministerstva Prosveshcheniia SSSR
ot 16 sentiabra 1983 goda No 30/1 (izvletseniia): Ob
opyte uglublennogo izucheniia russkogo iazyka v
shkole-internate   Nr   111   imeni   Panfilova   g.
Tashkenta.   Biulleten'   normativnykh   aktov
Ministerstva Prosveshcheniia SSSR, 1984, 1, Moskva:
Izdatel'stvo 'Vysshaia shkola';
Volodin, O., Predmet vseobshchei zaboty i vnimaniia.
Narodnoe obrazovanie, 1979, 62, 9.
    47. Useinov, A.,   Voprosy   bez   otvetov.
Uchitel'skaia gazeta, 1982, 58, March 6, 1982.
    48. Shamsutdinova, S.S., (1979) op cit;
Shamsutdinova, S.S., (1983) op cit.
    49. Krasnov, N.F., Resheniia iiun'skogo Plenuma
TS.K. KPSS i zadachi novogo uchebnogo goda. Vestnik
vysshei shkoly, 1983, 8.
    50. Kuznetsov, G.D.   and   Chekhoeva, S.A.,
Natsional'naia shkola RSFSR v sovremennykh
usloviiakh. Sovietskaia pedagogika, 1982, 46, 11.
    51. Schiff, B., Einheitlichkeit und nationale
Differenzierung als Determinanten des sowjetischen
Schulsystems. Bildung und Erziehung, 1979, 32, 6.
    52. Prikaz Ministerstva vysshego i srednego
spetsial'nogo   obrazovaniia   SSSR,   No   1116.
Biulleten' Ministerstva Vysshego i Srednego
Spetsial'nogo Obrazovaniia SSSR, 1979, 2, Moskva:
Izdatel'stvo 'Vysshaia shkola'.
    53. Solchanyk, R., Russian Language and Soviet
Politics. Soviet Studies, 1982, 34, 1, pp 23-24.
    54. Shermykhamedov, S.,   Vtoroi   rodnoi.
Izvestiia, August 6, 1983, p 3;

Tairov, L., Ia russkii by vyuchil . . . <u>Pravda</u>, August 22, 1983.

55. Amonashvili, S., Takoe umnoe detstvo. <u>Pravda</u>, March 19, 1981.

56. Kreindler, I., op cit, p 14.

57. ibid, p 27.

58. Simon, G., op cit.

59. Lewis, E.G., op cit.

60. Chekhoeva, S.A., op cit.

61. Lewis, E.G., op cit.

62. ibid, p 298.

63. ibid.

64. Baltabaev, M., op cit.

65. Lewis,E.G., op cit, p 392.

66. Dzhafarov, I.B., Prevrashchenie russkogo iazyka vo vtoroi rodnoi iazyk narodov SSSR. <u>Sotsiologicheskie issledovaniia</u>, 1982, 9, p 16.

67. Anweiler, O., Russifizierung durch Unterricht: Fakten und Hypothesen. In: Kreindler, I., op cit, pp 41-51; Bilinsky, Y., Haste makes waste, or the political dangers of accelerated Russification. In: Kreindler, I., op cit, pp 63-69; Friedgut, Th.H., The unity of languages and the language of unity. In: Kreindler, I., op cit, pp 79-89; Solchanyk, R., op cit.

68. Bennigsen, A., Langues et assimilation en URSS. In: Kreindler, I., op cit, pp 57-61.

69. Rywkin, M., op cit.

70. Protchenko, I.F., Iazyk druzhby narodov. <u>Sovietskaia pedagogika</u>, 1983, <u>47</u>, 11.

71. Fierman, B., The view from Uzbekistan. In: Kreindler, I., op cit, pp 71-78.

72. Kuznetsov, G.D. and Chekhoeva, S.A., op cit.

73. Zaslavskaia, T.I. and Ryvkina, R.V., A.G. Vishnevskii. Vosproizvodstvo naseleniia i obshchestvo: istoriia, sovremennost', vzgliad v budushchee. <u>Voprosy Filosofii</u>, 1983, <u>38</u>, 12, p 154,.

74. Anweiler, O. and Kuebart, F., op cit.

CULTURAL IDENTITY AND EDUCATIONAL POLICY: THE GERMAN
DEMOCRATIC REPUBLIC

Witold Tulasiewicz

Introduction

Some of the differences, political, cultural,
economic, religious to name but a few, in the
territories which now constitute the two Germanies
pre-date the emergence of the two states after the
second World War. Indeed, cultural separatism is as
much part of the German tradition as is a common
German identity. Important differences which
distinguish between the territories of the present
GDR and FRG exist, in matters of religious
affiliation, for example, or have existed until
recently, such as the distinctive agrarian structure
and a more right wing political culture in the
east. [1] Regional differences in Germany are
emphasized and new ones emerge, particularly when
they become differences between more or less
independent provinces or indeed independent states.
It is in the thirty-five years since the two
Germanies have existed side by side as states and
developed different socio-political systems and
opposing alliances, that significant contrasts
between them have become evident. The existence of
the 'traditional German way of life' in the GDR is
partly due to her political reluctance and economic
inability to construct a 'cosmopolitan',
sophisticated culture, and this may in turn account
for the close personal ties continuing to exist
between ordinary people in that country. Unlike the
FRG, there is less anonymity, more caring contact in
small communities and a 'sentimental' neighbourly
attitude reminiscent of the pre-computer era in the
GDR. The GDR's commitment to sponsoring the
independence of former colonial nations, as shown in
accounts of her ten years United Nations
membership, [2] contrasts with the FRG's
controversial decision in February 1981 when her

education ministers agreed to showing Germany's 1937 boundaries in school atlases.

An aspect of identity which marks the growing divergence of the two states is their different attitude to the concept of German nationhood. A united Germany rather than Prussia or Saxony used to be a goal aspired to by statesmen and artists alike for centuries in what has been called a Kulturnation, [3] a Germany which is not a political but a cultural entity only. However the words "state of German nation" used in both the 1949 and 1968 GDR Constitutions to refer to the GDR ("a socialist state of the German nation") and found also in the FRG's Grundgesetz of 1949, were dropped in the 1974 Constitution in favour of: "The GDR is a socialist state of workers and farmers". [4] GDR patriotism is being encouraged, a trend which has grown stronger since the introduction in 1978 of pre-military training in schools in the GDR and which contrasts with the FRG's population's often ambivalent commitment to the Federal Republic. [5] In the GDR the "bourgois" nationality concept was discarded in favour of the Marxist-Leninist view which distinguishes between a uniting proletarian national culture in each nation and a divisive bourgeois one. [6] The GDR now enjoys a "socialist national culture" [7] which traces its origins to radical elements in the common German past which as late as the 1960s were neglected, if not actually suppressed, in the FRG.

The different evaluation of the German past prevalent in the two states is revealing. In what was to become the FRG the concept Stunde Null, [8] was used to mark the new beginning of a country not only purged of fascism, but one which had turned its back on a good deal of its 'progressive' history as well. In the GDR links with Germany's socialist past - not just the short-lived Weimar Republic, but the previous 150 years of working class movement and its political and cultural expression: uprisings, strikes, soviet republics as well as life styles and cultural achievements: indeed earlier revolutionary events, like the Peasants' Revolt with which the figure of Luther has recently been more positively identified than before the quincentenary, the dialectic "Reformation und Bauernkrieg" forgotten, [9] as well as links with foreign and international happenings, like the Russian October Revolution - are not only acknowledged as anticipating the German socialist present, but actively promoted throughout the education system starting in the first school grades. [10] The GDR's establishing its roots in the socialist-national and international traditions has included re-interpretation and appropriation of historical events and figures of the national heritage, for example the wars of liberation in the nineteenth century or the humanist writings of poets like Goethe and Schiller, seen as a harbinger of socialist art. [11]

The close ideological and cultural ties which bind the GDR as a socialist country to the USSR and the Soviet bloc are a function of her political, social, economic and military status. But they are also in part a result of the now rediscovered class struggle concerns and experience of the ruling political party of the GDR, the Socialist Unity Party (Sozialistische Einheitspartei Deutschlands), SED, its acknowledged predecessor parties, the present government and the working people. The GDR's relationship with the socialist bloc and the USSR in particular, is expressed in the Constitution of 9 April 1968 which replaced the Weimar type "bourgeois"-democratic one of 1949 and which had no mention of it. [12] Its sixth article reads: "The GDR develops, in accordance with the principles of socialist internationalism, comprehensive co-operation and friendship with the USSR and other socialist states". Military partnership was mentioned in article 7. [13] The revised Constitution of October 1974 emphasizes this point with further qualifications like: "forever and irrevocably allied with the Union of Soviet Socialist Republics" [14] and "the GDR is an inseparable part of the community of socialist states" (article 6). Friendship treaties, like the USSR-GDR one of October 7, 1975 and those with other Warsaw Pact states, bind the countries together so closely that German reunification no longer receives mention in either the 1974 Constitution or the 1975 Treaty, although article 8 of the 1968 Constitution still had a reference to reunification and the 1964 draft of the USSR-GDR Treaty, when 'rapprochement' with the West was still considered a possibility, had a similar clause. Indeed, the current Treaty provides for "cooperation of production" between the two countries lasting well into the 1990s, while certain economic links and socio-political exchanges are contracted for various longer terms, reaffirmed and extended in 1984 during celebrations of the thirty-fifth anniversary of the republic.

This chapter accepts a modified interpretation

of the reciprocal relationship between the economic base and its statal superstructure and argues that cultural, ideological, educational ties follow political, military and economic alliances. The different identities of the two German states are thus in large measure due to their present different social and political systems, though there exist remnants of former regional differences. These, like the evidence of Prussian tradition recently surprisingly commemorated in exhibitions in Berlin and Potsdam, and found in the armed forces of the GDR for example, cannot be completely discounted. In the fourth decade of the GDR's existence as an independent state however the socialist characteristics tend to be emphasized, with official sources pointing out the working class origins of the GDR's new officer corps. [15]

If the social ownership of the means of production in the GDR determines that country's economic structure: collective farming and 'nationalized' industries for example, then the way of life, indeed the 'different' language associated with that economic structure are part of the new national identity of the GDR. Its manifestations are indeed numerous: people's attitudes and manners, the country's economic and social priorities - many of which must be included in a broad concept of cultural identity. A comparison between the school systems in the two Germanies, or an examination of advertisements or theatre bills in the two German capitals, yield examples of cultural identity - features absent in one country- being jealously guarded and preserved in the other.

For the purpose of this chapter the interpretation of cultural identity will be confined to five aspects, which can be taken to derive directly from educational policies: viz, the Soviet example, the role of Marxist-Leninist ideology, the link between education and the economy, the structure of the education system and cultural policy, and two, the leading role of the SED and the changing language, which are less directly dependent on these policies, but which are nevertheless an integral part of education. In conclusion practical examples of GDR cultural identity will be given in a brief analysis of a work of fiction.

Educational politics is particularly influential in the GDR. In socialist countries or countries becoming socialist the 'comprehensive' way of life associated with the construction of a new society uses education·in its widest sense to help

build the new society. Indeed this was a task
recognized by Soviet leaders immediately before and
after the October Revolution. [16] Thus the link
between educational policies and cultural identity
is particularly close with cultural practices,
structures and offices seen to result directly from
educational and political directives. The GDR can
be referred to as an "Erziehungsgesellschaft", [17]
an educational society in which all education is
'socialized' and all social institutions
'educationalized' with society a school for
political and economic development and an educator
for socialism, but which has no links with the
utopian self-contained paedagogische Provinz,
"pedagogical province", of German philosophers and
writers. Thus, it may be more appropriate to speak
of a "gebildete Gesellschaft", an educated society.
This has the advantage of reflecting Lenin's
declaration that only an educated people can build
socialism, and which combines high general
educational standards with ideological
commitment. [18] Because in the GDR the desire to
break with the fascist past was strong and
encouraged by the international political
circumstances in the area after 1945 it was easier
than in those socialist countries which did not have
the fascist stigma to put an entirely new education
system into operation and meet with little
opposition from various sections of the population.
    Though it is possible to distinguish between
two cultural periods in the history of the GDR, viz:
(I) Pre-1952 (or 1948) when more attention was given
to similarities between the two Germanies: The old
common anti-fascist front, the challenge of a new
start after the defeat of Hitler and the fact of
being part of a world-wide political constellation
and (II) The period of socialist construction in the
new GDR and a conscious abandoning of the
"imperialist" West - the difference between them
mirrors only the degree of emphasis and the speed of
the process of socialist construction, since in both
periods, ever since 1945 in fact, efforts were made
to establish a distinctive, new future society in
the GDR, accompanied by attacks on the allegiance of
the FRG to outgrown and outworn political systems.
In the GDR, where the Stunde Null concept never
found acceptance, the search for German and
international antecedents of socialism is the only
position officially tolerated.

The Soviet Example

In the GDR the Soviet model, the USSR being the first and most powerful of the socialist states, is one of the main ingredients of her specific cultural and national identity. In the near identical political systems of the two unequal partner countries, it is the USSR which is the more influential and whose own changes trigger off changes in the other. The Soviet example is probably the most important outside factor for change in the GDR, though the very close alliances within the Soviet Socialist bloc make many of her 'internal' innovations eventually also traceable to the USSR, like the social courts and conciliation and arbitration commissions. [19]

The cultural domain is as affected by this phenomenon as are the others. There is the prominent position given to the Russian language, the first foreign language in the GDR and a compulsory subject for all children, but really more influential as the language of international socialist communication. Soviet politics affect GDR policy making to the extent that most cultural, political, social, economic decisions in the USSR are enacted in the GDR with the minimum of delay. The postponement in late 1984, of the GDR's First Party Secretary's visit to Bonn can only be regarded as part of a global Soviet strategy towards the West, which the GDR follows, as she did earlier liberalization and freeze initiatives under Kruschev in 1963 and 1964, of which the New Economic System (Neue oekonomische System) of 1963 is an indirect result, and the Brezhnev-led invasion of Czechoslovakia in 1968 a direct one. Soviet models affect work practices, the planning discussions in the system of production in the factory as well as cultural manifestations at the place of leisure. They pervade shopping patterns, the education of children or the format and appearance of newspapers. The fact that since the VIII Party Conference in 1971 the GDR is in the process of further "developing" established socialism is the main reason for both voluntary and enforced borrowing from the USSR, acknowledged to have been through the same experience one generation earlier.

The Soviet example is rapidly replacing a common German national identity in the GDR (the FRG still clings to a national ideal), putting a socialist identity in its place. In this section an attempt will be made to isolate the all-pervasive Soviet model as a superordinate category responsible for a variety of changes, and to confine it to cultural concerns which have contributed to a change of the GDR's cultural and educational identities. The pre-eminent function accorded to education and the eminent position of educational functionaries, the introduction of socialist - realist rather than proletarian traditions in art are well known Soviet models. Though in this respect the GDR is no different from other socialist countries, clearly, because of her peculiar political culture, she is less immune from this influence. There is, to be sure, the very strong socialist tradition in Germany, the land of Marx and Engels. There exists, as has become well known in the 1980s, a different relationship between the government and the churches than in Hungary or Poland for example, a relationship which has made more believers declare themselves on the side of the government, despite recent peace initiatives independent of the state and the anti-abortion campaign of the Christian Democratic Union, Christlich-Demokratische Union, (CDU) of the sixties. The desire, officially encouraged, to create in the GDR an identity distinct and different from that of the other German state still associated in the eyes of many GDR citizens with Nazi guilt is a powerful factor conducive to a ready acceptance of Soviet models.

In order to maintain a more "bourgeois" democratic front when reunification was still a possibility, Soviet pedagogical influence which has made the GDR's educational system totally different from that in the FRG, and which in the course of time also departed from the much vaunted heritage of the educational policies of the Weimar period, was not loudly proclaimed until 1948/1952. The first educational impact was the Soviet Union's responsibility for educational decrees of the Military Administration on the re-opening of schools, [20] less directly the "Law on the Democratization of German Education" in May of the following year. [21] However on September 20, 1948 the Central Secretariat (later Politburo) of the SED voted for the intensive study of the Short History of the Communist Party of the Soviet Union (B) by all party members, [22] and in November Hans Siebert, the Central Secretariat's official responsible for education, in a speech made at the meeting of teacher activists in Leipzig, announced that socialist movements would be "helped in their task by following the Soviet example, since German socialists were aiming for the same ideals as their

Soviet brethren". [23] * In another speech on August
23, 1949 Siebert declared that "Soviet education
represents the sum total of educational knowledge
and research, not only socialist but of all
mankind".* In the circumstances it clearly made
sense to follow the Soviet model. If despite such
sentiments the model was introduced cautiously this
was because after the foundation of the GDR in
October 1949 the SED preferred the GDR to appear as
an autonomous Socialist state with its own reform
programme. The most powerful man in the SED
hierarchy at the time, Walter Ulbricht [24] however
insisted in July 1950 that the first Five Year Plan
would ensure "the success of the school reform and
further the appropriation and exploitation of Soviet
cultural experience and expertise".* His practical
suggestion was to use Soviet pedagogical manuals in
teacher education and to "let children learn the
lives of Lenin and Stalin and to be brought up to
love the USSR".
    The three resolutions of the Central Committee
and the Politburo of the SED of January 19, 1951 for
improving educational work demanded that schools
transmit the results of USSR "progressive scientific
achievements and spread a knowledge of Marxism-
Leninism and Soviet education among teachers,
students and others concerned with education and
vocational training".* The greatest impact of the
Soviet model has been on the structure of the
education system and its ideological and economic
relevance. The Ministry of Education itself
(Ministerium fuer Volksbildung) and the entire
system were restructured after January 1, 1953 to
achieve a closer link between the school and
practical work after a resolution of the Politburo.
The resolution called "Zur Erhoehung des
wissenschaftlichen Niveaus des Unterrichts und zur
Verbesserung der Parteiarbeit an den
allgemeinbildenden Schulen" of July 29, 1952 [25]
was based directly on Soviet models. It included
curricular guidelines for the teaching of all
subjects and the role of the Party in schools. The
first book on educational theory which appeared in
1950, was a Soviet adaptation. Its preface declared
tnat "Soviet education is the model, the lode star .
. . of the development of educational science in
Germany". [26]
    After Stalin's death German sources began to be
used. The Minister of Education, F. Lange, at the
5th Educational Congress on May 15, 1956 referred to
the rich and respected traditions of German

education and declared that Soviet education itself had developed and continued German humanist, democratic educational ideas, thus indirectly justifying the continuing dependence on Soviet models*, though Soviet experiences and innovations were not to be applied schematically. In March 1962 at a ministerial conference educational problems in the GDR were to be examined in the light of discussions of the XXII Party Congress of the Communist Party of the Soviet Union, (CPSU) and the 14th Plenum of the Central Committee of the SED. The programme discussed and passed by the XXII Congress should be a guideline for the German nation and its working class. "The tasks of improving education, teacher preparation and educational science can only be solved by learning from the Soviet Union."* The most important Soviet feature is the exclusive competency and responsibility of the SED for education and its presence at all levels of education structures in the form of party branch organizations. There are SED representatives usually in the post of deputy head teacher in schools, dean or director of university departments, a process completed after the re-organization of the Education Ministry and educational organs in local government in 1953. [27] The involvement of the SED in matters of education grew with its own ascendance as the main political force in the GDR.

In higher education the Soviet model began to be seen in the establishment of introductory university study faculties in 1949, called Arbeiter und Bauern Fakultaeten, workers' and peasants' faculties, for those who had been educationally disadvantaged; they were closed in 1964. The establishment of a Secretariat of State for Higher Education, (ordinance of February 22, 1951 on university reorganization) [28] and the appointment of pro-rectors in universities responsible for the production of specialist political and economic cadres, after a resolution of the SED Central Committee of January 19, 1951 [29] show the close control by the Party and government of the higher education sector. The introduction of compulsory Marxist-Leninist studies [30] and on September 6, 1952 of the official Free German Youth movement (Freie deutsche Jugand), FDJ-led seminar groups of 30 students in all faculties, [31] the interference of socio-political organizations (SED and other allied parties) in university life, senate and deanship elections are examples of direct ideological control of students and university teachers. [32] Kruschev's higher education reforms: previous experience of productive work for all applying students, and a close link between studies and professional life were immediately introduced in the GDR in 1957. That Soviet examinations are recognized by German universities shows the unprecedented integration of the two systems.

Schools also followed the Soviet model, the "learning school" took over from the Weimar "discovery school" after the January 19, 1951 resolution [33] and the debates on polytechnical education followed Russian discussions in every detail. [34] To be sure the ten-year polytechnical upper school (zehnklassige, allgemeinbildende, polytechnische Oberschule), POS, [35] was a case of a Soviet model being introduced in the GDR before its full implementation in the USSR, though it had Weimar antecedents. Detailed educational aims and curricula too were similar, for example, the introduction of apprentices' and pupils' learning and behaviour rules on August 19, 1954,* the position of Russian, the celebration of compulsory school holidays commemorating Soviet heroes, USSR-GDR friendship or the Day of the Soviet Army. [36] Text books use German examples and themes and are not copies of Soviet models but the general syllabuses, for example in history teaching follow the Soviet outline. [37] After the early 1960s (resolution of the SED Politburo of May 17, 1960*) professional education was integrated with school education and school leaving certificates linked with professional certificates. As in the USSR this is now limited to certain options, though proportionately greater numbers are involved in the GDR. The special schools for the gifted have no Weimar precedent, educational studies and research have became Soviet-inspired, and their application similar in both countries.

Many more laws and innovations can be traced to Soviet models, such as the 1974 "Youth Law" which brings young people within the interest sphere of the Party. [38] Even so certain national characteristics, the absence of school uniforms, the starting and leaving ages, have remained different in the GDR. Though the presence of youth organizations and uniformed children in school had occurred at other periods of German history, the FDJ and the Pioneer Organization (Jung Pioniere), (JP) are modelled on the Soviet system.

Marxist - Leninist Ideology in Education

The Komsomol greeting at the start of every lesson in the classroom and the FDJ and JP corners in every school lend a specific cultural-political identity to educational establishments in the GDR.

The SED is a Marxist-Leninist party of the new type; [39] teaching its ideology is therefore part of the process of strengthening the conviction of existing members, gaining new recruits, and getting the rest of the population from an early age to accept its role in the land. The political manifesto of the pre-war Communist Party (Kommunistische Partei Deutschlands), KPD and the Social Democratic Party (Sozialistische Partei Deutschlands), SPD of October 18, 1945* did not envisage a Marxist system of education, neither did the school law of May 1946. The main political emphasis was on anti-fascism, "bourgeois" democracy, with ideals like freedom, humanism to strive for, the terms themselves to begin with being left largely undefined. [40] This has changed, as a look at any recent dictionary will reveal. Walter Ulbricht however, even before the foundation in 1946 of the Socialist Unity Party, in a speech made to the first KPD functionaries' conference on June 25, 1945 demanded "a knowledge of socialism in the Soviet Union by the German working class" and an acquaintance with Marxist-Leninist philosophy as a base for the development of a new party.* Soon, particularly the teachers as future purveyors of ideology were expected to learn their new subject together with pedagogical science from Soviet books, of which by the late 1940s some 100,000 copies had been sold in translation, [41] with German produced books following later. The SED demanded the introduction of Marxism-Leninism at all levels of education, only in this way "would schools become institutions with a working class and partisan character" declared Hans Siebert to teacher activists in November 1948. In particular they must be staffed by ideologically trained teachers, capable of indoctrinating youth. [42] By August 1949 the SED and the 4th Educational Congress on the following day (August 25) had put ideology as a higher curricular priority than ordinary subject knowledge in schools. [43]

Since then the content and aims of education have had to be expressed in ideological terms, as in the USSR. The terms used vary, especially frequently used are formulations like "formation of an all-round socialist personality", education in "socialist morality", "democratic socialist patriotism" or simply "love and respect for work", the latter summing up the aims in succinctly practical words. Recent compendia on school curriculum and education repeat the well known aim of a scientific, modern, partisan education. [44]

Moral education was codified by Ulbricht in the form of ten commandments at the V Party Congress of July 1958.* Socialist education starts with a knowledge of Marxist-Leninist theory the most important item being the recognition that "the only scientific, progressive philosophy is dialectical materialism. Only he acts morally and in accordance with humanism who fights to bring about a socialist victory." Thus there can be no ideological co-existence", stated Lange at the 5th Education Congress on May 15, 1956. This view permeates all education and training; all scientific work must back it in theory and it must be applicable in practice; it must also be partisan: comply that is with the directives of the "party of the working class". Patriotism is not the same as national feeling alone [45] which is a "bourgeois" concept, but is linked with a grasp of the class struggle and socialist feeling and reasoning. Education for patriotism includes "education for hatred" of everyone who denies the truth of Marxism-Leninism and the victory of a Socialist-Communist order of society. After the construction of the Berlin Wall (August 13, 1961) new methods for education for patriotism were discussed in the Central Pedagogic Institute at a conference in October 1961. The director stressed that patriotism is synonymous with the civic consciousness of being a citizen of the workers' and peasants' state; it encouraged love for Germany and its language, culture and people, love and solidarity with the working class of all Germany and a will to fight for Socialism in all Germany. These all-German references have been dropped in more recent statements, indeed in the final demand that patriotism means love of the Party and its leaders [46] there are implications for a personality cult and an identification confined to the GDR. Since GDR school textbooks devote very little space to the FRG, Moscow or Warsaw are closer in young people's minds than Bonn or Munich. Love and respect for work is an important aim of education in that it encourages production. Only an overproduction of material and spiritual goods can bring about Communism, only overproduction can demonstrate the superiority of socialist society

declared Ulbricht on October 17, 1958, stressing the
importance of the economy in educational aims.
 Ideological education (dialectical and
historical materialism) is an integral part of the
curriculum in all educational work. Formal
courses [47] and the Jugendweihe, a secular
equivalent of 'confirmation' and preparation for a
socialist life, [48] the activities of the FDJ [49]
are meant to teach the theoretical aspect of
ideology, while participation in production, a year
being expected of all prospective students for
example, [50] ensures an introduction to "practical
socialist life". Celebrations of patriotic
festivals cater for the emotional side of
ideological education. Ideological knowledge and
attitudes have a place in school examinations,
school holidays, free-time activity and pre-military
preparaton. Admission to continuing education and
the award of extra grants are decided by referees
from the mass (ideological) organizations, like the
FDJ, the Democratic Women's Federation,
Demokratischer Frauenbund Deutschlands (DFD) and the
Society for Sport and Technology, Gesellschaft fuer
Sport und Technik (GST) according to an ordinance
(Stipendienordnung) of December 17, 1962*.
Makarenko's belief [51] was acknowledged as early as
the 1946 School Law; the involvement of parents has
brought education and ideology teaching of pupils
into the home. The participation of students in FDJ
teacher-led students' councils with pupils
collaborating in the running of the school is
another feature. [52] Parents' councils
(Elternbeiraete) and Aktive of 'committed' parents
have been an integral part of education since the
ordinance of January 7, 1960 of the Council of
Ministers. [53] The 4th Education Congress of August
1949 [54] finally abolished the artificial
separation of education from politics: education was
to be linked with political re-education, the
collectives of parents, pupils, teachers being the
instrument to achieve this. Aktive of participants
with military trappings, a system of praise and
punishment, collective responsibility, duty and
competition, teach discipline, ideology and some
subject matter. All this can be done linked with
holiday or sporting activities, for example
organized by the GST inviting mass participation and
instilling a sense of ideology through physical
activity. Participation in the various activities
and formal teaching together cater for the all-
sided, cognitive, attitudinal and practical skills,

moral-spiritual Marxist-Leninist education of a socialist personality. [55]

Education and the Economy

A distinctive feature of education in the GDR which owes much to the Soviet Marxist model is the closest interdependence between economic needs and educational planning. The training of cadres for the preparation of a strong economic base for the construction and maintenance of Socialism in the country [56] and the involvement of the entire educational system, general as well as vocational, in the task, is a feature of the process of transformation. The school is to raise its productivity in the same way as an industrial enterprise. In a non-planned free market economy education often seems distanced from work; certainly pupils in the GDR show a purpose in going to school. The fact that because of its specific demographic situation, unemployment is unknown in the GDR is a further factor accounting for the business-like movements of people observed going about their work. The country urgently needs the well qualified, skilled workers, the education system is meant to produce.

Impressive is the fact that two thirds of research potential in the country is committed to industry, some 170,000 people of whom 90 per cent actually work in Kombinate, several linked factories of one branch of the economy which operate independently. Specialists carry out applied and basic research and collaborate with technical college and university-based teams. Research collectives investigate what are likely to be the vital supply needs affecting a complete branch of industry.

The unity of economy and social policy has been especially close since the VIII Congress of the SED in 1971 which restated earlier resolutions to raise material and cultural production to improve national income and develop Socialism. The close link between the needs of the economy and education is seen in the fact that the 1400 educational centres for the reception of polytechnical pupils are all factory-sponsored, but with use made only of available existing resources for local production experience. Thus only 50 per cent of "polytechnical cabinets" (centres) have metal working, 14 per cent agriculture, and 9 per cent electronics facilities, and not all pupils can receive practical experience of all skilled trades in their area. However the training for a limited number of 'convertible' basic trades (Grundberufe) since 1967 in the vocational schools is claimed to be superior to vocational training in the FRG which requires more frequent re-training. [57]

The link between economy and education was announced in the earliest resolutions of the first two vocational education congresses in the Soviet Zone of Occupation and was followed by concrete steps to improve training facilities. In contrast to German tradition vocational and professional preparation was not to be carried out in vocational schools only, but in all educational establishments as stated by Siebert to the teacher activists in 1948. [58] Subsequent plans show that this necessitated a major reorganization especially of the content and structures of the general education schools and the establishment and promotion of adult and higher education geared to the needs of the economy especially during the first Two Year Plan. This involved in the first instance the creation of ten-year schools, initially intended as preparation for engineering and similar study. In the early days according to Ulbricht teachers were simply expected to exhort their pupils to "study harder and to introduce economic problems into mathematics and German teaching to make pupils aware of the country's economic needs". This rather unsystematic method was used in what in the early days passed as polytechnical education too. Not until the Politburo resolution of July 29, 1952 were its methods and content scientifically discussed and as a first task the preparation of a suitable natural sciences syllabus demanded. [59] Provision for instruction in the principles of production was made at the time, but the concept of the "weekly day in production", and the link between the worlds of work and education through new school subjects: introduction to socialist production and technical drawing, were only established on July 30, 1958. [60] The introduction of basic vocational training in grades 11 and 12 (in 1960/61) and grades 9 and 10 (in 1963/64) of the ten-year polytechnical upper school was an important landmark. [61] The special classes in mathematics and science established in September 1964, which admit particularly bright children after the seventh grade also have an economic purpose, since pupils are given extra tuition in those subjects directly helping both industrial and agricultural branches of the economy. After the passing of the new 1965

"Socialist Education Law" other school subjects were included in the intensive study programmes. [62] Vocational and professional preparation was to be the main route to higher professional and university education and extended upper school leaving certificate (Abitur), classes were established in vocational schools. After the publication of the "Theses of the SED Central Committee" of January 15, 1959*, other measures improved the balance between general polytechnical and vocational education in favour of vocational preparation within general education. [63] Preparation for "the modern world of work and first-class mathematics and science" was equally furthered, but in a speech in praise of the 1965 Education Law in the Volkskammer (People's Chamber - Parliament) on February 25, 1965, Politburo philosopher Kurt Hager compared the "bourgeois" emphasis on languages, art and literature with: "The transformation of science into a productive force which requires the new science subjects".* The important role of the general school in training a skilled work force is shown in the provision of vocational and professional guidance to pupils in the eighth grade, after the First Party Conference resolution of January 28, 1949. Earlier guidance was resolved jointly by the Politburo and Council of Ministers meeting of July 3, 1963 and initiated by the Council of Ministers. Talks on work preparation were thus offered in the sixth grade, given by school teachers together with employment guidance officers. Plans for vocational education must be decided four years in advance to ensure correct vocational advice to pupils currently in the eighth grade. The last word was left to Ulbricht who demanded at the VIth Party Congress, January 1963, "expanding polytechnical education into a preparatory vocational education"* and ensuring good education with facilities for introduction to and practice of "those trades available in each area of the country". Individual choice was further limited by allowing only two basic professions per class in grades 9 and 10 (resolution of July 3, 1963)*, however relevant out of school professional work was to be made available to each pupil.

Adult vocational education and training developed so much in the 1950s especially in further education (Volkshochschulen), that in 1962 the local Volkshochschule was given the task of coordinating all teaching for state adult qualifications in each district (Kreis). Significantly adult education was

renamed "further adult qualification" (Ausbildung).
Higher education was similarly brought into the
service of the economy after the already quoted
Central Committee decision of January 19, 1951.
This fixed admissions to the various university and
college faculties according to economic need. The
content and scope of courses were scrutinized to
serve these needs.* University study itself was
tightened up by a system of intermediate
examinations and a change over to a ten-month
academic year, as in the USSR. Another Soviet
model, the "aspirantura" included the new
'progressive' research scientists and future
university tutors. 1965 saw the establishment of a
central admissions office which abolished individual
applications for places in higher education.
Earlier than the schools did universities and higher
technical colleges after the reorganization
ordinance of January 19, 1951 and the directive of
October 1957* adopt the principle of a link between
theory and practice, the latter including production
experience. Such professional experience could be
taken in the form of work practice periods during
university study, and/or a practical year of work
before study. Sponsorship of higher education
studies by factories and enterprises (including
selection of students to be sponsored) in 1957
strengthened the close link between employment and
study. Students were required after the late 1950s
to sign acceptance papers of a post allocated them
on completing their studies before embarking on
their studies. Firm contracts with concerns, like
"associations of nationalized enterprises"
(Vereinigung Volkseigener Betriebe), VVB, had to be
made by students shortly before completing their
studies, those failing to finish being calculated as
"non fulfilment of economic plans". [64] There was
rapid expansion particularly in 1964 of 'distance
studies' in technical schools and universities so
that there were more distance and evening than full
time students enrolled in all professional technical
and university economics faculties in that year,
showing concern with 'in service' training.
The central State Planning Commission
(Staatliche Plankommission), SPK, became closely
involved with education. Since the decree of
February 22, 1951 reorganizing higher education* it
had the right to participate in the drawing up of
university and college study and examinations,
regulations and the nomination of professors and
lecturers; assuming a good deal of control of the

work of higher education. It is the state's
graduate employment organization responsible for the
drawing up of legally binding labour contracts for
graduates and their allocation to various branches
of the economy. The State Secretary for Higher
Education submits his plans for graduate employment
to it. Its scope was widened after a resolution of
May 14, 1964* when the SPK was made responsible for
planning and directing all professional preparation,
its content, development, organization and
financing, including all vocational/professional
work in the ten-year general POS. Its policies must
be accepted by state economic organs. It is
empowered to discuss with the Ministry of
Education [65] pedagogic questions and the
organization of the POS, where the vocational
preparation element impinges on general education.

The Role of the Socialist Unity Party
      The Socialist Unity Party's leading role in all
aspects of the nation's affairs is probably the most
important example of the Soviet model, the role of
the CPSU having similarly evolved in the USSR as
expounded in the Short History of the Communist
Party of the Soviet Union (B), and a distinctive
feature of GDR identity. When the Second Conference
of the SED in July 1952 decided on "constructing
Socialism in the GDR and on taking all necessary
measures to achieve this objective" state government
became Party dominated and the country became an
integral part of the Socialist bloc. Though the
merger of the German Communist Party (KPD) and the
Socialist Democratic Party (SPD) on April 21, 1946
in what later became the German Democratic Republic
can be interpreted as a legacy of the pre-war left
wing "Common Front" policy, this was hardly
practised during the Weimar period. The first step
to Socialism in Germany can thus be said to have
been taken after the war at the inaugural meeting of
the Cominform in September 1947 when the Soviet
delegate Andrei Zhdanov announced "the split of the
world into two irreconcilable camps". In response
to this the SED Party's executive (Vorstand) decided
during the summer of 1948 to transform the SED into
a "party of the new type". [66] The SED further
established a Political Bureau (Politburo) in
January 1949 which in turn established its
Secretariat which directs the work of the Central
Committee (previously Vorstand) between plenary
sessions (Plenen). These changes were approved
subsequently by the Third Party Conference in July

1950. The IV Congress approved the third version of the Statute which made the Party's organization identical to that of the Communist Party of the Soviet Union after the XIX CPSU Congress in October 1952 with a first secretary (Ulbricht) appointed in lieu of a general secretary. The fourth revision of Statutes (1963) which agreed separate Party organizations and leaders for the industrial and agricultural sectors of the economy also followed the Soviet model, as did the appointment of the Council of State in 1960 instead of a president as head of state, and the limitation on committee membership tenure in 1963. [67]

Though the formal endorsement of the leading position of the SED did not happen until the IV Congress in 1954, it had assumed the leadership of the "National Front", "the alliance of all forces of the people which had found its organized expression .... for the development of socialist society", [68] and which consists of the SED and the other four political parties, The Christian Democratic Union (CDU), The Liberal Democrats Liberal-Demokratische Partei Deutschlands (LDPD), The National Democrats National-Demokratische Partei Deutschlands (NDPD) and The Democratic Peasants' Party Demokratische Bauernpartei Deutschlands (DBD), plus the main mass organizations: the Confederation of Free German Trade Unions, Freier Deutscher Gewerkschaftsbund (FDGB), the Democratic Women's Federation (DFD), the Free German Youth (FDJ), and the Cultural Alliance Kulturbund der DDR (KB), well before that date. [69] Thus the Third People's Congress in 1949 which set up the GDR held single-list elections. The 1950 and subsequent state elections were held in the same way. Since the political composition of the mass organizations is mainly socialist, there are over 2,172,000 members of the SED, the Party is only nominally in the minority, with 25 per cent of the 500 seats in the Volkskammer. With its allies it represents a large majority, which becomes a clear hegemony with the support of the allied parties which centre round it in the National Front. Only the SED maintains local branches (Grundorganisationen) in the ministries, the army, police, schools, universities, factories, transport, arts, shops and other parts of the economy, politics and culture and has an overview and control of all organizations in the state united in the National Front. The Constitution states that the GDR is a Socialist state, the Republic is described as a political "organization of working people in town

and countryside, led by the working class and its
Marxist-Leninist party". [70] The latter as the
vanguard of the progressive majority class has a
clear claim to leadership because as the party of
the working class, as Lenin had stated, it alone
knows what the interests of the workers, and this
includes the collective farmers, the intelligentsia
and other progressive groups, are. If according to
the former SPD leader Grotewohl, the 1949
Constitution had established the supremacy of
parliament in the country as a first response to
fascist totalitarianism, this could not be
maintained since in the GDR all political power is
exercised by the working people who are at the
centre of all efforts of socialist society. [71] The
role of the SED consists in mobilizing the entire
population into participating fully in shaping the
political, economic, social and cultural life of the
socialist community and state (arbeite mit, plane
mit, regiere mit). [72] Socialist democracy can only
develop by getting the masses to participate. Full
turn out at elections is therefore essential and
ordinary citizens' involvement, not confined to flag
waving and listening to speeches, is characteristic
for the country's concept of socialist democracy.

   The participatory concept is located in the
source of social reproduction processes, ie, work,
which in the GDR (as in the USSR) is not only a
citizen's right but his duty. [73] This points to an
elimination of one aspect of the "bourgeois division
of political power", which in the GDR is firmly
concentrated in the SED and the National Front, and
which involves practically every citizen over 15
years of age, if not younger. Strong leadership and
planning combined with the "fullest participation of
the people" not confined to the role of an accepted
executive, is served by the principle of "democratic
centralism". [74] This system operates at all levels
of government. Elections proceed from the bottom
up. Apart from general parliamentary elections
where everyone votes, often only delegates elect the
next highest party organization and its secretary
who obtains orders from the next highest body, the
Central Committee of the SED for example. All
candidates are selected and proposed by the National
Front. The Party Congress elects the State Council
and the Central Committee, which in turn elects the
Politburo and the Secretariat of the Central
Committee. Government proceeds in the reverse
direction. The Volkskammer which is at the same
time more and less than a Western parliament, unites

legislative and executive powers when, since the
Party, its state and government are one, it passes
SED approved laws.
    It is in this process that the "mobilization of
the masses for leadership" takes place. Although
nothing that can be interpreted as anti-working
class is permitted, within the SED/National Front
hegemony, more organizations than in the West take
the initiative in proposing laws [75] and many more
again are consulted, discussing and criticizing them
before they are passed on with amendments. The
"1974 Youth Law" on political participation and
involvement, [76] was called a "youth law proposed
by youth". It was discussed by over 5 million
citizens in all sorts of committees, who proposed
4821 amendments to it of which 200 were actually
approved. [77]
    Local government consists of regional (Bezirk)
and district (Kreis) parliaments (Tage) elected in
the same way as the central Volkskammer, and
delegate elected councils (Raete) which may
interpret, but mainly execute central government
orders according to local conditions, particularly
in matters of health, education, housing, policing
and social security. The communities (Gemeinden)
are similarly administered. The state and Party in
the GDR are the "instruments and organizers of
societal development, whose driving force is the
coincidence of all political, material and cultural
interests of the workers and the collective farmers
with the demands of society". This paragraph (4) of
article 2 in the 1968 Constitution [78] was deleted
in 1974. It may be it pointed too much to the
stateless future under Communism, a phase whose
arrival, except during Kruschev has never been
loudly proclaimed. Be that as it may, the state
cannot be seen as threatening the right of any
individual, for socialist democracy is seen as being
carried out by the workers, their Party and their
trade union. The trade unions are a workers'
organization and the participation of FDGR in the
National Front has a Soviet model. [79] The
Constitution in Article 44 defines them as an
"independent organization" but the FDGB's own
constitution in turn acknowledges the leadership of
the SED under whose direction the FDGB helps to
shape socialist policies, carry out the scientific-
technical revolution, while fulfilling societal
construction plans - the broad principles of which
are handed down from above and discussed at each
executive level. In the Volkskammer the FDGB is the

second largest party. The FDJ, which is similarly
represented, has its own parliaments (Parlamente)
which vote support for SED policies in their own
activities, as in the slogan "FDJ Auftrag - IX
Parteitag".

The figures for citizens' participation in this
form of government are most impressive. Involvement
in collaboration links the SED and the National
Front with the people who by their participation are
seen to give their approval to the Front's policies.
The National Front has 205,242 citizens, that is
every eightieth citizen of the GDR, as deputies in
national and local parliaments and councils, with an
additional over 500,000 working in local and
national parliamentary commissions, 680,000
represented in parent teacher advisory councils and
225,500 working on 25,350 conflict conciliation
commissions which have the function of local
magistrates law courts. There are over 8 million
members of the FDGB, hundreds of thousands of lay
officials, (277,850 grievance officials and 241,350
work protection shop stewards alone) and nearly
30,000 deputies and delegates. 2.1 million members
of the FDJ have nominated 19,365 of their own
members as deputies to local parliaments and 40 into
the Volkskammer. [80] It is right to use this verb
since the vetted and approved nominees are virtually
certain to be elected. [81] This staggering
involvement of nearly half the citizens of the GDR
in some local, political or cultural work at any one
time, more than anything else determines the
identity of the GDR. "They are all in government".
Citizens who become local secretaries of the Party
and other executive officers however are
professionals and specialists in their fields. This
applies to ministers and councillors.

The Council of State (Soviet Presidium) which
acts for the Volkskammer between sessions, which is
most of the time since the latter only meets for
about one week in the year, issuing ordinances with
the force of law, the Council of Ministers which
issues decrees which the citizens are expected to
operate or the Central Committee and Politburo which
can act between Party Congresses are examples of
democratic contralism in operation.

With the SED's concentration of powers all
aspects of civic life in the GDR are affected by its
decisions. Its leading position has been re-stated
on numerous solemn occasions, since 1971 with its
sole and supreme aim of consolidating Socialism in
the country. To this purpose it activates in

addition to the usual governmental policies known in
the West its control over such parts of daily life
as education, the arts, youth and family policies.
The SED's grip on education which has been discussed
in previous sections is closely linked with its
interest in youth. The SED has overall control over
the FDJ and JP organizations through its maintenance
of a presence in them. These organizations, through
the usual state and Party offices, eg, State
Secretaries, receive and transmit Party policies and
see to it that they are carried out. The major
separate laws affecting youth, apart from article 20
of the Constitution are the Youth Law of 1974 and
the Education Law of 1965 which affect the lives of
all young people at school, at leisure, at work or
in training, and which spell out rights as well as
duties and obligations. Participation is but one of
them. With regard to education (and youth) matters
the SED and its government do not just provide the
outlines of policy, but prescribe in detail the
methods and syllabuses to be used, for example in
school programmes. [82]
    The judiciary seems to be less under the
control and influence of the SED. The minister of
justice and a number of judges are not Party
members. However the lay magistrates and
conciliators appear to be mainly drawn from the SED.
    An interesting comment on GDR cultural identity
is the fact that in the 1940s the SED took an early
initiative partly no doubt to establish itself as a
leading and credible political force in the new
Germany. Unlike the Verordnung ueber die Erhaltung
and Entwicklung der deutschen Wissenschaft und
Kultur of March 31, 1949* the SED's own resolution
at the First Party Conference of January 25-28,
1949* does not mention the Soviets. History
programmes for schools of 1951 too emphasized the
leading role of the SED, the organ of the German
working class movement, in establishing a new
democracy in the eastern part of Germany with only
"help from the Russians".

The Identity of the GDR Education System
    The education system was among the first
institutions to be radically transformed after the
Soviet entry into Germany. This confirms the
importance that attaches to education, in particular
to the aim of eradicating all traces of fascism in
the country. Thus when the schools reopened in the
Soviet Zone of Occupation, on October 1st, 1945,
their primary aim was education for a democratic

political system. The replacement of 78 per cent of all teachers who may have been tainted by fascist ideology by emergency-trained, democratically oriented teachers was an indication of the stress laid on the new teacher identity. 15,000 teachers were ready by October 1945. The most important of the early educational decrees was the "Law for the Democratization of German Schools" with its programme of a secular, all-through comprehensive single basic school and the abolition of educational privilege. Soon however, education and the schools came under the purview of the KPD and Marxist ideology. Significantly the posts of chief civilian education and police officials in the German administration in the Soviet Zone of Occupation went to communists. After the merger of the KPD and SPD the SED continued to have responsibility for education and youth policy. Only one youth organization, the FDJ, was allowed to be registered on March 5 1946 by the Soviet Military Administration [83] to prevent the various political parties, including the KPD, and religious groups, from having their own separate organizations, thus creating a multiplicity of groups likely to lead to disunity – which would make it more difficult to re-educate youth.

Universal State Schooling:

Direct Soviet and communist influence was strong on educational legislation in preparation for the intended future construction of Socialism. It was Paul Wandel the communist education official who produced the Law for the Democratization of German Schools, the draft for a school reform in the countryside in June 1946*, as well as publishing a month later on July 1, 1946* the first teaching programmes and syllabuses for schools especially in history. These as well as later measures, like the decree for the introduction of Marxist-Leninist ideology, lend the GDR education system its identity, as revealed during the 3rd and 4th Education Congresses in 1948 and 1949. The near total institutionalization of education, in which a school pupil's self image is different from that of a child educated at home: 80.6 per cent of the youngest children are pupils in before-and-after school centres, is typical. [84] (a) <u>Kindergartens</u> were meant after the 1946 Law merely to prepare children for school. With the governmental regulation of September 1952 they were given the important task of ideological education: "The pupils must become active builders of a peace loving,

democratic Germany, patriots capable of becoming
Socialists". [85] The kindergartens and boarding
schools were intended for pupils aged 3-6. Weekly
boarding facilities (Kinderwochenheime) for the 3-12
year olds and the fact that in the Education Law of
February 25, 1965 creches were also brought into the
state system are examples of institutionalization.
(b) General Education. Throughout the aim was for a
single school for everyone, reflected in the
education laws of 1946, 1959 and 1965, [86] but not
generally introduced till after the final abolition
of the 8-year basic school followed by four years of
secondary upper school in 1964. The school leavers
of the 10-year school were intended for semi-skilled
professional work in industry and agriculture,
traffic, police, as well as education and nursery
work. In the ninth year vocational practice was
introduced. The schools called Mittelschule in
1955, polytechnische Mittelschule in 1956, became
the general polytechnic upper school,
Allgemeinbildende polytechnische Oberschule (POS),
with children starting of the age of six and
variously staying on until the age of nineteen.
Children of workers and peasants in specially
defined categories were given priority for
admission.
The Polytechnical Principle:
     The second distinctive feature is the reform of
the 1950s which introduced polytechnical and work-
linked education. Discussions started in July 1952
in the Politburo and lasted six years. [87] At the
5th Educational Congress on May 15, 1956, the
minister of education, Lange, spoke in favour of
handicraft work (wood, metal) and polytechnicism in
schools. In April 1958 the SED schools commission
for socialist education of youth demanded a day of
production visit with teachers in socialist
enterprises and productive work experience for grade
7-12 pupils. [88] Ulbricht's paper (Der Kampf um den
Frieden, fuer den Sieg des Sozialismus, fuer die
nationale Wiedergeburt Deutschlands) reiterated the
commission's demand at the V Congress in 1958 for
part of every pupil's education to be completed in
production. Polytechnical education was announced
by the Ministry on July 30, 1958 for the following
school year 1958/1959. Grades 1 to 4 would receive
handicraft practice, (elementary polytechnicism), 5-
6 vocation-related handicraft practice, grades 7-12
"a day of production" plus theoretical introduction
to socialist production. [89] Gradually all school
subjects would have a polytechnical profile as they

have today. [90] After strong criticism that the extended upper school Erweiterte Oberschule/Abiturstufe, did not include polytechnic instruction grades 11-12 were made less academic. [91] Further strong criticism of half-hearted polytechnicism voiced by W. Ulbricht at the VI Congress in January 1963* brought in July 1963 basic vocational preparation and a general technical education in grades 9-10. Thus in the top two grades of the 10-year school there was differentiation: polytechnic education directly preparing for professions, a basic vocational preparation only or a special general polytechnical education for gifted pupils, which was taken over into the 1965 School Law. [92] Central schools were established in the coutryside following the Soviet model and according to demand and circumstances which offered an agriculture-biased polytechnical education different from town schools. Detailed syllabuses, regulations for oral and written intermediate and after grade 10 final leaving examinations in POS, published by the Ministry of Education on January 18, 1964* reflect nation-wide, state-directed curricular aims. Ordinances of 1959 and 1974 determined plans for work collaboration between schools and factories, the tasks and duties of teachers, headteachers and others to achieve uniformity. The vocational schools in collaboration with factories prepare qualified workers in theory courses of 6-13 weekly periods for which the practical work takes place on factory premises or in workshops. The law requires that all vocations for which training lasts between 2-3 years are codified in profiles as to content and demand made on students. The compulsory older vocational school for those who did not proceed to the secondary level lasted 3 years after the 8 years of basic school. With the introduction of the 10-year school the vocational component was reduced to two or even to one year if the school offers basic vocational preparation. [93] After a June 30, 1960 ordinance by the Council of Ministers* and a directive by the Ministry of Education of July 6, 1960* at least 20 per cent of all POS students going for vocations after 1965 should do so via a school leaving certificate (Abitur) class, thus entitling them to both a professional and a general school leaving certificate with which the leavers could study any university discipline they wished. Conversely academically qualified school leavers could leave with a vocation. The improved curricula meant that

vocational time available in these 3-year courses
was only 6 per cent less than in purely vocational
schools. After the 1965 Education Law the courses
were reduced to two years. [94] The result of these
measures was to provide good general education
combined with vocational preparation, and an
additional more vocational sector which does not
foreclose further study.

Adult Education is concerned exclusively with
further professional qualifications and re-
qualifications of workers according to principles
laid down by the FDGB confirmed by the Council of
Ministers in 1960 and organized by the Council on
September 27, 1962* and coordinated in industrial
areas by socialist enterprise colleges,
Betriebsakademien, and in the countryside by village
colleges, Dorfakademien. The remaining institutions
are coordinated by Volkshochschulen. There are also
radio and television academies. Higher vocational
schools (Fachschulen) educate the middle ranking
technical, economic, educational (including physical
education), arts, library sector workers who have
successfully completed a vocational education. They
are under the control of appropriate enterprises
which may delegate students; fees must be paid.
Teacher Education:

Plans of the 3rd Educational Conference in 1948
to give all teachers a university education were not
realized. Until the early 1950s most teachers were
educated in short courses as democratic teachers
were urgently required. After July 29, 1952 the
Politburo decided to follow the Soviet model of
educating teachers, pioneer leaders and educators
according to their destination school - implementing
the measure as of May 15, 1953*. Thus, Kindergarten
teachers are trained in special schools, but can
obtain a further certificate by the special schools
department of Humboldt University. Pre-school
teachers may still study at a four year institute
for teacher education (Institut fuer Lehrerbildung),
which has a higher status than in the USSR, being
partly higher education. [95] POS teachers (up to
grade 10) study for four years at pedagogical
academies (Paedagogische Hochschulen) and senior
class teachers in universities or Paedagogische
Hochschulen. Study at teachers' institutes starts
after the tenth school year, entrants to the other
two types must have completed the 12-year school
with Abitur. After a state examination the teachers
are qualified, but opportunities for upgrading
exist. Potential teachers with production

experience have been encouraged to study in distance
courses, thus assuring an ideologically reliable and
polytechnically qualified teaching force.
Out of School Education:
      The   fourth   feature   of   GDR education is the
system   of   'supplementary'   school   subject   and
ideological   training,   and   · the   SED   and   its
organizations' involvement in it. (f) Out of School
Work, organized by the FDJ and JP who provide study
groups,   courses,   clubs   in   school   subjects
(especially mathematics and science), sport, art,
technology   and   ideological work in youth clubs and
youth 'palaces' are an integral part of education.
They   were   organized in detail as part of socialist
education by the Ministry of Education's directive
on   extra-curricular   education   of   July 30, 1963*.
According to the directive pupils of different ages
are   allocated to interest groups such as gardening,
animal   care,   (grades   1-2);   communications,
electronics,   construction   technology,   modelling
(grades   3-6).   The   oldest   pupils   obtain   more
comprehensive   exposure   to   one   area   of organized
leisure   and   join   para-military,   sporting   and
technological   activities   (young   sailor,   young
rifleman), some organized by GST. Since   the   1960s
military   preparation,   for   the honour to serve the
national people's army (Nationale Volksarmee), NVA,
is   part   of education given by teachers who qualify
specially for this work.
      Pupils not taking part   in   FDJ   or   JP summer
camps   have   since a Central Committee resolution of
January 19, 1951* been sent on   organized   holidays:
Ferienfreundschaften, with detailed tasks determined
centrally   by   state   economic   organizations.   The
"Youth Law" envisages state   mass   organizations   as
holiday   planners   and   the   enabling law on holiday
activities of scholars and apprentices of April 10,
1963 [96] emphasizes socialist moral and ideological
training with young people.
The Role and Control of Higher Education:
      The   number   of   universities   after   1946   has
remained   unchanged   but   the   number   of   tertiary
colleges   with   one   faculty   and   university status
increased   by   1964,   with   the   addition   of   nine
technological   colleges,   one   pedagogical   college,
nine pedagogical institutes, three medical academies
plus tertiary schools for agriculture, art, sport,
party   political,   military   and   police   education.
Student numbers grew till 1970 with engineering and
technology   students   the   most   numerous, followed by
education, economics and medicine.

The full autonomy and independence of universities was guaranteed by the 1949 Constitution but over the years erosions occurred; student intake became planned and no individual applications accepted, student representatives and self management offices were curtailed after October 1948 when "democratic blocs" were founded in universities. [97] Teaching activities and the political stance of professors were scrutinized, and the SED became represented on university bodies, with industrial branch type cells directly responsible to the Central Committee, which after the reform in 1951, implemented Party policy. The new organization of higher education (February 22, 1951*) and the further "socialist" reorganization of higher and professional education (February 13, 1958*) brought further changes in the autonomy: limiting the self management rights of non-Party university bodies, and introducing a veto by the Higher Education Secretariat's representative. The rector was no longer chosen by the council but the wider university senate, his election had to be confirmed by the Ministry of Education or the Secretary of State for Higher Education. The pro-rectors were nominated directly by the Secretary of State after an examination of cadre requirements. [98] The senate and deanships are no longer exclusively composed of members of the university, but now have representatives of the state and the economy. The control of the students' union was explicitly allocated in the Education Law of February 1965 to the FDJ. "Students enjoy their rights for self-determination through their own social organization, the FDJ, whose members attend meetings of the university group". [99] The secretaries of these FDJ "seminar groups", whose membership remains constant as a collective during the entire period of study, as stipulated by the Secretary of State on September 6, 1952, report on each student's fulfilment of his working assignments, performance and ideological discipline. [100]
   As the central body responsible for training cadres the Secretariat of State responsible for universities and professional colleges aims to have a reliable, political, scientific-technical and pedagogic leadership in each university, as well as politically and scientifically well prepared students, researchers, professors and other workers. According to an ordinance of The Council of Ministers of February 13, 1958* it ensures the

universities' collaboration in developing science
and research commensurate with their role in the
development of socialist society. The Secretariat's
tasks were confirmed in an ordinance of June 3,
1965*; these are: passing on Central Committee's
views and deciding on all planning and management
duties necessary to carry them out; communicating
its decisions to the rectors. To link the
universities to the economy - all must prepare work
plans for the year as in the USSR, following the
State Secretary's framework. After June 5, 1964*
the regulations envisage 37-38 teaching weeks,
including practical work and examinations, 4 weeks
holiday, 3 weeks harvest gathering or similar work
and military training in the academic year. The
Secretary of State submits plans for graduate
employment to the State Planning Commission, SPK.
Since 1958 the tasks of higher education have
remained the same - training qualified personnel,
true to the workers' and peasants' state who can put
their knowledge at the disposal of Socialism,
reiterated in the Education Law of February 25,
1965.

Cultural Policy
     Like education, cultural and artistic policy in
the GDR assumed a new direction in June 1952 with
the proclamation of Socialism. Artists were asked
to search their consciousnesses and to prove the
truth of the claim that only the artistic method
demanded by the SED would lead to a rise in the
level of German culture. [101] Previous attempts at
defining a common German art were dropped in favour
of socialist art, music, literature, sculpture and
painting, (Sozialistische Nationalkultur), the
promotion of which concerned the German Academy of
Art in Berlin. It was accepted that the SED, which
controls all aspects of national life, including the
cultural, can use its powers to further its efforts
without opposition. Art, properly controlled, can
bring about a new awareness in man and make its own
particular contribution in the programme of
construction. The example to be followed was the
one of the First Congress of Soviet Writers in 1934,
which introduced "socialist realism" (the term was
coined by the novelist Maxim Gorky) and the
unconsolidated period of struggle between various
'reactionary' artistic movements in the 1920s,
including a "proletkult" . [102] The use of
"socialist realism" has never been repealed, though
its application has been relaxed at times for the

168

sake of "gaining ideological allies", as during the
second World "Patriotic" War in the USSR and several
periods of "thaw" since then in various countries.
    Cultural agencies of national life allied with
the SED are engaged in the process of promoting
"socialist art". These agents include the Cultural
Alliance (KB), the literary societies and many
others. The Federation of Trade Unions (FDGB) too
is linked with this by sponsoring artists, by
involving them in the process of socialist
production - inviting working writers to spend time
in a factory and to write about their experience
afterwards. [103]
    The first major cultural meeting of the SED in
May 1948 specifically to discuss culture, had
demanded a real (not fanciful, fantastic), realistic
and popular form of art, suggesting Soviet art as an
example, though only the III Party Congress in July
1950 demanded the Soviet example to be made
obligatory. [104] With this the battle of the Party
against "cultural barbarism" (resolution of the III
Congress) was on and pointed the way to things to
come. The resolution of the Central Committee
accepted at the 5th Plenum, March 15-17, 1951,
however, is the document whose message is still
valid today in all artistic matters. [105] With the
economic base alone falling behind in the production
of socialist man, the "superstructure" (the correct
form of art in this case) could be used to speed up
the progress of Socialism. Thus the role of art,
"to the extent the artist shapes the new, the
progressive in the development of humanity, he is
helping to educate millions to be progressive human
beings". [106] The mass organizations of the
National Front help the construction of Socialism by
developing realistic art which can cummunicate the
essence and meaning of the Two Year Plan and similar
future economic ventures and create an exemplary
hero. [107] As the documents show, the economic
"base" in tbe GDR as in the USSR before that had to
be secured first, the demand for new art following
the major changes in the ownership of the means of
production in agriculture and industry and also the
reform of the educational and legal
"superstructures". Cultural policy of the nation
means educational policy in the first place. Art in
the GDR follows politics and all the events,
statements, decrees concerning it have political or
economic antecedents: such as the moves against
formalism, formalism being pronounced anti-
bolshevik, or the demand for partisan didactic art

in March 1951, the call to use Soviet models, art being national in form but socialist in content. The Bitterfeld plan in art coincided with polytechnism on the educational-economic front, while that of anti-coexistence had the political background of 1963. [108] The periods of "thaw", usually coincided with Soviet moves, as during the period of the 4th Writers' Congress in 1956 the anti-personality denunciations of the XX CPSU Congress, and that of 1961 following the XXII CPSU Congress and Ulbricht's report to the 14th Plenum. [109]

The setting up of a Ministry of Culture on January 7, 1954 was intended to sponsor "socialist realism" ideologically, materially and organizationally; it supplemented the Ideological Commission at the Politburo. This was necessary because 'deviations' occurred, since "socialist realism" had never been adequately defined by the Marxist classics in their Critique of Political Economy, though Lenin in 1905 in Party literature and party organization defended socialist literature as partisan and dedicated to the proletarian cause. After the 11th Plenum in December 1965 Ulbricht's successor as Party secretary, Erich Honecker [110] gave a full definition of partisanship and optimism in art. There is a mixture of ideology and pragmatism in the mobilization of citizens for the production of worthy artistic objects, poems in praise of the National People's Army, the Five Year Plan or peaceful coexistence. It is easy to see all socialist art as 'conformist' and 'non-conformist', depending on the more or less eager acceptance of SED directives. Child mentions the SED's official responses to departures from prescribed "socialist realist", writings, such as the re-establishment of the State Commission for Art in September 1968 as a sign of 'tightening up' after its dissolution in June 1953. [111] In June 1957 a commission responsible to the Central Committee was said to have kept a check even on Johannes Becher, the Minister of Culture.

Socialist realism has brought with it a surge of interest in Russian art, books, films and plays which has meant a relative diminution of interest in Western works. It has also meant a reinterpretation of the classics, highlighting their espousal of ideals, like freedom, in the case of Schiller, which in the hostile socio-political context of their own time could obviously not find practical acceptance. [112] The GDR has cultivated a positive attitude to the artistic heritage, particularly the socialist progressive one, with interpreters preferring to discuss their authors' socio-political position to detailed considerations of style. With the sharpening of the socialist course, the interest in 'old' socialist art has diminished somewhat if not that in the appropriated classics: The architecture of the bombed cities has been carefully restored.

The rules of "socialist realism" in art state: it must be: a) <u>True to life,</u> a true reproduction of reality in its revolutionary development (including a future perspective). This produces a dynamic optimistic picture of reality when showing historical themes, the historical-materialist development of class society leading to Communism, b) <u>Popular</u>; to be able to influence people it must be understood by them. Stylistic experiments and innovations are not encouraged, but workers as writers reproducing their own environment are. Ulbricht's message to workers was to "turn their socialist work brigades into cultural work brigades" (April 24, 1959), [113] c) <u>Typical</u>; socialist realism does not attempt to portray average personalities but the model (=typical exception) which shows development to Socialism and which is characteristic for a particular historical and social period. "Objective art prevents the involvement of workers", and does not encourage imitation of positive examples. The prescriptive concept of socialist culture is responsible for the changes that have occurred in GDR art, which is working class, revolutionary, representing the class struggle - in its statement of aims it is art which makes its demands and message quite clear. The publishing houses attached to a party, church or mass organization exercise control over quality of production. The GDR Writers' Federation, <u>Schriftstellerverband der DDR</u> and the <u>Kulturbund</u> also have a supervisory power.

Language and Identity

Language is an integral part of every nation's or nationality group's cultural identity. However, though it can be stunted or encouraged in its growth by governmental policies and decrees it is not wholly determined by external political and educational measures.

The GDR lies across several German dialect areas and some, like the Saxon variety, are almost entirely confined to the territory of the present

GDR. This alone would account for important linguistic differences between the two German states. However language must be seen as an indispensable instrument of socialist communication in the Democratic Republic. Her socialist language policy encourages the preservation of minority languages, like Sorbian, only where this does not threaten the efficacy of the national medium of communication. There is in socialist countries a move to make language more 'equal' by discouraging the use of dialect. Educational policy is not only to use the standard language as the sole medium of instruction in schools, but the sole medium of daily intercourse as well. Though dialects exist and speakers' use of them can be detected, they tend to be relegated as lesson material or preserved for national festivals and folklore functions only. This GDR policy reflects to some extent Soviet efforts at "Sovietization of culture" in the USSR rather than Russification, if standard German is taken as the overall medium and the dialects represent the national languages. To the extent then that language represents cultural and educational policy the separate development of language in the two Germanies attracted scholars' attention on a somewhat wider scale in the 1960s, their investigations perhaps not entirely free from ideological prejudice. In the GDR language separation was denied to begin with; in the 1970s on the other hand it was the GDR which took the initiative in proving divergence, as in the case of a 'socialist' literature. In the FRG the insistence on the existence of a united 'national language' has been wholly consistent with her "one German nation" policies.

Political changes in the GDR have favoured the development of a distinct linguistic medium, a 'socialist' version of German, the language itself also changing in response to deliberate language policy, such as the principal position of Russian and the use of dialect. A socio-political system as centralized and omnipresent as that of the GDR is bound to affect its language which is its medium of communication.

Comparing language changes reflecting socio-political changes, new social aims and expectations, can be used to assess different cultural identities. [114] Changes to the vocabulary, lexis being the most 'open' linguistic system, are the most likely, with existing words changing their meaning when used in new contexts and new or adapted words coined to reflect socialist political needs. There are thousands of such words now in popular use in the GDR which are German and recognized as such, but which are not used, sometimes not even properly understood in the FRG. The two Duden dictionaries of Leipzig (GDR) and Mannheim (FRG) since 1951 and 1954 respectively (the last common Duden was published in 1947) have registered an ever increasing number of new words or words with different meanings, found in only one of the German nations. Certainly concepts like "unemployment benefit", "employee", "school fee" or "social market economy" would be unknown in the GDR, with her different political system and there would be 'no words' for them in the Leipzig edition. Conversely, the socialist concepts of "planning", "formation" or "mass initiative" would be absent from FRG dictionaries, though in both cases the words themselves could be found with different meanings and be generally understood in their basic common meaning; for example, 'initiative'. The world of socialist work and participatory politics throws up terms like Brigade, Brigadier in a civilian construction context (it is the smallest work team unit) or Aktiv. Some words are also current in Russian: Diversant, Kombinat and indeed Aktiv. Old words with new meanings would be Demokratie, Propaganda, Perspektive (an optimistic outlook), while Blasphemie would be stripped of its religious connotation. There are purely Russian words like Datscha and Kolchos(e). However, vocabulary change alone does not make a new language, more profound morphological and syntactical changes are necessary for that. These are emerging, in the shape of distinct plural forms, (for example, Aulen = Aulas), the Russian "i" plural ending, or syntactical changes, in the use of cases. West German has acquired new Anglo-American phonemes 'dzh' (manager), East German has Russian 'zh' 'shch' and 'tsh'. The Soviet practice to use initials (ABF, VVB) is more often found in the GDR than in the FRG.

Further speculation underlines the division between the languages spoken in the two countries. Language change is recognized as a change in thinking and conceptualization. Volksfeind, Volkseigentum (words with Volk (people) are particularly popular in the GDR) denote concepts which in the FRG would not be understood without some effort, as would be the case with Volksheld, a popular hero label not likely to be given to a pop star. Such terms not only refer to GDR specific

ideas or institutions, they are very particular GDR
linguistic formations, concrete rather than
metaphorical, clear and precise. The frequent use
of the Russian genetive case model is another
example of the same trend, as observed by Raddatz in
expressions like: "storming of the pinnacles of
culture". [115] Raddatz quotes investigations which
prove that the language in the GDR is more likely to
be used for 'teaching', 'converting' and must
therefore be clear, expressive and concrete. The
two languages result in different partnerships; if
the language is there to change and to convince it
must use means enabling it to do so efficiently.
The use of compound words is of course known in
German as well as Russian. In the attempt to go too
far in this direction GDR language has been called
naive in its translucence. [116]
   Speculation on 'different ways of thinking' in
a different language is difficult, as it is
impossible to measure this objectively. Language
exists to change man's consciousness, overcome
(bewaeltigen) obstacles and fight (kaempfen) for a
new future. Users of GDR German seem more active,
participating, as when young pioneers halten
Freundschaft mit den Kindern der Sowjetunion und
aller Laender. [117] In an investigation of GDR
cultural identity semantic changes are a more
fruitful area than the use of regional 'accents'.

Cultural identity in a work of fiction
   A recent work of fiction, Dietrich Hohmann's
Blaue Sonnenblumen published in December 1982 by
Neues Leben Podium, Berlin, provides an artistic
illustration of the cultural identity of the GDR.
This set of six 'average' stories probably is more
suitable for the illustration of identity than the
work of a well known and acknowledged 'great' artist
since it describes rather than creates characters
and situations. The stories in the volume, while
depicting the characters' individual circumstances
and problems, see them against the canvas of
contemporary GDR society, the canvas being taken,
unvarnished, from socialist reality.
   (a) In the first story the unmarried mother is
very much her own woman, while the young men in her
life, including a successful industrial scientist
and communist who has risen to the top, are shown as
wanting in some social and personal respect. (b) In
the second a newspaper reporter writes a glowing
public portrait of a 'veteran' factory worker. Will
he change it when he discovers what a domestic

tyrant the man is, or is the reporter one himself? (c) This story, in which the pre-war 'exploiters' who have done very well in the FRG return to 'their' villa in the GDR and meet the new occupants, several families in fact, confronts the two Germanies. The characters speak 'different' languages, there are mutual suspicion and false expectations. (d) A bureaucratic 'unreasonable' works manager fails to appreciate the excellent production performance of a worker who expects more indulgence under Socialism for his somewhat undisciplined behaviour. (e) The fifth story analyzes the 'petty bourgeois', selfish, behaviour of a family of former garden nursery owners who become state employees after the war. Their son, after hesitation, joins the (official) trade union work safety inspectorate. His girl friend, whose father is a dedicated communist and teacher, loses her university place because of "Western" contacts. (f) The last story too concentrates on the difference of human attitudes and values in pre-war and post-war, capitalist and socialist Germany, describing a long-lasting feud betweens two neighbouring villages which has become a feud between families and which their grandchildren manage to overcome.

All the stories are "socialist realist", reality being shown in its revolutionary progress, which includes the defeat of fascism and the change to social ownership of the means of production, with "typical", positive heroes. Situations which are not exemplary are clearly overcome. The style is simple and entertaining, but didactic and convincing at the same time, without the new "perspective" becoming too obtrusive. The book reflects GDR reality, particlarly the emphasis on the 'new', the change to Socialism not only in the new ownership relations, but conditions of work, education, cultural and leisure pursuits which together make up her socialist cultural identity. The surprisingly 'down to earth' narrative with topics of drink, sex, jealousy, petty desires and squabbles, which could easily be found in Western popular fiction, illustrate the common 'human identity'. GDR identity shows through in the new socio-political and economic conditions: the country's concern with production yields and good production methods, the analysis and fulfilment of production plans, optimal exploitation of raw materials, the link of work and education in sponsorship contracts between schools and factories (Patenschaftsvertraege), the education of cadres for various tasks (Marx and Engels are

175

cited in this context), socialist competition at work; the independent position of women, social welfare provision, opportunity for relaxation after work in cultured surroundings, pride in and membership of communist youth organizations with their ceremonies, loss of party position and its effect on the individual.

These stories clearly illustrate the new morality which emphasizes optimism and progress, belief in man's capabilities starting with the assertion: der Mensch kann alles, good neighbourly relations, socialist attitude to work, including affectionate references to machinery and products, Ziegelchen, good collaboration and common achievement, patriotic behaviour is another aspect. A third is the new political reality; with references to the noble cause (grosse Sache) of Communism and its ultimate victory. "Ideological help" in case of "objective difficulties" (= lack of partisanship) may be necessary. There are opinion forming propaganda apparatuses jokingly referred to as the Meinungsfront, looking for heroic stories, there is fear of non-Marxist-Leninist world views but much friendship and technical assistance to Tanzania. Friendship with and interest in the USSR is frequently mentioned, Freundesland and das Land Lenins, as well as high regard for Soviet biologists. "Searches through antique myths" turn out to be Russian.

Everyday life experiences are very different — ranging from communal living conditions in flats, relations with other socialist countries — invitations to Bucharest, student exchanges with Kiev university, flights between Moscow and Berlin. The foreign words to be read turn out to be Ukrainian. Manners are different, modes of address: Genosse Tissula and "the comrades of the people's militia" are normal. People celebrate holidays like: the eve of the First of May and 'The Day of the Republic', they use different consumer goods: Trabant cars, and children learn 'study of contemporary society' at school. All of this is reflected in language. One finds Olga or Wladimir as first names, Mischkabaer instead of Teddybaer, while the very large number of new officials, and offices give rise to new titles and concepts: Konfliktkommission (conciliation commission working between workers and 'management'), Klassiker (of Marxism), Verkaufsstelle (point of sale, not shop!). Frauensonderstudium shows women's extra educational opportunity, while Kaderakte is a citizen's

confidential dossier which accompanies him on his
road to promotion or party membership. Oberschule,
Kombinat, Parteisekretaer, Jugendweihe would not be
immediately accessible in the FRG, while words like
Basis (work face!), Agitprop — (political
demonstation and education centre) require a more
complete adjustment.

Some references would be totally
incomprehensible, if it were not for the great
interest in the GDR in Federal Germany: 'made in
Adlershof' (Soviet HQ), Zwei Engels (banknotes with
the head of Engels), Dame Berolina (travel firm),
Blauhemd (the blue shirt, colour of youth, worn by
young pioneers) or Taigatrommel (a reference to the
Moskvich car) are but a few examples.

The third story in the collection (Hoher
Besuch, Distinguished visitors) confirms what has
been said above. It takes the reader through the
political developments to the emergence of the new
Republic, emphasizing the Neue Zeit, with the
construction of Socialism, not forgetting the
difficulties to be overcome, such as the plight of
war refugees. The emotions stirred by assertions of
not going back, "we don't live in the nineteenth
century" and the statement "there is no 'revanchism'
in the GDR", contrast with fanning of false hopes in
the FRG to break up the post-war order in Europe.

The private fortunes of the original
businessman owner of the villa who has escaped to
the West and those of the new owners and their very
difficult living conditions to begin with are played
out against this political canvas. Everyday life in
the provincial town of the GDR includes concern with
freedom fighters (Angela Davis), references to
scientific progress (flight of Soyuz 2), while
complaints of housing shortages (applicants for
flats) are balanced by technical-commercial study
opportunities for girls (BMSR Student: Betriebs,
Mess, Steuerungs und Regelungstechnik in grade 12)
and a mild anti-religious jibe (monastery in Rila).
The original owner's wife speaks of the "peace of
conscience" which the GDR caretaker counters with
the visitors' unspoken hope for eventual recovery of
their private property. The figure of the daughter
Bibi is that of an optimistic girl firmly rooted in
and identified with the GDR, but ignorant of the
West. Particularly the younger generation, the two
girls find it somewhat difficult to converse. Bibi
does not know an Opel car, her speech includes
several Russian expressions, khorosho, and she
refers to her teacher as uchitiel, partly to

177

underline the difference between her and her FRG
visitor; note her joke "take me to your country".
The expression 'Westler' shows the disdain of the
GDR family for the FRG. They live in a totally new
world (eine andere Welt) and are beginning to doubt
the common Germanness (Deutsche, vielleicht!) of
themselves and their visitors. The FRG is of course
neither home nor abroad, but drueben, 'over there',
an adverb used in the same way in the FRG for the
GDR. At the end of the visit the GDR family are
pleased to be alone: "da waeren wir ja wieder
beisammen".
     The collection confirms the very different
self-image, the new cultural identity of the German
Democratic Republic.

Conclusion
     The Russian presence whether physical in the
shape of Warsaw Pact soldiers or the military
headgear worn by the GDR's own Nationale Volksarmee
or cultural in the form of imported plays and books
- and a German speaking society where Moscow though
over 1,500 kilometres away is somehow nearer than
Bonn which is less than one third that distance, are
features which any visitor is quickly made aware of.
To write about these was not the main purpose of
this chapter which concentrates on more specific
aspects of a distinctive socialist cultural identity
which began with economic and political change. The
emphasis was on education which is a characteristic
feature of the country, with 2,529 marks spent on
the education of every school pupil, excluding
salaries, in one year [118] and a school system
which employs some 70 per cent more teachers than
its immediate neighbour. Education has a clear
political and economic aim which in turn lends a
specificity to the GDR's cultural identity: the
transmission of new values, a sharing, more
conforming attitude amongst people where a 'victory'
has to do with harnessing the resources of nature.
The emphasis on construction, building "the new"
which is the outcome of an education and re-
education process linked with a very strong
remembrance of the horrors of the fascist past is
one of the lasting impressions one has of the GDR
and its people.
     The attitudes of teenagers sampled in a survey
conducted by two FRG researchers who compared the
views and priorities of 15 year olds in the two
German states are revealing: teenagers in the GDR
were much less "ich-bezogen", concerned with their

178

own selves and much less consumer goods oriented. [119] If the second may be understood in the context of GDR economy the first was a most surprising revelation when communicated by the author of this chapter to a group of British student teachers.

The case of the GDR confirms that her cultural identity is a "sum total" of a country which has embarked on a new course. This accounts for the pervasive presence of the SED party which is largely responsible for the new image, and the spread and completeness of its appearance, to the extent that newspapers for dog owners and breeders are not exempt let alone the distinctive image of schoolbooks. Here a survey of texts revealed the ignorance of average citizens of one German state of the other. [120]

The separate cultural identity of the dissidents and misfits does not alter the picture. The GDR is distinctive enough to prove the point that political separation has reinforced the differences between the two German territories, despite their common language and tradition. The late political unity of Germany, the verspaetete Nation, has no doubt helped in this process.

Notes and References

1. Krejci, Jaroslav, Social structure in divided Germany. Croom Helm, 1976, gives statistics of the voting patterns in the present three divisions of the former Reich and a brief introduction to the GDR.

2. The German Democratic Republic, 10 Years of United Nations Membership. Verlag Zeit im Bild, 1983.

3. A recent use of this term is found in Schweigler, Gebhard, Ludwig, National Consciousness in Divided Germany. Sage Publications, 1974. In the GDR the adjective gebildet (cultural) has been appropriated for the socialist republic.

4. The Constitution of the German Democratic Republic. Staatsverlag der Deutschen Demokratischen Republik and Verlag Zeit im Bild, 1974, Article 1.

5. Liedtke, Klaus, Muss die Welt die Deutschen fuerchten? Stern, Nr 18, April 26, 1984.

6. Lenin, V.I., Questions on National Policy and Proletarian Internationalism (from Progress English translation of Lenin's works), Progress, 1977.

7. Socialist national art was preceded by

socialist and bourgeois art. For example socialist
literature in Germany dates back to 1830. Earlier
periods anticipate and 'pre-figure' the present.
    8. The "zero hour" after the German collapse
in 1945, after which all political and cultural
counting starts anew.
    9. Cf the documentation by Kobach, Manfred and
Mueller, Ernst, Der Deutsche Bauernkrieg in
Dokumenten. Hermann Boehlau Nachfolger, Weimar,
1977, with recent references in Christians and
Churches. Panorama DDR, Verlag Zeit im Bild, 1983.
    10. See textbooks in the Heimatkunde and
Lesebuch series, published for each grade of the
polytechnical upper school by Volk und Wissen
Volkseigener Verlag in Berlin.
    11. The best known early interpreters of the
two classics were Alexander Abusch and Johannes R.
Becher.
    12. Cf the draft Constitution, Entwurf einer
Verfassung fuer die Deutsche Demokratische Republik
of 1946. JHW Dietz, Nachf., Berlin, 1946.
    13. Gesetzblatt der Deutschen Demokratischen
Republik. 1968, Teil I, p 199 foll. Verfassung der
Deutschen Demokratischen Republik vom 6 April 1968,
Staatsverlag der Deutschen Demokratischen Republik,
Berlin, 1968. (Abbreviated to Gesetzblatt, below.)
    14. The Constitution op cit.
    15. Cf Forster, Thomas, Manfred, The East
German Army: The second power in the Warsaw Pact.
Allen & Unwin, 1980.
    16. Cf the famous "learn" exhortations of
Lenin; as in The Tasks of the Youth Leagues and
other speeches. Lenin, V.I., On Youth. Progress,
1977;
It was Fidel Castro who declared "Revolution and
Education are the same thing" in a speech in 1961.
Universidad Popular, 6th Series, Educacion y
Revolucion, Imprenta Nacional de Cuba 1961, p 271.
    17. This is a general philosophical pedagogical
term not used to refer to a particular phenomenon,
but convenient to emphasize the education of
citizens in 'progressive periods', encyclopaedism or
neo-humanism, and which aptly illustrates the
socialist society in its various stages of
development.
    18. Lenin, V.I., op cit. Cf the references to
Marx's insistence on the inclusion of the
'bourgeois' heritage.
    19. The latter had a place in trade union
legislation of the Weimar Republic but were further
developed in the USSR, while the social courts

involving lay persons (gesellschaftliche Gerichte),
well known in the USSR have been introduced more
recently in the GDR.
    20. The order (Befehl) Nr 40 of the Soviet
Military Administration in Germany of August 25,
1945. See Schneller, Wilhelm, Die deutsche
demokratische Schule. Volk und Wissen Volkseigener
Verlag, 1955.
    21. Gesetz zur Demokratisierung der Deutschen
Schule. Grundlage fuer gemeinsame Gesetzesvorlage.
In: Adomeit, Heinz, ed., Karteibuch des Schulrechts
der Deutschen Demokratischen Republik - Recht der
Schule. Deutscher Zentralverlag, 1951 foll. (1-
142);
continued as Adomeit, Ursula, ed., Bildung und
Erziehung - Loseblattsammlung gesetzlicher
Bestimmungen.
    22. Ueber die Verstaerkung des Studiums der
'Geschichte der kommunistischen Partei der
Sowjetunion (Bolschewiki) - Kurzer Lehrgang',
Beschluss des Zentralsekretariats der SED vom 20
September 1948. Dokumente der Sozialistischen
Einheitspartei Deutschlands. Vol 2, Dietz, 1951.
    23. Siebert, Hans, Neue Lehrer in Kampf um die
Erfuellung des Zweijahrplans, reprinted in Baske,
Siegfried and Engelbert, Martha, eds., Zwei
Jahrzehnte Bildungspolitik in der Sowjetzone
Deutschlands. Dokumente (I & II), Quelle & Meyer,
1966. Other documents quoted and there reprinted
are marked with an * in the text and will not be
referred to in this section unless an additional
commentary or source are provided.
    24. Walter Ulbricht (1893-1973) co-founder in
the USSR of the National Committee for a Free
Germany in 1943 and largely responsible for
rebuilding the administration in Berlin. Elected
general secretary of the SED Central Committee in
1950, chairman in May 1971.
    25. Dokumente Dietz op cit, vol 4, 1954.
    26. Dorst, Werner, Erziehung, Bildung und
Unterricht in der Deutschen demokratischen Schule,
Grundlagen. Volk und Wissen Volkseigener Verlag,
1953, p 76.
    27. Cf note 25.
    28. Gesetzblatt 1951, Nr 23. Verordnung ueber
die Neuorganisation des Hochschulwesens, vom 22
Februar 1951.
    29. Gesetzblatt 1951, Nr 62. Einsetzung von
Prorektoren fuer besondere Aufgabengebiete, vom 21
Mai 1951.
    30. Gesetzblatt 1951, Nr 94.

Gesellschaftswissenschaftliches Grundstudium an den
Universitaeten und Hochschulen, vom 4 August 1951.
    31. Bildung und Aufgaben der Seminargruppen,
Anweisung Nr 26 des Staatsekretariats fuer
Hochschulwesen vom 6 September 1952. Das
Hochschulwesen, Wissenschaftspolitische Rundschau,
1955, 3, 1.
    32. Hager, Kurt, Der Kampf fuer die weitere
sozialistische Umgestaltung der Universitaeten und
Hochschulen der DDR. In: Lange, M., ed., Zur
sozialistischen Kulturrevolution. Dokumente, Vol I,
Aufbau, 1960.
    33. Dokumente Dietz op cit, Vol 3, 1952.
    34. Anweisung zur Durchfuehrung des Schuljahres
1958/59, vom 30 Juli 1958. Karteibuch
Loseblattsammlung 124, op cit.
    35. Gesetzblatt, 1955, Teil I, Nr 48.
Anordnung ueber die Umwandlung von Oberschulen in
Zehnklassenschulen, vom 11 Mai 1955;
Efforts to introduce the 10-year school started in
1950. See Guenther, Karl-Heinz and Uhlig, Gottried.
Geschichte der Schule in der Deutschen
Demokratischen Republik 1945 bis 1968. Volk und
Wissen Volkseigener Verlag, 1969, p 92.
    36. Anweisung zum Ablauf des Schul-und
Lehrjahres 1964/65 an allgemeinbildenden
Oberschulen, kommunalen Berufsschulen und
Volkshochschulen, vom 5 Juni 1964. In: Adomeit,
Ursula, ed., Bildung und Erziehung,
Loseblattsamnlung 54. Nachtrag C/1c/29. (See note
21)
    37. Neuner, Gerhart, ed., et al.,
Allgemeinbildung Lehrplanwerk Unterricht. Volk und
Wissen Volkseigener Verlag, 1973;
Bereday, G.Z.F. and Pennar, J. eds., The politics of
Soviet education. Fr. Praeger, 1960.
    38. Gesetzblatt, 1974, Teil I, Nr 5.
Jugendgesetz der DDR, Ueber die Teilnahme der Jugend
an der Gestaltung der entwickelten sozialistischen
Gesellschaft und ueber ihre allseitige Foerderung in
der Deutschen Demokratischen Republik, vom 28 Januar
1974. This supersedes all previous laws. Also
available in: Jugendgesetz. Staatsverlag der
Deutschen Demokratischen Republik, Berlin, 1984.
    39. This is a party which has adopted the
philosophy of Marxism-Leninism and democratic
centralism as its form of organization and
procedure. It is not a 'factional' party of several
in parliament, but a cadre party of activists
recruited in their place of work rather than one of
mass membership with only a territorial organization

based on members' domicile.

40. Cf also Groth, W., Zur Schulpolitik der Partei in der gegenwaertigen Situation. Einheit, Theorie und Praxis des wissenschaftichen Sozialismus, 1949, 10.

41. Jessipow, B.P., and Gontscharow, N.K., Paedagogik (1948) and Ogorodnikow, I.T., and Schimbirjew, P.N., Lehrbuch der Paedagogik (1949) both by Volk und Wissen Verlag.

42. See note 23.

43. Schulpolitische Richtlimen fuer die deutsche demokratische schule (SED Executive and 4th Education Congress versions). Der 4. Paedagogische Kongress vom 23. bis 25. August 1949. Volk und Wissen, VerlagsGMBH, 1949.

44. Neuner, Gerhart ed., et al., op cit. Pp 38 foll. sum up the inseparable unity of socialist ideology and modern scientific discovery which forms the base of every subject taught in GDR schools'.

45. See note 25.

46. Neuner, Gerhart, Ueber die Erziehung junger sozialistischer Patrioten. Deutsche Lehrerzeitung 1961, 8, 43.

47. Cf the role of the social sciences in the curriculum, Neuner op cit, pp 244 foll. and any of the Volk und Wissen published Heimatkunde, Geographie, Geschichte school text books for higher grades. 1-2 hours a week are given to the social sciences;
Ministerium fuer Volksbildung, Lehrplan der zehnklassigen allgemeinbildenden polytechnischen Oberschule. Volk und Wissen Volkseigener Verlag, 1959 (and foll).

48. The Jugendweihe has been taken since 1954 by most youth aged 14 and marks their entry into GDR society. It is meant to be independent of social origin and outlook of candidates. A boy or girl who has undergone Jugendweihe is accepted as an adult. The Jugendweihe has its roots in a German working class 'coming of age' celebration going back to 1859.

49. See note 31;
Cf the resolution of the Central Committee of January 19, 1951: Die naechsten Aufgaben der allgemeinbildenden Schule. Dokumente Dietz op cit, vol 3;
Dokumente zur Geschichte der Freien Deutschen Jugend. Vol 1, Neues Leben, 1960.

50. Gesetzblatt, 1957, Teil I, Nr 69. Anordnung ueber das praktische Jahr der Studienbewerber an Universitaeten und Hochschulen,

vom 17 Oktober 1957, is a directive of the Ministry
of Work and Vocational Training.

51. Makarenko, A.S., The Collective Family. A
Handbook for Russian Parents. Peter Smith,
Gloucester, Mass, 1973.
52. Dokumente Neues Leben, op cit;
Deiters, Heinrich, Die Schule der demokratischen
Gesellschaft. Dietz, 1948, p 113.
53. Ichenhaeuser, Ernst, A., Das Elternaktiv.
Volk und Wissen Volkseigener Verlag, 1983.
54. Paedagogischer Kongress, op cit.
55. Cf Neuner, op cit, note 44;
Waesch, G. Der Klassenleiter und die
ausserunterrichtliche Taetigkeit aelterer Schueler.
Volk und Wissen Volkseigener Verlag, 1976;
Pigors, Paul and Waesch, Gerhard, Klassenleiter und
FDJ Gruppe. Volk und Wissen Volkseigener Verlag,
1983.
56. Gesetzblatt, 1965, Teil I, Nr 6. Gesetz
ueber das einheitliche sozialistische
Bildungssystem, vom 25 Februar 1965. From the
preamble to the 1965 Law.
Cf also Guenther op cit, 1969;
See also: Klein, M.S., The Challenge of Communist
Education. East European Monographs, Boulder, 1980.
57. Gunther, Karl-Heinz, et al., Das
Bildungsewesen der Deutschen Demokratischen
Republik. Volk und Wissen Volkseigener Verlag,
1983, pp 95 foll.
58. Siebert, Hans, op cit.
59. Dokumente Dietz op cit, vol 4.
60. Lehrplan der zebnklassigen Oberschule, op
cit, note 47;
Karteibuch, op cit, note 34.
61. Dokumente Dietz op cit, vol 8, 1962;
Gemeinsamer Beschluss des Politbueros des
Zentralkomitees der SED und des Ministerrates der
DDR ueber die Grundsaetze der weiteren
Systematisierung des polytechnischen Unterrichts,
der schrittweisen Einfuehrung der beruflichen
Grundbildung und der Entwicklung von Spezialschulen
und -klassen, vom 3 Juli 1963. Deutsche
Lehrerzeitung 1963, 10, 29.
62. ibid; and 1965 Law, op cit.
63. Frankiewicz, Heinz, Sozialistische
Bildungstheorie und polytechnische Bildung.
Paedagogik, Zeitschrift fuer Theorie und Praxis der
sozialistischen Erziehung, 1965, 20 6;
Frankiewicz, Heinz, Einige Grundfragen der
Weiterentwicklung der polytechnischen Bildung und
Erziehung. Paedagogik, op cit, 1962, 17, 5.

64. Arbeitsrichtlinie der Staatlichen Plankommission und des Staatsekretariats fuer das Hoch - und Fachschulwesen zur Durchfuehrung des Berufsansatzes der Hochschulabsolventen, vom 9 Mai 1960. Das Hochschulwesen, Wissenschaftspolitische Rundschau, 1960, 8, 7/8.

65. Gesetzblatt, 1964, Teil II, Nr 61. Gesetz ueber die Verbesserung der Planung und Leitung der Berufsbildung in der Deutschen Demokratischen Republik, vom 14 Mai 1964.

66. See note 39.

67. Statut der SED. Dietz, 1976.

68. Cf article 3 of the (1974) Constitution, op cit.

69. The exact dates for the formation of the National Front are uncertain. The 'collapse of fascism' and the 'democratic and socialist construction' quoted are later formulations since a 'Front' had come into being during the war within the "National Committee for Free Germany", Nationalkomitee Freies Deutschland. In this the KPD as the party of the revolutionary working class was the senior and majority partner. The SED replaced it as the leader and thus assumed its rightful role in the state of workers and collective farmers. The reason for an alliance of parties is that the overthrow of fascism was a common effort and it, rather than a workers' party-led revolution, preceded the construction of socialism. The "United Front" of July 14, 1945 of the four then existing political parties (KPD, SPD, CDU and LDPD) anticipated the later constituted Democratic Bloc, Demokratischer Block of parties in the Volkskammer.

70. Cf article 1 of the (1974) Constitution, op cit.

71. ibid, article 2.

72. ibid, article 21(1).

73. ibid, article 24(1) & (2).

74. ibid, article 47(2); Sontheimer, Kurt and Bleek, Wilhelm, The Government and Politics of East Germany. Hutchinson University Library, 1975, pp 57 foll.

75. These are listed in article 65 of the (1974) Constitution.

76. op cit.

77. Details taken from DDR-Gesellschaft-Staat-Buerger. Staatsverlag der Deutschen Demokratischen Republik, Berlin 1979, p 184.

78. Verfassung der Deutschen Demokratischen Republik, vom 6 April 1968, op cit.

79. Haney, Gerhard, Demokratie - ein Begriff

und seine Wahrheit. Staatsverlag der Deutschen Demokratischen Republik, Berlin, 1973.

80. Figures taken from DDR-Gesellschaft-, op cit.

81. Cf notes 31 and 49 and ops cit.

82. Cf Neuner, op cit, note 44.

83. See notes 49 and 52 and ops cit.

84. Statistical Pocket Book of the German Democratic Republic, Staatsverlag der Deutschen Demokratischen Republik, Berlin, 1983.

85. Gesetzblatt, 1952, Nr 134. Verordnung ueber die Einrichtungen der vorschulischen Erziehung und der Horte, vom 18 September 1952.

86. See Guenther, op cit, note 57, for the major school reforms.

87. See Dokumente Dietz op cit, vol 4.

88. Vorschlaege der Schulkonferenz der sozialistischen Einheitspartei Deutschlands zur sozialistischen Erziehung der Schuljugend, vom 24 und 25 April 1958. Zur sozialistischen Kulturrevolution, op cit, vol II.

89. Guenther op cit, note 57.

90. Cf Neuner op cit, notes 37 and 44.

91. Frankiewicz, 1962 op cit.

92. Law 1965 op cit.

93. Gemeinsamer Beschluss des Politbueros und des Ministerrats, op cit, see note 61.

94. Law 1965 op cit.

95. See Grant N., in: Goodings, R. et al., eds., Changing Priorities in Teacher Education. Croom Helm, 1982.

96. Gesetzblatt, 1963, Teil II, Nr 45. Fuenfte Durchfuehrungsbestimmung zum Gesetz ueber die sozialistische Entwicklung des Schulwesens in der DDR. Feriengestaltung der Schueler und Lehrlinge, vom 10 April 1963.

97. The founding of the political bloc in Berlin is mentioned in Forum, Zeitschrift fuer das geistige Leben an den deutschen Hochschulen, 1948, 2, 10.

98. Gesetzblatt, 1953, Nr 124. Bearbeitung der Kaderangelegenheiten der Universitaeten und Hochschulen, vom 10 November 1953.

99. Law 1965 op cit.

100. Bildung und Aufgaben der Seminargruppen. Hochschulwesen, 1955, op cit.

101. W. Ulbricht, in: Theater der Zeit, 1952, 15.

102. A narrow, dogmatic strictly proletarian working class culture, which discards all bourgeois influences, rejected by Lenin in 1920 as non-Marxist

cultural separatism.

103. This was sponsored by the Bitterfeld literary movement, <u>Bitterfelder Weg</u>, which encouraged industrial reality in art with the slogan '<u>Greif zur Feder, Kumpel</u>' of April 23, 1958; also 1964.

104. cf Alfred Kurella, in: <u>Neues Deutschland</u>, May 17, 1958. Beilage.

105. In: <u>Einheit</u>, Theorie und Praxis des wissenschaftlichen Sozialismus, 1951, 8/9.

106. Gaertner, Hannelore, ed., (for Autorenkollektiv) <u>Die Kuenste in der Deutschen Demokratischen Republik</u>, Henschelverlag Kunst und Gesellschaft, 1979.

107. Hager, Kurt, Kunst ist Waffe fuer den Sozialismus. <u>Sonntag</u>, October 20, 1957, uses a slogan of the 1920s for the propagation of socialist art.

108. <u>Neues Deutschland</u> Nr 94, April 4, 1963.

109. <u>Neues Deutschland</u> Nr 327, November 28, 1961.

110. Erich Honecker born 1912, secretary of Communist Youth before the war. First (General) Secretary, SED Central Committee since 1971, chairman, Council of State, <u>Staatsrat</u>, since 1976.

111. Childs, David, <u>The GDR: Moscow's German Ally</u>. George Allen & Unwin, 1983.

112. For different interpretations of modern GDR literature in the FRG, see: Tulasiewicz, W.F., <u>Modern Languages</u>, 1976, <u>57</u>, 4.

113. Dialektik des Neuen. In: <u>Neues Deutschland</u>, Nr 132, May 15, 1959.

114. Hillerer, W., in: <u>Sprache im technischen Zeitalter</u>, 1961, 16.

115. Raddatz, J., <u>Traditionen und Tendenzen</u>, Materialien zur Literatur der DDR. Suhrkamp, 1972.

116. Johnson, Uwe, et al., Sie sprechen verschiedene Sprachen - Schriftsteller diskutieren. In: <u>Alternative</u>, 1964, 38-39.

117. Reich, Hans, H., Sprache und Politik. Untersuchungen zu Wortschatz und Wortwahl des offiziellen Sprachgebrauchs in der DDR. <u>Muenchener Germanistische Beitraege</u>, 1968 <u>1</u>; Korlen, Gustav, Zur Entwicklung der deutschen Sprache diesseits und jenseits des Eisernen Vorhangs. In: Handt, Friedrich, ed., <u>Deutsch gefrorene Sprache in einem gefrorenen Land?</u> Polemik, Analysen, Aufsaetze, Literarisches Colloquium, Berlin (West), 1964.

118. Calculated from the Statistical Pocket Book, op cit.

119. Jaide, Walter and Jaide, Hille, Barbara, eds., Zukunftsvorstellungen von 15 Jaehrigen in der DDR und der BRD. In: Jaide, Walter, Jugend im doppelten Deutschland. Westermann, 1977.

120. Siebert, Horst, Der andere Teil Deutschlands in Schulbuechern der DDR und der BRD. Buchmarkt - Forschung, 1970.

CRITICAL EDUCATION AND ISLAMIC CULTURE

Paul Hurst

    Muslim   societies   throughout   the   world   are
currently   undergoing   a   profound   cultural   crisis
brought about by their adoption at various levels of
scale   of   Western   educational   patterns   in   order   to
acquire modern technology and knowhow for   the   sake
of   economic   development.   At   the   same   time   this
Western system of education is   secular   in   nature,
and   both   critical   and   speculative   in its approach.
As such it runs directly counter   to   and   threatens
much   that Muslims value in their traditional system
of beliefs and culture.   As a consequence it had led
to dualistic educational provision   on   the   ground,
with   a   modern   Western-style   schooling   system
existing alongside a traditional Islamic   system   of
muktab [1]   and   madrasah, [2]   and   virtually   no
contact between the two.   The modern   school   system
in   Muslim countries is seen to be in an ethical and
spiritual vacuum and, at the same time, as a   feeble
and   ,inefficient   copy   of   Western   models.   The
traditional Islamic system is often considered to be
out-of-date,   backward-looking   and   intellectually
stagnant.   From   a   wider   point   of   view   than
education, the current   cultural   crisis   in   Muslim
societies   is a complex of alienations, from Western
materialistic   individualism   which   is   morally
decadent, from Marxist materialism which is godless,
and   from   Muslim   pietism   which   is   mentally   and
materially backward.
    Some Muslim scholars hold out the view   that   a
synthesis   is   possible, in which Western scientific
thought will be sanitized and rid of its secular and
amoral accretions.   It   will   be   reformulated   and
reconciled with the essential precepts of Islam, and
will   thus   serve   as   the   basis   for a new type of
education which will resolve the cultural crisis and
act   as   the   springboard   for   autonomous   Islamic-

189

scientific advance. In this chapter it is proposed
to examine the assumptions underlying this
programme, and it will be argued that it rests on a
fallacy, namely that the product of scientific
enterprise can be separated from the mode of its
acquisition. It is no historical accident that
scientific method has a secular and sceptical
character, and the same must be true of educational
systems which seek to promote it. There is, it will
be argued, a fundamental contradiction between
revelation and research, and the painful conflict
between the two is as evident in the history of
Islamic science and philosophy as it is in that of
the Christian West. While scientific knowledge up
to a given point in time can no doubt be treated as
a corpus of doctrine or lore and vetted according to
Islamic (or indeed any other) moral principles, and
in fact has been so scrutinized by various religious
and political authorities in the past, this is
inimical to the further development of that
knowledge.

The Cultural Crisis Viewed by Muslim Scholars
It is perhaps more appropriate to present
perceptions of the crisis in Islamic cultural
identity through the words of Muslims themselves,
and accordingly there follows a sequence of brief
excerpts from relevant works. Along with Hossein
Nasr's Islam and the Plight of Modern Man, [3] one
of the most perceptive recent studies is Husain and
Ashraf's Crisis in Muslim Education. [4] This book
picks up most of the themes that are discussed in
this debate, and presents them in an articulate and
cogent manner. One of the most common themes is the
impious and sceptical emphasis in Western culture.

> Modern Western education places an exaggerated
> emphasis upon reason and rationality and under-
> estimates the value of the spirit. It
> encourages scientific enquiry at the expense of
> faith; it promotes individualism; it breeds
> scepticism; it refuses to accept that which is
> not demonstrable; it is anthropocentric rather
> than theocentric. Even where it does not
> directly challenge faith it relegates it to the
> background as something less important than
> reason.... The Muslim World too has been
> invaded by this Western form of civilization.
> This feeling of rootlessness has already
> entered society because our intellectuals are
> now being educated in the West, being

brainwashed and returning to their own
countries after reading textbooks which are all
filled with ideas in conflict with their
traditional assumptions. Even in Muslim
countries the traditional Islamic education
system has been superseded by a modern one
which has been borrowed from the West. [5]

Western culture and the educational system
which transmits it is therefore lacking in a fixed
sense of moral values, which cannot be adduced by
rationality but must be divinely revealed. As a
consequence, Western culture presents a spectacle of
moral anarchy and degeneracy, both public and
private.

Thus what distinguishes the Islamic system of
education from the modern Western System is the
importance it attaches to faith and piety as
one of its fundamental aims. In the West, the
aim of education is spoken of as being to
produce a good individual and a good citizen,
both of which aims Islam can accept. But
having secularized education completely, the
West fails to indicate how in the absence of a
set of moral values, either of those aims can
be realized. Western society is today in
danger of disintegrating. There is nothing to
hold it together except state laws, and when
the justice of the state laws is in question,
moral anarchy and urban lawlessness are the
response. [6]

Nevertheless, Western culture cannot simply be
rejected outright, since the benefits of
technological advance are too important to
repudiate.

Much as the Muslim, anchored in faith,
disapproves of the spiritual nihilism of the
West, he himself, because of his neglect of
science and technology, has created around his
society a suffocating atmosphere as oppressive
as the spiritual sterility of the West. Want
and poverty, disease and epidemic, colonialism
and economic humiliation have forced him to
realize that it is only by mastering science
and technology that he can escape these
problems. [7]

But when the Muslim turns to Western culture,

the result is alienation.

> The Muslim, when exposed to Western thought,
> thus finds himself confronted with something
> which repudiates the basic premises on which
> the whole edifice of his religious and cultural
> life rests. This is the reason why the
> alliance from without between the modern system
> and the Islamic system does not seem to work.
> The Islamic system tries to impart a set of
> values which are contradicted by the modern
> system and people feel often bewildered and
> confused. But since the modern system is
> better geared to the kind of life that
> industrialization has created, the tendency on
> the part of a Muslim youth exposed to it
> without adequate precautions would be to assume
> that the old system which he has inherited from
> his own past is totally irrelevant to his
> modern needs. [8]

Is it possible to overcome this dilemma and
reconcile Western scientific advances with Islamic
spiritual values? It is important to recall here
that early Islam set great store, perhaps too much,
upon the acquisition of scholarship and consequently
it is a tenet of Islam that the pursuit of learning
is in itself an ethically superior activity. The
Quran, Hadith [9] and other sources contain numerous
injunctions and sayings to this effect, such as:

> The ink of the scholar is even more precious
> than the blood of martyrs.

> Seek knowledge from the cradle to the grave.

> Seek knowledge, even if it be in China.

We must remember too that Islam, unlike early
Christianity, but like late mediaeval Christianity,
was very much an educational enterprise, in the
widest sense. The culture into which it was
introduced was largely pre-literate and oral, and it
is truly astonishing that the messenger who brought
into the world this complex code of jurisprudence,
political economy, religious practice, tolerance of
other religions, military strategy, (far more
complex than the other-worldly simplicitudes of
Christianity) and many other matters besides, was

himself an illiterate. Thus it is not surprising to find Muslim scholars arguing that the spiritual bankruptcy of Western science is not a by-product of the quest for knowledge itself.

Can we discover a means of isolating the sterile values which have so warped Western life from the knowledge which they corrupt? Knowledge, Muslim scholars believe, cannot by itself be harmful or dangerous. It is the extraneous values and assumptions which man imparts into it which cause it to produce a spiritually harmful fall-out. [10]

And just as it is The Book - that which is written - which came to play such a dominant role in the development of Islam, so too it is the impurity of the modern textbook which is seen as central to the current cultural crisis.

They [Muslim Scholars] have all tried to isolate what is basic and fundamental in Muslim education and what outward trappings from the Western System can easily be dispensed with. They maintain also that as long as Muslim society continues to rely upon textbooks borrowed from the West, the problem will stay with us, because textbooks, whether they are textbooks on Physics or Chemistry or Political Science, are imbued with the ethical values of the writers and the only way in which this problem can be tackled is by Muslim writers coming forward to produce their own textbooks which will be free from the kind of bias which informs Western writings. [11]

The relative backwardness of Muslim Society in terms of material progress and indeed other forms of development is not always seen as entirely due to the ungodly unacceptability of Western culture, at least not by a minority of observers. Mohammed Wasiullah Khan is more scathing than most, but such a note of Muslim self-criticism is by no means unheard of.

Originally Muslims, by implementing Islamic injunctions in their individual and collective lives, achieved the highest social economic, and political stature in their contemporary world. However, over succeeding centuries of ideological degeneration and despotic or colonial rule, a grossly individualist interpretation of Islam has prevailed.... With the exception of practising certain rituals, the masses of Muslim countries and their self-styled leaders hardly see any virtue in such values as efficiency, diligence, orderliness, punctuality, frugality, scrupulous honesty, fairness and impartiality, rationality, lack of prejudice, preparedness and adaptability to change, alertness, opportunity, energetic enterprise, integrity and self-reliance. Commitment to ideology has been reduced, at least at the level of the masses, to wishful thinking and day-dreaming which sometimes drift into feelings of false pride. [12]

Schooling in Muslim countries also comes in for a share of criticism, as in these remarks by Basheer El Tom:

Muslim schools tend to discourage intellectual nimbleness to such an extent that the pupil's uncritical mind accepts whatever is promised to him. From the very beginning he is expected to know things by rote rather than through understanding and critical appraisal. Desire for intellectual initiative is withheld from him and any talents he may have are wasted. Other qualities of value such as self-reliance and moral courage are also killed by the lethal educational fare that he is made to swallow; moreover Muslims do not have the polytechnic schools of whose graduates and functional activity we stand in dire need. [13]

The proposed solution to this acute and complex problem of the clash of incompatible cultural elements finds its roots in the traditional Islamic binary polarity haram-halal (forbidden/permitted).

Modernization as a package is being transferred into the Muslim world with all its evils as if there could be no selection; and as if the entire prescription was indispensable. This surely is a result of a failure on the part of the Muslim intelligentsia to evolve a rational outlook which ensures on the one hand the acceptance of the beneficial, the permissible and the universal elements of modernization, and their assimilation into Islamic culture so that they no longer remain features of a

foreign culture and, on the other, a total
rejection of forbidden and subversive elements.
Presumably, it is still possible to modernize
the Muslim World upholding the values of the
Quran and the Sunnah. But for that an
ijtihad [14] of the entire Ummah [15] is
essential....... [16]

It is surely strange that the 'outlook' which
will successfully discriminate between the
beneficial, the permissible and the universal from
the forbidden and the subversive is described as
'rational' when it appears to have been the
rationalist emphasis in Western culture which
created the problem in the first place. In fact,
one may detect in many such writings that the
authors are returning (sometimes apparently unaware
that they are so doing) to themes addressed by the
great Muslim thinkers of the golden age of Islamic
philosophical and scientific endeavour, between the
third and ninth centuries after the Hegira.
It is little realized or appreciated in the
West that we owe an immense debt to early Arab
scholars in the fields of philosophy, science,
mathematics and medicine. The Dark Ages are often
presented historically as an interregnum between the
Graeco-Roman period and the Renaissance with the
Christian Church keeping the torch of scholarship
alight. In fact, it was Arab scholars who played a
major role, not merely in passing on the hellenistic
tradition through translations, but also in
developing it and adding to it; for instance,
developing empirical experimental methods in
branches of physics such as optics. [17]
As Jolivet [18] has pointed out, Islamic
philosophical enquiry began during the third century
of the Hegira [19] when the Abbasid dynasty had
superseded the Ummayads, and the Muslim empire by
then incorporated Syria, Egypt and Persia, all
regions that had been strongly infuenced by Greek
thought since the time of Alexander, as well as
having a strong oriental element in their cultures.
When the works of Plato, Aristotle and some neo-
platonists began to be studied by Muslim
intellectuals it created an immediate and, as it
transpired, an enduring problem.

When philosophy came on the scene and claimed
its place, for one thing there was no need to
look for a rule of life any more since the
coming of the Arab Prophet, for the Koran

contained everything in the way of knowledge
needed to ensure salvation, plus the essentials
in the field of belief and rules of behaviour.
For another, the practice and even the theory
of social organization, and personal and
property problems, were dealt within the
science of law itself, based on the Koran, the
traditions of the Prophet and his companions
and the judgements and decisions of the early
caliphs. [20]

More significantly, hellenistic philosophy
contained elements which ran directly contrary to
Islamic doctrine. Aristotle for instance held the
view that matter is eternal whereas Islam teaches
that God created the world. Some of the neo-
platonists subscribed to polytheism, which, of
course directly opposes the central Islamic concept
of tawheed [21] the uniqueness and unity of Allah.
Jolivet distinguishes two schools of thought which
developed in reaction to this problem. The first -
that of the falasifa [22] attempted to show that
there were no fundamental contradictions between
Greek philosophy and Islamic doctrine. Two of the
principal exponents of this school were al-Kindi
(who died in 873 AD) and ibn Sina (Avicenna, who
died in 1037 AD). As we shall be mentioning the
views of Popper, Kuhn and Lakatos in due course, it
is worth mentioning here that al-Kindi believed that
man cannot know the entire truth; he only knows what
has been accumulated over generations and passed
from one culture to another. From this principle he
adduced the corollary that the correct scientific
and philosophical method consists of setting out
what is already known and adding what one has
discovered.
    This is very different from the Islamic concept
of absolute truth being revealed by the divinity to
a chosen human messenger, although al-Kindi argued
that philosophy itself led to awareness of the
divinity. Similarly, and in a much more equivocal
way, Avicenna sought to adumbrate a cosmology which
synthesized Islamic revelation and hellenistic
philosophy. The other school - principally al-
Farabi (who died in 950 AD) and ibn Rushd (Averroes,
died in 1198 AD) - were much less concerned with
religious thought and carried on the hellenistic
tradition in a more secular manner. Nevertheless it
was the judgement of al-Ghazzali (who died in 1111
AD), and much later, that of the famous historian
ibn Khaldun (1332-1400 AD) which prevailed in

subsequent Muslim scholarship. They held that revelation reigned supreme over reason.

> [There is] ...... a long, complex, extremely rich doctrinal evolution in which Greek philosophy and Islamic religion were mixed and intertwined together in a variable and problematic way. It is absolutely correct, again from a strictly historical point of view, to say that this philosophy or philosophies grew up as a function of Islam, both because it gave them a locus in which to develop and an equally fruitful source of both inspiration and problems, and also because even in al-Farabi and Averroes (as could be demonstrated) they were not fundamentally separated from it. It is equally true, and from just as strictly historical a viewpoint, that the synthesis al-Kindi and Avicenna dreamed of and sought to achieve never really worked, because Avicenna was regarded by the men of religion as too philosophical and by the philosophers as too religious. [23]

There are of course other reasons why Islamic research and scholarship went into a period of long decline, other than the triumph of the revelationists. Political and religious dissensions led to very heavy emphasis on the acceptance of orthodox dogma, particularly as the State (or ruler) was at once the chief political, military and religious authority. Such heterodoxies as Sufism [24] and the Ikhwan-as-Safa [25] provoked an authoritarian reaction which attacked independent intellectual speculation. Nor were the factors making for decline entirely endogenous. Much has been made by Muslim scholars of the ravages of the Mongols, the neglect of the Ottomans, and the exploitation and cultural rape of the European colonial period. It is an exaggeration to claim that the Europeans attempted to destroy a vibrant and flourishing Islamic culture, but it is undoubtedly the case that European colonialism did nothing to foster it, except in provoking Muslim reaction to its own excesses.

Critical-Speculative Education and Islamic Culture

We have seen how unpalatable to Muslim thinking is a form of scientific inquiry which casts doubt upon that which is already known, and which seeks new knowledge through an interplay of criticism and

imagination using purely human faculties, without
reference to any divine guidance. By the same
token, an educational system or other mechanism of
cultural transmission, for example broadcasting,
which reflects a similar sceptical and secular
approach is bound to be viewed with moral distaste.
The pious Muslim is not a person who can develop a
cultural schizophrenia, suspending his traditional
beliefs while operating within the Western
intellectual paradigm and vice versa, which people
in some other cultures do, changing mental sets as
easily as they change from traditional to modern
dress. The central concept of tawheed implies that
either Western science can be reconciled with God's
will as communicated through the prophets, or it, or
at any rate some parts of it, must be forbidden.
Either science is part of, and subordinate to,
religion, or it is haram. [26]

And yet, according to philosophers and
historians of science such as Popper, Kuhn and
Lakatos, scientific knowledge advances through the
critical discovery of weaknesses in existing
knowledge and the production of new theory by means
of imaginative speculation which is itself subject
to critical assessment, of conjecture and refutation
as Popper has summarised the process. Nor is the
critical-speculative method distinctively 'modern'
or 'Western'. Many Muslim scholars like to believe
that Western science went off the rails about the
seventeenth century AD, when it progressively lost
its Christian character and became increasingly
secular or even atheistic, with Western society and
culture as a whole following suit. From this
perspective Western secularism appears as a fairly
recent and possibly temporary aberration. However,
if we consider the experiments in geometrical optics
of ibn al-Haytham (Alhazen) and al-Farisi, for
example, it is clear that it was these early Arab
scientists who were engaged in the generation and
testing of mathematical propositions about the
properties of light. Indeed Alexander von Humboldt
in the last century asserted that empirical
experimentation was itself an invention of the
Arabs. The method of systematic doubt was not a
late European creation, whenever it was invented.

There is of course no necessary reason why
people who practise the critical-speculative method
of enquiry and education should be irreligious.
Many scientists believe in divine creation. But it
is no more than that - a belief, a cosmological
theory which is conceivably erroneous. It matters

little with what degree of conviction such beliefs
are held. From the critical-speculative viewpoint
any proposition about the world is potentially
false, in whole or in part. Whether or not its
truth or falsity is testable is another issue.
Untestable propositions may still be true or false,
or partly both, and few would nowadays agree with
the logical positivists that untestable propositions
are meaningless.

This brings us back to the crucial dilemma
which not even a mind as subtle as that of Avicenna
could resolve. If some propositions about the world
are potentially erroneous, and if scientific
knowledge proceeds by cumulatively uncovering the
error and correcting it, why (if there is no
contradiction between revelation and research) are
some propositions in a reserved category, whose
truth is unquestionable? If we create an
educational system (as we presumably wish to) which
successfully transmits the critical-speculative
method to at least some of its graduates, they will
be bound to ask why there are some propositions
(other than tautologies, which are not about the
world) which are necessarily true, when all the rest
are falsifiable in principle. To reply "because God
uttered them" is not calculated to satisfy a mind
imbued with the critical-speculative ethos. It is
regrettable that the moral relativism to which the
critical-speculative method leads should create such
confusion and even despair in immature minds. For
this, modern education bears a heavy responsibility,
since it teaches some of its 'brightest sparks' to
think critically, but often cannot enable them to
put anything constructive in place of what they
criticize, with the result that some turn to drugs,
hooliganism and terrorism. It would be a blessing
in many ways if we could restore the simple
certitudes of religious piety; but once a mind
acquires the critical habit it will not stop
questioning simply because the authorities say so,
whether they be ulama, bishops, kings or commissars.
Galileo showed this in his day, Sakharov in ours,
and the same is true of much lesser intellects.

The programme of Islamicizing the modern
curriculum seems therefore doomed to failure.
Either it will produce a curriculum that is
moribund, in which case it will produce no one
capable of outstanding research, or it will succeed
despite itself in producing people who are genuinely
capable of critical-speculative thinking. In which
case they will waste no time in throwing it out and

replacing it with a better one.

Notes and References

1. Muktab (Maktab): A place for teaching boys and girls, like an elementary school. It represents an advance on the Kuttab which is an attempt to provide early education for Arab children destined to receive training as religious leaders. The Muktab is administered by a Sheykh who collects fees, receives grants from religious endowments and subsidies from public funds. Boys are admitted at the age of four or younger and continue for two to four years before being transferred to one of the other types of elementary school.

2. Madrasah (School): A higher school than the Muktab, still under Islamic supervision.

3. Nasr, Hossein, Islam and the Plight of Modern Man. Longman, 1975.

4. Husain, Saijid and Ashraf, Ali, Crisis in Muslim Education. Hodder and Stoughton / King Abdulaziz University, Jeddah, 1979.

5. ibid, pp 2-3.

6. ibid, p 38.

7. ibid, p 39.

8. ibid, p 57.

9. Hadith: The Holy traditions of the Messenger Mohammad, which are the outcome of God's revelation to the educated person that is the prophet Mohammed Al-Rassol (messenger).

10. ibid, p 40.

11. ibid, p 59.

12. Khan, Mohammed Wasiullah, ed., Education and Society in the Muslim World. Hodder and Stoughton / King Abdulaziz University, Jeddah, 1981, p 3.

13. El Tom, Basheer, Education and Society. In ibid p 41.

14. Ijtihad: The Islamic intellectual abilities exhibited by the adult Moslem, who really knows the principles of the Islamic religion; a specialist on the principles of the Islamic law and Sharyaa. The person who can derive the answers and the rules from these, and has the ability to explain new situations in Islamic society such as the impact of economic and social development.

15. Ummah: People who comprise a local community celebrate the customs and the principles of their culture.

16. Saquid, Gnulam Nabi, Modernization of Muslim Society and Education: Need for a Practical

Approach. In: Khan, M.W., op cit, pp 48-49.

17. Rashed, Rashdi, Islam and the Flowering of the Exact Sciences. In: Islam, Philosophy and Science. UNESCO, 1981.

18. Jolivet, Jean, The Development of Philosophical Thought in its Relationship with Islam up to Avicenna. In ibid.

19. Hegira: Relates to the transfer of the prophet of Islam Mohammad and his companions, and the Moslem people, from Mecca to El-Madynah in Saudia Arabia. The Messenger Mohammad also used the term Hegira as meaning the transfer of any person from one situation to another.

20. ibid, p 40.

21. Tawheed: Asserts that the One God is the sole unchallenged originator of this world and is in full control of its affairs and destiny. A Moslem expresses this commitment in a simple phrase testifying- La ilaha illa Allah (there is no God but God).

22. Falasifa: Islamic philosophers well known in medieval Europe, such as Alpharabius, Ibn Khaldum, Al-Ghazali and Al-Farabi.

23. ibid, p 60.

24. Sufism (Al-Sufia): An Islamic principle, though not from the Holy Koran, involving interpretation and definition of Koranic rules.

25. Ikhwan-as-Safa: A group of Arab scientists having their own interpretation of natural phenomena and the nature of man. To some extent of historic interest only, though some of their ideas have been incorporated in modern educational approaches in Islamic states.

26. Haram: A pre-Islamic concept, though now incorporated, and signifying something that is forbidden.

EDUCATION POLICY AND CULTURAL IDENTITY IN ISRAEL

Yaacov Iram

Background

Israel is a young immigrant country. Its society is pluralistic. This pluralism is evident in almost every aspect. Nationally it has a Jewish majority, constituting 84 per cent of the population, and a non-Jewish, predominantly Arab, minority of 16 per cent. The non-Jewish minority is religiously diversified: Muslim (13.5 per cent), Druze (1.5 per cent), Christian (1 per cent). The two languages spoken are Hebrew and Arabic. Set up as a home for all Jews, the national, religious and linguistic pluralism of Israel has caused three separate educational systems to emerge: Jewish, Arab and Druze. [1]

The Jewish majority itself is diverse ethnically, religiously, culturally as well as educationally. Ethnically - in the sense of country of origin, [2] 48 per cent of Israel's Jewish population are Israeli born, 25 per cent are 'Orientals', Sephardim born in African, Asian and Middle-Eastern countries, while 27 per cent are 'Westerns' or Ashkenazim Jews, born in America, Europe and South Africa. [3] The other nationalities similarly are not all autochthonous.

As far as their religion is concerned, Israeli Jews are divided into 'religious', strict observers that is of Jewish practices and religious commandments (Mitzvot), [4] and 'non-religious', namely non-observers of Mitzvot in daily life, although most of them may honour some Jewish customs and obligations. [5] Culturally - the different ethnic groups brought along with them from their countries of origin different customs, ceremonies, attitudes, values and ways of life.

Alternating periods of harmonious cooperation and tension, coexistence and conflict between

202

Sephardim and Ashkenazim on issues of socio-economic equality and cultural identity, as well as between religious and non-religious arise frequently. Two grass roots ethnic conflicts between 'Orientals' and Ashkenazim may serve as examples of socio-economic tensions: the Wadi-Salib slum neighbourhood riots in Haifa of July 1959, and the subsequent development of governmental and public awareness of the ethnic problem; [6] and the 'Black Panthers' street protests, demonstrations, and clashes with police in Jerusalem during March-August 1979. [7] A political example would be the various attempts to form political parties on an ethnic basis and a platform to work within the political system, such as the partly successful attempt of the Tami party in the 1981 elections, which won 2.3 per cent of the vote and three seats in the Knesset. [8]

The tensions between religious and non-religious are more enduring but the strife is mainly in the political and judicial arenas of religious legislation and court appeals. The conflicts are related to the resilience of the religious status quo, accepted as a political arrangement for peaceful coexistence and the avoidance of a Kulturkampf in matters of personal status such as marriage and divorce, and the observance of Sabbath and religious holidays in public. [9] However, along with the legitimate orderly and democratic struggle, from time to time small radical groups on both sides resort to violence and confrontation. In the 1960s the League Against Religious Coercion held demonstrations and clashed with religious groups and police. In the 1970s the Committee for the Defence of the Sanctity of the Nation, an ultra orthodox group, was very active. [10]

Differences in the approach to religious observance have caused the development of three Jewish educational subsystems: those of State Education, State Religious Education and the Independent Education of Agudat Israel, [11] that maintains its educational system under the category of 'non-official recognized schools' of the State Education Law of 1953. [12] The heterogeneity of the Israeli society has posed a dilemma regarding the socio-cultural function of education: should education serve as a 'melting pot', assimilate that is the immigrants into the dominant ruling groups, or rather, see itself as an instrument of social integration within a pluralistic society, and encourage cultural identity of the different groups? These two conflicting attitudes have found their expression in different strategies of immigrant absorption, as well as changes in educational policy. [13]

This chapter will try to describe and analyze the impact of educational policy on two major issues that are most prominent on Israel's socio-cultural and educational agenda, their recent developments and current status, namely: religio-national identity and ethno-cultural integration.

Religio-National Identity

An American anthropologist concludes his study on the children of a particular kibbutz by stating:

In effect, the sabras [14] feel no tie ....
with much of Jewish tradition or with peculiar Jewish values; they want little to do with the last 2000 years of the Jewish past; and they wish to dissociate themselves from those Jews, who, actually or symbolically, represent those values and that past. [15]

Ten years later a French-Jewish sociologist called his book, written following a visit to Israel: The End of the Jewish People? His own answer to his rhetorical question is that

A new people is being created every day in Israel; a young people that is neither an appendage nor the centre of the now-legendary 'Jewish people'. [16]

These impressions were not just those of outside observers who may lack an intimate acquaintance with Israeli youth. Inside Israel too there was felt a growing concern during the years following the establishment of the State, at the negation of the past by many Israelis, along with an anxiety about a possible estrangement of Israeli youth from their Jewish heritage. Indeed, this tendency was expressed by an extreme, though small group of young intellectuals who called themselves 'Young Hebrews' or as they were sometimes called by others, 'Canaanites'. This group would wish to sever all links between Jewish people and Jewish history of the last two thousand years in the diaspora. Its members regard themselves as Hebrew, as distinct from Jews, claiming direct spiritual descent from the indigenous population of the land of Canaan. [17] Various studies conducted during the 1950s have shown that most non-orthodox youngsters

born in Israel tend to define themselves primarily
as Israelis rather than Jews or Hebrews, and that
their Jewish identity was weak or non-existent. [18]
    Paradoxically, the roots of this estrangement
from the past may be found in the Zionist movement
which strove to re-establish the integral national
identity of the Jewish people. [19] In this process
Zionism was torn between rebellion against the past
and the desire to be rooted in it. [20] The revolt
was against Jewish diaspora existence and its
inherent defects and anomalies as viewed by the
Zionists. At the same time, however, Zionist
leadership was dependent upon the political and
economic support of affluent and influential Jewish
groups in the Western world. While the older
generation in general showed a sentimental
attachment to the life style and culture of the
Jewish communities in Eastern Europe, particularly
after its tragic destruction during the Nazi
Holocaust, most of the youth did not share these
feelings. A similar ambivalence characterized
Zionists' attitude to the Jewish tradition and
cultural heritage. Zionism, essentially a secular
national movement, sought for roots in national
history and heritage, which was predominantly
religious in character. Thus the Zionist dilemma
was how to continue a history and heritage against
which it was in open revolt. [21] A partial solution
was found through selective emphasis on those
elements in the Jewish tradition and heritage which
could be secularized, such as the revival of the
Hebrew language or the attachment to the natural
environment of the ancestral homeland. Another way
out of the dilemma was to stress elements that lent
themselves easily to modern and secular humanistic
re-interpretation [22] and to universal, social and
moral ideals of national self-preservation and
physical survival. For expositions of modern
Jewish-national thought see note 23. [23]
    No such ambivalence characterized the attitude
of the majority of young Israelis towards their
brethren's life in the diaspora, nor to their
religious traditions and heritage. The only
exception are the youngsters from orthodox Jewish
homes, whose adherence to the religious way of life
enables them to cope with the twin problems of
continuity with the Jewish religious past and of
affinity with the Jewish people in the diaspora.
Thus:

    Not only do the religious students feel more

Israel

Jewish and value their Jewishness more under
all circumstances, but they feel closer to, and
have a greater sense of identification with
Jews everywhere. [24]

In the case of the religious students, home, school
and youth movement mutually reinforce one another in
an integrated outlook on Jews and Jewishness as a
set of values and a code of behaviour. Indeed, the
state religious schools include in their curriculum,
in addition to the subjects taught at secular
schools, intensified courses of study in Bible and
Talmud, and instruction in religious observance.
However, only between 22 and 25 per cent of all
children in state schools (figures for 1970/71 and
1981/82 school years respectively) avail themselves
of this instruction. [25]
    The weakness of the Jewish identity of non-
orthodox young Israelis alarmed Israel's political
and cultural leadership, as well as educators. [26]
Indeed, article 44 of the principles and declared
policies of the 1955 Coalition Government's Platform
presented to the Knesset reads:

In primary, secondary and higher education, the
Government will endeavour to deepen the Jewish
consciousness of Israel's youth, to root it in
the past and the historical heritage of the
Jewish people, and to strengthen its moral ties
with World Jewry founded upon the recognition
of the community of fate and of the historical
continuity which unite Jews throughout the
world in all generations and countries. [27]

This government led by the Mapai (Labour) Party and
headed by Prime Minister David Ben-Gurion was
presented to the Knesset on November 3, 1955. To
implement this stated policy, the Ministry of
Education and Culture proposed to introduce in
schools a detailed curriculum for the cultivation of
'Jewish-Israeli consciousness' in the State
elementary school system.
    Mr Zalman Aranne, the Minister of Education and
Culture, summarizing the parliamentary debate on
this issue in the Knesset on June 15, 1959,
reiterated the rationale of the programme by saying
there was an urgent need to face 'four baffling
problems' which he listed as follows; one: how to
foster in Israeli youth the feeling of belonging to
the Jewish people, despite the fact that the
majority of this people live outside the boundaries

of the State; two: how to root the youth in the
history of the Jewish people, when half of that
history occurred outside the boundaries of the
State; three: how to reconcile Zionist teaching of
'negation of the diaspora' with the need to
inculcate in Israeli youth an awareness of the unity
of the Jewish people; four: how to bring closer to
children educated in secular schools a culture
permeated with religion. [28]

Following lengthy political, public and
educational debates, the Ministry of Education and
Culture in September 1959 introduced a programme for
'deepening of Jewish consciousness in the State
schools'. [29] These directives were a
crystallization of an earlier programme issued in a
Circular by the Director General of the Ministry of
Education and Culture in 1957. Its threefold
expected aims were:

a) Improved acquaintance with the Jewish past
in the diaspora achieved by emphasizing certain
periods, events and personalities in Jewish
history, thus deepening awareness of the
continuity of the Jewish people.
b) Improved acquaintance with diaspora Jewry.
This aim to be achieved by a systematic study
of Jewish communities in the diaspora, their
socio-economic structure, their political and
legal status, their culture and customs and
their ties with the State of Israel.
Particular emphasis is to be laid upon the
unity and solidarity of the Jewish people
throughout the world and strengthening
emotional ties with diaspora Jewry.
c) Familiarizing the pupils in non-religious
schools with the spiritual heritage of the
Jewish people which is religious in character.
This is to be achieved by the study of prayers,
rites, customs, folklore and religious symbols,
and creating a 'Jewish atmosphere' at school
especially around the Holy Days and the
Sabbath. [30]

This programme encountered opposition both from
anti-clerical left wing and from religious parties.
The 'secularists' denounced it as an attempt to
introduce religious education into secular State
schools, while religious teachers denied the
possibility of teaching 'Jewish consciousness', not
based upon belief in divine revelation of the
Scriptures and upon religious observance of the

practical precepts of Judaism. Indeed the Minister of Education stated in the Knesset debate:

> It would constitute a gross injustice if there were any compulsion, either religious or anti-religious ... love and respect for tradition must permeate our national schools not in order to educate for religion but in order to uphold the national character of our educational system. [31]

To eliminate doubts, the Ministry's directives made it clear that:

> the new programme in no way changes the essential nature of the State School system. Inasmuch as it has not hitherto educated in favour or against religious observance, so it will continue not to educate for or against religious observance. [32]

In 1964 the Ministry of Education established the Centre for Promotion of Jewish Consciousness as an independent unit within the Ministry, to coordinate publication of curricular materials, textbooks and guides, and to oversee initial and in-service training of teachers. The Centre was closed formally in 1975 because of administrative, personnel and pedagogical reasons, [33] but the activities aimed at fostering the Jewish identity in its threefold dimension, viz. the past, the diaspora and the tradition did not cease. In answer to the question, did the Jewish Consciousness Programme succeed?, two recent studies [34] claim that the great expectations of the initiators to solve the religio-cultural debate over the Jewish-Israeli identity did not materialize. Nor did this programme and the Ministry's education policy create a national consensus towards the issue of the proper place of Jewish culture, essentially religious in character, in the State of Israel. Indeed, the fragile status quo between religious and non-religious in national politics and in daily life is being shattered more often in the 1980s than before. The complex issue of 'Who is a Jew?' which has direct implications in matters of citizenship and personal status and the problem of observance of the Sabbath in public life have been written about and documented in the Israeli and the international news media a good deal recently. [35]

It would seem that the failure of the Programme

stems from its evasion of the crucial issue of
defining the content and substance of Jewish
identity; its initiators have stressed instead the
aspects of imparting knowledge and gathering and
disseminating of information. It is in this respect
one must admit, that the Programme of Jewish
Consciousness as a subject of school instruction,
achieved a modest success in eradicating common
ignorance of the Jewish past and Jewish life outside
the boundaries of Israel, and in creating an
awareness of the variety of Jewish tradition. Even
so, the crucial issue of what is desirable and what
is feasible in the realm of cultural identity of
young Israelis remains unresolved. [36]

Ethno-cultural Identity and Integration

We turn now to the analysis of educational
policy in regard to another major issue, namely
educational equality and ethno-cultural integration
of the two numerically almost equal components of
the Israeli society, Jews of Afro-Asian origin
(Orientals or Sephardi) - numbering 51 per cent and
those of Euro-American origin (Ashkenazi) -
numbering 49 per cent. [37]

We repeat: Israel is a young immigrant society.
Although the foundations of the modern Jewish
community in Israel (Palestine) were laid in the
latter part of the nineteenth century, mass
immigration only started following the establishment
of the State in 1948. The first three and a half
years of Israel's existence witnessed an influx of
about 750,000 immigrants which more than doubled the
original Jewish population of 649,600 to 1,404,400,
more than tripled it by 1961 and almost quintupled
its Jewish inhabitants by 1975. [38] This was an
outcome of Israel's Law of Return: one of Israel's
earliest constitutional acts under which every Jew
everywhere has the inalienable right to immigrate to
Israel and the automatic right to Israeli
citizenship upon his arrival in the country. This
declared open-door policy of almost unrestricted
Jewish immigration, the policy of KIBBUTZ-GALUYOT or
in-gathering of the exiles was in accordance with
one of the cardinal aims of Zionism, and of the
State of Israel which was established by Jewish
immigrants with the expressed purpose of absorbing
further immigration. [39]

The large waves of immigration brought about an
incisive change to the fabric of Israeli society,
namely its ethnic or geocultural composition.
Whereas almost 90 per cent of Jewish immigration to

209

Israel before 1948 hailed from Europe, more than half of the immigrants to Israel after its establishment, came from underdeveloped, semi-feudal, traditional societies in the Middle East and in Africa, north of the Sahara. [40] As a result the Jewish population of Israel underwent a radical change from being preponderantly European in origin before 1948 to achieving a numerical majority of Orientals by the early 1960s. [41] This trend of 'orientalization' became a crucial issue for Israel. Having been built up by immigrants from Europe, despite her Middle Eastern geographical location, Israel has always been oriented towards the modern Western and European civilization with its characteristic elements of rationality, planning, future-mindedness, technological and scientific progress. [42] The 'orientalization' of its population thus presented Israeli society and its education system with the challenge of MISUG-GALUYOT or, 'the fusion and integration of the exiles', namely the rapid modernization and 'westernization' of the Asio-African immigrants and their linguistic, cultural, ideological, political and socio-economic integration into a modern type technological and scientific civilization with a democratic civic culture and national aspirations and solidarity. The immigrants from the Middle-Eastern and North-African countries were members of large families, poor, many of them without any formal education and unprepared, therefore, for a life in a western industrial economy. Consequently, many of them were at an a priori social, political and economic disadvantaged position within the modern Israeli society. The immediate result was the development of a number of persistent and growing socio-economical gaps, mainly in material well-being, occupational and professional distribution, political power and in education. [43]

Educational Gap

The commitment of the Israeli society to 'bridging', 'narrowing' and even 'closing' the ethnic socio-economic gap is expressed in the platforms of all political parties and by the Government. For example, one of the 'basic principles' of the 1969 coalition led by the Labour Party and headed by Prime Minister Golda Meir indicates:

The Government will work systematically for the merging of all communities (eg, Orientals and

Ashkenazim), veterans and newcomers. All communities will be assured of equal opportunities for full integration in Israel's economy and society, in education, culture and social life, and steps will be taken to remove economic gaps between communities. [44]

The same is true of the Likud (Conservative) Party's Government formed in 1977 and 1981, led by Prime Minister Menachem Begin. [45]

To cope with this evolving and dangerous gap, Israel has tried two mechanisms: the first was the enactment of massive social welfare programmes (housing, employment, health care); the second was the provision of a free universal and open school system. Although the welfare measures improved the socio-economic status of the oriental immigrants, they were not enough to overcome the continuing phenomenon of adverse correlation between oriental origin, poverty and educational underachievement. [46] Education was therefore conceived as the main tool for the social, cultural and political integration and for the forging of a unified society out of the diversified ethnic groups.

However, the mere expansion and growth of the educational system did not diminish the gap. The disparity in educational attainment between students of Asian-African origin and students of European and American origin is shown in their median school attendance, which in 1961 was 5.9 years for the Orientals, and 9.1 for European-American immigrants aged 14 and over. [47] In 1975 the situation improved slightly: 7.1 compared to 9.8; but the percentage of Ashkenazim with at least some college education was about three times greater than that of Orientals. [48] This situation has not changed to date as indicated by figures presented to the Conference on 'Ethnic Gap and Higher Education', held by the Parliamentary Sub-committee, Alienation among Ethnic Groups in Israel, convened in the Knesset on May 29, 1984. [49]

To bridge this gap more radical changes than legal-administrative measures of expanding educational opportunities were needed. There was a need to change the philosophy of the system which was founded on a uniformity of educational procedures and structures fused with high-level educational contents and demands. [50] The new efforts to narrow the gap in achievements and to bring about equal educational opportunities were of

Israel

two kinds: different programmes of compensatory
education were introduced at the elementary level
and with the passage of the School Law Reform of
1969, in the junior high school as well; [51] at the
secondary school level, various new types of schools
were initiated to cut the drop-out rate which during
1953-1962 was of the order of between 45 and 37 per
cent and even higher among students of low socio-
economic and oriental origin. Most of the new or
modified school programmes were of a less academic-
demanding nature than those of the existing academic
high schools. The most significant of these were
different types of vocational education and
training, which brought their own social
implications. [52]

    As a result of these efforts, the growth rate
of students of oriental origin in post elementary
education, vocational and academic high schools that
is, rose from 17 per cent in 1956/57 to 36 per cent
in 1966/67 and to 50 per cent in 1976, and was much
greater than the rate of growth of youth of oriental
origin in the respective age groups in the
population at large. [53] During the early 1960s the
ethnic gap at the primary school level disappeared,
while during the 1970s, following the 1969 School
Reform the gap at the post-elementary school level
narrowed from -14.3 per cent in 1966/67 to -5.4 per
cent in 1979/80. However, a further differentiation
between vocational and academic post primary
education shows that in academic streams which lead
to higher education, Orientals were still
underrepresented by -17.4 per cent in 1980. Thus
the gap at higher education level persists, for
while Orientals constitute 56.4 per cent of the 20-
24 age group, university students of oriental origin
were only 19.2 per cent of the student population.
The ethnic gap indicator in higher education
diminished very slightly from 44.4 per cent in 1965
to -36.3 per cent in 1979. [54]

Ethno-Cultural Integration
    Since 1975 the Ministry of Education and
Culture has launched various programmes aiming at
the 'cultivation, preservation and revival of the
oriental communities' heritage and their cultural
assets'. [55] The immediate goals of the programmes
were to strengthen the feeling of Jewish unity, to
improve the self-image of these communities and to
impart their cultural heritage to all students.
These programmes tend to emphasize the cultural
pluralism concept rather than the uniformity which

was more stressed in the past, and which alienated some segments of the population of oriental origin in Israel.

The ideological assumption which guided Israeli society as well as the Ministry of Education policy was that the ethnic problem was one of inequality in level of education, standard of living, and exercise of political power. Though there was a broad consensus which negates ethnicity, it was felt in educational circles that in order to foster a positive self image of oriental children, their culture, traditions and their literary creation, as well as the customs of oriental Jewry, should find their due place in the curriculum which was entirely European.

It was hoped in this way to restore the pride of the oriental children, to mitigate their feelings of inferiority in relation to the culturally and economically dominant European group and to minimize feelings of alienation from the Israeli society. Some steps in this direction had been made within the context of the Jewish Consciousness Programme in the 1960s, but it was not enough. [56] In 1976 the Ministry of Education and Culture announced its intention 'to widen the integration of the spiritual heritage of Oriental Jewry into education and culture'. [57] This programme reflected a definite change in social policy towards ethnic integration, although the stated target of the Israeli society remained ethnic integration and uniculturalism with only minor subcultural pluralism.

Still it is a modification of the melting-pot idea of MISUG-GALUYOT, of unity via uniformity rather than unity within diversity and cultural particularity. The basic ideology adopted in 1976 was that the historical encounter of various ethnic groups in Israel must lead to a cultural synthesis, provided each group will have the opportunity to conserve and develop its cultural heritage. The aim of cultural integration remained, but its product should be, by different means, dialectical integration, through selective cultivation of particular identities. A major criterion for selection of these particular components is their relevance for a modern Israeli society. Intellectuals of oriental origin, as well as university centres for the study of Oriental Jewry were among the first movers in this direction. Indeed, in 1977 the Ministry of Education and Culture decided to establish an administrative and curriculum special unit within the Ministry, the

Israel

Centre for Integration of Oriental Jewry's Heritage
which was charged with the task of:

> the cultivation, preservation and advancement
> of the oriental communities' heritage and their
> cultural assets. [58]

The immediate goals of the educational programmes
were the imparting of cultural assets; an awareness
of Jewish cultural variety; understanding, tolerance
and mutual respect among the ethnic groups; the
value of Oriental Jewish heritage; the discovery of
common elements in the traditions, customs and
values of Jewish ethnic groups, while stressing
their particularities; strengthening the self image
of members of the various ethnic groups while
striving for mutual cultural enrichment based on
internalization of concepts, values, feelings and
attitudes; an awareness by school of the importance
of the socio-cultural background of each student;
the latter's identification with the modern society
and a deepening of his feeling of belonging to the
Jewish people and the State of Israel. [59]
    At present it is too early to assess the merits
of these programmes and the possible outcomes of
this change in ethnic policy in Israel.

Notes and References

    1. This chapter does not deal with the non-
Jewish minorities in Israel. For a discussion of
the social status of the Israeli Arabs, see:
Stendel, O.M., The Minorities of Israel. Jerusalem:
Israel Economist, 1973 [and];
Smooha, Sammy, Israel: Pluralism and Conflict.
Routledge and Kegan Paul, 1978.
    2. Herman, Simon N., Israelis and Jews : A
Continuity of an Identity. Random House, 1970.
    3. Additional internal subgrouping exists
within Jewish ethnic groups. 'Orientals' and
Ashkenazim are internally divided among people
hailing from about a hundred countries of origin.
For comprehensive introductions dealing with various
aspects of pluralism in Israel see, for example:
Weingrad, Alex., Israel : Group Relations in a New
Society. Pall Mall Press, 1965;
Patai, Raphael, Israel between East and West.
Greenwood, 1970.
    4. Mitzvah (pl. Mitzvot) - a commandment,
precept or religious duty. Traditionally there are
613 biblical commandments, which are divided into

248 positive mandates and 365 prohibitions. In addition there are rabbinic commandments. A further division is between those regulating conduct 'between man and his Maker' (ritual) and those 'between man and his fellow' (social).

5. Herman S.N., op cit, uses another classification within a division of three categories: religious, traditionalist and non-religious. On the importance of the religious variable in determining the Jewish identity of the Israeli see Herman pp 20-23. For a general description and discussion of religion in Israel, its status, organization and services, see: Don-Yihye, Eliezer, Religion in Israel, Jerusalem : Government Printer, 1975. (Hebrew).

6. Eisenstadt, S.N., Bar-Josef, R. and Adler, Ch., eds., Integration and Development in Israel. Jerusalem University Press, 1970.

7. Peres, Yochanan, Ethnic Relations in Israel. Tel-Aviv: Sifriat-Poalim and Tel-Aviv University, 1976.

8. Peres, Yochanan and Shemer, Sarah, The Ethnic Factor in the Elections to the Tenth Knesset. Megamot Behavioural Science Quarterly, 1984, 28 2,3.

9. Herman S.N., op cit.

10. Don-Yihye E., op cit.

11. Agudat Israel (lit: Association of Israel) is a political party representing ultra-orthodox Jews. Founded in 1912 in Katowice, Poland as an anti-Zionist movement it rejected the establishment of a secular Jewish state not based on the Torah. In the mid-thirties and particularly after the Holocaust Agudat Israel moderated its position. Following the establishment of the state of Israel it has participated in elections and joined government coalitions. See:
Eisenstadt S.N., Israeli Society : Background, Development and Problems. Weidenfeld and Nicolson, 1967;
Don Yihye E., op cit.

12. For an English translation and interpretation of the laws and regulations concerning education, see: Stanner, Ruth, The Legal Basis of Education in Israel. Ministry of Education and Culture, Jerusalem: Government Printer, 1963.

13. Eisenstadt S.N., The Absorption of Immigrants. Greenwood Press, 1975.

14. Sabra (pl. Sabras), literally : cactus fruit; a nickname for youngsters born in Israel.

15. Spiro, Melford, Children of the Kibbutz. Harvard University Press, 1958, p 388.

16. Friedmann, Georges, The End of the Jewish People? Doubleday, 1967, p 238.

17. Kurzweil, Baruch, The New Canaanites in Israel. Judaism, 1953, 2, 1.

18. Herman S.N., op cit.

19. Hertzberg, Arthur, ed., The Zionist Idea. New York : Atheneum, 1969;
Lacqueur, Walter, A History of Zionism. Holt, Rinehart and Winston, 1972.

20. Katz, Jacob, Zionism and Jewish Identity. Commentary, New York, 1977, 63, 5.

21. Avineri, Shlomo, Varieties of Zionist Thought. Tel-Aviv: Am-Oved, 1980 (Hebrew).

22. Schweid, Eliezer, Judaism and the Secular Culture. Tel-Aviv: Ha-Kibutz Ha Meuhad, 1981 (Hebrew).

23. Kleinberger, Aharon, F., Society, Schools and Progress in Israel. Pergamon Press, 1969;
Rotenstreich, Nathan, New National Thought. In: Aspects of Judaism, Tel-Aviv: Machbarot Le-Sifrut, 1953 (Hebrew);
Rotenstreich, Nathan, Jewish Existence in the Present Age. Tel-Aviv: Sifnat-Poalim, 1972 (Hebrew);
Hertzberg A., op cit;
Avineri S., op cit;
The educational implications are discussed by Kurzweil, Z.E., Modern Trends in Jewish Education. New York: Thomas Yoseloff, 1964 pp 278-279;
Schweid E., op cit.

24. Herman S.N., op cit, p 115.

25. Israel, Ministry of Education and Culture, Educational Statistics, Jerusalem, June 1982 (mimeo, Hebrew).

26. In the early 1950s Ernst Simon, a prominent Israeli educator raised the question "are we still Jews?" which may be seen as an indication of the feeling among many educators in Israel. See:
Simon, Akiba Ernst, Are We Still Jews? Ha'Aretz Almanac, 1951-2, 5712, (Hebrew);
Reprinted in: Are We still Jews? Essays. Tel-Aviv: see: Sifriat Poalim, 1982.

27. Israel Government, The policies and principles of the Coalition Government. Israel Government Year Book 1955-1956, Jerusalem: Keter Publishing House, 1956.

28. Kurzweil, Z.E., op cit, pp 278-279.

29. Israel, Ministry of Education and Culture, Deepening of Jewish Consciousness in the State Schools. Directives and Syllabi. Jerusalem Government Printer, 1959 (Hebrew).

30. Israel, Ministry of Education and Culture, Director General's Circular 18/5, November 7 1957, Jerusalem: Government Printer, 1957.

31. Israel, Ministry of Education and Culture, 1959, op cit.

32. Israel, Ministry of Education and Culture Supplement A to Circular 18 article 714 (September 1958), Jerusalem: Government Printer, 1959, p 19 (Hebrew).

33. Navon (Phima), Chaim, Jewish Consciousness in State Education, unpublished MA Thesis, Ramat Gan: Bar-Ilan University, 1982 (Hebrew).

34. ibid; Ben-Bassat, Nurith, The Development of Jewish Identity in Israel General Schools, unpublished Doctoral Dissertation; Ramat-Gan: Bar-Ilan University, 1980 (Hebrew).

35. Time, September 7, 1981. See for example New York Times Magazine, March 7, 1982, New York Times, May 3, 1982, US Navy and World Report January 3, 1983, Commonwealth, July 15, 1983, Ha'Aretz Weekly, March 2, 1984 (Hebrew).

36. Ben-Bassat (op cit) attempts to offer a structural model for the fostering of Jewish identity based on five essential elements derived from the thought of Jewish philosophers. These elements are: 1) faith in god, 2) the uniqueness of the Jewish people, 3) the unity of nation, Jewish ethics and way of life, 4) the study of Jewish literary sources and 5) national Zionism.

37. Peres Y., op cit, p 45; cf also Smooha S., op cit, p 280-281 tables 7-9; also for the historical background with regard to the ethnic separation among Jews which began with their territorial dispersion, see Smooha, S., op cit, p 48-61.

38. Israel, Central Bureau of Statistics, Statistical Abstracts of Israel, 1-27 (1950-1976), Jerusalem: Government Printer, 1976.

39. Eisenstadt S.N., (1967) op cit; Eisenstadt S.N., (1975) op cit.

40. Israel, Central Bureau of Statistics, Statistical Abstracts of Israel, 18 (1967), Jerusalem: Government Printer, 1976, p 89.

41. Full figures on Jewish immigration to Palestine and Israel can be found in Smooha S., op cit, p 281, table 9; for changes in the demographic ratios of 'Orientals' and Ashkenazim, ibid, table 8.

42. Kleinberger A.F., op cit.

43. Smooha S., op cit;

Peres Y., op cit.

44. Israel Government, The Basic Principles of
the New Government. Israel Government Year Book
1969-1970, Jerusalem: Keter Publishing House, 1970,
p 27.

45. Israel Government, The principles of the
Likud Government. Israel Government Year Book 1981-
1982, Jerusalem: Keter Publishing House, 1982.

46. Adler, Chaim, Social Stratification and
Education in Israel, Comparative Education Review,
1974, 18.

47. Israel, Central Bureau of Statistics,
Language, Literacy and Educational Attainment.
Jerusalem: Government Printer, 1963, p 98 (Hebrew);
Kleinberger A.F., op cit, pp 51-86;
Smooha S., op cit, pp 159-163.

48. Israel, Central Bureau of Statistics,
Statistical Abstracts of Israel, 27 (1976) op cit, p
589.

49. This conference was attended by the author.
Mimeographed data compiled by The Central Bureau of
Statistics, Jerusalem: May 29, 1984.

50. Adler C., op cit.

51. The educational ladder was restructured to
run from 8 + 4 years to 6 + 3 + 3 years of full time
education, ie, a junior high school was added;
see: Glasman, Naftaly, S., Israeli Political Effects
of two Educational Decisions. In: Thomas, R.
Murray, ed., Politics and Education. Pergamon
Press, 1983, for a recent discussion of the Reform.

52. Iram, Yaacov, Vocational Education in
Switzerland and Israel : A Comparative Analysis.
Canadian and International Education, 1980 9, 1.

53. Israel, Central Bureau of Statistics,
Statistical Abstracts of Israel, 28 (1977)
Jerusalem: Government Printer, 1977.

54. Israel, Ministry of Education and Culture,
Educational Statistics, op cit, p 24-25.

55. Israel, Ministry of Education and Culture,
Director General's Circulars. Integration of
Oriental Jewry's Heritage in Educational
Institutions, Jerusalem: Government Printer, 1979
(Hebrew).

56. Kleinberger A.F., op cit.

57. Israel, Ministry of Education and Culture,
Director General's Circulars, November 1 1976,
Integration of Oriental Jewry's Heritage in
Educational Institutions, Jerusalem: Government
Printer, 1976, (Hebrew).

58. Israel, Ministry of Education and Culture,
1979, op cit.

Israel

59. Israel, Ministry of Education and Culture, Director General's Circulars, December 1983, Integration of Oriental Jewry's Heritage in Educational Institutions, Jerusalem: Government Printer, 1983, p 3 (Hebrew).

EDUCATION CULTURAL IDENTITY, AND THE STRUCTURAL
INTEGRATION OF INDIANS IN THE PERUVIAN HIGHLANDS

Erwin H.   Epstein*

Introduction
        Education wherever obtained is a natural
vehicle for the development of cultural identity.
In culturally more or less homogeneous societies the
promotion of a common identity is much simplified,
but in heterogeneous countries, where forging a
common identity is essential to nationhood, the
school is usually the State's most powerful
socializing institution and therefore assumes great
strategic importance. This chapter will examine how
education has been used to forge a sense of
nationality in Peru, where a large indigenous group
has lived on the margin of national culture for
generations.

Educational Policy and Cultural Dualism in the
Colonial Period
        However important the school is in fostering a
sense of nationality, there is often strong
disagreement about how it should be used for that
purpose. Such discord has existed in Peru since
before nationhood.   Many of the Spanish conquerors
of early Peru viewed the large Indian population as
no more than beasts of burden with little capacity
to learn.   Being close to the lands of their tribes
they did indeed prove more intractable. The Church
regarded schools primarily as a means to
christianize the Indians and to teach them como
vivir en policia, how to live within a peaceful,
orderly society. [1] Yet some Spaniards viewed the

----

*   The author wishes to acknowledge with thanks
     the able assistance of Jeffrey Ahrens and
     Donald Lane.

Indians as having considerable intellectual capability, and sought to preserve their self-identity, especially by advancing the most widely spoken aboriginal language, Quechua. This was particularly true of Fray Domingo de Santo Tomas, founder of the University of San Marcos, the oldest university in the Americas.

Fray Domingo was the first European to master Quechua by reducing it to grammatical rules and patterns. By 1551 there were professorial chairs of Quechua in the Cathedral of Lima and in the most important convents of the city. By 1579 courses in Quechua were compulsory for students who aspired to become priests. In the seventeenth century Quechua became a full-fledged literary language, with prayers, hymns, poems, sermons, narratives, and even plays produced in that language by Spanish and mestizo as well as Indian authors. [2]

Nevertheless, however much advancement of Quechua nurtured Indians' self-identity, it also provided an efficient way by which European ideas could permeate Indian society. Quechua became no longer the exclusive domain of Indians, but a bridge between Indian and European cultures. Inevitably, Church schools also taught Spanish and Christian doctrine along with simple arithmetic and music, and in some cases a manual skill or trade. The attempt to mingle the two cultural streams was no more evident than in early plans to provide education to the sons of the Inca nobility. In 1576 Viceroy Toledo entrusted Jose de Acosta, one of the most brilliant minds of sixteenth century Peru, with the task of formulating objectives and a curriculum for a highly selective school for the Indian aristocracy. The school was to be bilingual and include, besides language studies in Quechua and Spanish, music, religion, history, hygiene, and the principles of both Spanish and Incan public administration. According to Acosta (quoted in Martin from de Egana) [3]

> The Indian students should not be deprived of the laws, customs, and methods of governing accepted in their provinces, if they are not contrary to Natural and Christian Law. It is not suitable to attempt to turn them completely into Spaniards because, besides being very difficult and an occasion of discouragement for the students, it will also be very harmful for their own republic and government.

Peruvian education must be understood against a backdrop of cultural dualism reflecting the imposition of Spanish civilization and an opposing tendency toward preserving Indian traditions. On the one hand, for example, the encomienda, on which the contemporary hacienda system is based, was introduced into the highlands - where most Indians live - very soon after the Spanish conquest. The encomienda entrusted Indians of a given locale to a 'worthy and loyal' conquistador, who had the right to exact the crown's tribute as well as personal service for himself from his Indian charges. In return he was obligated to educate them in Christian ways and beliefs. This obligation was often neglected in favour of more selfish ends. Although encomienda holders had no claim to Indian lands, they soon abused their mandate and took possession of their charges' property. Eventually, encomiendas were passed on to heirs or sold to the highest bidder. The trust to collect crown tribute and instruct Indians in Christianity was transformed into the hacienda system, an agricultural enterprise modelled on the feudal manor complete with a resident labour force. The hacienda's Indians were part of its assets, the right to their labour being transferred with the land itself. Despite occasional attempts at reform, the hacienda remained a prominent force in highland society for nearly five centuries, culminating in land reform legislation of 1969.

On the other hand, existing in tension with the Spanish hacienda was a system of Indian communities, whose origins were in the ancient Incan Empire. Some of these settlements, or ayllus, were given to Spanish overlords in the form of encomiendas, yet others in more remote areas were left relatively untouched. These latter tended to guard their autonomy jealously, and to remain geographically, economically, socially and politically isolated.

Indian Ethnicity

The tension between Hispanic and indigenous traditions, spanning almost half a millenium, has produced a structure of ambiguous relations among cultural groups. For one thing, it is no longer easy to describe Indian ethnicity. Indians display several distinctive characteristics, only one of which, language, is currently recorded in census reports. The 1940 census was the last to enumerate population by ethnic group, and that enumeration showed Indians to be 46 per cent of the total, [4]

Amerindian Peru

representing a gradual but steady decline from the
58 per cent estimated by the 1876 census. [5] From
current census data on languages spoken we may infer
that Indians now comprise only about 20 per cent of
the nation's inhabitants, but the difficulties of
identification make this figure highly approximate.
Moreover, the highlands is a vast area that displays
considerable cultural variation. The northern part
is more exposed to outside influences than the
mancha india, literally, 'Indian spot', in the
south, and even in this latter region outside
influences vary greatly according to the extent of
the communities' physical isolation. But what is
more important, scholars have not always agreed on
the nature of Indian ethnicity - in Peru as in
Mesoamerica generally - in large part because that
ethnicity has changed considerably since the Spanish
conquest. Indeed, Indian ethnicity is not a stable
property, but a dynamic by-product of pre-Hispanic
customs mixed with colonially created identities and
national ideology, economics, and politics. Some
anthropologists have observed so much change among
Indians that they challenge the appropriateness of
viewing them as a distinctive ethnic group. [6]
Others, such as Warren, [7] while denying that
Indian identity is an indigenous set of beliefs,
social forms and techno-economic adaptations,
nevertheless claim that such identity constitutes a
source of values contrasting with those of non-
Indian society, and that it does not operate as an
exclusively negative definition of what Indians lack
with respect to the broader society. Indeed,
Miracle [8] finds that among Aymara Indians in
Bolivia, interlocking cultural patterns growing out
of childrearing practices and events, myths, games,
and language acquired largely outside the school
produce a shared cultural perception that is
markedly different from Hispanic culture and
perception. Consequently, schools in Bolivia, which
are orientd to Hispanic values, are incongruent
with Indian culture and are marked by poor
attendance, high attrition levels, a low rate of
scholastic success, and little impact on illiteracy
rates.
      Most observers have found that Indians in
Mesoamerica generally tend to be group-oriented and
reconciled to the "given order of things" in the
community. [9] However, when Indians move from a
traditional to a Europeanized mestizo world view as
a result of schooling, travel, and work in non-
agricultural jobs, many become aggressively

223

individualistic and seek freedom from group demands. Such change encourages the atomization of indigenous communities. [10] On the other hand, Indians who display the individualistic behaviour of mestizos tend to be regarded with contempt by the outside world. Faron [11] reports that in Peru the serranos, highland Indians, who migrate to the coast in search of work are considered beasts of burden. Their social status is below that of black Peruvians and descendants of the despised Chinese and Japanese immigrants who were forcibly imported during the nineteenth and twentieth centuries, and also below the descendants of the original Indians of the lowland coast who pridefully label themselves as cholos - people who have adopted competitive Europeanized economic practices while having retained Indian dress and language to distinguish themselves from the serranos. The pervasive consciousness of this racial and ethnic hierarchy severely limits social mobility and contributes to the formation of a system of rigid stratification, with the highland Indians at the bottom.

National Policy towards the Indians
        The arrival of independence from Spain in 1826 altered official views of the Indians in one important respect: the urgent need to promote nationhood made integration of the large Indian population a primary consideration. During the colonial period treatment of Indians was regarded exclusively as an economic or moral issue; rarely were the Indians considered amenable to or capable of full political integration. Their social institutions were to function concurrently with European forms or to disappear completely under Spanish domination.
        The options faced by republican leaders were more numerous but more difficult. [12] First, they could try to integrate the Indians forcibly by systematically destroying their institutions and culture, thereby converting them into dark-skinned copies of their former masters. Many leaders favoured this alternative, but others were vigorously opposed, remembering that the Spaniards had often pursued a similar policy and failed because of the Indians' fierce resistance and the material difficulties of forced imposition in remote areas. Another option was to leave the Indians completely alone or even to segregate them on reservations as was done in the United States and Chile. This was not seriously advanced except by

224

some <u>indigenistas</u> - members of an early twentieth century movement that publicly condemned the exploitation of Indians. [13] Given that such a solution would have required a complete change in the structure of economic and social relationships, which relied on a steady supply of cheap Indian labour, its lack of support was assured. A third alternative was to allow the Indians to integrate themselves peaceably, while the government provided protection for their lands and traditions through legislation. Although this policy usually prevailed in theory, it assumed that the Indians would enthusiastically cast off their way of life in favour of assimilation. An outstanding example of this policy was under the administration of Peru's first civilian president, Manuel Pardo (1872-76), who sought to establish a free and universal system of primary education and to end the linguistic isolation of monolingual Indians. In March, 1874, contending that the government should

> facilitate the study of the Quechua language and spread Spanish among those Peruvians of the interior who do not yet possess it, [14]

Pardo ordered the state press to print one thousand copies of a Spanish-Quechua dictionary. [15] Another example was the National Plan of Integration of the Aboriginal Population under the regime of Manuel Prado (1956-62). It sought to improve living conditions by extending free and compulsory education, better medical care and economic opportunities, and by formal recognition of Indian Communities. [16] In practice, however, these policies failed because of considerable political and Church opposition, preventing Indians from exercising their rights under the law even when legislation was passed, and their enduring distrust of government efforts to integrate them.

The persistent failure of integrationist policy was usually attributed to a lack of government vigour, thus tending to encourage increased efforts by succeeding administrations to extend services, and especially education, to the Indians. However, from 1968 to 1980 a reformist military regime introduced a novel twist to integrationist policy: Indians were no longer to be regarded as a culturally distinct population but simply part of the larger peasantry, consisting of landless peons, sharecroppers, and small landowners living on <u>haciendas</u> or indigenous settlements. [17] 'Indian

Amerindian Peru

communities' were redefined as 'peasant
communities', and St. John's Day (June 24) was
celebrated as "the day of the peasant" instead of
"the day of the Indian". Large haciendas were
expropriated and reconstructed as a component of a
new "social property" economic sector based on
peasants' collective ownership of the means of
production, thus irreversibly shifting the balance
of socio-economic power in the highlands away from
the landed elite. [18] To be sure, government
references to the Indian past became common, and
Quechua was made an official language along with
Spanish, to be taught in schools and used in court
proceedings. [19] Nonetheless, acknowledging the
indigenous past and emphasizing native language
instruction was aimed not at strengthening a sense
of Indian ethnicity but at expediting literacy in
Spanish and inspiring nationalism in the society at
large. For Indians, Quechua was considered the
preferable medium for 'easing' children into
education, until they were sufficiently comfortable
to be taught Spanish and learn most subjects in that
language. [20] For the larger society, appropriation
of a glorified Indian past was to provide a unique
and powerful marker of nationality, one that would
serve to unify the country at large rather than the
purposes merely of a discrete segment.

Education for National Consciousness
    However sensitive previous administrations were
to the absence of national unity, they lacked the
authority and sense of purpose to effect a
consistent unification policy. The military regime
lacked neither. In 1970 the government established
a Commission for Educational Reform that issued a
comprehensive plan to create "tne new Peruvian man
in a new Peruvian society". [21] To accompany a
revolutionary change in the nation's social and
political structure, the Commission proposed a
programme for radically transforming attitudes and
values. It was to be a transformation brought about
by means of concientizacion, a concept borrowed from
the Brazilian scholar and activist, Paulo
Freire, [22] and defined by the regime as an

    educational process whereby individuals and
    social groups gain a critical awareness of the
    historical and cultural world in which they
    live, shoulder their responsibilities and
    undertake the necessary action to transform
    it. [23] (Author's translation)

226

It was to be, in other words, an unabashed joining
together of education and politics, engaging the
active participation of the entire community in a
struggle against the conditions of internal
domination that had for so long been a part of
Peruvian life. It embodied a strong nationalistic
tone and harsh rejection of prevailing educational
practices. In the document that officially
introduced the reform, several inadequacies of
traditional Peruvian education were identified,
including insufficient attention to the needs of
children from marginal social classes; a system that
favoured a privileged elite; the use of methods that
had no connection to social reality; excessively
pedantic practices; and a lack of Peruvian
'feeling'. In regard to the latter, the document
said:

> There exists a very serious defect, one that
> has profoundly negative consequences in the
> orientation of our education, that is, its lack
> of feeling for national reality, and the
> reinforcement of alienation that the Peruvian
> man suffers. Our education is only
> superficially Peruvian; in truth it does not
> contribute to a knowledge of the problems,
> necessities and rights of Peru as a nation.
> Its apparent Peruvianism consists of a merely
> rhetorical use of symbols that masquerade as
> the essence of the Peruvian condition. It
> applies foreign social models or otherwise
> systematically transfers norms of authority and
> subordination that benefit the dominant groups
> or the world's hegemonic powers. Consequently,
> it inspires in Peruvian children and youths
> neither a sense of personal but unavoidable
> struggle against injustice and oppression, nor
> an eagerness to affirm and advance the Peruvian
> nation's truly positive achievements. [24]
> (Author's translation)

Included among the goals of the reform were the
institution of the new educational system in all
parts of the country, concientizacion of all
Peruvians, and extension of instruction to the
entire highland peasantry.

The reform's goals were further broadened by
its architect, Salazar Bondy, [25] who argued that
education must contribute to breaking the chains of
economic and cultural dependency, relate to the
particular realities of its participants, be

connected to the total life of the individual and
the community, and be directed by the community as a
whole. These goals were to be achieved by creating
nucleos (community organisms), established to
coordinate and manage education within specific
geographical areas. They were the principal means
by which control of the schools was to be
transferred to the people, and they were to monitor
the local system and create programmes based on
community needs. Organizationally, the director was
to be chosen by the Minister of Education, while a
council was to be elected from teachers, parents,
and local officials.

As part of this national mobilization effort,
concientizacion was to be carried out on several
levels. At the top, entrenadores (trainers),
selected by virtue of their strong support of the
government, were sent to various parts of the
country to familiarize teachers and the public with
the aims of the educational reform programme. The
entrenadores were also to marshal public opinion
against the social and political system as it had
operated during previous administrations.
Subsequently, zonal offices were established to
recruit volunteers from the community, endow them
with an understanding of the ideological and
political implications of the reform, and instruct
them in the use of appropriate teaching
techniques. [26]

Since entire communities and not only children
had to be educated, schools were not to spearhead
the concientizacion campaign. Instead, primary
responsibility was given to SINAMOS, the regime's
ideological arm, whose objective was to transform
the local community into a school without walls.
The name SINAMOS itself meant 'without masters', and
was designed to convey the idea that mass
participation was the remedy for the oppressive
dependency on the domestic oligarchy and foreign
interests that had characterized the past. SINAMOS
was created because Peru's humblest classes, in view
of their inexperience in self-government, needed
lessons in "ideo-political capacitation" before they
could be expected to participate responsibly and
constructively in national life. The agency was to
initiate this educative process by helping the
people become 'concienticized' and involving them in
affairs that directly affected their lives at work
and in the local community. In theory, the SINAMOS
would eventually fade from existence, as the masses
became full participants in national politics and as

the nation was transformed into a "social democracy of full participation". [27]

SINAMOS was to provide an institutional framework for achieving the people's political goals but the organization would be useless to them unless they became 'concienticized', which required literacy to break the ties of dependency on the dominant classes. Operation ALFIN - which stands for Alfabetizacion Integral, or Integrated Literacy Programme - was created in 1973 to teach the most marginal illiterates not only work skills but also reading and writing. [28] ALFIN differed somewhat from the Freire method of concientizacion by emphasizing the socio-economic problems of the nation more than local issues and the community context. Yet its focus on developing critical consciousness leading to collective action and a radical transformation of society clearly distinguished it from conventional literacy programmes, such as those sponsored by UNESCO which tended to preserve the status quo. It was highly nationalistic, insisting, for example, on the use of domestic over imported reading materials, the latter considered as alienating and culturally imperialistic. Since concientizacion was aimed at direct socio-political intervention in people's own affairs, literacy was to be achieved not only in Spanish but also in the indigenous language of the local community.

Consequences of Educational Policy

Most ethnographic evidence indicates that the Indians benefited little from the military government's concientizacion campaign. [29] Elsewhere I have extensively discussed why the regime's educational programme failed. [30] In brief, the government promised more material rewards than it could deliver, was unable to reconcile participatory goals with autocratic rule, and failed to recognize the strength of Indian ethnicity. To be sure, the Indians were rarely able to exercise control over community schools because they had more basic priorities than education and because they lacked training and experience in self-leadership. But the regime's failure must be blamed largely on its own policies. Although the new pedagogy encouraged communities to prepare their own educational materials in order to inspire collective action and insure that these materials were appropriate to local realities, the ministry continued to crank out nationally uniform curriculum

Fig. 1. <u>Estimated public expenditure on
education as a percentage of GNP</u>

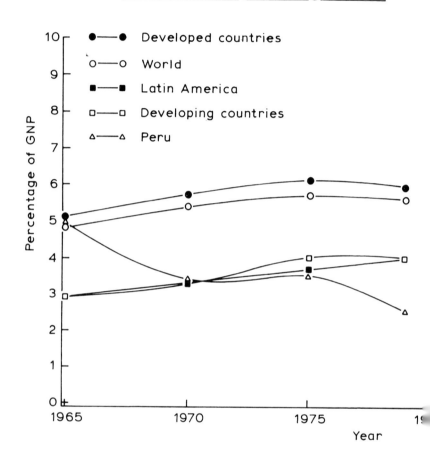

materials using behavioural objectives, much as it had done under previous regimes. Other inconsistencies that tended to undermine the government's programme became increasingly apparent. The regime alienated many teachers in 1978 when it formed an 'official' teachers' union after declaring illegal a strike called by a teacher-organized union and deporting its leaders. Teacher retraining programmes, consisting largely of short courses organized at the local level and designed to induce teachers to draw on community issues for instruction, tended to be doctrinaire in style and content. Moreover, these programmes seemed to go against the grain of revolutionary rhetoric, which called for national, not local, unity. Although local participation was intended to support national ideology, the regime's approach appeared contradictory and was difficult to implement.

By increased reliance on local resources and total community participation the regime evidently hoped not only to curry favour with peasant communities but also to reduce the educational budget. Hence the government cut back drastically on education relative to other expenditures. As Figure 1 shows, total expenditure on education as a percentage of GNP by the end of military rule was half of that just prior to the military's takeover. During the previous administration the percentage of Peru's expenditure on education had been above that for the world overall and Latin America in particular, and virtually identical with that for developing countries, but during military rule, that percentage dropped markedly below the figures for the world, developing countries and Latin America.

The reduction in material support to education had practical repercussions throughout the system. Figure 2 shows that the pupil-teacher ratio at the primary level increased during military rule. Figure 3 indicates that the number of post-secondary students in education, after rising during the regime's initial years, declined eventually to about one quarter the number just prior to military rule. Since the number of vacancies in fields of study was not affected by the number of qualified applicants but controlled by the government to satisfy estimated needs in particular fields, [31] this reduction of education students was deliberate. Furthermore, the reduction of education students plausibly influenced the percentage of female students in higher education. Although both male and female enrolments rose under military rule,

Fig. 2. **Pupil-teacher ratio**

At first level of education

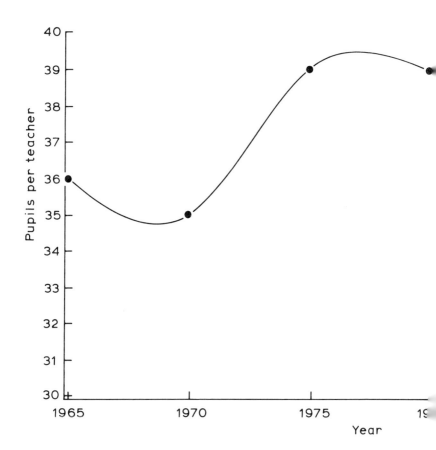

Figure 4 shows that female enrolments increased considerably less; in 1970, 588 more males than females per 100,000 inhabitants were enrolled in higher education, but that figure almost doubled to 1,072 by 1978.

Figures on female enrolments are highly meaningful. Educating girls may be one of the most effective investments a country can make in future economic growth and welfare even if they never enter the labour force. Most girls become mothers, and a variety of studies have shown that their influence on their children's health and fertility is crucial. [32] In Peru the continued disparities between males and females in education under military rule were displayed not only in higher education but, more importantly for Indians, in illiteracy rates. Figure 5 shows that although these rates gradually but steadily declined, the gap between males and females in rural areas, where Indians predominate, remained virtually unchanged.

Current Educational Policy
In 1978, in response to widespread discontent, the military government allowed free elections to be held to elect a constitutional assembly. That assembly promulgated a new constitution in 1979 and civilian rule under Fernando Belaunde Terry - the same individual the military deposed 12 years earlier - was reinstated in July 1980 after general elections were held in May of that year.

The education reforms instituted by the new administration have been far less pervasive than were those of the military regime. The most important changes have been largely cosmetic, such as an administrative re-ordering of the system, especially at the secondary level. Higher schools of professional education were created, and the last three years of the five-year secondary school curriculum [33] have been divided into five distinct tracks: agricultural, artisan, commercial, industrial, and scientific-humanistic. Belaunde promised a broad programme to expand and improve education and expressed the hope that his administration would be remembered as the five year period of education. However, such radical and extensive measures as consciousness-raising campaigns are no longer official policy, and the government seems content to pursue integrative goals with more traditional methods.

The present administration's more conservative posture may be attributed to several causes. First,

233

Fig. 3. <u>Number of students at the third level</u>
<u>of education</u>
By selected fields of study

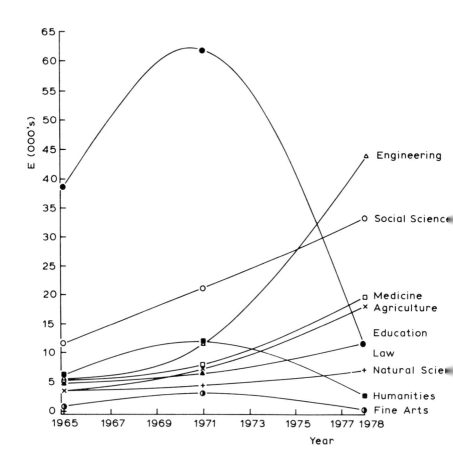

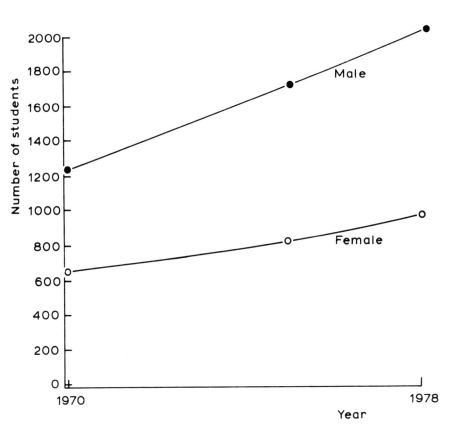

Fig. 4. Number of students enrolled
At the third level of education per
100,000 inhabitants by sex

Amerindian Peru

Belaunde's objectives, though ambitious, are not
revolutionary. As in his earlier term he professes
a desire for steady but gradual progress. [34]
Second, the new administration clearly wishes to
avoid the excesses of the past. Military rule,
failed on many fronts, not the least failure being·
as I have shown, in education. The military
inherited a foreign debt of less than $1 billion
in 1968, but left the new civilian government a debt of
about $9 billion in 1980. Inflation was about 19
per cent in 1968; it was 67 per cent in 1979. The
Peruvian sol was valued at about 44 per US dollar in
1968, but declined in value to about 260 per US
dollar by mid-1980. In 1968 there were 364 major
strikes affecting 108,000 workers; in 1975 there
were 779 strikes affecting 617,000 workers [35]
Finally, it is the immediacy of large-scale economic
and political problems which has captured the
administration's attention, eclipsing the urgency of
educational reform.

Recent economic setbacks have been especially
serious. Gross domestic product is estimated to
have declined by about 10 per cent in the 12 months
ending March 1983, and gross external debt increased
to about $12 billion in October of that year.
During the first half of 1983 these difficulties
were compounded by drought, floods, and landslides
which disrupted transportation and oil field
operations and caused losses in tropical food
production. Oil and copper exports also suffered
lower international prices. But much of the blame
must be attributed to administrative policies. For
example, the military, who encumbered enormous debts
from arms purchases in the mid-1970's have pressured
the current civilian government to increase its
expenditures on military arms and facilities. It is
estimated that security of one kind or another
absorbs as much as one-third of the government's
$3.5 billion annual budget. This comes at a time
when the country is experiencing its worst recession
since the 1930's. Indeed, near the end of 1983
inflation was running at an annual rate of about 130
per cent, and the sol had devalued to more than 2200
per US dollar. The combination of heavy military
expenditures and a sharp decline in income because
of economic recession obligated the government to
reduce its normal budget for schools and other
public service investments by about 40 per
cent. [36]

Political pressures on the administration have
been no less disturbing. In particular, a small but

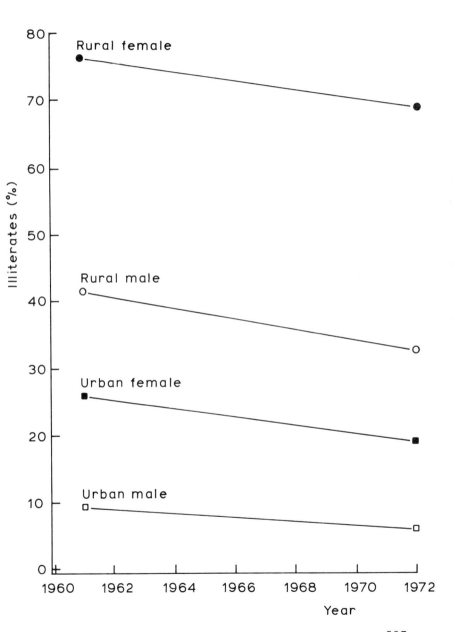

Fig. 5.   Percent of illiterates in population
15 years of age and over by sex and residence

rapidly growing Maoist guerrilla group, Shining Path, is waging a violent war against the government. The group was initially organized by university students for upper middle-class white and mestizo families of the coast who learned Quechua and indigenous customs and traditions, and gradually became accepted as an integral part of the Ayacucho Indian community in the central highlands. Recently the group expanded its operations to the north and south, including disabling attacks on Lima, the capital. According to a poll taken in mid-1983, Peruvians fear Shining Path more than the economic crisis or the severe floods and drought which have paralysed large regions of the country. [37] The government in response has taken vigorous measures. Balaunde placed the country under a state of emergency during part of 1983 and ordered security forces to crush the group. One result of the government's campaign against the guerrillas was a vigorous condemnation by Amnesty International, which charged that security forces during the first half of 1983 kidnapped, tortured and murdered hundreds of Indians in the anti-insurgency area of the highlands. [38]

By the end of 1983 the government's position had deteriorated measurably. In municipal elections held in November, Belaunde's Popular Action Party suffered an overwhelming defeat, losing almost all the country's 1,800 local elections, with the United Left, a coalition of six Marxist parties, and the centre-left APRISTA (Alianza Popular Revolucionaria Americana) party as the definitive winners. [39]

Conclusion

Highland Indians, who constitute a large segment of the Peruvian population, have posed a dilemma for governments since the Spanish conquest. To integrate them forcibly into the national political and cultural mainstream would be to deprive them of their traditional ways and indigenous identity. Yet not to integrate them would be to deprive them of the rewards and opportunities of the larger society, and assign them perpetually to an underclass and impoverished condition. This dilemma was magnified once Peru achieved its independence from Spain, since the very definition of nationhood had to account for the indigenous population.

Successive Peruvian administrations have ordinarily sought integration, although with varying commitments to this goal. Education has usually played a prominent role in integrative efforts, since it represents a moderately forceful method when universal schooling is obligatory. Furthermore, as a socializing device it has the potential of going beyond political and economic structural integration to win the allegiance of the Indians, and inducing favourable changes in belief systems and value orientations. Nevertheless, however advantageous the school may be as a potential integrative instrument, its effects tend to be gradual, becoming manifest only over generations of schoolchildren.

The slow pace of educational effects moved one administration - the military regime that ruled during the 12 year period, 1968-80 - to introduce more forceful tactics. Rather than rely on schools alone to induce a change in beliefs and attitudes, the regime mandated collective education, with the participation of whole communities. But Indian participation was to be without a separate ethnic identity. In an extraordinary move the regime actually attempted to eliminate the Indians' cultural isolation by decree, by redefining them as peasants and claiming for the nation at large their ethnic and historical heritage, and hence displacing them as the rightful heirs of their Incan ancestors. The Indians, to be sure, were to share in the nation's glorified past, but only as integrated members of the society. Their language, customs, and traditions were no longer to be uniquely theirs; as systematic educational campaigns were waged to arouse their consciousness and sense of Peruvian nationality, their culture was to be absorbed into the larger society. When the government expropriated foreign holdings, the action was couched in terms of Indian rebellions of the past to show that expropriation was not simply the pursuit of self-interest, but part of the sacred mission of an oppressed Peruvian nation. In this way the regime linked the past oppression of Indians with the present cause of the people as a whole. By this association the government sought to divest Indians of their communal identity as it integrated them structurally, and concurrently providing the country with a powerful marker of identity and source of solidarity. In the end the regime failed. Relatively few Indians benefited materially from the government's programmes, and they tended to resist the imposition of external authority. Even worse, the military regime passed on a legacy of political and economic dislocation to the succeeding civilian adminstration, a legacy that has diminished hope for lasting reform. The present government faces problems of such magnitude and immediacy that it is largely unable to pursue its professed ambitions for educational changes.

Yet even if Peru's economic and political difficulties were not so severe, the dilemma of Indian integration would remain. In my study of Indian schoolchilren's identity just prior to the military takeover in the 1960's, I found that pupils in geographically and culturally less remote areas displayed a weaker sense of Peruvian nationality than more isolated children. [40] An explanation for these surprising findings is that the isolation of Indian children makes it easier for them to accept myths about the national society promoted by the schools. Pupils living in towns are more exposed outside their schools to the realities of national life and are consequently less likely to believe such myths. Hence, as long as communities remain isolated, and education represents virtually the only exposure children have to the larger society, the school may be effective in inducing national allegiances and identity. Yet, ironically, as the government strives to end Indians' isolation by introducing Europeanized forms of commerce and politics, the school, with its mythologized image of national life, will plausibly become less effective as a socializing instrument. In short, structural integration may work at cross purposes with the school's acculturative function, and the impact of education may become weaker if the government succeeds in establishing Europeanized mestizo institutions and ways of life in Indian communities.

Notes and References

1. Vargas Ugarte, Ruben, Historia de la Compania de Jesus en el Peru. Burgos: Imprenta de Aldecoa, 1963, I.

2. Martin, Luis, Indian Education in Colonial Peru. Indian Historian, 1973, 6.

3. Ibid.

4. Nyrop, Richard R., ed., Peru: A Country Study. Washington: US Department of the Army, 1981.

5. Mishkin, Bernard, The Contemporary Quechua. In: Steward, Julien, ed., The Andean Civilizations. Vol.2 of Handbook of South American Indians. Washington: US Government Printing Office, 1942, pp 411-70;

Kubler, George, The Indian Caste of Peru, 1795-1940:

A Population Study based upon Tax Records and Census Reports. Washington: US Government Printing Office, 1952.

6. Friedlander, Judith, Being Indian in Hueyapan: A Study of Forced Identity in Contemporary Mexico. St. Martin's Press, 1975.

7. Warren, K.B., The Symbolism of Subordination: Indian Identity in a Guatemalan Town. University of Texas Press, 1978.

8. Miracle, Andrew W., Jr., The Effects of Cultural Perception on Aymara Schooling. Unpublished Doctoral Dissertation. Gainsville: University of Florida, 1976.

9. Escobar, G.M., Organizacion Social y Cultural del Sur del Peru. Mexico: Instituto Indigenista Interamericano, 1967.

10. Coy, P.A., A Watershed in Mexican Rural History: Some Thoughts on the Reconciliation of Conflicting Interpretations. Journal of Latin American Studies, 1971, 3; Reck, G.G., In the Shadow of Tlaloc: Life in a Mexican Village. Penguin, 1978.

11. Faron, L.C., Ethnicity and Social Mobility in Chancay Valley, Peru. In: Goldschmidt, W. and Hoijer, H., eds., The Social Anthropology of Latin America: Essays in Honor of Ralph Leon Beals. University of California Latin American Center, 1970.

12. Davies, Thomas M., Indian Integration in Peru: A Half Century of Experience, 1900-1948. University of Nebraska Press, 1974.

13. Dobyns, Henry E. and Doughty, Paul L., Peru: A Cultural History. Oxford University Press, 1976.

14. As quoted in Davies, op cit, p 32.

15. San Cristoval, Evaristo, Manuel Pardo y Lavalle: Su Vida y Su Obra. Lima: Editorial Gil, 1945.

16. MacLean y Estenos, Roberto, Indios de America. Mexico: Instituto de Investigaciones Sociales, Universidad Nacional Autonoma de Mexico, 1962.

17. Alberti, G., Peasant Movements in the Yanamarca Valley. Sociologia Ruralis, 1972, 12; Fuenzalida, F., Mayer, E., Escobar, G., Bouricaud, S., and Mar, J. Matos, El Indio y El Poder en el Peru. Lima: Moncloa, 1970.

18. Knight, P.T., New Forms of Economic Organisation in Peru: Towards Workers' Self-Management. In: Lowenthal, A.F., ed., The Peruvian Experiment: Continuity and Change Under Military

Rule. Princeton University Press, 1975;
Novitski, J., Peruvian Regime Woos the Masses. New York Times, April 18, 1971.
    19. Peru. El Proceso Peruano: Lecturas. Lima: INDICE, 1974.
Werlich, D.P., The Peruvian Revolution in Crisis. Current History, 1977, 72.
    20. Chiappo, L., Liberacion de la Educacion. Participacion, 1973, 2;
Drysdale, R.S. and Myers, Robert G., Continuity and Change: Peruvian Education. In: Lowenthal, A.F., ed., op cit.
    21. Delgado, C., El Proceso Revolucionario Peruano: Testimonio de Lucha. Mexico: Siglo Vientiuno Editores, 1976, p 221.
    22. Freire, P., The Pedagogy of the Oppressed. Seabury, 1970.
    23. Peru. Ley General de Educacion, Decreto Ley No. 19826 Lima: Ministerio de Educacion, 1972.
    24. Rueda, Sanchez, G., ed., Reforma de la Educacion Peruana: Informe General. Lima: Ediciones El Peru y Sus Leyes, 1971, pp 8-9.
    25. Salazar Bondy, A., La Educacion del Hombre Nuevo: La Reforma Educativa Peruana. Buenos Aires: Editorial Paidos, 1975.
    26. ibid.
    27. Delgado, op cit.
    28. Lizarzaburu, A., ALFIN: An Experiment in Adult Literacy Training in a Society in Transition. Paper presented at the International Literacy Symposium, Persepolis, 1975.
    29. Barndt, D., Education and Social Change: A Photographic Study of Peru. Kendall/Hunt, 1980;
Conlin, S., Participation Versus Expertise. In: van den Berghe P.F., ed., Class and Ethnicity in Peru. Brill, 1974;
Guillet, D., Agrarian Reform and Peasant Economy in Southern Peru. University of Missouri Press, 1979;
Kleymeyer, C.D., The New Patrons of the Peruvian Peasantry: An Analytical Description of Maintenance and Change in Power Relations. Paper prepared for the meeting of the Rural Sociological Society meeting, Madison, Wisconsin, September, 1977;
Primov, George, The School As an Obstacle to Structural Integration Among Peruvian Indians. Education and Urban Society, 1978, 10;
van den Berghe, Pierre F., Education, Class, and Ethnicity in Southern Peru: Revolutionary Colonialism. In: Altbach, P.G. and Kelly, G.P., eds., Education and Colonialism. Longman, 1978.
    30. Epstein, Erwin H., Peasant Consciousness

Under Peruvian Military Rule. Harvard Educational Review, 1982, 52.

31. Gray, Collen, Peru: A Study of the Educational System of Peru and a Guide to the Academic Placement of Students in Educational Institutions of the United States. Washington: American Association of Collegiate Registrars and Admissions Officers, 1983.

32. Isenman, Paul, et al, World Development Report, 1980. Washington: The World Bank, 1980.

33. The entire secondary level lasts about five years. There are three different systems operating concurrently: the upper cycle in the 'traditional' system is for 15-16 year olds, 15-18 year olds in the 'reform' system, and 14-16 year olds in the 'new' system.

34. Woy-Hazleton, Sandra L., The Return of Partisan Politics in Peru. In: Gorman, Stephen M., ed., Post Revolutionary Peru: The Politics of Transformation. Westview Press, 1982.

35. Fitzgerald, E.V.K., The State and Economic Development: Peru Since 1968. Cambridge University Press, 1976;
Palmer, David Scott, The Post-Revolutionary Political Economy of Peru. In: Gorman, Stephen M., op cit;
Sulmont, Denis, Historia del Movimiento Obrero Peruano, 1840-1977. Lima: Tarea, 1977.

36. Ashehov, Nicholas, World Bank Pressures Peru to Reduce Navy Port Plan, Costly Arms Purchases. Wall Street Journal, November 1, 1983;
Lindow, Herbert, U.S. Exports to Peru on Downtick. Times of The Americas, October 26, 1983.

37. Laux, Emily, Seudero: Peru's Cancer. Times of The Americas, October 12, 1983;
Schumacher, Edward, Suddenly, Little-Known Rebels Force Grim Choices for Peru. New York Times, June 5, 1983.

38. El Mundo, Medellin, Colombia. September 21, 1983.

39. Times of the Americas, November 23, 1983.

40. Epstein, Erwin H., Education and Peruanidad: 'Internal' Colonialism in the Highlands. Comparative Education Review, 1971, 15.

THE AUTONOMOUS BASQUE COMMUNITY OF SPAIN: –
LANGUAGE, CULTURE AND EDUCATION*

Norma Bernstein Tarrow

Introduction
    Sensational newspaper accounts of bombings,
assassinations, arrests, and other terrorist
activities in San Sebastian, Bilbao, and other urban
centres familiarize us with the struggle for
identity, language and values of the Basques in
Spain. Their efforts, far from being extinguished
during the years of repression by the Franco regime,
were indeed rekindled by that very repression. The
struggle has continued through the first years of
Spain's new democracy and even into the present era
of its first socialist government. It is being
played out in the ministries, legislatures, in the
media, as well as the formal and informal
educational settings of the Basque country, where
curriculum, teacher training, methods and materials

----
*   Research for this chapter was carried out under
     a grant from the US–Spanish Joint Committee for
     Cultural and Educational Cooperation.
     The author wishes to express appreciation to
     the US–Spanish Joint Committee for Cultural and
     Educational Cooperation and to California State
     University, Long Beach for their support and
     to: Professor William Douglass, Dr Dorothy
     Legarreta and Professor Roslyn Frank for their
     critical suggestions; to Selma Margaretten for
     help in interviewing; to research assistants
     Gretchen Holbert and Laurie Ravazzani; to Josu
     Legarreta for invaluable contacts, information
     and logistical assistance in the Basque
     country; and to innumerable school children,
     educators and adminstrators there and in
     Madrid.

of instruction are being determined at least as much, or possibly even more by political rather than educational considerations. This chapter considers various historical, political and cultural factors and the role of education in the Basques' effort to re-establish their cultural identity.

The Basques: Historical and Socio-political Aspects

Although the historic Basque homeland is split by the Spanish-French national border, there are strong ties that have led and still lead some Basques to dream of a unified, independent Basque nation-state. On the Spanish side, the coastal and industrial historic territories of Guipuzcoa and Vizcaya, and the primarily rural territory of Alava have constituted since 1979 the Basque Autonomous Community, Comunidad Autonoma Vasca, with a total population of approximately 2,200,000, while Navarra, prompted by strong loyalties to its own historic Kingdom of Navarra and greater acceptance of Spanish language and culture, has opted to remain outside it. Figure 1 shows the Basque region including the three historic provinces of France, Navarra, and the Autonomous Community.

The question of Basque origin has puzzled ethnologists for two centuries and is still an enigma. Considered fully autochthonous, since neither people nor language can be traced to any other region, [1] there is evidence of the presence of a Basque population for many centuries before the creation of modern Spain; through the Roman and Visigoth eras, the Muslim conquest and the Reconquest. Since the Middle Ages the legal and administrative structure of the Basque region was based on an elaborate system of fueros [2] specific to each of the territories, which reinforced both the ethno-cultural and linguistic distinctiveness of the Basques and their inter-territorial differences. [3] The history of the nationalistic movement involves conflict with the increasing centralizing tendencies of the Spanish state and internal dissension based on the historic economic, social class, political, geographical and philosophical differences. Since Basque nationalism has leaned heavily on linguistic identification, the attempt to destroy the Basque language as a functioning medium of communication, was the highest priority under the Franco regime's concerted programme of cultural repression intended to crush the nationalist spirit. Repression also extended to execution and imprisonment, the only escape from

Figure 1

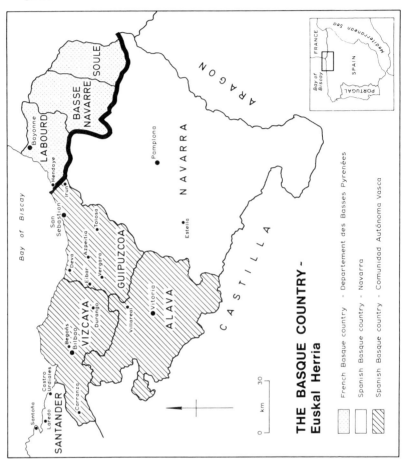

which was exile. [4] In the Autonomous Community today, the major political camps are: the Partido Nacionalista Vasco (PNV), founded in the nineteenth century with intent to restore autonomy and regarded as moderate; the separatist Herri Batasuna (HB); and the Partido Socialista de Euskadi (PSE), the regional branch of the current socialist government in Spain. The hard line of that government towards Basque terrorists, and what the PNV-controlled Basque Government sees as a regression in the extension of the autonomy granted by the first post-Franco government, has led to a distinct worsening of relations between Madrid and Vitoria. [5] In the second elections since the formation of the Autonomous Community, on February 26 1984, held in the aftermath of the assassination of a socialist minister, the PSE gained ground with 23 per cent of the vote, while the PNV with 41 per cent, was unable to obtain the clear majority that would allow it to rule unilaterally. The radical HB garnered 14.5 per cent of the vote. In interpreting these results and predicting the future course of events, the consensus of political analysts appears to be that the nationalists will have to think in terms of compromise with the socialists in Madrid, perhaps cooperating in the repression of ETA (Euzkadi Ta Azkatasuna) [6] while the socialists in Madrid will have to seek some kind of political compromise with the nationalists if they want this cooperation. Yet, the situation is seen as so unstable, and feelings are so irrational that compromise appears unlikely and ETA will probably continue to defy all political or military solutions, and so threaten the democracy of Spain.

> ... the 'Basque problem' in Spain is actually many problems rather than one. The Basque problems involve the history of the Spanish nation-state, the economic history of the Basque country, pervasive centre-periphery conflicts between the Basques and the rest of Spain, elements of class conflict both within the Basque country and within Spain as a whole, and the complex cultural issue of the legitimacy of government. [7]

Language and Language Policy

The ancient and non-Indo-European Basque language of Euskera has been the focal point of much nationalist sentiment and activity as well as

internal dissension and conflict with the central
government. As a function of its dyglossic
situation, [8] its not being associated with upward
social mobility, the influx of many immigrants into
the rapidly industrializing Basque region and the
paucity of a written literature, [9] the language
began to disappear by the nineteenth century. The
last hundred years have witnessed successively the
rise of nationalism with its concurrent attempt to
revive the language, the repression by the Franco
government, a second, clandestine revival movement,
and ultimately the recognition of Euskera as a
protected regional language, though Euskera could be
taught in elementary schools since 1968.

In the 1970s, various government policies and
laws were passed providing for the protection of
regional languages. Article 3 of the 1978 Spanish
Constitution gave co-official status to these
languages in their regions. In 1979, the Statutes
of Autonomy (Article 6) established Euskera as a co-
official language, [10] with the Basque Government
policy on bilingualism instituting programmes of
instruction in Euskera at all levels in the state
schools. The 1982 Basque Government's Basic Law for
the Normalization of the Use of Euskera [11] set up
a policy for use of the language in all aspects of
economic, social, political and cultural activities.
The resurgence of language use is evident in the
slow reversal of the trend towards a decline in the
proportion of the population speaking Euskera.

A recent study commissioned by the Basque
Government Uso y Conocimiento del Euskera [12]
provides data on various levels of 'Basque-speaking'
proficiency and on inter-territorial differences.
Only in Guipuzcoa is the active user of Euskera;
that is one able to speak, speak and read, or speak,
read and write it in the majority (over 56 per
cent), whereas in Alava combining all groups with
any active knowledge of Euskera produces a maximum
of only 13.07 per cent and in Vizcaya 28 per cent of
the population of adults over the age of 18. This
is not surprising in a region where more than half
the residents are non Basque immigrants.

From its inception the Basque Autonomous
Government has embarked on a policy to 'rebasquize'
its public officials and administration with the
goal of servicing its citizenry in both official
languages. It is evident, in 1984, however, that
there are wide differences in the attainment of, or
movement towards this goal in the various
departments of the Basque government. Spanish is

still predominant in public meetings, newspapers and
official conversations. Heads of departments and
political appointees appear to be primarily Spanish
speakers. Although a recent poll indicates that a
majority of citizens interviewed in each of the
three territories believe that all public officials
should have to learn Euskera, [13] there are
criticisms from both extremes. Radicals demand that
knowledge of Euskera should be an immediate
requirement; others see it as unnecessary and
discriminatory to otherwise competent Spanish
speaking officials.

Cultural Identity

Political theorists have pointed out that the
centre-periphery dichotomy can exist in all or any
of three different domains: political, economic and
cultural. Based on concepts of distance, from the
geographic centre of power to the peripheral region;
difference between the peripheral group and the
dominant society; and dependence of the peripheral
area on the central seat of power; peripheral
societies possess some sense of separate identity
but this is constantly threatened by central
agencies. [14] The Basques represent a politically
mobilized peripheral collectivity whose members
share a distinctive self identity. As a distinct
ethnic group with a shared sense of peoplehood and a
degree of autonomous political power, they appear to
exemplify the progression from the status of a
subordinate minority in their own region to one of
nationhood. [15] While the Basque language is viewed
as a badge of that nationhood [16] and serves as the
most distinguishing feature of Basque ethnicity,
other aspects of cultural identity include history,
traditions, art forms and communications. [17]

Repressed throughout most of the Franco era,
there has been since the 1960s a reawakening of
awareness and participation in relation to those
cultural experiences which are not seen as
threatening the state and which, if not actually
encouraged, at least are not hampered by the central
government. At the time of the establishment of the
Basque Autonomous Community, the Department of
Education and Culture in Vitoria was created.
Government authorities indicate that first priority
was given to the collection, revival and nurturing
of traditional cultural forms such as chisto music,
ritual dances, choral groups, poetic improvisation
and the theatrical form of the pastorale, followed
by the establishment of a formal structure for a

variety of activities throughout the region. [18] With limited resources, relatively little support has been provided for extra-curricular cultural activities for the young still at school, under the assumption that the school pupil population is being offered formal instruction in Euskera language and culture within the education system.

At present, official efforts, focussed directly on children, or indirectly, on the teachers who influence them, are largely limited to the formal educational structure. These demonstrate an almost single-minded concern with implantation of the language, although a number of educators have indicated that a more effective approach to recouping the language and to the broader goal of rebuilding a sense of cultural identity would be through the teaching of Basque history and a broad concept of native culture. [19] Teachers who are largely from outside the region or who are products of an era in which the educational system was forbidden to deal with Basque culture, have neither the knowledge nor motivation to teach these subjects. In particular they are hampered by the scarcity of available books and other materials. Extra-curricular activities for children thus tend to concentrate on sports, organized by parent groups, rather than on excursions and other activities and experiences that would enhance a sense of cultural identity. Willingness on the part of school parent associations to organize the latter type of activity frequently meets with rejection on the part of teachers. [20]

An examination of newspaper articles and announcements in journals indicates that some of the following activities are being organized to foster a sense of cultural identification: Basque cinema festivals; competition for places in touring groups of musicians, actors and dancers; musical events on school premises after school hours; the funding of scholarships for research into themes relating to the Basque region; courses for teachers in Basque history, language and literature; programming for the new Basque television channel Euskal Telebista, the latter including cartoons, news, music, telenovels, sports and films, with subtitles in Spanish; plus radio transmissions in every municipality.

In general, however, media use of Euskera is limited in both time and space allotted, and is confined almost exclusively to Batua [21] rather than the dialects spoken by many of the native speakers. Obviously the majority of printed and oral communication via the media is being offered in the dominant language, Spanish. However, since motivation to become fluent in a language is linked to the necessity for using it as a means of communicating and receiving information, media representatives are being encouraged to expand the use of Euskera and their coverage of the fields of education and culture. There are three weekly papers published exclusively in Euskera. Most daily Spanish language papers published in the Basque region have one or more articles in Euskera.

Education
The remainder of this chapter describes the current educational situation in the Basque region and the impact of political, cultural and linguistic factors. The first section presents an overview of the Spanish national educational system, followed by a consideration of the special features in the implementation of that system in the Basque Autonomous Community. The third section provides an analysis of two crucial but currently contested education laws, one at the central and one at the regional level, while the final section is devoted to a consideration of current problems and issues from the perspectives of instructional programmes, professional staff, parents and students.
Overview of the Spanish National Education System:
The structure of the Spanish educational system was established by the 1970 Law of Educational Reform and modified by the 1980 Organic Law for State Regulation of Schools (Ley Organica Estatuto de los Centros Escolares) (LOECE), and the 1983 Law setting out the Right to Education (Ley Reguladora de Derecho a la Educacion) (LODE). [22] Figure 2 gives a summary of the details.
The Spanish education system consists of eight years of free and compulsory schooling between the ages 6 - 14 in three cycles of Elementary General Education (Educacion General Basica, EGB). This is preceded by voluntary pre-school education, ages 2-5, free of charge in state schools or with state aid in private schools. Secondary schooling is offered in two tracks:
(a) Academic: three years of General Certificate Work (Bachillerato Unificado Polivalente, BUP) and one year of University Preparation Courses (Curso Orientacion Universidad, COU) or
(b) Vocational: two years of Vocational Work (Formacion Profesional, FP) at the first level

Figure 2 The structure of the Educational System in
Spain

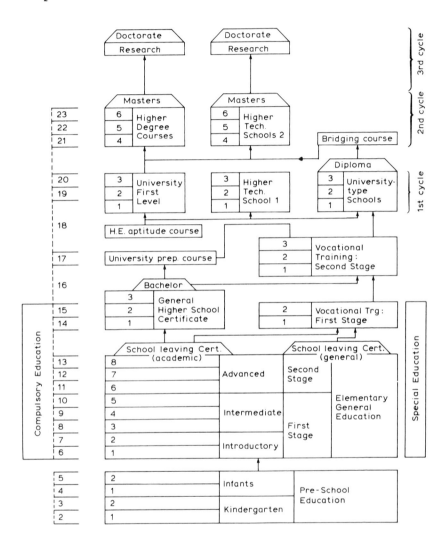

followed by three years of second level.

Those who complete the academic track may move into higher education <u>via</u> universities, technical schools or specialized university colleges, including teacher training institutions, and on to postgraduate work, the second cycle of university studies. Students who complete the vocational track may move directly into appropriate specialized University Colleges (<u>Escuelas Universitarias</u>), or (more often in theory than practice) after completion of a year of COU, into Higher Technical Schools (<u>Escuelas Tecnicas Superiores</u>) and Universities.

University Colleges (<u>Escuelas Universitarias</u>) are administered by a university, and offer post-secondary (first cycle university) work in a number of areas including teacher training for pre-school and Elementary General Education in <u>magisterios</u>. COU, BUP or FP students can develop advanced skills in Higher Technical Schools in such disiplines as electronics and engineering. Other University faculties provide the option of further study for certification or <u>carrera</u> (degree) at a state or private university in other disciplines. University graduates who wish to teach at the level of <u>ensenanza media</u> or above (grade 6 or higher) are in theory required to complete an additional year of pre- pedagogical training in CAP (<u>Curso de Adaptacion Pedagogica</u>). [23] Post graduate study such as <u>licenciado</u>, a master's degree, is available in the second cycle.

Under the terms of the Spanish Constitution of 1978, the Central Government retains responsibility for and control over certain areas of the educational enterprise. These have been interpreted to include the establishment of minimum standards of a core curriculum, the certification and payment of teachers, the provision of free, compulsory public education without discrimination, including academic freedom and the right of inspection. All of these were confirmed by LOECE. Virtually all other educational responsibilities were transferred to each of the regional governments under their respective <u>Statutes of Autonomy</u> and <u>Transfer of Educational Services from the State to the Autonomous Community</u> (transferencias). [24] The <u>Organic Law of University Reform</u> of 1983 (LAU) established conditions for extending regional authority to the area of higher education. [25]

<u>Education in the Basque Country: Implementation</u>

and Special Features:
        Since the education system in the Basque region
conforms to the national Spanish model described
above, this section is limited to aspects of its
implementation in the Basque region at each
educational level and to special features of
education peculiar to this region.
(a) Pre-school to University: Recognizing early
childhood as the optimal period for implanting
language proficiency, state schools in the Basque
region have channelled major efforts and resources
to pre-school and Elementary General Education.
Three models of instruction for implanting fluency
in Euskera have been established: Model A
(instruction in Spanish with Euskera as a second
language); Model B (bilingual instruction in both
languages); [26] and Model D (instruction in Euskera
with Spanish as a second language). Currently the
predominant model is A (mandating a minimum of three
hours weekly of instruction in Euskera) with models
B and D seen as long term objectives except where
children are already fluent in Euskera. [27] Despite
efforts by the authorities there were in 1983 still
significant numbers of children who were not
receiving instruction in Euskera.
        At the secondary level, both nationally and
regionally, an inordinate number of students opt for
the academic General Certificate BUP schools, the
completion of which prepares them for nothing but
university entrance. However, relatively few choose
this particular destination. The total enrolment in
1982/83 was 128,727 for the Basque Community of
which 79,898 were in BUP. [28] Recent increases in
attendance in FP schools especially in Guipuzcoa,
where they are in majority, however, may indicate a
growing awareness of the value of vocational
education. Unique to the region are a number of
independent technical schools based on a philosophy
of Christianity, work and service to the community
intimately linked to the industrial cooperatives
that have dominated the economy in some of these
areas since the 1950s.
        Magisterios in the Basque country, are
available in the public as well as the private
sector for the training of teachers in pre-school,
elementary and special education. in both Spanish
and Euskera. The latter attract people committed to
'rebasquization' through teaching. [29]
        University education which has not been a
tradition in the Basque country, as it was in
Catalonia is also available through private as well

as public institutions. The State University now has three branches, in San Sebastian, Vitoria, and Lejona (near Bilbao), each with its own specialized faculties. As yet, the newer state campuses, such as San Sebastian, offer only minimal resources and encouragement to faculty or students for research. Courses for the preparation of university graduates for teaching careers are offered by the Pedagogical Institutes (ICE) in Deusto, Bilbao's Jesuit University, and Lejona. Newspaper announcements advise candidates of student or faculty vacancies and grants and scholarships. In May, 1983, the first investiture of doctoral candidates from the State University was hailed as a symbol of cultural rebirth. An open university, Universidad Nacional por Educacion a la Distancia (UNED) also provides opportunities for university level study to aspirants in all parts of the region.

(b) Ikastolas: A unique feature of the Basque education scene is the increasing support of a parallel private educational system, in addition to church schools, arising from the establishment of individual schools at the community level. These schools, or ikastolas, are dedicated to the revival of Euskera as a language of daily use and its employment as the major medium of classroom instruction. Operating as clandestine institutions during the Franco regime, they launched a cultural revival movement regarded as spearheading resistance to the dictator. Parent financed, with strong church support, and parent involvement in matters of curriculum and administration, this movement has proceeded through four stages of development and is about to embark on a fifth.

Stage One: Pre-Civil War.
In the 1920s several small bilingual schools opened in Vizcaya with regular instruction in Euskera for the first time. Between 1932 and 1936, twelve of these schools were created with a total of 1200 students; an important step marking the beginning of national consciousness and spirit.

Stage Two: The Clandestine Era: 1960-1968.
Instruction in Euskera was made illegal, and classes were conducted secretly in private homes or churches after normal school hours; students, parents and teachers alike risking imprisonment. These classes were an island of Basque identity in an otherwise Castillian world, since all instruction was in Euskera. These schools functioned only at the pre-school and elementary levels. However, adult literacy programmes were also offered to teach

reading and writing skills to Euskera speakers, plus oral language skills for those who had no knowledge of the language. Cost, and fear of government reprisals kept the movement small. During the Franco era, many teachers went into exile. [30]

Stage Three: The Era of Tolerance: 1969-1978.
During the 1970s officials began to look the other way as long as political activism was not encouraged. Enrolment rose steadily, although figures differ depending on the source. There were over 40,000 students by 1977. [31] The ikastola system represented a true popular movement and by 1975 the Franco government, recognizing the inevitable, began to give it official acknowledgement.

Stage Four: The Era of Recognition: 1978-1983.
Originally a private system of schools servicing a rural monolingual Basque speaking population, since official status has been granted, it is intended to serve a wider public, that is to say an indigenous Basque, monolingual Spanish, urban population within a complex pluralistic society. [32] Consequently the ikastolas have been experimenting with a typology based on different methods of second language and bilingual instruction. [33] Staffed by enthusiastic and dedicated Euskera speaking teachers who usually do not hold official teaching credentials awarded by the Central Government upon passing national examinations, oposiciones, nor receive the salary scale which is uniform for all teachers in state schools in Spain, these schools are housed in premises that range from superior to totally inadequate.

Stage Five: The Present Situation.
The ikastolas are, at present in a state of transition as the Basque Government moves towards granting the ikastolas public school status with private school privileges. Ramifications of the law, EIKE, are discussed in the section on educational legislation.

(c) Other Factors Impacting on Education in the Basque Country: The church, immigration and dispersal policies, the role of parents and private schools have all had a significant effect on the Basque educational system.

The Catholic Church, which has traditionally exercised great influence and is closely woven into the social fabric of the Basque country, has played a significant role in promoting local interests. The links between clergy and parishioners have been closer and more intense than elsewhere in Spain. Although a relatively small number of Basque clergy have Marxist leanings and have assisted extreme groups such as ETA, and though an even smaller number has taken the espanolista or Central Government position, the overwhelming majority are Christian Democrats who have not only supported but also spearheaded nationalist activities, cultural and language revival, and other educational efforts. [34]

The huge influx of immigrants in the 1960s and 1970s wrought a change in the balance of Basques to non-Basques and Euskera speakers to non-Euskera speakers, and resulted in the increased growth of what is now a large industrial working class or terciarizada. The newcomers were primarily from provinces with a strong Castillian culture which tended to discourage rather than encourage assimilation. This of course led to a further decline in the distinctively Basque identity of the region. It also had the effect of intensifying the efforts of nationalists to 'rebasquize' the area, thereby encouraging a polarization between the indigenes and the immigrants. This tendency is reinforced by the social geography in that the immigrants are for the most part isolated in separate new housing tracts with Spanish speaking schools. Indeed, the influx of labour increased the demand for school places to such an extent that there was unprecedented overcrowding, the employment of underqualified teachers, and a general lowering of standards. [35] With the end of the immigration that accompanied the industrial recession of the late 1970s and 1980s, educators, no longer plagued by the problems of finding accommodation and teachers, were able to concentrate their attention on improvement of instruction, and the quality of education in general. With particular reference to the effects of the Franco government policy of dispersal of Basque educators and priests, and the importation of neutral, non-Basque replacements, (intercambio), these are still being felt. Coupled with the closing of universities in the Basque region the result was a generation of teachers with little Basque cultural identity, many of whom are still on the staffs of schools today.

The Basque country with its high level of political and national awareness, resistance to centralization throughout history and a tradition of local responsibility for its educational services has also enabled the parents to play an energetic

role as curriculum planners, financial
administrators and staff. This is particularly true
of the large private sector rather than the public
one where parents' activities are more likely to be
confined to sports activities and advisory
committees. [36]
    Data supplied by the Basque Government shows
that Guipuzcoa is the only territory where enrolment
in the private sector for pre-school and elementary
general education has been consistently higher than
in the public sector. This is also true of the
vocational sector, but here the other territories
show a similar trend. The ikastolas had 39.22 per
cent of pre-school pupils, the state schools 35.63,
with 25.24 per cent for other private pre-schools,
including church schools. There were 21.61 per cent
of pupils in ikastolas at the EGB level, with 40.61
per cent in state maintained establishments. These
figures show the strong support for private schools,
especially the ikastolas, probably not unconnected
with the fact that Guipuzcoa is the only territory
with a majority of Euskera speakers. [37]

Educational Legislation
    The centre-periphery dichotomy and the internal
dissension within the Basque community have both
come to a head over two current pieces of
legislation which would have a major effect on
educational policy; the Central Government's bill
regulating the right to education (LODE) and the
Basque Government's EIKE law establishing a National
Institute of Ikastolas.
(a) Ley Reguladora de Derecho a la Educacion (LODE)
    On July 12 1983 the central socialist
government, winning some surprising last minute
support even from the nationalist Catalan sector
managed to win approval of the Cortes (parliament)
for one of the most controversial pieces of
legislation in recent years - referred to by the
Basques as the "infamous LODE". LODE is the
socialist government's version of the educational
reform law (LOECE) passed in 1980 by the previous
government over the objections of the then minority
socialist party.
    Apart from leaving open future legislation for
raising the school leaving age, LODE recognizes for
the first time the right of students to form
associations and provides a more democratic,
participatory system of local and regional councils
as organs of the government of education. The most
problematic item is its classification of local

centres, and the criteria used for their public
financing. [38] The generic concept upon which this
law is based is that an educational centre
subsidized by public funds must abide by the
conditions of management which it shares with other
public centres. It must satisfy the requirements of
scholarship, and must offer free education, given
without discrimination or preference of any kind -
ethnic, linguistic, intellectual or religious.
Describing the educational situation of recent years
as a history of failure, the Government pointed out
that it spent 75 billion pesetas in 1983 on an
educational system without exercising what is seen
as the right and obligation of government to improve
the system's deficiencies. [39] The classic
socialist argument is put thus: the private sector,
particularly the church, has monopolized education,
profited and aided in establishing a mechanism of
social inequality and class dominance. The
principle of freedom of choice of schooling is being
used by the private sector to affirm the right of
each centre to prove its own educational and social
ideology, expecting the state to abandon its rights
and responsibilities at the school gate while at the
same time letting it foot the bills. The Autonomous
Community rejects LODE as a denial of freedom of
educational choice which it sees as an attempt to
limit the rights of the Autonomous Government. LODE
is also opposed by powerful associations
representing the private sector and the church
affiliated schools. Major demonstrations against
the law have been held in Madrid, [40] with every
major educational organization and political party
expressing an opinion. [41] Professional educators
and administrators have lined up on their respective
sides. Basque representatives point out the
deteriorating relationship between the Central
Government and the Basques in the first year of
socialist government, noting a growing feeling of
separation, of "making us feel disassociated" [42]
and decrying the Central Government's use of the
media to create a general feeling of aversion to the
Basques. Ministry of Education spokesmen deny the
accusation that LODE would spell the death of the
ikastolas. Provided cultural rather than political
ideas are transmitted and assuming that there is a
willingness to meet the criteria of public schools,
the ikastolas could be classified as centros
concertados according to the Central Government.
This is a new category of school under Article 10
whereby private centres become eligible for state

financing by agreeing to conform to certain minimum
curriculum, governance and teacher selection
standards, and to the acceptance of students at
compulsory education levels free of charge,
discrimination or preference.
(b) Euskal Ikastolen Erakundea - Instituto Vasco de
Ikastolas y se aprueba el Estatuto Juridico de
Ikastolas (EIKE)
    The expected enactment of LODE by March, 1984,
was delayed by a constitutional challenge. The
classic tug-of-war between centre and periphery
placed Madrid on the defensive in the battle with a
nationalistic and linguistically different ethnic
nation on the offensive. The roles are reversed in
the current battle over the Basque Government's EIKE
law, Euskal Ikastolen Erakundea - Instituto Vasco de
Ikastolas y se aprueba el Estatuto Juridico de
Ikastolas, establishing legal public status for the
ikastolas. [43] On July 27, 1983, fifteen days after
the socialist government in Madrid won approval of
its education law, LODE, and, after months of
discussion, controversy and modification in the
Basque region, the Basque Parliament approved this
controversial law to establish an autonomous
organism, EIKE, the Institute of Ikastolas and the
statutes to govern its member schools. [44]
    Critics of this law both within and outside the
Basque community see it as a blow to the
consolidation of a public school network fostering
divisiveness and confrontation. [45] Defenders
interpret the Constitutional statement that each
parent has a 'right' to send his child to the school
of his choice, to mean that this 'right' extends to
the right to receive this education in publicly
financed schools. Brandishing the virtues and
undeniable contribution of the ikastola movement to
the revival of Basque language and culture, they
create a mystique around the ikastolas justifying
the use of public funds to demonstrate respect for
their accomplishments, and guaranteeing resources
for their maintenance, protection and
expansion. [46]
    EIKE, in both its original form and with its
modifications, was opposed by both left and right
Basque political parties. The modifications include
statements to the effect that the law is a
transitional step towards the consolidation of
ikastolas as Basque state schools; further that it
is a compromise on the proportional representation
of parents in education; also that new legislation
for all education up to university level is on the

way in any case. The political opposition once again demonstrates the intensely political basis for educational provision in this region, and the ability of the PNV to ward off blows from all sides in these internal battles. Some of the modifications in EIKE, and the coincidence of the passage of this law immediately after the approval of LODE in Madrid, indicate a sense of urgency to make some concessions to certain features of LODE as a realistic political manoeuvre.

On November 2, 1983, the Council of Ministers of the socialist Central Government approved a challenge of constitutional legality against a whole series of articles of the Basque regional Constitution based on the Central Government viewpoint that the Basque Parliament had exceeded its authority and contradicted the legal status of public schools established by the LOECE law. [47] The Basque Government on the other hand acts against the challenge by the Central Government, which it sees as opposed to the ikastola movement and a Basque national model. [48] This law also awaits the decision of a Constitutional Tribunal.

Current Problems and Future Directions

This final section considers issues in the educational system of the Basque Autonomous Community from the perspectives of quality of provision, the appropriateness of the curriculum, the training of professional teaching staff, students and parents; as well as the larger issues affecting control of this system by different tiers of governmental authority.

Education is a major preoccupation of both the regional and the central governments. Their responsibilities intertwine sufficiently for both to take credit for the gains and blame the other for the weakness of the system. With over 44 per cent of the entire 1983 budget of the Basque Government earmarked for education, authorities have continued efforts to modify and renovate educational structures in order to bring them up to at least minimum standards. This has been a primary concern ever since responsibility for schools was transferred to the regional government and it will continue to require attention for years to come in order to improve the physical standards of schools. Little attention has so far been given to the outdoor environment at educational centres. Recreation periods take place on empty concrete school yards with an occasional basketball net in

the better equipped schools. The lack of equipment
and of specialists in physical education provides
evidence of the neglect of this area in the
elementary schools.

Subject matter specialists are also needed at
the advanced cycle of Elementary General Education
(Grades 6-8), where attention is also being directed
to such problems as failure rate, the absence of a
stage of professional orientation to help students
discover their realistic potential, the misfit
between the rigid cognitive learning syllabuses and
the reality of the jobs to which the majority of
students will go, and the inordinate number of ill-
suited students who go on to the baccalaureate.
These problems have been articulated at both central
and regional levels. It remains to be seen whether
pending reform programmes will be implemented and
whether or not they will correct the situation. At
the vocational preparation (FP) level, with the
exception of the cooperatives, there is little
liaison between schools and industries to either
ensure educational programmes suited to the reality
of the workplace or to cooperate in developing new
approaches of industrial development and future jobs
in a period of mass unemployment.

At the present time there is little evidence of
efforts made by the Department of Education to
coordinate or focus research efforts of academics in
the areas that need investigation. Support and
direction for such research would appear to be a
first step followed by efforts at disseminating the
results of such research and applying the findings
to the improvement of instruction. In the field of
language instruction, the teaching of foreign
languages (primarily English) utilizes methods and
materials which fail to develop communicative
ability. As for the goal of bilingualism in Spanish
and Euskera, educational authorities acknowledge
that this cannot be accomplished nor expected with
Model A. They claim that the use of this model is
merely transitional until school children are
sufficiently competent in Euskera to participate in
programmes under Models B or D. One must recognize,
however, that the Autonomous Community is not a
homogenous Basque society. There are many children,
parents and indeed teachers who have little interest
in learning Euskera. In most of the region, the
environment is largely Castillian with films,
television, newspapers and radio primarily
communicating in Castillian Spanish. Preparation of
books and materials for the teaching of Euskera has

been left largely to commercial publishers. Dissemination of some of the excellent materials prepared by Pedagogical Institutes (ICE) staff and students and a greater responsibility to be assumed by the Department of Education for the preparation of materials would appear to be indicated.

Involving teams of teachers in the development of instructional material would offer the double benefit of providing economic reward for their creativity and ensuring a higher level of commitment of teachers to the effective use of the materials they have helped to create. Teachers, after all, play the most significant role in determining the effectiveness of implementing mandated syllabuses. On the other hand, it must remembered that in a system which does not require teachers to upgrade their education, it is difficult to develop a corps of teachers from the existing teaching body who can teach Euskera or in Euskera. The rights of those experienced teachers who do not wish to learn Euskera (more than 70 per cent, according to some sources) must be safeguarded. Although some of the magisterios are producing new teachers competent in Euskera, the job prospects of graduates of magisterios which do not stress Euskera are also a concern. Reform plans of the Basque Department of Education which address some of these issues include programmes for professional improvement (Plan de Perfecionimiento de Profesorado), (PPP), a programme to 'rebasquize' teachers (IRALE), and a programme of bilingualism (Plan de Bilingualismo). [49]

No reform measures in any school system can truly be effective without focussing on improving the attitudes, methodology and professionalism of teachers. This is a delicate situation in the Basque region since teachers receive their accreditation via oposiciones. They are then considered paid employees of the Central Government, governed by its policies that require no probationary period to determine effectiveness and which grant jobs for life immediately upon employment. There are no courses, workshops, in-service or any other type of professional improvement required. In any case, incentives for advanced study do not exist. There is no assessment of teachers' competence in facilitating student learning progress, and teachers enjoy the considerable protection of teacher unions. In addition, a policy that encourages teacher transfers fosters tremendous teacher turnover which particularly affects rural schools. These often

have the additional problem of having to close down
when teachers are ill due to a lack of a system of
substitute teachers.

The problem of non-certificated teachers also
merits attention. Many unprepared teachers were
placed in classrooms during the period of teacher
shortage. They feel no need to upgrade themselves,
nor are they required to do so, and in the Basque
area there is often mistrust of qualifications
awarded by Central Government. A system of economic
incentives plus a requirement of continued upgrading
for new teachers could redress this situation.
Especially, it might resolve what could be a major
issue if and when LODE is implemented - the status
of the non-certificated teachers in the ikastolas.
More effective preparation of new teachers should
also provide more opportunities for supervised
practice teaching in the schools. At present, there
is little or no supervision provided by the teacher
training institutions since teaching faculty from
these institutions would not presume to enter the
public school classrooms and since there is also no
communication between the two. With the
implementation of the University Reform Law, it
remains to be seen if transfer of authority for
institutions of higher learning to the Autonomous
Government will lead to improvements in the training
of teachers for pre-school and elementary general
education levels (magisterios), and if CAP
programmes of the universities will be made
mandatory by law as well as by practice in the
preparation of teachers for secondary schools.

Parent involvement is another problematic area.
Parents have indicated that most public schools make
no effort to capitalize on their knowledge of
language and culture or special skills or to
actively involve them in setting policy or
educational goals. Greater respect for the role of
parents as the primary educators of their children
could lead to meaningful cooperation and shared
responsibility for that education. Recognition that
formal language instruction is only one means for
implanting cultural identity could also lead to more
effective utilization of parents. The media, the
Department of Culture, and society as a whole cannot
relegate the implanting of cultural identity to the
schools alone.

The larger issues involve the internal
dissension within the Basque community and the tug-
of-war over control between the Basque Government
and Madrid. For some, 'rebasquization' is seen as

justifying almost any means even in a society where Basques make up less than 50 per cent of the population. They are convinced that the Central Government will stop at nothing to ensure that the Basques will be deprived of their ikastolas. Others are more willing to agree with the socialist government's argument that to qualify for support from public funds schools can attend to the implantation of cultural identity, cannot include political indoctrination and must be free, open to all without discrimination, while meeting minimum standards of curriculum and teacher preparation.

Years of oppression have led to increasing sensitivity and defensiveness. Hard won concessions to autonomy will not be relinquished without a fight; and the Central Government (regardless of party) is suspected of having as a primary motive the chipping away at Basque autonomy. Educational decisions are made on national and regional levels as well as individual territorial and even municipal levels. In some areas, the interests of children are best served by having certain minimum standards imposed centrally so that the accident of attending school in a richer or poorer area has as little effect as possible on the kind of education received. In other issues, the interests of children are best served by having decisions made by those most familiar with the unique conditions of the individual educational centre; thus the municipalities can probably respond most effectively. In all cases, the interests of children are best served when municipalities, territories, autonomous communities and central government operate from a foundation of mutual trust, when developmental and pedagogical concerns play a greater role than party political ones in determining educational policy and practice. This must remain a hope, although the present in-battles over legislation give rise to considerable anxiety. [50]

Notes and References

1. Gallop, R., A Book of the Basques. University of Nevada Press, 1970.
2. Fueros were agreements with or grants by the Crown conceding certain privileges, such as local autonomy or exemption from military service, and devolving many rights and responsibilities to local authority. These ended in 1876 although the provinces which supported Franco like Alava and

Navarra had some minor privileges reinstated.

3. Frank, R.M., The Politics of Language and Ethnicity in the Basque Country Today. Paper presented to the European Studies Conference, Omaha, Nebraska, October 1981;
Heiberg, M., Urban Politics and Rural Culture: Basque Nationalism. In: Rokkan, S. and Urwin, D. eds., The Politics of Territorial Identity. Sage Publications, 1982.

4. Legaretta, D. The Guernica Generation University of Nevada Press, 1985.

5. Kurlansky, M.J., Madrid's Relations with Autonomists Reach Low Point in Post-Franco Era, Chicago Tribune, June 30, 1983.

6. A militant, revolutionary group founded in the late 1950s dedicated to the creation of an independent Basque nation-state. The name translates as 'Basque land and liberty'.

7. Greenwood, D.J., Ethnic Regionalisms in the Spanish Basque Country: Class and Cultural Conflict. Iberian Studies, 1976, 5, 2; p50.

8. Frank, R.M., Eguzkitza, A. and Bloom, L., The Basque Language. Past, Present and Future. Word, (in printing).

9. Medhurst, K., The Basques and Catalans, Minority Rights Group: London, 1977.

10. The Estatuto de Autonomia para el Pais Vasco was passed on December 18, 1979. The same law also granted similar rights to Catalonia. See also Heiberg, M., op cit.

11. The Ley 10/1982 Basica de Normalizacion del Uso del Euskera; November 24, 1982 owes its origin to Basque sensitivity to the fact that although both Spanish and Basque are recognized official languages the citizen has the duty to know Spanish, but only the right to use Euskera. Thus Basque can be used in official business. The policy of 'Basquization' of officials is lawful, as are measures to achieve progressive equality. In education, instruction in both languages is compulsory up to university level. Knowledge of Euskera is mandatory for certain teaching posts. The frequently used word 'rebasquization' is something of a misnomer since Euskera was never in the past the language of public officials.

12. This investigation into the use and knowledge of Euskera commissioned by the government of the Basque Autonomous Community in 1982 classified the population of the whole Community and of the three territories separately according to their ability to use the language skills in

different age groups. The percentages showed a decline from 41.5 per cent for those born before 1908 to 20.8 per cent for those born between 1958 and 1964. The native inhabitants showed a slightly higher percentage, 59.9 per cent and 23.5 per cent respectively while their children registered an encouraging 58.1 and 35.3 per cent, proof that efforts since 1968 to revitalize the language have not been entirely unsuccessful. These figures appear in J. Ruiz de Olabuenaga. El Euskera en la Comunidad Autonoma Vasca. KIMU, 1983 (May) p 28; According to Beltza, El Nacionalism Vasco, 1876-1936, Editorial Txertoa, 1976 and Urizar, P. de, Los Dialectos y Variedades de la Lengua Vasca (quoted in Clark, R.P., Language and Politics in Spain's Basque Provinces. West European Politics, 1981, 4, 1, p 91, and the Annuario Estadistico Vasco 1982 (Basque Autonomous Community Government Department of Statistics, San Sebastian 1983) of the total population of 2,145,000 (excluding Navarra) there were 697,000 Basque speakers (32 per cent), compared with 455,000 (19.8 per cent) in 1970, but 500,000 (41.7 percent) in 1930.

13. Goni, E.O., Euskaldunizacion del Funcionariado. KIMU, 1983, (May). Goni also reports details of language courses and language policies of various agencies.

14. Rokkan, S. and Urwin, D., Economy, Territory, Identity. Sage Publications, 1983.

15. Ross, J.A., The Mobilization of Collective Identity: An analytical overview. In: Ross, J.A., Cottrall, A.B. et al., eds. The Mobilization of Collective Identity: Comparative Perspective. Lanham, Maryland, University Press of America, 1980.

16. Medhurst, K., op cit.

17. Clark, R.P., The Basques: The Franco Years and Beyond. University of Nevada Press, 1979.

18. Interview with Imanol Olaizola, Cultural Delegate, Guipuzcoa, 1984.

19. Interviews with Julio Serrano, University of Pais Vasco at San Sebastian; Fermin Goicochea of the Instituto Solicianas Colegio Nacional; and Tomas Uribeetxebarria of the University of Pais Vasco at Lejona, in 1984.

20. As reported by a Parent Association (Asociacion de Padres) meeting at the Colegio Nacional Javier Ibarra in Bilbao, in January 1984.

21. Euskera Batua is a unified, modern literary language created by scholars out of a vast number of existing dialects. See Frank, R.M., Eguzkitza, A., and Bloom, L., op cit.

22. LOECE (Ley Organica 5/80 Estatuto de Los Centros Escolares) of June 1980 the product of the Suarez Government spells out the central government powers over education: raising the leaving age; parents' rights to their children's education according to philosophy or religious belief; and the prohibition of discrimination on the basis of language. Its replacement by LODE (Ley Reguladora de Derecho a la Educacion) was delayed by a challenge of the constitutionality of the latter.

23. These preparatory pedagogical training courses (CAP) are offered through Institutes of Educational Science (Institutos de la Ciencia de Educacion, ICE) at various universities. However, since university graduates can obtain teaching jobs without CAP, enrolment in them is directly related to teachers' employment prospects.

24. Under this royal decree (Nr 2808) of September 26, 1980 Traspaso de Servicios del Estado a la Comunidad Autonoma en Materia de Ensenanza (Transferencias) all aspects of education not reserved to the state were transferred to the autonomous provinces, and lend further legitimacy to the formulation of plans for the teaching of Euskera at all levels.

25. Implementation of Ley Organica 11/1983 de la Reforma Universitaria of August 25, 1983 was delayed by the new socialist central government.

26. Bilingualism is interpreted widely, and can mean different subjects being taught in different languages, according to the availability of teaching materials.

27. These pupils account for between 12.54 per cent of all school students in EGB in the first year, where model A is the most popular (55.92 per cent), rising to 23.89 per cent (64.93 in model A) in year eight. Except in the first year, model B accounts for less than 10 per cent, while model D varies from 18.32 per cent (year one) to 8.68 per cent (year eight). This confirms the trends noted by the Government (see Ruiz de Olabuenaga J.I., op cit). At pre-school level in year one, 14.53 per cent have no Euskera, but school models B and D each have over 20 per cent of the total number of pupils, and model A claims 41.51 per cent.

28. Figures supplied by the Departmente de Educacion, Comunidad Autonoma Vasca, Vitoria.

29. Interviews with Maria Karmen Garmendia, Magisterio Diocesana, and Jesus Garmendia, Magisterio Escoriasas, in 1984.

30. Escuelas Vascas Origen de las Ikastolas.

KIMU, 1982 (Nov/Dec).

31. Clark, R.P., 1979, op cit.

32. Askoren A., Colloquio Sobre Bilinguismo en las Ikastolas. Jakin, 1981, 19/20.

33. See for example: Zammalloa, K.A., Problematica Psychopedagogica del Bilinguismo en el Pais Vasco. Bilinguismo y Biculturalismo. Instituto de la Ciencia de la Educacion, 1978; Torrealdai, J.M., Ikastola Euskal. Jakin, 1981, 19/20; Lasa, M., Analisis Critico de la Politica Linguistica de las Ikastolas. Jakin, 1981, 19/20.

34. Medhurst, K., op cit.

35. Arpal, J.P., Asua, B. and Davila, P., Educacion y Sociedad en el Pais Vasco. Editorial txertoa, San Sebastian, 1982.

36. See: meeting of Asociacion de Padres, op cit.

37. Government, Basque Autonomous Community, Planning Service Department of Education, Students in pre-schools and EGB, 1982-83, San Sebastian; Government, Basque Autonomous Community, Department of Statistics, 1978/79, San Sebastian 1981/82.

38. Equipo de Educacion del PSE-PSOE, La Lode y La Legislacion Actual. HITZ, 1983, 12zb.

39. Ensenanza Obligatoria, Historia de un Fracaso. Comunidad Escolar Especial LODE, January 1984.

40. Manifestaciones Contra la LODE en Varias Ciudades. Comunidad Escolar, January 1/15, 1984.

41. Opiniones Sobre el Proyecto de Ley. Comunidad Escolar Especial LODE, January 1984.

42. See: interview with Tomas Uribeetxebarria, op cit.

43. Ley 15/1983 por la que se crea Euskal Iskatolen Frakundea – Eike Instituto Vasco de Ikastolas y se apprueba el Estatuto Juridico de Iskatolas provides for the establishment of an Institute which would bring the ikastolas under Basque local government control.

44. The main purpose of this law is to provide machinery for coordinating the work of the ikastolas, the establishment of new ones, the promotion of the teaching of Euskera and the development of the language, the setting up of minimum government standards of education and the reform of teacher training and pedagogical research.

45. Gurrutxaga, X., Se Approbo la Ley del Eike. HITZ, 1983, 12zb.

46. Arregi, M., El Eike y la Lode, Elija. Usted su cole. HITZ, 1983, 12zb.

47. "Prosigue en Euskadi el Debate Sobre las Ikastolas". Comunidad Escolar, December 15/30, 1983.

48. Interviews with Jesus Legarreta, Director of KIMU in 1984 and Tomos Uribeetxebarria, op cit.

49. Interview with Jesus Garmendia, op cit, Maria Karmen Garmendia, op cit, Tomas Uribeetxebarria, op cit, and Maria Jose Armandariz of the Department of Education, Basque Autonomous Community, in 1984.

50. Meister, S., Basques - A Dilemma for Spain. Los Angeles Times, March 2, 1984.

AUSTRALIAN IMMIGRANTS AND INDIGENES IN THE CONTEXT OF CULTURAL REAFFIRMATION: SPECIAL OR GENERAL EDUCATIONAL NEEDS?

Philip de Lacey and Anthony Fielding

Introduction

While evidence suggests that Australian Aboriginals as a minority group are engaged in the process of cultural reaffirmation, there remains a great deal of uncertainty as to how this process may be encouraged through reforms in educational practice. Whether or not cultural reaffirmation can be achieved alongside pressures in Australian society which urge Aboriginals to become anglicized, remains very much an unanswered question. Most of the former colonies are now peopled both by the descendants of the colonists and by those whose forebears were the original population. After the arrival of colonists, indigenous people tend to undergo a particular series of changes in condition and behaviour that has been documented. [1] At first, typically, indigenes try to resist colonization or invasion by others; but the invaders, usually Europeans in recent centuries, tend to subjugate the indigenes through their superior technology.

The period of subjugation is frequently characterized by military defeat, disintegration of many structural and cultural elements, material poverty, disease - especially exotic disease, and a falling birth rate. This period may continue for many decades, after which the social, physical and cultural decline results either in the extermination of the indigenes, as in Tasmania at the hands of Europeans or in New Zealand where the Moriaris were annihilated by another wave of Polynesians, the Maoris. A different process is what Berry calls 'reaffirmation'. This term implies a termination of the decline, followed by a biological and psychological revival, which in turn is manifested by the re-establishment of a cultural ethos with the reappearance of original or borrowed cultural arts and artifacts, a rising birthrate, the identification of social objectives - particularly valuable objectives like access to political decision-making and property, including land, and a gradual improvement in the general conditions of living. This reaffirmation process is currently in progress in several countries, including the United States, Canada, South Africa, New Zealand and Australia.

In Australia, for example, in a number of towns in western New South Wales where Aboriginal artifacts no longer existed, models were copied of boomerangs and music sticks from Central Australia. From such beginnings the process of cultural revitalisation appears to occur. Contact with traditional cultural artifacts and the skilful ways these may have been used in the pre-colonial environment may be part of the instrumental means of embarking on cultural reaffirmation. Perhaps of greater national importance though, has been the number of organised campaigns aimed at allocating ancestral lands to the Aboriginal people. In the mid - 1980s, Australian Aboriginals have succeeded in regaining control over such lands in South Australia and the Northern Territory. The impact of these developments is yet to be observed in terms of distinctively Aboriginal involvement in shaping the economic future of Australia and the restoration of cultural experience in respect of Aboriginal spirituality and art forms.

The indigenous people, adjacent to or integrated with the dominant Europeans - whether the latter are less numerous as in South Africa, or more numerous as in North America - inevitably also belong to other social groups. These may be based on ethnic origin, country of origin, material wealth, religious affiliation or place of residence. This ambiguity or plurality of group membership is important, since, if it is not carefully identified, it can lead to fundamental logical errors in social analysis and in inappropriate recommendations and policies towards the indigenous populations on the part of the dominant majority. This point is taken up again later in the chapter.

The Indigenous Australians - Aborianials and Lifestyle

In Australia, there is no one lifestyle that characterizes the decendants of the original inhabitants - the Aboriginals. The anthropologist

Rowley has identified four principal life styles of Aboriginal people: the city dwellers who live with the 80 per cent plus of the Australian population that is urban; the fringe dwellers who live mainly on reserves near many country towns; the mission people who live on remote church missions or government settlements; and those fewer tribal people in the north of central Australia and the north-west of Western Australia, some of whom made their first contact with white people as recently as the 1950s. [2]

In the decade since Rowley's work, some changes associated with the reaffirmation process have occurred in each of these groups. The proportion of middle class urban Aboriginals, though still quite small, has increased as a result of more public service jobs being made available to Aboriginals on a positive racial discrimination basis. More fringe dwellers have moved into nearby country towns, while the titles to several of the reserves, on which some of them have been living, are being invested in Aboriginal groups. These reserves were originally set aside for short stays by itinerant stockmen and their animals. Especially in more remote areas the reserves are furnished with only the most basic accommodation, though some amenities have recently been improved, for example the addition of some water supplies and sanitation facilities.

The Government and even some local administrations are supplanting church administration in many of the outback missions, though the churches generally retain their pastoral, teaching and caring roles. A few mission stations which have included several tribal groups, as at Hermannsburg in Central Australia, have undergone decentralization; some tribal groups returning to outstations on lands formerly occupied by their forebears. Among the few remaining people living in tribalized communities, more access is being made available to the products of modern (Western-style) living, in so far as these are welcomed by the Aboriginal people themselves.

Australian Population Characteristics - a Brief Overview

In the last four decades there has been a substantial increase in the heterogeneity of Australia's population. So much has this been the case that the indigenous population, the largest for some years after colonization, at the last estimate numbered only 300,000. [3] This is less than two per

cent of the total population, and leaves the
indigenes outnumbered by several non-Anglo ethnic
groups. Of this two per cent, over half have
European as well as Aboriginal ancestry. [4]

The greatest population change has been the
inclusion of several hundred thousand immigrants
from southern Europe, principally Italy and Greece,
as well as about as many thousands from northern and
eastern mainland Europe. These movements have
resulted in an increase to about 30 per cent in the
proportion of the population at least some of whose
forebears came from countries other than the United
Kingdom. [5] Despite the substantial cultural
variation that has occurred as a consequence, it is
still the case that the Anglo-Celt base of
Australian culture and population remains dominant.
This is so, not only because nearly half the total
immigrant numbers have continued to come from the
United Kingdom, producing a 'recharging' effect, but
also because immigrants from other countries have
filtered into the country over several decades, and
have thus differentially been subjected to
progressive anglicization. While it is true that
tight affiliations among immigrants from some
national backgrounds have often resulted in
resilient cultural maintenance, this is less true of
their children, whether they were born in Australia
or not. These children accept progressive
anglicization more readily, even though, for them
too, this can be a slow and sometimes traumatic
experience.

In sum, Australia's population is culturally
diverse, but dominated in terms of power, status,
population characteristics and size by its Anglo-
based community. Among its major ethnic groupings,
Australia's Aboriginal population has declined in
relative size to the point in the mid-1980s where it
appears to be about the same size as, for example,
the Italian-based group.

Thus, from being the sole inhabitants of the
Australian Continent, Aboriginals now compete for
resources, power, status and cultural identity with
numerous ethnic minorities as well as with the
dominant Anglo-based group.

Minority Group
In this chapter we adopt the qualitative
criterion suggested by Megarry et al as a means of
identifying minorities; that is:

We are using the word 'minority' to refer not

to relative numbers but, to 'the condition of
being inferior or subordinate'; groups who are
disadvantaged by differences of culture and
language, especially ethnic minorities who do
not possess the background, attributes and
skills of the dominant group and are thus
distanced from the sources of power and status
in the country they inhabit. [6]

It seems incontestable that Aboriginals
constitute that minority group among the Australian
population most distanced "from the sources of power
and status in the country they inhabit". Arguably,
Aboriginal culture is as different as that of any
minority group from the culture of the dominant
Anglo-based group. Aboriginal history, cultural
attributes and living skills are anchored in an
anthropology which is yet to be comprehended by the
non-Aboriginal population; Aboriginal skills for
living are remote in kind from those which evolved
in the sociogeographic environments of Europe and
Britain; and Aboriginal spirituality is itself
remote, so far as we understand, from the stylised
and formalized practices of the Judeo-Christian
tradition brought here by the colonists. It appears
to these Anglo-based writers that European
understanding of the nature and experience of
Aboriginal culture and society has advanced only
marginally during the two hundred years since White
settlement. And this despite a long history of
'research' and theorising about these important
matters. Some attempt is necessary, at this point
in the chapter, to try to explain why this is so.

An Anthropological Illusion

So far as Anglo-European views about the nature
and history of Aboriginal culture are concerned, it
seems safe to say that these views have been, until
very recent years, in the main profoundly misguided.
They have been frequently based on unsupported
opinion, and distorted by the application of methods
of enquiry and conceptual analysis having their
origins in the traditional Western European
scientific worldview.

Goodall [7] captures the essence of this
difficulty for Anglo-Europeans by pointing out the
ethnocentrism representative of anthropological
thought during the period of the late 1930s to the
late 1950s. That thought:

cemented the illusion that the aborigines had

never taken part in the white economy or done anything else since the white invasion except sit around in a depressed state [8]

Even if this attitude is placed in the context of the period, during which Australia with much of the world suffered the Great Depression and World War Two, the extent to which it evidences a western ethnocentric bias remains high, for as Goodall is quoted as claiming:

.... aborigines had not only fought consistently for independence (during the nineteen thirties), but also had undertaken highly successful farming ventures that were systematically crushed. Their lands were seized so that they could not develop an economic base [9]

Such views as the one critized by Goodall, even if developed with the best of intentions, and during a period of intense economic uncertainty and World War, arguably have become 'cemented' into an Anglo-European ethnocentrism which has given rise to palpably unsupportable views about Aboriginals and their cultural anthropology. But of course the history of the impact of this ethnocentric view goes much further back in time. For example, as early as the mid-seventeenth century, Abel Tasman described Aboriginals as:

.... naked, beach-roaming wretches, destitute of rice and not possessed of fruits worth mentioning, excessively poor and of a very malignant nature [10]

Tasman, one of the first to betray a Western European ethnocentric bias in his declamations about Aborigines, has his successors down through the generations. As late as 1893, the anatomist Fiske made the following extraordinary claims, (cited in Jack):

If we take into account the increasing cerebral surface, the differences between the brain of a Shakespeare and that of an Australian savage would doubtless be fifty times greater than the difference between the Australian's brain and that of an orangutan. [11]

Despite the appearance of studies which hinted

at a totally different reality, [12] Anglo-European
views about Aboriginals have been dominated, even
until the present time, by a prevailing Western
world ethnocentrism which by its nature has
virtually precluded anything better than marginal
success at understanding the existential basis of
Aboriginal culture. Without a written history
available for study; without any real appreciation
of the customs and mores of Aboriginal people; with
the biased belief that Anglo-European civilization
was the zenith in sociocultural evolution; and with
the accompanying belief, widespread among the White
populations of the world even to the late decades of
the twentieth century, that Black peoples are
inferior representatives of the species, it is safe
to claim that in the 1980s Anglo-European
understandings of Aboriginal life and society are
conceptually primitive and in the main lacking in
objective content.

Adding to the impact of Anglo-European
ethnocentrism on the development of the kind of
cultural anthropology described above has been the
factor of geography. Geographically, Australia's
non-Aboriginal population is concentrated in a few
large conurbations while its Aboriginal one is
dispersed among sparsely populated and frequently
inaccessible rural areas. Contact, therefore, at
any level, between Aboriginals and Whites is
infrequent and when it does occur tends to be
transitory. Even in rural communities where there
is both a settled White and Aboriginal population
such contacts are minimal; the preference on both
sides being to keep largely to themselves, with the
exception that contact with Government agencies is
often maintained by Government officials. These are
usually educated Whites who may well not reside in
the community to which they provide Government
services.

Finally there is apparently a supreme irony in
most of the documented Anglo-European writings about
Aboriginals. Moorehead, in an attempt to portray
the historical tragedy of white-Aboriginal contact,
identifies the essential basis of this irony in his
claim that:

> The important thing about the Australian
> aborigines was not that they were so very
> different to these first white men who came
> among them, but that they were so very similar.
> Cook and Banks in fact were observing a
> primitive manifestation of themselves, and

Dampier was absolutely wrong. [13]

Under such a view whereby when Anglo-Europeans come into contact with Aboriginals they are in contact with a historically distant version of themselves, they are so distant that there is no recognition of this. Instead, ethnocentrism is asserted; differences rather than similarities become emphasized. Rather than understanding that the particular form of Anglo-European civilization which the Whites represent is but one possible future destiny that Aboriginals may select for themselves, the dominant Anglo-European culture takes it to be 'cultural given' that Aboriginals will select this destiny. This has given rise to the doctrine of cultural assimilation so much supported in Australia in the decades preceding the mid-1970s. The irony is further evidenced by Moorehead:

> In Australia prior to white settlement there had been no need for the aboriginal to develop; the climate was warm enough for him to do without clothes or houses, there was sufficient food to be had without forcing himself to the hard labour of tilling the ground, no wild animals threatened him, and he was so few in number ... that he was not often obliged to resort to drastic tribal wars to defend his hunting grounds. Cook and Banks saw him as he had ever been, in a state of balance with nature, not entirely freed from want ... but able to survive without extreme neurosis or fear, and his codes of behaviour were, on the whole, very sensible. [14]

Aboriginals and Anglo-European Education

The first Anglo-European school for Aboriginal pupils was probably the one established at Parramatta, just west of Sydney, by Governor Macquarie in 1815. According to Budby:

> ... this school was destined for failure as it attempted to impart westernised values onto the very tribal Aboriginal community. The school soon had to be disbanded because of the lack of interest on the part of the Aboriginal community as a whole. [15]

Mission schools soon followed, set up on

Government reserves or church mission land. Until
as late as the 1940s the policy in most Australian
states had the effect of discouraging the
involvement of indigenes in schooling, even to
providing that they could be expelled from school on
the basis of complaints from non-aboriginal parents.
After the Second World War, however, there was a
major effort made to enrol Aboriginal children in
schools, with a view to encouraging their
assimilation into the majority culture as much as
possible.

But even then the participation rate was
modest. The 1976 Census showed that 12 per cent of
Aboriginal children never attended school, by
comparison with 1 per cent of non-Aboriginals. By
1970s there had commenced a few intervention
programmes aimed at the pre-school age group. An
example of such a programme which has survived to
the present is 'Project Enrichment of Childhood Pre-
school', at Bourke in north western New South Wales.
Funded by both State and Federal Governments, this
project has continued for fourteen years. Follow-up
studies over a decade indicate for example, that
some pre-school pupils show over twenty I.Q. points
of gain. This is claimed by the researchers
involved as being a direct consequence of the
enrichment programme. [16]

In recent years, the National Aboriginal
Education Committee, [17] consisting of Aboriginals
from all states, has produced periodic comment and
statements on Aboriginal educational issues,
including suggestions about the four life style
categories and schooling options for Aboriginal
communities. The four categories, based on the work
of Rowley, [18] were 'rural traditional', 'rural
non-traditional', 'urban condensed' and 'urban
dispersed'. In the first three categories, special
schools for Aboriginals are possible. Budby [19]
favours Aboriginal control of some schools in order
to guarantee the survival of Aboriginal culture.
This view is on the grounds that the contemporary
state and Catholic school systems have failed to
provide a context for the formal education of
Aboriginal children, because they are not attuned to
the 'learning styles' of these children. It should
be noted that administrators and teachers control
schools, not Aboriginals. These personnel typically
are not Aboriginals though there are now some
trained Aboriginal teachers and teacher aides,
especially in the northern parts of Queensland and
the Northern Territory.

The movement towards gaining greater assistance for the education of Aboriginal children has been lent impetus by the coincidental movement to obtain more facilities for the education of other minorities; indeed the two movements have largely pooled their resources. Administratively, English as a Second Language (ESL) and Aboriginal English (AE) sections have, for example, been combined within the New South Wales State Department of Education. ESL and AE programmes are essentially the same as employed in Australia as a whole which in turn are very similar to programmes used in other English speaking countries. Teacher training for ESL work is carried out in Universities and Colleges of Advanced Education through methodology options and specialist diploma and degree programmes.

But there is by no means unanimity about modifying existing sructures and curricula to accord with the wishes or needs of minority groups. On the one hand, some writers argue that the overarching basis for considering different needs is not so much culture as socio-economic circumstance. Consequently low-income Anglo-Celts, have at least as legitimate a claim for schooling to be modified in the direction of enhanced opportunities for socio-economic improvement. [20] On the other hand, there is a strong and clearly recognizable, if cautiously expressed, opinion among some educators and politicians that the first and over-riding responsibility of a school system lies in the direction of responding to the needs of the majority. Furthermore, in circumstances of limited available resources, if there is conflict between the responses to majority and minority needs, the majority needs must have precedence. Thus, while there are powerful arguments for allocating substantial resources to minority groups who either find schooling unusually difficult or who wish to enjoy an alternative form of educational experience, it is hard to argue that any one group that is disadvantaged should have precedence over any other, historical antecedents notwithstanding.

But to take the opposing view, it is manifestly the case that among minority groups Aboriginal are unique in that they are both the indigenous inhabitants and were 'conquered' as a result of the 'invasion', during the late eighteenth and early nineteenth century, by the technologically superior Anglo-Europeans. And it is a mark of the extent to which a society can regard itself as 'civilized' that it relinquishes the role of conquerer as early as possible and replaces this with the role of partner with the 'conquered' in the task of social reconstruction and the achievement of inter-cultural harmony. Put differently, we are arguing here that Anglo-European society should place no hurdle in the ways of Aboriginal self-determination and cultural reaffirmation. And if this means that some of the resources which otherwise would have been enjoyed by the majority culture must be allocated to Aboriginals then this is the price to be paid as a means of demonstrating that the dominant culture is indeed 'civilized'. But of course these statements open up yet a further controversy.

That controversy concerns whether it is appropriate to regard contrasting cultures as merely different, [21] or hierarchical. In respect of the assumption of cultural hierarchy, de Lacey [22] argues that a 'deficit hypothesis' does not necessarily imply derogation of that culture which, as a minority, compares unfavourably with the dominant culture in terms of its capacity for self-maintenance. On the contrary, the so-called deficit hypothesis can be a legitimate response to social reality, recognizing that, for better or for worse, there is in our Western society powerful support for the argument for the need to possess certain skills, particularly those based on numeracy and literacy and derived abilities, as prerequisites to such social participation as entry to the effective work force, giving point, however, to the central aspects of this controversy, are views firmly opposed to this argument. [23] This is quite different from a derogatory kind of deficit view of former times, which often regarded some ethnic groups as genetically inferior, even sub-human, as indicated earlier in this chapter. The non-derogatory, pragmatic variety of deficit hypothesis, it is argued here, can be both realistic and constructive as a basis for educational programmes tailored more to the needs of groups which are disadvantaged, in conceptual and linguistic development, in terms of comparable developments in mainstream children. It is our view that such an understanding of 'deficit' can be instrumental, if adequately implemented in educational practice, in ensuring that Aboriginals, for example, have some certainty of maintaining their parent culture and in articulating among themselves and to the dominant culture their programme to reinstate their parent culture by, for instance, the process of cultural reaffirmation.

The question arises; how do Aboriginal parents

feel about the 'compensatory' style of education which is designed to help overcome learning deficits? As might be expected, the answer to this question is far from being definitive and, not surprisingly, still requires a great deal more enquiry than has already been made. Two contrasting views appear to have emerged in the past decade. In the tribal situation in Central Australia, Seagrim and Lendon [24] report that many Aboriginals hope that schools will teach their children, not the 'bush' English they use, but the 'secret' English of the written literature - analogous to the more meaningful and esoteric 'language' of the 'secret' ceremonies of their own culture. The experience of de Lacey and his co-workers, covering the past fourteen years of field studies at The Bourke Pre-School, indicates that successive years of pre-school parents, Aboriginal and White, of children at the school have consistently voted the most important goal as being 'to help my child do better at school', vindicating in this context-rural non-traditional-the heavy emphasis placed by this pre-school on 'majority style' concept and language development. [25] In contrast to these reports, Fesl, [26] in a study of literacy and educational perceptions of three Aboriginal communities (Dandenong and Shepparton in the State of Victoria, and Bourke in New South Wales), found that, "Most Aborigines do not view literacy or the need for it in the same way as non-Aborigines or educators. The dichotomy is epitomized when a person with an obvious literacy deficiency does not view it as a 'problem'." In reviewing the research report the author makes the following pertinent observations:

- ... Aborigines are not particularly interested in becoming 'assimilated' into a society which has signified it does not want them anyway;
- ... the written word...contains little of relevance to Aborigines and their lifestyles ...
- ... different values (are) placed on literacy in English between the Anglo and Aboriginal groups ...
- ... the tradition of oral transmission (has) served Aborigines well for over 40,000 years, and (is) continuing to do so. [27]

All this said, it is probably unlikely that schools are going to change substantially from responding to the demands of the culturally dominant group, despite urgings that they do so by cultural minorities such as Aboriginals. It is reasonable, and expected, that provision for children of all minority groups should have increasing assistance with their schooling as a means of ensuring that they become both better understood by the majority culture and better able to articulate to themselves their own needs for cultural reaffirmation. Nonetheless the hard fact remains that the pressures for learning achievements based on western technological society are so strong and so insistent as to severely limit the implementation of changes directed at accommodating the reaffirmation desires of minorities. The way ahead for Aboriginal adults and their children would therefore seem to be a twofold strategy. First, they need to extract the maximum accommodation possible from the school system. This is particularly important in respect of teaching strategies and content appropriate to Aboriginals, as has been suggested by Burney [28] and Watts. [29] Second, there is a need to redouble the present rather tentative efforts at providing that type of compensatory education for such clientele that is manifestly capable of making a substantial difference in the rate and level of cognitive development in children who can be regarded as less disadvantaged by dominant-culture criteria.

Notes and References

1. Berry, J.W., Human Ecology and Cognitive Style. Wiley, 1976.
   2. Rowley, C.D., Aboriginal Policy and Practice. Australian National University Press, 1971.
   3. Australian Information Service, The Australian Aboriginals, Canberra: Australian Government Publishing Service, 1980.
   4. Gray, A. and Smith, L.R., The Size of the Aboriginal Population, Australian Aboriginal Studies, 1983, 1.
   5. Price, C., The Australian Population. In: Falk, B. and Harris, J. eds., Unity in Diversity. Carlton, Victoria: ACER, 1983.
   6. Megarry, J., Nisbet, S., and Hoyle, E. eds., World Yearbook of Education: Education of Minorities. Kogan Page / Nichols, 1981 p 9.
   7. Goodall, H., Sydney Morning Herald, August 6, 1983.

8. ibid, p 33.
9. ibid.
10. Jack, R.L., Northernmost Australia. Melbourne: George Robertson, 1921, p 64.
11. Ibid, p 66.
12. Haddon, A.C., ed., Reports of the Cambridge Anthropological Expedition to the Torres Strait. Volume 2: Physiology and Psychology. Cambridge University Press, 1901; Fowles, H.L., Report of the Psychological Tests of Natives in the North West of Western Australia. Australian Journal of Science, 1940, 2.
13. Moorehead, A., The Fatal Impact: An Account of the Invasion of the South Pacific, 1767-1840. Penguin Books, 1975, p 153.
14. ibid.
15. Budby, J.R., Aboriginals and Schooling. Unicorn, 1983, 9, 3, p 202.
16. de Lacy, P.R., and Ronan, N.M., Verbal I.Q; Gains From Early Intervention Pre-schooling. Research Report. University of Wollongong, 1984.
17. The National Aboriginal Education Committee was set up in 1977. Members, all of whom are Aboriginal, are elected from State Committees to advise the Federal Minister of Education on policy matters relating to education.
18. Rowley, C.D., op cit.
19. Budby, J.R., op cit.
20. For example, Jacubowicz, A., Ethnic Welfare: Problems in Policy Formation and Implementation. Social Alternatives, 1983, 3.
21. Kelly, M.E. and McConnochie, K.P., Compensatory Education: A Subtle Term for Racism? Australian Journal of Education, 1974, 18.
22. de Lacey, P.R., Compensatory Education: A Basis for More Equal Opportunity. Australian Journal of Early Childhood, 1979, 4.
23. Fesl, E.D., BALA BALA: Some Literacy and Educational Perceptions of Three Aboriginal Communities. Canberra: Australian Government Publishing Service, 1982; Fesl, E.D., The Irrelevance of Literacy. Educational News: Journal of the Commonwealth Department of Education and Youth Affairs, 1983, 18, 5.
24. Seagrim, G., and Lendon, P., Furnishing the Mind. Sydney Academic Press, 1980.
25. de Lacey, P.R., and Ronan, N.M., op cit.
26. Fesl, E.D., (1982), op cit.
27. Fesl, E.D., (1983), op cit, p 14.
28. Burney, L., Teaching Strategies for

Aboriginal Australia

Aboriginal Children. <u>Education News: Journal of the Commonwealth Department of Education and Youth Affairs</u>, 1982, <u>18</u>, 1.
    29. Watts, B.H., Aboriginal Futures: Review of Research and Developments and Related Policies in the Education of Aborigines. Brisbane: <u>Schonell Educational Research Centre</u>, 1981.

UNITED STATES EDUCATIONAL POLICIES AND BLACK CULTURAL IDENTITY

Nathan Kravetz

Introduction
      The development of concepts of ethnic identity
is not new in the United States. The recognition
and maintenance of ethnic cohesiveness stems from
group insistence upon the common backgrounds,
traits, traditions, and even the appearance of its
members. The common standing of ethnic groups has
tended to reinforce both the validity of group
consciousness and the opportunities of group members
for seizing advantages in economic, social, and
political contexts. While in the United States
Black ethnic and cultural identity would be
difficult to deny, the current emphasis on Black
identity with Blacks striving for appropriate
participation in the social, economic, and political
spheres is of eminent importance. Insofar as 'Black
Cultural Identity' has been related to the
facilitating effects of educational policies, it is
these policies that are seen as governing the rate
of progress of Black development in the United
States.
      This paper will review the background of Blacks
in the United States and the elements which have
become the concepts of 'Black Cultural Identity'.
It examines the events and the circumstances which
have tended to form and give focus to Black
identity, and to emphasize those elements in
national educational policy that have most recently
had their impact. Finally, it will attempt to
suggest the further developments which may
reasonably ensue from the continuity of anticipated
events.

Background and Development
      From the earliest days of colonization in the
New World, the use of imported slaves was seen as a

286

necessary practice in the zones of greatest
agricultural development. Although at first, in
some few instances indigenous people were placed in
service as slaves for the agricultural needs of some
regions, this did not develop as a viable activity.
The importation of African Blacks laid the
foundations for the development of the institution
of slavery in the colonial period and in the newly-
established United States. Due notice must be taken
that in some regions, like the northern and New
England states, slavery was not seen as a necessary
or even economically feasible condition. With the
early establishment of trade, commerce, and the
rudiments of industrialization, European immigrants
and their employers, usually of similar background
and cultural source, developed the manpower status
which could and did function without the requirement
for the kinds of labour that was provided by Blacks
in the South.

The original importation of Blacks, therefore,
was for labour in the agriculture of the colony, be
it French, Spanish, or English and with particular
reference to those lands and those crops which could
not feasibly be managed by family farmers with white
hired labour or by tenants. Slave labour was
frequently imported and traded in North America by
the businessmen of New England, but they did not
intend that slavery itself should become implanted
in their region.

When New Englanders, New Yorkers and
Pennsylvanians observed the practices of slavery,
they were certain that it had serious moral
impediments, particularly those observers with
religious and ethical convictions. They were
appalled, if not horrified, at the conditions of
labour, the situation of the slave quarters, the
relations of slaves and their families, and no doubt
at the relations between masters and slaves.
Nevertheless, the 'trade' continued, beginning with
the delivery in West African harbours of prisoners
of tribal wars, of Arab slaves, and even a minority
of willing impoverished tribesmen who believed they
would find some opportunity to renew their lives,
even as slaves in a new world. Most were, however,
captured in organised raids by slave traders. The
traffic encompassed the miserable conditions of the
voyage, including considerable loss of life, the
separation of families both in the transport and in
ensuing slave sales, and the profound hypocrisy of
those who engaged in and fostered slavery while
proclaiming their deep ethical and religious values.

Black USA

In the development of the United States as a nation, the continued economic growth of the southern agricultural regions tended to depend upon the holding and employment of slaves. Until the time of the Civil War, discussions and arguments resounded over the ethics of slavery as an American institution. Some concerns also were beginning to be expressed with regard to the economic validity of working slaves on southern lands. There were indeed the costs of maintaining slaves to be compared with the productivity of such labour. With the development of new technology in farm equipment, there might have been an excess of labour intensive activity when capital investments might have proved more profitable. At the same time, however, the principle of who may make decisions other than the individual states appears to have become more important than economic or ethical issues. The question was, does a state have the right to choose slavery or is this to be decided by the pressures of other states, or by the federal government itself, thus pre-empting the rights of the individual states.

It would be naive to assert that the American Civil War was fought to free the slaves, much as this may still be a popular concept among certain segments of American and world society. With the quarrel over states' rights, the ultimate right to be determined was that of the right to secede from the Union. It was over this that the Civil War was fought. The abolition of slavery was an issue for certain inspired individuals and groups, and for the eventual enshrining of President Lincoln, whose own declarations were that the Union must be preserved. As an astute politician and a statesman of the highest rank, he could not order the draft of thousands of Whites into military service so that they could be killed or wounded in order to free the Blacks of the Confederacy from slavery.

With the coming of freedom, Blacks could leave the farms of their servitude, the households where they had helped to raise white children and provided for the needs of white families, the workshops where they had practised the skills of carpentry, blacksmithing, animal and veterinary husbandry, and the numerous other crafts and occupations which they had learned and cultivated over several generations. They could travel freely to the urban centres and cities to seek employment, medical care, and educational chances for their children as if they had never experienced the conditions of slavery.

288

They might also remain close to the farms and be hired for pay where they had previously been slaves. But with their new status of hired labour, they could not expect to receive the usual treatment that wise owners gave to their valued property.

Blacks were thus involved as manpower in much the same way as were Whites of the same economic category. In many instances, Blacks were able to offer skills well beyond those of available white labour. Yet, given their lack of education and the persisting attitudes of Whites, employers as well as workers, towards Blacks, former slaves could not easily improve their economic status or move forward. At the same time, Blacks who had never been slaves lived somewhat more easily in the northern states, able to attend schools · for some years, and to move freely to places where they might be employed, while possessing the status of citizenship on the same basis as other residents of those states. [1]

These conditions, however, changed drastically with the arrival of southern Blacks, former slaves, in their midst. [2] This loss of distinction by northern Blacks had a dual effect. On the one hand they appeared to be like the new arrivals and thus had to forego privilege. On the other hand, those Blacks with more education and more experience of community life were more affluent, more susceptible to leadership roles, and more likely to wish to keep their distance from their southern brethren.

The Concept of Identity

Throughout the period of Black participation in the development of the United States, concepts of cultural identity have been based upon several factors. These include, first and most visibly, race: characteristics of hair, skin, and general appearance. Acceptance of race as a form of cultural identity may, for some observers, lead to attempts to make similar definitions for other groups, where in fact cultural determinations are generally not linked to physical traits, but rather to ethnic and historical experience and development. Astute consideration, nevertheless, will reach the conclusion that in the case of Blacks, Orientals, and some Hispanics, racial characteristics may be fairly noted as, in effect, 'cultural'. A major force for this is in the ready practice of those who themselves are not members of a minority group to assert race as a characteristic for members of such groups. [3]

A second cultural attribute is in the recognition that one's group or entity derives from a particular region or area in another part of the world. For Blacks, their origin in West Africa remains an essential element in the definition of cultural identity. They may, if they wish, relate to the kingdoms and other political establishments of that area in Africa. They determine, if they can, the exact territory and even village from which their slave ancestors were kidnapped and thus attempt to name a tribe which may provide them with the richest possible inheritance of culture. Locale thus becomes a focus for a unifying cultural attachment of all or most Blacks who come from slave ancestry. Coming out of their historical experience of being enslaved in Africa and then sold in the New World, Blacks in the United States are able to assert such aspects as being inherent in their cultural identity. And it is from these origins that Blacks refer to such specifics as the language spoken in their African homeland; the elements of music, art, and drama which may be found on those sites or in museums; the poetic, and mythological works that may be found within the regional or localized tribes of African origin. [4] From such sources, American Blacks have sought to re-establish the strength of their cultural determinations. Researchers have examined the files and archives to identify and establish Black origins and to name the kings and heroes, the historical events that gave them the needed sense of continuity, and the specifics of language and the arts with which the ancestors communicated. [5] Thus, without reference to their experiences in the New World, American Blacks can define with satisfaction certain specifics of their cultural identity. Indeed, at this point, such specifics may in fact pertain to the Blacks in the region who never left Africa at all.

Blacks have been able to focus on the cultural identity which derives from their history before their entrance into slavery in North America. In addition, the experiences of slavery and then of the period from the end of the Civil War to the present time also constitute for American Blacks a tapestry of culture. From their forced arrival in the Americas, Blacks initially depended upon their sense of common origin to maintain and strengthen the efforts which made for physical survival. In time, the generations left and lost their knowledge of their African culture, with no attempts made by

sympathetic Whites to help them sustain it.
Instead, Blacks at work on plantations or in
industry developed new aspects of culture: language,
musical and other artistic expression; American
Black heroes; literary and historical continuities.
Central to all this were aspirations for improved
economic, political, and social standing.

Education and Identity
      In fact, it was in the struggle for such true
participation in the overall culture of the American
society that Blacks gained what might be called a
new essence of Black culture: that of mutual self
identity in the struggle for equality. The
perception by Blacks that they have a total and
dynamic culture has stimulated and enhanced their
efforts to gain more opportunity and status within
the American social condition. Where once it was
conceived as proper that Black children should
attend school in facilities that were like those for
Whites, yet specifically separated, the Brown
decision [6] has brought change. The battle for
desegregation meant that the deliberate
establishment of separate school and other public
facilities for Blacks was nullified.
      Beyond that battle was the one for integration.
This meant that since Black children could not be
isolated within Black-only situations, they must
further be placed into Black-and-White classes and
schools where the numbers did not once more reach a
condition of apparent segregation. The Congress and
recent administrations supported both the
desegregation and the integration of black children
by establishing that children could be transported
by bus across ethnic 'divides' to avoid segregation
in specific schools and school districts. For the
most part where 'bussing' occured, it was the black
children who were transported rather than the white.
This came about due to several factors which
prevailed in the most populous cities. In
particular, White flight from public schools to
private ones left few white children in some
communities who could be transported into Black
neighbourhoods. However, the overwhelming numbers
of black children in the inner cities could not be
placed on buses, or otherwise exchanged with equal
numbers of white children so as to achieve
integration in white or black segregated schools.
Black parents in some ghetto areas objected to
having their children travel away from their
communities. They asked that the funds so expended

291

be spent on improving the segregated Black schools they knew. Thus Black control of their community schools has been a frequent and increasing demand by Blacks.

The minority of black children who did leave their home neighbourhoods met with their age peers in integrated schools. This development did not necessarily enhance black cultural identity, but it provided for black children to be educated with white children, by white teachers, in school environments that were generally of better quality than those in Black neighbourhoods. Not surprisingly there were some murmurings regarding the assumption that black children could only learn well if taught by white teachers in the presence of white children, and away from their home neighbourhoods. There were complaints by equally qualified black teachers who felt that their abilities, qualities, and dedications were being disregarded, indeed denigrated. [7] Furthermore, some parents did not want their children to travel for schooling in this way, since it was not entirely clear that their education was significantly improved in the integrated school, if at all.

Nonetheless, for many Blacks so affected the education of their children together with Whites represented more opportunity for advancement and social mobility. It was also noted that white children could benefit from attending school with children of another culture, of different backgrounds, and with different life experiences. [8] These benefits to white (and black) children are described more often than objectively validated. The establishment of 'magnet' schools which all children may attend by choice has tended to offer integrated situations based upon a special curricular focus such as science, the arts or technology.

An additional contention was that with Black children attending integrated schools, the contents of the curriculum should also provide for their own improved self image, their better understanding of their origins, and their opportunities for self-expression in their own unique ways. Without special efforts these images would be lost in the integrated schools. Thus, Black history with its acknowledgement of the evils of slavery, and of the slave owners, was introduced. Much study and research was needed to bring this into the school curriculum. Books, pictures, and special displays were prepared for use in the schools. White

teachers had to re-learn their history of the United
States and discover that Blacks hardly figured in
their existing texts, indeed one would suppose that
Blacks had been non-existent in American history for
generations!

While Black Studies at the post-secondary level
has been a new curricular area, it is in the lower
schools that Black heroes, folk tales, music, and
other images of strength are incorporated into
social studies materials and language arts
activities. There are supportive teachers' guides
on these themes. This particular area of curriculum
development stems from the 1973 Ethnic Heritage
Studies Amendment to the Elementary and Secondary
Education Act, and is a good example of the
legislative approach to positive discrimination
favoured in the USA. It also illustrates an aspect
of federal government involvement in this field.

Attention was paid as well to what many Blacks
considered to be an important cultural resource,
namely the language of their ancestors in Africa.
Thus Swahili was brought into some schools, though
with little success, despite considerable effort in
the preparation of texts and other teaching
materials. It is not a West African language, but
regardless of this the acknowledgement of an African
language for American Blacks was for a time a part
of the overall concept of 'Black Cultural Identity'.
Of somewhat greater impact for Blacks was the
recognition that black children in the ghetto tended
to speak a variety of English that was unique. Some
linguists and academics argued that Black English
was a viable language and should be given
appropriate time and attention in the schools. [9]
This argument brought with it problems of too few
trained, knowledgeable teachers of the language as
well as the concerns of educators that Black English
would displace standard English in the experience of
black children. There were fears that Black English
would become a bilingual issue, over which general
area considerable disagreement already exists, [10]
for example in respect of Hispanic Americans.

The increased attention given to Black cultural
interests in American education brought more than
new language and history into the curriculum. It
focussed attention also on the literary and artistic
works of creative Black Americans past and present,
thus bringing forth not only appreciation and
understanding, but seeding the development of new
efforts by American Black poets, dramatists,
musicians, and other artists. Such works were often

created to represent Black issues and brought a
further strengthening of Black self-perception and
esteem. [11]

The growth of 'Black Cultural Identity' was
accompanied by a parallel development of political,
economic, and social opportunity for all Americans.
The legislation and court decisions that have
proceeded into implementation since the Brown
decision, have underlined new perceptions of human
rights, economic fairness, and societal
obligations. [12] Attention was particularly paid to
the needs of all ethnic groups for recognition and
enhancement. While Whites were considered to be
already generally favoured, ethnic minorities were
to be clearly identified, counted, and provided with
affirmative support as a means of righting the
wrongs which had been done them throughout the
history of the United States. [13]

Throughout the great portion of Black history
and experience in the United States, educational
policies may be said to have been structured so as
to minimalize the involvement of Blacks. When
special efforts were undertaken for elementary and
secondary schooling, these activities tended to be
restricted to those states and regions with small
Black populations of long standing. In the tertiary
sector too, education in the several Black colleges
and universities since the late nineteenth century
which often served as important steppingstones for
some upward mobility of Blacks was rare. Indeed,
such mobility was further limited to those few
Blacks entering the 'genteel' professions: teaching
and the ministry.

The policies of the more traditional states did
not distinguish Blacks from any others, either in
their conceptualization as policy or in their
implementation in statutes. Thus the 'invisibility'
of black Americans was ensured until the major court
decisions required change. [14] Nevertheless it must
be said that under precisely such conditions, with
well nigh minimal expressions of policy, this kind
of 'neglect' of Black educational opportunity
allowed some Blacks in several states to finish
secondary school, participate in the professional
development offered in post-secondary education, and
join the Black middle class. [15] From 1865 onwards,
Negro institutions of higher learning were
established in seventeen southern states, under the
Morrill Land Grant Act.

However, the most favourable conditions were
clearly in the northeastern and mid-western states,

where neither demography nor former conditions of servitude hindered Blacks from entering the common school and experiencing individual success. In 1900 the New York State legislature enacted a law providing that no one should be denied admittance to any public school on account of race, colour, or previous condition of servitude. A similar Massachusetts statute dated from as early as 1855.

The Impacts of Policy Change

Educational policy in the United States made a spectacular turn with the advent and conclusion of the Second World War, impacting profoundly upon Blacks, Whites, and national institutions alike. The enactment of the 'GI Bill of Rights' offered hitherto unknown opportunities to Blacks and Whites who, though often having served in segregated units, found convergence in their common post-war interests. [16] This legislation opened up schools and universities that were high-cost and even exclusive. For underprepared ex-servicemen assistance in the preparation of entry-level skills was provided. Extensive job benefits and opportunities also followed.

With further legislation and court decisions responsive to developing needs in American society, [17] a succession of events affected educational policy so as to impinge upon all ethnic elements, including Blacks. Court decisions with regard to desegregation and integration of school children eventually reached out toward the need to respond to conditions in society which went beyond the provision of education. Thus the concept of affirmative action was born and written into law with regard to education, job rights, housing opportunities, and the various aspects of participation in the human affairs of the nation. [18] Associated with affirmative action was the need to offer some form of compensation for the effects of slavery, post-slavery poverty, and the conditions of alienation prevalent in Black communities. Blacks received opportunities to come 'to the front of the line', ahead of numerous others, since they had for so many generations been 'at the back of the bus'.

The effectiveness of judicial determinations with regard to affirmative action now provided many more Black youths with admissions to professional schools and a pathway toward social and economic mobility. The objections of other youths who may have been passed over were seen as having little

force of argument in the contentions which made
affirmative action necesssary.

It was in the self-conscious feelings of
achievement; of the openings of previously closed
doors; of an inherent strength that had previously
been only hinted at, that the concept of Black Power
was fostered and given form. Black Power meant the
demands and rights of Blacks to be more than just
those of another underprivileged class. [19] It
meant being provided with opportunities identical to
those of other identifiable groups in the United
States; it meant being reckoned with socially and,
of course, politically. So new educational policies
that expanded to include 'Black Studies' at all
levels of the curriculum, brought into the schools
the history and needs of the past as well as the
demands and pressures of the present. 'Open
Admissions' policies meant that all applicants of a
certain age could attend post-secondary educational
institutions regardless of current academic
standing. [20] The success of 'Open Admissions' as a
means of opening previously closed doors to
education, expanded Black, as well as other ethnic
enrolments in higher education. It stimulated the
extension of the various curricula to include ethnic
studies, and struck fear in the hearts of ensconced
academics whose grading and evaluation practices
were out of touch with the new students now being
enrolled. Black Power that brought students into
post-secondary education also brought Black
personnel into employment. Though some Blacks were
introduced as teaching faculty members, most entered
as counsellors, advisers, in effect special human
resources for Black students and for Black ethnic
curricula.

Demands were necessarily also made for the
improvement of education for Blacks in the secondary
and elementary levels. With attention focussed upon
generally low achievement of Blacks in higher
education, the lower schools must be improved for
the benefit of on-coming age groups, since
otherwise, the advantages of open admissions, of
Black-oriented curricula and of increased numbers of
personnel in schools at any level, would be a matter
of temporary value, good only for a few Black
citizens, but with no lasting effect.

There has been a cumulative series of
'recognitions' of Black standing in American culture
concurrent with the activities of the current
national presidential administration seeking
reelection. Many of these have been outside the

immediate purview of educational policy, focussing
on civil rights in general, job and seniority
rights, cultural distinctions in the arts, and
extending the opportunities for participating in the
economy. While educational policies are not
directly affected, the definition and implementation
of Black opportunities in a number of situations
have had their horizontal impacts on education as
well. This is a measure of increased Black ethnic
standing in the community at large.

Major efforts to increase the registration of
eligible Blacks as voters have brought in young
activists as participants in the task. High school
and college students have accumulated 'field
experience' in civics and sociology as one by-
product of their active involvement. They have
indeed been educated in communicating with the
community, in recognizing the volatile touchpoints
in Black areas and in White ones, in discovering the
competitive rise of other ethnics engaged in similar
campaigns. [21] Suffice it to say that ethnic
minorities, or majorities, often view with some
alarm the increasing numbers of eligible voters
among other ethnic groups! The relatively recent
cases of Black mayors being elected in major cities,
such as Atlanta, Chicago, Newark and Cleveland, may
be indicative. Yet Blacks acknowledge that such
successes in politics would not have been possible
without the active, positive engagement of Jews and
other 'White ethnics'. This connection represents a
historic support for civil rights expansion,
particularly for Black rights, which had tended to
become corroded and somewhat unsure in recent
years. [22]

Another major recognition for Blacks and for
the enhancement of Black Cultural Identity has been
the acceptance and overwhelming absorption of the
elements of Black-based art, particularly music,
into the American culture. Music, dance and drama
have each received new infusions of the long-
standing concepts of Black culture. [23] They are of
long-standing because Black expression has come from
the days of slavery, rising from Black labour in the
fields, Black worship with music and ritual movement
in the churches, Black labour in the mills, on the
rivers, and in services, all appearing as 'private',
unique, and a source of curiosity for the white
population, regardless of the latter's own
ethnicity.

Post-bellum and continuing into the present,
Black ghettos have attracted curious onlookers and,

paradoxically, well-wishers, would-be participants, and enthusiastic imitators. Thus today, though radio and television commercials may not always have Black performers, musical and linguistic observers have noted the Black cultural derivation of even this form of expression. [24] The same may be said of Black music, once jazz but not so any longer, and 'music video', the most widely acclaimed performances in current experience. Again, it would be difficult to relate these developments in American culture to specific educational policy. However, observations in schools at almost any level will verify that the music taught there no longer rests on Mendelssohn, Stephen Foster, and the "old Kentucky home"!

Nor is it entirely facetious to note that in such nationally popular sports as baseball, football, basketball and athletics, the Black presence as 'stars' far outweighs their proportion in the total population who watch the games. In this regard, educational policy in the provision of physical education and recreation offers a powerful underpinning for Black identity. Schools are the original sites of black children's acquisition of these skills for personal accomplishment and group recognition. It is in the secondary schools that universities find, cajole, solicit, and bribe the young often Black, athletes to enter the halls of academe as a means of escaping the perilous pathways of ghetto life and indeed as a means of bringing glory to the Alma Mater through their prowess and special abilities. Within this ever more selective process, Blacks in high schools become candidates ready for training for athletic fame in higher education. Admitted in large numbers, smaller numbers participate sufficiently to be visible to the ultimate authority, the main stage upon which Black athletes can establish themselves for life: the professional world of sports and entertainment. [25]

Thus, the educational policy of open admissions, with special attention to those with weak qualifications lends basic support to Blacks who wish to pursue academic careers. It is in the arena of athletics that such opportunities are often visibly pursued. There is the notorious instance of the Black athlete at a major university who, upon his commission of a felony, was discovered to be in a state of illiteracy. [26]

A recognition of considerable importance to Black identity, primarily in school contexts, is the

enactment of 'Black History Week' (or Month) in
several states. In these circumstances, recognition
of Black status in as many facets as possible has
become frequent in the school curriculum: arts,
history, heroes, social problems and current needs
are underscored with the use of newly developed
teaching materials. The effective dissemination of
Black history information depends not only upon the
variety and quality of such materials, but upon the
motivation and preparation of individual teachers
and school officials. Thus, although the instances
of school policy where Black history is incorporated
within the curriculum are becoming more numerous,
there are variations in the actual relevance of the
activities themselves. What might be legislated by
local education authorities to an on-going, all year
round consideration of the Black condition in
American culture often becomes but an annual pause
to remember, as fleeting as St. Valentine's day and
as profound as Halloween.

    Yet, one cannot remain unimpressed by the very
existence of such programmes and activities, aimed
at enhancing Black self-identity and at sharing the
essence of ethnicity in America with all elements in
the population. The establishment of a national
observance on January 16 each year for the birthday
of the assassinated Reverend Martin Luther King,
Jr., is in itself a most remarkable development,
since no other American hero has been so honoured.
It does reflect upon the strength of Blacks as a
community within the total American entity. It also
expresses the sense of common adherence of all in
that entity to the principles and ideals espoused by
Dr. King. It remains for the citizenry as a whole
to choose to experience the holiday in its most
profound sense, or merely to find it a convenient
day to attach to a free week-end as is the case with
other public holidays.

    Of perhaps lesser value in the establishment of
Black identity in America may be the designation and
successful participation of a Black in American
space efforts. While the ethnic derivations of
other astronauts have not been noted though the sex
of one has been, the ethnicity of Astronaut
Bluford [27] has indeed been brought to the fore,
particularly during the actual flight, though since
that time there have been few notices in the media.

    The presence of a Black presidential candidate
in the 1984 campaign has been a serious
preoccupation of the media and of students of
political phenomena in the United States. The

Democratic Party, opposing an incumbent Republican president, was faced with the interesting dilemma of encouraging the full participation of Blacks in the election process and at the same time acknowledging almost overtly that a Black candidate would have no place on the Democratic ticket. The Reverend Jesse Jackson as an articulate, attractive campaigner further complicated the situation. Nevertheless, that he has taken his candidacy so seriously as to take vehement stands on specific, not necessarily Black-oriented issues, may have meant that he was not truly a candidate, but testing the waters, experiencing the power of the media, assembling and forming up alliances, and amassing the attention of politicians and ordinary citizens alike. [28] The presence of such a phenomenon on the political scene, is not directly traceable to educational policy. Nonetheless, the interests of all voters in finding a congenial candidate may have given to Blacks the impetus toward registration as voters in far greater numbers than they have hitherto, as well as providing a stimulus for achieving higher goals.

Looking Forward

The continuity of a relationship between educational policy and 'Black Cultural Identity' may have reached a plateau. The early momentum of the Johnson and Nixon administrations has produced significant Black progress in the political sphere. Progress in the social area has been subtle and long-established, but it has only been in the last twenty years that ethnic powers have been yielded to Blacks in educational institutions and their processes. Thus the recognition of Black identity and the sharing of that identity through integration in schools has become overt and a matter of policy.

The plateau was further emphasized with the reduction by the Reagan administration of Federal funds for programmes which formerly supported special activities in poverty, particularly Black, areas. The assignment of such funds, in lesser amounts, as block grants to the states permits a greater variety of allocation and may include considerably more division among clamouring groups in each state. In any case it has always been a feature of Federal grants to local educational initiatives that they have largely gone to already comfortable districts and schools. This is because of the fact that such places have been more aware of the mechanisms for application and have, to a greater extent than their poorer neighbours, the

300

expertise necessary to formulate a potentially successful proposal. This is not to say of course that there have not been important initiatives in some Black school districts that have been Federally funded. But it is doubtful that future allocations will return to the levels and for the type of programmes previously carried out: States will therefore require fewer employees to administer and implement Black-focussed activities. A momentum may be created, with the lessening of support in schools, in the aspects of public housing, and in the protection of families with working mothers and dependent children.

With Rev. Jackson's somewhat grander entry onto the national political stage than American Whites, and other ethnics had previously witnessed, the effect of the 1984 campaigns did go some way to clarify the role of Black candidates for high national office; for there has been no Black senator in recent years. The difficulties that still remain for American Blacks may be compounded by the growing populations of Commonwealth West Indian Blacks, of Haitians, of immigrants from Southeast Asia, and of Hispanics. Questions of pluralism may become more in need of attention along with the possibilities of coalitions of non-Anglo ethnic groups for the purpose of achieving power in the educational context as elsewhere. For American Blacks, traditionally associated with White liberals, Jews, and Democratic party builders, the struggle for attention and power may be disruptive of previously successful efforts. In reaching toward the political spotlight, some Blacks, notably the Rev. Jackson, have attempted to establish a commonality of interest with third world issues which may in fact be ultimately irrelevant to realistic concerns of American Blacks. Indeed, Black identification with such international issues may further diffuse the efforts to achieve ethnic parity in the United States. The assumption that there is a commonality of interests and of history, enslavement, and tradition with Arabs, Filipinos, Black Africans, Salvadorans, and the populations of South African Bantustans is, to say the least, speculative in respect of popular support in America. It may, indeed, place American Blacks in the position of affiliates with many who are in themselves without a democratic experience or tradition. The espousal of such causes as 'Black Causes' is likely to mislead American Blacks and their allies into byroads which may prove deceptive and ultimately spurious.

The needs of American Blacks for education, housing, economic, social, and political achievement are unique, being based upon the Black experience in the American Commonwealth and in no other. Looking forward, then, is a task of sober consideration for all concerned. The problems which remain have been identified; they have even been to some extent shifted, reduced, and diminished if not subjugated. To move forward toward their complete resolution calls for the realistic assessment of the identity and status of all ethnic groups, of every ethnicity, and for the realization that the answers may lie less in the grasping for exclusive power and more in its sharing. Educational policy at all levels of the American system will have as significant an effect on the outcome of the next phase of Black development as it clearly has had at important stages in the past.

Notes and References

1. Lieberson, Stanley. A Piece of the Pie: Black and White Immigrants Since 1880. Berkeley: University of California Press, 1980.
2. Steinberg, Stephen. The Ethnic Myth. New York: Atheneum, 1981.
3. Killian, Lewis M. The Impossible Revolution. Washington: University Press of America, 1975;
Also Morgan, Gordon D. America Without Ethnicity. Port Washington, NY: Kennikat Press, 1981.
4. Silberman, Charles E. Crisis in Black and White. Random House, 1964.
5. Goldstein, Rhoda L., ed. Black Life and Culture in the United States. Thomas Y. Crowell, 1971.
6. United States Supreme Court, Brown v Board of Education (1954).
7. Morgan, G.D., op cit.
8. Besag, Frank P. and Nelson, J.L. The Foundations of Education: Stasis and Change. Random House, 1984.
9. Vansertima, Ivan, African Linguistic and Mythological Structure in the New World. In: Goldstein, op cit.
10. ibid.
11. Goldstein, R.L. op cit. See Chapters 4, 10, 17, 18, 19.
12. ibid.
13. Steinberg, S., op cit.
14. ibid.

15. Ploski, Harry A., ed. <u>The Negro Almanac.</u> New York: Bellwether Co., 1971.

16. <u>The Servicemen's Readjustment Act</u> popularly known as the 'G.I. Bill of Rights' provided benefits to those who served in the armed forces of the United States, and became law in 1944.

17. Besag, F.P. and Nelson J.L., op cit.

18. United States Supreme Court, <u>Regents of the University of California v Bakke</u> (1978). In this controversial case, the Court agreed that Bakke, a White American, had suffered discrimination because of his race, but stated nonetheless that race could be taken into account in university admissions.

19. Killian, L.M., op cit, enlarges the substance of a definition of Black Power and extends it to reflect an assumption of strength that is both <u>new</u> and <u>black.</u> Killian describes the rise of the slogan as having numerous contexts: "political, economic; violent, non-violent; loving, hostile ..."

20. 'Open Admissions' became a policy at major institutions of higher education around 1970, when students (of all ethnic groups) would be admitted and then where necessary assigned to remedial courses and centres. They would be required to show achievement in literacy and numeracy before being enrolled in college or university classes.

21. Steinberg, S., op cit.

22. ibid.

23. Goldstein, R.L., op cit.

24. ibid.

25. The national adulation in respect of the performances of Carl Lewis in the 1984 Los Angeles Olympics is a recent example of this, to say nothing of the incredibly lucrative contracts that were specifically dependent on the winning of Gold medals by this athlete and others. It is an interesting example of the re-assertion of the competitive ethic, after the stage of positive discrimination has played its part.

26. This was the case of a football player who was enrolled at a branch of the University of California.

27. Guion S. Bluford was a member of the American space mission launched on August 30, 1983.

28. Reverend Jesse Jackson maintained his candidacy vigorously through to the convention where, though unsuccessful, he was widely acclaimed to have made not only the best address, but also the most unifying address in respect of the multiethnic nature of Democratic support and the American population in general.

COLONIALS SUBORDINATES, OR SUPERORDINATES: PUERTO RICANS AND EDUCATIONAL POLICY ON THE UNITED STATES MAINLAND

Elizabeth Sherman Swing

Introduction
        As R.A. Schermerhorn has shown, [1] peaceful social integration may involve both centripetal and centrifugal trends: at one extreme, assimilation of minorities; at the other the existence of mutually tolerated communities in a pluralist society or even of separatist enclaves. Puerto Ricans in the United States exist at all points on this spectrum, although the question posed by their activists is whether even peaceful coexistence will suffice. Hispanics in an English language world, colonials in a democracy, American citizens with the status of immigrants, they are marked by language, by the indefiniteness of racial designation, and by an energy which has already transformed the educational structure of the cities in which they are clustered. Willing gadflies, they are far from satisfied with a subordinate role. Indeed, the designation of roles is a matter Puerto Rican activists will not leave to Anglos.

The Basis of Power on the Mainland
        Unlike immigrants who have left a distant land or who for legal or political reasons cannot easily return home, Puerto Ricans are American citizens, internal migrants who can travel without restriction between island and continent in a matter of hours. Many make the trip every year - a reality well known to teachers and administrators of schools in Puerto Rican neighbourhoods on the mainland where the turnover of students in a single academic year may approach one hundred per cent. [2] This "circularly migrating labour force and community" [3] actually live in two worlds, one English, the other Spanish. It is not possible to understand the pragmatic design of the educational programmes Puerto Ricans

304

are likely to champion without reference to this fact.

The emergence of large settlements of Puerto Ricans on the mainland of the United States is a post World War Two phenomenon, [4] an analogue to the accelerated arrival of Mexican 'wetbacks' in the southwest of the United States, of 'guest workers' in European Economic Community countries or New Commonwealth immigrants in Great Britain during the same era. There were, of course, Puerto Ricans in the United States much earlier: in the nineteenth century, small groups of middle class political activists in New York whose concern was to end Spanish rule; in the early years of the twentieth century, migrant workers in isolated settlements, which in the years prior to World War Two gave way to fast growing urban communities. After World War Two, however, mass exodus from a poor, overpopulated island to the booming economy of an industrialized nation in need of workers began in earnest. The Puerto Rican component of this mainland labour force became increasingly clustered into a number of cities, especially New York, and despite the recession of the 1970s had by 1980 reached a total of 2,013,945. [Table 1 (b)]

That these two million Puerto Ricans have managed to make their voice clearly audible amid competing voices in a nation of over 226 million reflects considerable political and organizational talent. It also reflects their membership in a much larger, equally strident identity group. Hispanics in the United States now number 14,608,673 [Table 2], by far the largest linguistic minority. They are well organized, youthful – a median age of 23.8 in contrast with a national median of 31.2, and energetic, especially in matters pertaining to the education of Spanish-speaking children. And their ranks continue to grow. Their communities are constantly being replenished by immigrants, both legal and illegal, from Central and South America. Even more important, Hispanics have the highest fertility rate in the nation: 106.6 live births for one thousand women between eighteen and forty-four years of age in comparison with a national average of 71.1, and the white and black rates of 68.5 and 84.0 respectively. [5] The fact of membership in this fast-growing ethnolinguistic community provides Puerto Ricans, even though they are outnumbered by other Hispanics seven to one, with a seven-fold leverage.

Another factor contributes to the visibility of

Table 1

(a) Persons of Puerto Rican Birth in the Continental
United States 1910-1940

1910	1920	1930	1940
1,513	11,811	52,774	69,967

Source: United States Department of Commerce, Bureau
of the Census. United States Census of Population:
1950. Special Reports. Puerto Ricans in
Continental United States. Report P-E no. 3D,
Preprint of Volume IV, Part 3, Chapter D.
Washington: United States Government Printing
Office, 1953. 1970 Census of Population. Subject
Reports. Puerto Ricans in the United States.
PC(2)-IE. June 1973.

(b) Persons of Puerto Rican Birth and Parentage in
the Continental United States 1950-1980

1950	1960	1970	1980
301,375	892,513	1,391,463	2,013,945

Source: United States Department of Commerce, Bureau
of the Census. 1970 Census of Population. Subject
Reports. Puerto Ricans in the United States.
PC(2)-I.E. Washington: United States Government
Printing Office, June 1973. 1980 Census of
Population, V.I., Characteristics of the Population,
Chapter B, General Population Characteristics, PC80-
I-BI. May 1983.

Puerto Ricans. Puerto Ricans and persons of Puerto
Rican origin, have clustered in urban areas easily
serviced by charter jets from San Juan. The main
concentrations are listed in Table 3. Although
about 50,000 have ventured to the Los Angeles, Long
Beach, Anaheim area of California, this is the only
sizeable Puerto Rican group east of the Mississippi,
though a number now live in midwestern industrial
cities. The majority are concentrated on the
eastern seaboard: in New York, New Jersey,
Pennsylvania, Connecticut, Massachusetts, and
Florida [Table 4]. Puerto Ricans may in fact be an
'invisible minority' among Cubans in Miami, [6] or
among Mexicans in Hispanic communities in the
Midwest and Pacific regions, but in the Middle
Atlantic and New England area they outnumber all
other Hispanics combined [Table 5].

Puerto Rican USA

Table 2

Spanish Origin Persons in the United States: 1980

U.S.A. Totals	Spanish Origin Totals	Puerto Rican	Mexican	Cuban	Other
Population					
226545805	14608673	2013945	8740439	903226	3051063
Median Age					
31.2	23.8	23.3	22.1	39.1	26.6

Source: United States Department of Commerce, Bureau of the Census. 1980 Census of Population. V.1, Characteristics of the Population. Chapter B, General Population Characteristics. United States Summary PC80-1-B1. Table 48. Washington: United States Government Printing Office, May 1983.

Table 3

Concentrations of Puerto Ricans and Persons of Puerto Rican Origin in the United States 1980

New York-Newark-Jersey City (NY-NJ-Conn.)	1,129,211
Chicago-Gary (Ill.-Ind.-Wis.)	136,885
Philadelphia-Wilmington-Trenton (Penn.-NJ-MD)	91,768
Miami-Fort Lauderdale (Fla)	53,836
Los Angeles-Long Beach-Anaheim (Calif.)	48,521
Boston-Lawrence-Lowell (Mass-N.H.)	41,222

Source: United States Department of Commerce, Bureau of the Census. 1980 Census of Population, V.1, Characteristics of the Population, Chapter B, General Population Characteristics. Washington: United States Government Printing Office, May 1983.

Table 4

Persons of Puerto Rican Origin in
Selected States by Rank 1980

State	Rank	Number	Percent Distribution
United States		2,013,945	100.0
New York	1	986,389	49.0
New Jersey	2	243,540	12.1
Illinois	3	129,165	6.4
Florida	4	94,775	4.7
California	5	93,038	4.6
Pennsylvania	6	91,802	4.6
Connecticut	7	88,361	4.4
Massachusetts	8	76,450	3.8

Source: United States Department of Commerce, Bureau
of the Census. Census of Population. Supplementary
Report. Persons of Spanish Origin by State: 1980.
Table 8. Washington: United States Government
Printing Office, 1982.

    That Puerto Ricans are a dominant Hispanic
voice in their barrios in Spanish Harlem, Jersey
City, Newark, Hartford, Boston, and Philadelphia has
another significance. In these northeastern cities,
which have known wave after wave of ethnic power
brokers: Irish, Italian, Jews, [7] Puerto Ricans
have had ample opportunity to observe urban power
politics at first hand. Many, moreover, came of
political age participating in registration drives
and federal programmes during the 1960s. [8] For
redress of their very real grievances - 37.7 per
cent of Hispanics in the northeast live below the
poverty line; only 40.9 per cent of Puerto Ricans
have completed four years of high school or more,
[Tables 6 and 7], they have now begun to make
application of lessons learned. Schools are clearly
a major political issue, but the restructuring of
more than schools is at stake.
    To understand the urgency of what is at stake
requires historical perspective. Puerto Ricans,
like others involved in the bilingual education
movement, have focussed on the politics of language,
on the inadequacy of an English language curriculum
to meet the needs of non-Anglophone children. Like

Table 5

Ranking of Puerto Rican Population by Region
in Comparison With Other Hispanics, 1980

	Type of Hispanic Origin (in thousands)			
REGION	Puerto Rican	Mexican	Cuban	Other
1. Middle Atlantic	1322	71	163	749
2. East North Central	197	673	29	169
3. New England	172	17	13	97
4. South Atlantic	140	200	493	361
5. Pacific	120	3777	64	850
6. West South Central	31	2831	24	275
7. Mountain	14	959	7	463
8. West North Central	9	148	4	48
9. East South Central	9	66	5	40
Total: 14,609	2014	8740	803	3051

Source: United States Department of Commerce, Bureau of the Census. Statistical Abstract of the United States, 1982-1983, Table 39. Washington: United States Government Printing Office, December 1982.

Table 6

Characteristics of Hispanics and Others (Per Cent)

	All	White	Black	Spanish Origin
Below Poverty Line: (1981)				
U.S.A.	14.0	11.1	34.2	26.5
Northeast	11.9	9.5	33.2	37.7
Four Years of High School or More (1981)	69.7	71.6	51.2	44.5

Source: United States Department of Commerce, Bureau of the Census. Statistical Abstract of the United States, 1982-1983, Tables 224 and 729. Washington: United States Government Printing Office, 1982.

Table 7

Years of School, 1970 to 1981
Whites, Blacks and Hispanics
in the United States

	1970	1975	1980	1981
	Less Than Five Years of School (Per Cent)			
ALL	5.5	4.2	3.4	3.2
White	4.5	3.3	2.6	2.6
Black	14.6	12.3	9.2	7.9
Hispanic	19.5	18.5	15.8	15.6
Mexican	28.5	24.6	20.9	21.0
Puerto Rican	20.5	7.4	15.0	13.1
Cuban	8.2	7.3	5.7	5.3
Other	8.8	7.6	6.4	6.8
	Four Years of High School or More (Per Cent)			
ALL	52.3	62.5	68.6	69.7
White	54.5	64.5	70.5	71.6
Black	31.4	42.5	51.2	52.9
Hispanic	32.1	37.9	45.5	44.5
Mexican	24.2	31.0	38.9	39.3
Puerto Rican	23.4	28.7	38.3	40.9
Cuban	43.9	51.7	54.0	48.1
Other	44.9	58.0	60.2	58.9

Source: United States Department of Commerce, Bureau of the Census. Statistical Abstract of the United States, 1982-1983, Table 224. Washington: United States Government Printing Office, 1982.

other newcomers from the Caribbean, they have also shown considerable resistance to assimilation. [9] Puerto Ricans, however, have particular reasons for asserting their cultural identity. Not only are they American citizens, they are citizens with an ambiguous status as the "longest colonized people in the Western Hemisphere." [10] Reconciliation between educational policies on the mainland and the legacy of their colonial past shapes much of their political agenda.

The Colonial Legacy
    Puerto Rico became a colony of the United
States in 1898, a fruit of victory in the Spanish
American War. It has had an ambiguous status ever
since. Although the Organic Act of 1917 granted
American citizenship to Puerto Ricans, and the
Commonwealth Constitution of 1952 provided for a
degree of legislative autonomy, [11] in most matters
the Island has less power than states of the Union.
It is neither a territory, nor a state, and
certainly not an independent nation. Continued
Commonwealth status, statehood, and independence
represent hotly debated political positions.
    Whether Puerto Rico was technically a colony or
not, during the first half of the twentieth century
the United States promoted policies on this
Caribbean island which were virtually
indistinguishable from what Altbach and Kelly have
referred to as classical educational
colonialism. [12] This can be exemplified by the
organization of an American school system in 1899 by
Dr. Victor Clark in which English was to be the
medium of instruction because only through use of
English would it be possible to inculcate
'democratic ideas'. [13] Although Clark soon
retreated to acceptance of a modified bilingual
programme which would teach standard Spanish as an
alternative to the mother tongue patois of his
students (another prescriptive linguistic posture),
subsequent Commissioners of Education reverted to
Clark's initial programme, thus thrusting the issue
of the language of education to centre stage.
    Policies thereafter alternated between
prescriptive use of English in the schools and
reluctant acceptance of a bilingual pattern. [14]
From 1900 to 1905, Spanish was the medium of
instruction in elementary schools, English the
language of secondary schools. From 1905 to 1916 an
attempt to make English the sole language of
instruction and to force native teachers to learn
English was so unpopular that it gave impetus to the
movement for Puerto Rican independence and to a
reorganization of school curricula. From 1916 to
1934 elementary schools adopted a transitional
bilingual programme: use of Spanish as a language of
instruction for the first four years, of both
Spanish and English in the fifth year, transition to
English thereafter. By 1934, however, Spanish once
again had become the sole medium of instruction in
grades one to eight, although English continued as
the language of secondary schools.

Another swing of the pendulum occurred in 1937 when President Roosevelt, concerned over the number of Puerto Ricans who knew no English, appointed Jose Gallardo as Commissioner for Education, charging him to educate for bilingualism. Gallardo experimented with several schemes, including use of Spanish as a language of instruction in the early grades and of both Spanish and English in secondary schools. These policies, however, satisfied neither the Secretary of the Interior, Harold L. Ickes, to whom critics charged that there was not enough English, nor Puerto Rican Nationalists, who interpreted Gallardo's reforms as intrusive Americanization. Language of education had become an explosive political issue. By 1948 when Puerto Rico gained the right to elect its own governor, transition to full-time use of Spanish was already underway. By the time Puerto Rico attained Commonwealth status in 1952, Spanish had become the language of instruction in elementary and secondary schools, and even in the University of Puerto Rico at Rio Pedras.

Thus, the outcome of a half century of educational colonialism in Puerto Rico has been an ironic reversal: the establishment in this outlying area of the United States of monolingual linguistic policies similar to those found in Belgium and Quebec, sites of major language maintenance movements. [15] Indeed, the only way that Anglophones living on the island can now obtain an English language education for their children is to enrol them in private schools. That Title VII funds, [16] the same federal monies used on the mainland to fund bilingual programmes for Puerto Rican children, are also available in Puerto Rico to fund programmes that will provide transitional bilingual education for these Anglophones dramatizes the paradox in this reversal but does not change it. Even so, Puerto Rican activists are concerned that those who return from the United States will carry the 'contagion of English back to the island.' [17] Memories of the era of educational colonialism are very much alive.

The Language of Education on the Mainland

The triumph of monolingual territoriality in Puerto Rico at a time when mass migration to the mainland was just beginning has had consequences for mainland schools over and above the obvious consequence of the need to accommodate large numbers of monolingual Hispanic children. Puerto Rican language loyalists have shown themselves far from willing to abandon hard-won linguistic gains just because they have left the Caribbean. That an English based curriculum should deny their children opportunity to learn in the mother tongue, the official language of schools run by the United States government in their homeland, is an indignity to be borne with increasing impatience. That activists have not yet pushed this issue to the top of their public agenda is, however, a measure of their political astuteness. [18] Language maintenance may be a covert issue, but it is an issue nevertheless.

The United States has had a long tradition of bilingualism in education: three centuries of church related private schools, even German-language public schools in some parts of the country prior to World War One. [19] But the dominant ethos in the twentieth century prior to the emergence of the bilingual education movement in the late 1960s was assimilationist, the incorporation of immigrants into an English language world. By the time Puerto Ricans became a significant force in mainland schools, a number of states had even made it illegal, except in the modern language classroom, to use a language of instruction other than English. It is hardly surprising that J. Osuna's report in 1948 of a visit to New York City schools enrolling Puerto Rican children stresses the need to improve techniques for teaching English rather than a concern over preservation of Puerto Rican language and culture. [20] In the early years, learning English was the major concern.

Puerto Ricans began to challenge this assimilationist ethos long before bilingual education became a political issue. Sporadic experimentation with occasional bilingual programmes took place throughout the 1950s and early 1960s, particularly in New York City where most Puerto Ricans were concentrated. An Auxiliary Teachers' Program dates back to 1948, a school and community relations coordinator for bilingual programmes to the early 1960s. [21] There were schools using Spanish as a language of instruction for 85 per cent of the day in the 1960s in East Harlem and the Bronx. [22] These programmes, however, were voluntary, dependent on local good will, not on legislative safeguards, certainly not on legislative concern over language maintenance.

It is important to remember, moreover, that the first federal legislation affecting the language of education in schools where Puerto Rican children were enrolled, the Bilingual Education Act of 1968, Title VII of the Elementary and Secondary Education Act (ESEA), was part of President Lyndon Johnson's War on Poverty, not part of a language maintenance initiative. ESEA had already targeted funds for schools in low income areas where 'culturally deprived' children needed special assistance in learning to read. The new legislation expanded the concept of cultural deprivation by including among those entitled to benefits bilingual children of limited English proficiency from families below the so-called poverty line. As members of the poorest, least educated community in the northeastern cities in which they have settled, Puerto Ricans were a primary target of this legislation from the beginning, but not because of concern on the national level over their cultural identity.

Language maintenance did become an issue during debate over amendments to the Bilingual Education Act in 1974, the amendments which removed poverty as a requirement for participation in programmes funded by Title VII funds; but it was too explosive an issue to become an explicit legislative goal. [23] Even Lau v. Nichols, [24] the definitive Supreme Court ruling in the field of bilingual education, was not based on language maintenance concerns. Instead, it was based on a civil rights issue, the right of Chinese Americans of limited English proficiency to equal educational opportunities under Title VI of the Civil Rights Act of 1964, that is to say, the right to special instruction because of learning difficulties. The so-called Lau Remedies, formulated by the Office of Civil Rights in the wake of this case, made bilingual /bicultural education an alternative outcome. [25] But neither Lau nor the Lau Remedies were concerned with language maintenance.

That a number of Puerto Rican activists cannot reconcile a language deficit theory with their dedication to the preservation of the mother tongue is part of their ongoing struggle. [26] Bilingual education is nevertheless widely viewed as the major hope for reversing educational failure, as the key to upward mobility. [27] Programmes designed to provide cognitive development in Spanish of skills such as reading and arithmetic until the student is ready to join the English language mainstream may fall far short of language maintenance goals, but they receive strong support, as evidenced by protracted and determined litigation on behalf of bilingual education frequently pursued by Puerto

Rican action groups. [28] That this is a heartfelt issue, anyone who has witnessed spontaneous reactions of Puerto Ricans (among others) at meetings of the National Association for Bilingual Education can testify.

The Bilingual Education Dilemma

The dilemma posed by bilingual education for Puerto Ricans is not always apparent. If, however, language maintenance is indeed a covert goal, this dilemma is real. As an illustration, we may consider the ambiguities underlying the Aspira Consent Decree of 1974 in New York City, one of several legal actions brought by Puerto Rican groups in eastern cities. [29] This class action suit was brought by Aspira of New York, the Puerto Rican Legal Defence and Education Fund, and others against the Board of Education of the City of New York on behalf of 182,000 Hispanic students who knew little or no English. The issue was denial of equal educational opportunity. Specifically, the complaint charged that New York City schools had proved ineffective in educating Puerto Rican children, a charge substantiated by documentation of high drop-out rates, truancy, low stream in school, and low rate of admission to higher education. [30] Monolingual English instruction was an issue because imposition of an English language curriculum was the cause of these failures.

> Premature introduction of a second language can lead to intellectual impairment and to academic retardation that is often never overcome. [31]

The goal, however, was to force schools to compensate for these inequities, not to force the introduction of a language maintenance programme.

The programme imposed on the New York City schools in the out of court settlement announced on August 29, 1974, by Judge Marvin E. Frankel of the United States District Court, Southern District of New York, called for a transitional bilingual programme. Hispanic (or Hispanic surnamed) children

> whose English language deficiencies` prevent them from effectively participating in the learning process and who can effectively participate in Spanish [32]

would have initial reading instruction in Spanish and would use Spanish as a language of instruction in substantive areas such as mathematics, social studies, and science. But they would also have intensive instruction in speaking, understanding, reading and writing English. Use of Spanish was a temporary tool, not an end in itself. The ultimate goal was to ease Hispanic students into an Anglophone mainstream.

Despite the explicitness of this goal, the Aspira case was widely perceived as an example of "local support for ethnic language maintenance" [33] and as a special victory for the Puerto Rican community: an overdue "mechanism for social change", [34] an attainment through court action of what could not be gained through "traditional political channels", [35] a vehicle for bringing

> New teaching strategies, curriculum development, additional personnel, and most of all, community and professional spirit into the schools. [36]

Not all reaction was positive. The United Federation of Teachers (UFT) warned of the social consequences of "segregation of non-English language children into minority language streams", [37] of the danger that these children would not learn English, [38] and of the discrimination against monolingual teachers that could result from the creation of a bilingual teachers licence. The UFT correctly assessed the power conflict in which it was engaged, but even the embattled UFT saw the Consent Decree as a victory for language maintenance.

Administrators in the New York City schools, on the other hand, were less concerned about language maintenance outcomes than about the changes implied by Aspira's victory in this power conflict. They did not rush to embrace these changes. The plaintiffs have returned to Court twice since 1974, charging the Board of Education with non-compliance. [39] Indeed, officials at the Puerto Rican Legal Defense and Education Fund which now monitors the Consent Decree are certain that eligible students may still be overlooked. [40] The fact remains that Aspira has changed New York City schools. Prior to the Decree there was no widespread mechanism for ensuring special concern for Spanish dominant students with limited English skills. Aspira has supplied this mechanism.

Aspira has changed the structure of the New York schools in even more fundamental ways. To meet

the terms of the Decree, all newly registered
Hispanic, or Hispanic surnamed, students must be
tested before they are assigned to classes;
subsequently, all Aspira students must be tested
twice a year - a procedure which puts a tremendous
burden on school personnel. Spanish dominant
students found to be deficient in English must be
assigned to special classes, a procedure which can
mean reorganization of school structures. To meet
the needs of the children so assigned, schools have
had to change teacher hiring practices. In 1975
there were 728 bilingual teachers in the 32 school
districts in New York City; in 1981 there were 1709.
In 1975 there were 79 teachers of English as a
second language; in 1981 there were 188. If we add
to these figures high school bilingual and ESL
teachers, the total comes to 1886 and 295
respectively. [41] And even with these increases the
supply of bilingual teachers still falls short of
the demand, especially the demand for native
speakers of Spanish. Given the fact that bilingual
teachers now enjoy more job security than their
monolingual colleagues, it is small wonder the
United Federation of Teachers was concerned.

That the outcome of the Aspira programme has
neither fulfilled the hopes of language loyalists
nor substantiated the fears of their foes symbolizes
the bilingual education dilemma. Of the 239,386
students on the Hispanic register in July 1981, only
50,827 (21 per cent) were entitled to enrol in
Aspira classes. Only 74 per cent of the entitled
actually enrolled. When this group is augmented by
those who have 'opted into' a bilingual programme
including those enrolled only in ESL classes, the
total represents only 23 per cent of the total
number of Hispanic students. [42] It is possible
that some Spanish-dominant students with inadequate
English language skills are not identified because
of faulty testing procedures. But it is also clear
that even if the Aspira classes were designed to
produce language maintenance, they would represent a
small finger in the dyke of a language shift which
is already well underway. It is not that all the
remaining students are competent in English; but
even if they were, there are no institutional
safeguards to reinforce Spanish competency on the
part of the minority who could use such
reinforcement - and certainly no concern over long
range language maintenance goals.

If Rolf Kjolseth is right in his thesis that
bilingual education actually speeds the process of

assimilation, [43] language loyalists within the Puerto Rican community face a serious dilemma. Without bilingual education, there is no possibility of introducing Spanish as a language of instruction in mainland schools. But even with it, there is little probability of implementing long range language maintenance goals. By challenging the superordinates of the New York Public school hierarchy, bringing their suit to a successful legal conclusion and forcing administrative and personnel changes on the schools, Puerto Ricans proved their political power. But if language maintenance be the ultimate goal, they will have to find other programmes and tactics if they are to succeed. [44]

The Language Maintenance Issue

Just what language maintenance means to the Puerto Rican community is, however, shrouded in ambiguity. Spanish is needed for communication with relatives on the island and even sometimes for communication with an older generation on the mainland. But does such necessity support the widespread assumption that Spanish will survive as a primary language and as a political symbol? Tension exists between the role of Spanish, the language of personal communication, and the role of English, the language of the wider society in which Puerto Ricans would like to find a place. [45] This culture conflict impinges in unexpected ways: in the practical necessity to use an adolescent who knows English as an interpreter in a situation that undermines parental authority; [46] or in the temptation to abandon Puerto Rican naming patterns – the use of a double surname in which the name of a child's father precedes that of the mother – a practice widely misunderstood in many mainland schools.

Joshua Fishman writes of the necessity to compartmentalize languages in order to slow the process of language shift, even the occasional necessity for "a degree of physical withdrawal from establishment society." [47] There is, however, little evidence that even the most committed Puerto Rican activists seek such isolation, although it is not uncommon for adolescents, after going through an avid English phase, to rediscover their culture and language. [48] Nevertheless, outside the home, and often even within it, there exists a lack of rigid separation of contexts for each language, a bilingualism without diglossia. [49] When individuals operate in a world without societally

patterned allocation of different linguistic
functions, how long will it be possible to maintain
boundaries? In the political arena the lines are
drawn between assimilationist and nationalist
leaders, [50] and for the latter there is a
pervasive fear that national culture will one day
have to be expressed in English as well as in
Spanish. [51]

These concerns are exacerbated by the so called
Spanglish issue, the influence (or is it
contamination?) of English on Spanish lexicon and
vocabulary. On Spanglish the jury is still out.
Some tend to minimize this influence. Zentella, for
example, does not find evidence for widespread
replacement of Spanish lexicon with English
vocabulary items or for wholesale convergence of the
two grammars, although grammatical transfers do take
place. According to her, most code switching is a
conscious communicative choice rather than an
expression of a vocabulary deficit. [52] Other
intellectuals emphasize the reality of linguistic
change but tend to caution against value judgments,
although they, too, are wary of institutionalizing
unconsummated changes. [53]

One English language influence deserves special
mention: the impact of Black English vernacular
(BEV) on young Puerto Ricans. That this influence
should exist is hardly surprising, given the close
proximity between Blacks and Hispanics in urban
centres, plus the complex racial structure of a
Puerto Rican family in which black and white
siblings may grow up side by side. [54] But the
power of this vernacular is readily documented:
assimilation of linguistic terms, the leaving off of
end consonants, the use of verbal activities such as
ritual insults. [55] Black vernacular speech
patterns are not always happily accepted by an older
Puerto Rican generation concerned about the impact
of a stigmatized vernacular on upward mobility. But
for a younger generation the boundary between Puerto
Ricans and Blacks is frequently blurred. Perhaps
the incorporation of Black English within an already
complex bilingual repertoire is a way of coping with
these blurred boundaries.

Ultimately it is the Spanish language which is
the point of reference in this repertoire; but even
if Spanglish were not an issue, a serious identity
crisis remains. With which Spanish register are
Puerto Rican language loyalists concerned, the
Spanish spoken on their Island and implied in those
New York City public schools which use the term

Puerto Rican on official forms? Or does Spanish connote the language taught by departments of modern languages? That some directors of bilingual teacher training programmes have consciously selected a Puerto Rican register as the language of instruction [56] does not completely solve the issue. Nor do attempts to preserve the vernacular within the context of standard forms, in the way that Mark Twain imbedded his vernacular within the standard English of Huck Finn. [57] Language loyalists within the Puerto Rican community must eventually decide whether preservation of island culture is more urgent than the need to give individuals access to a Spanish of wider communication. [58] It will not be an easy choice with the resulting impact on the Puerto Ricans' cultural identity as enshrined in their language a far reaching one.

Notes and References

1. Schermerhorn R.A., Comparative Ethnic Relations. University of Chicago, (1970), 1978.
2. Personal communication, administrator in Potter Thomas Elementary School, Philadelphia, Pennsylvania;
Emigration Threatens Puerto Rico. Philadelphia Inquirer, November 4, 1983.
3. Macias, Reynaldo F., US Language-in-Education Policy: Issues in the Schools of Language Minorities. Annual Review of Applied Linguistics 1981, Newbury House, 1982.
4. For a more detailed account of this migration and its implications see Fitzpatrick, Joseph P., Puerto Rican Americans: The Meaning of Migration to the Mainland. Prentice-Hall, 1971;
Glazer, Nathan and Moynihan, Daniel Patrick, Beyond the Melting Pot: The Negroes, Puerto Ricans, Jews, Italians, and Irish of New York City. MIT Press and Harvard University Press, 1963;
Handlin, Oscar, The Newcomers. Negroes and Puerto Ricans in a Changing Metropolis. Anchor Books, Doubleday, (1959), 1962;
Mills, C. Wright, Senior, Clarence and Goldsen, Rose Kohn, The Puerto Rican Journey: New York's Newest Migrants. Russell and Russell, (1950), 1967;
Padilla, Elena, Up from Puerto Rico. Columbia University Press, 1958;
Sexton, Patricia Cayo, Spanish Harlem. Harper Colophon Books, Harper & Row, 1965.
5. United States Department of Commerce,

Bureau of the Census. Statistical Abstract of the United States, 1982-1983. Table 91. Washington: United States Printing Office, 1982.

6. Mackey, William F. and Beebe, Von Nieda, Bilingual Schools for a Bilingual Community. Newbury House, 1977.

7. See Glazer and Moynihan, op cit, also Handlin, op cit.

8. Estades, Rosa, Patterns of Political Participation of Puerto Ricans in New York City. Editorial Universitaria, Universidad de Puerto Rico, 1978;
Herbstein, Judith, The Politicization of Puerto Rican Ethnicity in New York. Ethnic Groups, 1983, 5, 1-2.

9. Mackey and Beebe, op cit;
Safa, Helen I. Caribbean Migration to the United States: Cultural Identity and the Process of Assimilation. In: Gumbert, Edgar B., ed., Different People: Studies in Ethnicity and Education. Georgia State University, 1983.

10. Traviesco, Lourdes, Puerto Ricans and Education, Journal of Teacher Education, 1975, 26, 2.

11. Puerto Rico is an autonomous political entity in voluntary association with the United States. An elected resident commissioner has a voice but no vote in the United States House of Representatives. The Constitution of 1952 allows for a tripartite government with executive, legislative and judicial branches. Senators, members of the House of Representatives, and a governor are elected every four years by popular vote. Supreme Court justices are appointed by the governor with the advice and consent of the Senate. The Constitution may be altered providing that it does not come into conflict with the Constitution of the United States or with the laws governing United States/Puerto Rican relations. The United States may not levy federal income taxes on income derived from island sources, but a federal court does have jurisdiction over the implementation of federal laws in Puerto Rico. Appeals may be carried to the United States Supreme Court. The federal government also assumes responsibility for currency, interstate commerce and defence.

12. Altbach, Philip G. and Kelly, Gail P., Education and Colonialism. Longman, 1978.

13. Cafferty, Pastora San Juan, and Rivera-Martinez, Carmen, The Politics of Language: The Dilemma of Bilingual Education for Puerto Ricans.

Puerto Rican USA

Westview Press, 1981.
14. See the following for a more detailed history of language and educational policy in Puerto Rico: Bou, Ismael Rodriguez, Significant factors in the Development of Education in Puerto Rico. In: Status of Puerto Rico, Selected Background Studies Prepared for the United States-Puerto Rico Commission on the Status of Puerto Rico, 1966; Cafferty and Martinez, op cit; Epstein, Erwin, ed., Politics and Education in Puerto Rico: A Documentary History of the Language Issue. Scarecrow Press, 1970; Kloss, Heinz, The American Bilingual Tradition. Newbury House, 1977; Leibowitz, Arnold, Educational Policy and Political Acceptance: The Imposition of English as the Language of Instruction in American Schools. Washington: Educational Resources Information Center, 1971.
15. For discussion of the implications of territoriality, see Kloss, op cit; McRae, Kenneth D., The Principle of Territoriality and the Principle of Personality in Multilingual States. International Journal of the Sociology of Language, 1975, 4; Swing, Elizabeth Sherman, Bilingualism and Linguistic Segregation in the Schools of Brussels. Quebec, Canada: International Center for Research on Bilingualism, 1980.
16. The Bilingual Education Act of 1968 (amended 1974 and 1978) provides through Title VII of the Elementary and Secondary Act of 1965 for financial assistance to local and state educational agencies for the establishment of bilingual educational programmes and to institutes of higher education for the establishment of training projects for bilingual teachers.
17. Centro de Estudio Puertorriquenos of the City University of New York, Language Policy Task Force, Language Policies and the Puerto Rican Community. Reprinted from La revista bilingue/The Bilingual Review 1978, 5, 1-2.
18. Santiago, Isaura Santiago, A Community's Struggle for Equal Educational Opportunity: Aspira v. Board of Education. Princeton, New Jersey: Office for Minority Education, Educational Testing Service 1978;
See also discussion of the debate over the 1974 amendments to the Bilingual Education Act in Schneider, Susan Gilbert, Revolution or Reform: The 1974 Bilingual Education Act. New York: Las

322

Puerto Rican USA

Americas, 1976.
    19. Fishman, Joshua A., Language Loyalty in the
United States. Mouton, 1966.
    20. Osuna, J., Report on Visits to New York
City Schools. In: Francesco Cordasco and Eugene
Bucchioni, eds., The Puerto Rican Community and its
Children on the Mainland: A Source Book for
Teachers, Social Workers and Other Professionals.
Scarecrow Press, 1972.
    21. Personal communication from participants.
    22. Kloss, op cit.
    23. Schneider, op cit.
    24. Lau v Nichols, 414 U.S. 563 (1974)
    25. Office of Civil Rights, Department of
Health, Education, and Welfare. Task Force Findings
Specifying Remedies Available for Eliminating Past
Educational Practices Ruled Unlawful Under Lau v.
Nichols. Washington: Summer 1975.
    26. Milan, William G., A Generative Analysis of
the Constituent Dimensions of Bilingual Education.
In: Fishman, Joshua A. and Keller, Gary D., eds.,
Bilingual Education for Hispanic Students in the
United States. Teachers College, Columbia
University, 1982.
    27. Centro de Estudio Puertorriquenos, op cit.
    28. Teitelbaum, Herbert and Heller, Richard J.,
The Legal Perspective. Bilingual Education, Current
Prospects: Law. Washington: Center for Applied
Linguistics, 1977.
    29. Philadelphia public schools now report
twice a year to the Office of Civil Rights on
provisions for providing students of limited English
proficiency and a dominant language other than
English with a bilingual education.
    30. Santiago, Isaura Santiago, Aspira v Board
of Education of the City of New York. New York:
Aspira of New York, Inc., 1977.
    31. Aspira of New York, Inc. et al. v. Board of
Education of the City of New York. Plaintiffs'
Memorandum of Law Regarding the Educational Programs
Appropriate and Necessary Pursuant to the Mandate of
Lau v. Nichols. May 20, 1974.
    32. Aspira of New York, Inc. et al. v. Board of
Education of the City of New York. Consent Decree.
August 29, 1974.
    33. Mackey and Beebe, op cit.
    34. Milan, William G. and Munoz-Hernandez,
Shirley, The New York City Consent Decree: A
Mechanism for Social Change. Bilingual Review,
1977, 43.
    35. Steinberg, Lois S., Can Federal Laws

Protect the Educational Interest of Language Minorities? Implementation of the Bilingual Education Act and the Aspira Consent Decree in New York City. ERIC, 1979.

36. Lourdes Traviesco, op cit, p 129.

37. United Federation of Teachers, UFT Position on Bilingual Education. October, 1974.

38. New York Times, June 21, 1976.

39. Aspira of New York, Inc. et al. v. Board of Education of the City of New York. Opinion. October 22, 1976; Aspira of New York, Inc. et al. v. Board of Education of the City of New York. Memorandum of Understanding, 1978.

40. Personal communication.

41. Santiago, Isaura Santiago, A Community's struggle for Equal Educational Opportunity. Office of Bilingual Education, Board of Education of the City of New York, City-wide Summary Lab Testing Procedures and Results; Spring 1981.

42. Office of Bilingual Education, Board of Education of the City of New York, City-wide Summary Lab Testing Procedures and Results; November 1979, Spring 1981.

43. Kjolseth, Rolf, Bilingual Education Programs in the United States: For Assimilation or Pluralism. In: Spolsky, Bernard, ed., The Language Education of Minority Children. Newbury House, 1972.

44. See Swing, Elizabeth Sherman, Flemings and Puerto Ricans: Two Applications of a Conflict Paradigm in Bilingual Education, International Journal of the Sociology of Language, 1983, 44, for a discussion of interethnic conflict and bilingual education.

45. Hoffman, Gerard, Puerto Ricans in New York: A Language Related Ethnography. In: Fishman, Joshua A., Cooper, Robert L., Ma, Roxana, Bilingualism in the Barrio. Indiana University, 1971; Wolfram, Walt, Objective and Subjective Parameters of Language Assimilation among Second Generation Puerto Ricans in East Harlem. In: Lourie, Margaret A. and Conklin, Nancy Faires, eds., A Pluralistic Nation: The Language Issue in the United States. Newbury House, 1978.

46. Schuman, Amy, Collaborative Literacy in an Urban Multiethnic Neighborhood. International Journal of the Sociology of Language, 1983, 42.

47. Fishman, Joshua A., Bilingualism and Biculturism as Individual and as Societal Phenomena. In: Fishman and Keller, eds., op cit.

Puerto Rican USA

48. Attinasi, John, Language Attitudes and
Working Class Ideology in a Puerto Rican Barrio of
New York. Ethnic Groups, 1983, 5, 1-2.
49. Tollefson, James W., Language Policy and
the Meanings of Diglossia. WORD, 1983, 34, 1.
50. Herbstein, Judith, op cit.
51. Centro de Estudio Puertorriquenos, op cit.
52. Zentella, Ana Celia, Spanish and English in
Contact in the United States: The Puerto Rican
Experience. WORD, 1982, 33.
53. Milan, William G., Contemporary Models of
Standardized New World Spanish: Origin, Development,
and Use. In: Cobarrubias, Juan and Fishman, Joshua
A., eds., Progress in Language Planning:
International Perspectives, Mouton, 1983;
Also Spanish in the Inner City: Puerto Rican Speech
in New York. In: Fishman and Keller, eds., op cit.
54. The US census does not differentiate within
the Hispanic community between races, but the
identity crisis suffered by darker members of a
single family is a sociological reality and an
important theme for Puerto Rican novelists. See for
example, Thomas, Piri, Down These Mean Streets.
Vintage Books, Random House, (1967), 1974.
55. Wolfram, Walt, Sociolinguistic Aspects of
Assimilation. Puerto Rican English in New York
City. Arlington, Virginia: Center for Applied
Linguistics, 1973.
56. The bilingual bicultural programme for
educators and other urban professionals at LaSalle
College in Philadelphia, Pennsylvania, has elected
to provide instruction in the Puerto Rican register.
57. Keller, Gary, The Ultimate Goal of
Bilingual Education with Respect to Language. In:
Fishman and Keller, eds., op cit.
58. Guitart, Jorge M., Conservative vs.
Radical Dialects in Spanish: Implications for
Language Instruction. In: Fishman and Keller, eds.,
op cit.

PRIVATE SUPPLEMENTARY SCHOOLS AND THE ETHNIC
CHALLENGE TO STATE EDUCATION IN BRITAIN

Martin McLean

Introduction
        A   significant   recent   development   in
multicultural   education   in   Britain   has   been the
growth of private classes run   by   ethnic   community
organizations   outside   normal   school   hours.   This
phenomenon is important for several reasons.
        Firstly, private classes have been   established
among   most   cultural   minorities   including both long
settled groups and the most recent immigrants.   The
total   number   of   children   in   these   classes   has   grown
quite dramatically in the last ten years.   Secondly,
the   classes   have   become   better   administered   by
effective   and   large   organizations, they use state
school   buildings,   have   regular   sources   of   finance,
and   the   children   receive   systematic teaching for
several   hours   a   week   over   a   number   of   years.
Thirdly,   the   curriculum   of   these   schools   includes
not only the ethnic community's   language,   religion
and   cultural   heritage, but, in some cases, attempts
to   duplicate   the   teaching   of   state   maintained
schools.
        These   developments   are   important not only in
themselves but because   of   recent   changes   in   the
philosophy,   organization   and   character   of   state
education.   There has been a tradition, in the past,
that state schools should not   invade   the   familiar
culture   or   preclude   possibilities   for parents to
seek private tuition for their   children.   But   the
development   of   the   common or comprehensive school
ideal has involved notions that all children   should
receive   similar   educational opportunities and that
social cohesion - even if based   on   mutual   respect
for differing cultures - can be encouraged by giving
all   pupils   a common experience in culturally mixed
institutions.
        The growth of the supplementary schools poses a

threat to the achievement of these ideals by state maintained schools as they are presently constituted. The supplementary schools themselves indicate that parents are not convinced by the claims of the state system to provide a complete education. State educators are faced with the choice, given that the aspirations demonstrated by the growth of supplementary schools are not likely to disappear, of attempting to satisfy these demands within state schools or of recognizing and working in partnership with the supplementary schools. The choice between these alternatives requires both a greater understanding of the supplementary school movement and the aspirations that lie behind it and of the present inadequacies of state schools which have prompted supplementary school growth..

The demand for supplementary school education
    Both the strength of demand and its character need to be considered in estimating the capacity for an accommodation between the supplementary school movement and the state school system. The volume of demand seems to have grown. A survey of three local authorities in 1981 suggested that between 26 per cent and 41 per cent of linguistic minority pupils were attending supplementary schools and that most schools were established after 1975. [1]
    The size of demand varies between cultural groups when measured by participation rates. Probably over 75 per cent of Japanese children and over 50 per cent of Jewish children in Britain attend supplementary schools. [2] The rates for Poles and Greek Cypriots [3] are around 30 per cent while for various groups from the Indian sub-continent and the Caribbean, where evidence of total provision is not easily collated, participation is less and in the West Indian case, probably not more than 10 per cent.
    There is a view that supplementary schools are a reflection of the nostalgia of first generation immigrants for the culture of the country of origin. It is then argued, usually by state school educators who are hostile to the supplementary school movement, that the children will reject this traditionalism and seek assimilation into the host culture. It is then claimed that these classes are inappropriate in content and methods to children in a British urban environment and will disappear after a few years.
    There is historical evidence in Britain of supplementary schools dying out with first

generation immigrants as in the case of nineteenth century Irish schools or those of Russians in the early nineteenth century. But there is also evidence of schools surviving and becoming stronger particularly in the case of the Jews who were late nineteenth and early twentieth century immigrants or Eastern European groups such as Poles and Ukrainians who arrived mainly in the 1940s. The supplementary schools of the main immigrant group of the 1950s and 1960s (West Indians, Asians, Chinese, Greek Cypriots) developed and grew mainly in the late 1970s and early 1980s at the very time when assimilationist theories would have predicted the beginnings of a decline.

However, it should not be assumed that all or even a majority of parents from a particular ethnic group will want supplementary schooling for their children. There are always likely to be differing attitudes within cultural groups towards the maintenance of the mother tongue or identity and assimilation into the host society. Some will reject traditional culture as irrelevant to their future lives while others retain it tenaciously even to the apparent detriment of their economic opportunities. But the pattern of acceptance of a traditional identity is not simple. Within most cultural groups there are traditionalists, liberals and apostates with movement of individuals from one grouping to another. While children of some ethnic minorities resent and resist parental attempts to send them to supplementary schools, the same protestors as adults and parents may re-integrate themselves into the traditional culture. [4] One of the main arguments for state support for supplementary schooling rather than a policy of teaching minority cultures in state schools is the variety and complexity of responses of individual members of ethnic groups to the preservation of their culture through education.

However a distinction should be made between the strength of motivation to maintain a group identity which affects latent demand for supplementary schooling and the opportunities for supplementary schooling which affects the degree to which latent demand becomes actual participation. Three major kinds of motivation seem to affect demand for supplementary schooling in Britain. There are in the first instance groups who want to become integrated economically, socially and politically into British society but also wish to maintain elements of the traditional culture, especially language and religion. Secondly, there are groups who set up supplementary schools in order to compensate for the failure of the state education system to provide adequate opportunities for their children to achieve economic integration into British society. Lastly, there are supplementary shools with the express purpose of preparing children for the return to their country of origin.

The phenomenon of ethnic minorities seeking economic integration while maintaining cultural separation has been described in race relations literature. Various cultural groups may retain their cultural identity and cultural exclusiveness but meet in the 'market-place'. [5] In other words, there is economic assimilation and economic success but cultural identity is preserved in non-economic areas. State schools provide avenues for desired economic assimilation while supplementary schools are agents for preserving cultural identity.

Most supplementary schools in comtemporary Britain fall into this category. They include those of the Jews, Poles, Greek Cypriots, Chinese and various groups from the Indian sub-continent. The culture that is transmitted in these schools consists of language, religion, and cultural heritage, such as music, dancing, art, festivals, drama or history. There are differences between these groups such as the degree of endogamy, the extent to which the group is economically self-contained and the emphasis that is placed in the traditional culture on language or religion, often with differences within groups as well as between them. Some of these groups, it will be seen, also use supplementary schools as a means to prepare for the repatriation of their children but the extent to which transmission of the mother culture is used within the context of aspiration of return to the country of origin or of permanent settlement in Britain varies both between and within groups.

The second motivation is to compensate for the failure of ethnic minority children to gain full economic opportunities in the state education system. This is indicated by the establishment particularly of West Indian supplementary schools to cater for a group of children whose underachievement in state schools has been marked and chronic. [6] This underachievement has been attributed to a considerable degree to discrimination by teachers and educational authorities. [7] West Indian parents do not feel that their children have a fair chance in the state system. Caribbean supplementary

schools are not intended primarily to transmit a
black culture - though this has some part in the
schools - but to cover the state school curriculum
so that the pupils' performance in external school
examinations and thus economic opportunities are
improved. There is deliberate duplication - and, in
the view of some parents, supplanting - of the work
of state schools.

However, the supplementary schools are not the
only means by which West Indian parents attempt to
improve the opportunities of their children.
Private tutors are used which seems to have some
effect on performance [8] as well as reflecting
traditions of the West Indies. Other parents are
prepared to make sacrifices to support their
children at full-time private schools. The West
Indian supplementary school movement is only one
indicator of a West Indian disenchantment with state
education and the adoption of the alternative course
of private schooling, not vast anyway, is big in
proportion.

The third kind of motivation is linked to the
first or is held by the same groups as the first.
It is to use supplementary schools as a means to
prepare children for a future in the country of
origin rather than in England. This function
traditionally has been carried out by full-time
foreign schools in Britain, - such as French, German
and American, and which have state maintained
status. It has been adopted more recently either by
groups for whom full-time mother culture schooling
is not available or, more commonly, by those who
prefer to keep options open for the children of
settlement in England or of return. The first group
includes the Japanese who are almost certain to
return and whose children need to prepare for
crucial examination for entry to Japanese middle
schools, upper secondary and higher education but
whose full-time Japanese schools in Britain provides
less than half the places for which there is a
demand. [9] The second group includes more
substantial minorities in Britain including Cypriots
(Greek and Turkish) and peoples from the Indian sub-
continent. In the case of Greek Cypriots, their
community in Britain is almost half the size of that
in Cyprus itself, travel is relatively easy and
their ranks have recently swelled by substantial
numbers of refugees from the 1974 Turkish invasion.
In the case of peoples from the Indian sub-
continent, patterns of caste marriage as well as
fears about their present and future treatment in

Britain make it wise to keep open possibilities for return through education.

Supplementary schools prepare for the possibility of return rather than its certainty, except for groups such as the Japanese. This option may never be exercised. There are groups of political exiles who would not consider repatriation a practical possibility, whose children however are increasingly being sent to visit relations in their countries of origin, for example Poland. Clearly it is difficult for governments to ascertain or predict the nature of this demand for repatriation and those that have organized schooling of immigrant group children on this assumption have been seen rightly to be discriminatory. [10] Supplementary schooling, as a private and reversable choice, offers much more flexibility.

Motivation alone does not determine attendance at supplementary schools. There are a number of contextual factors which appear to effect the extent to which latent demand is translated into pupil attendance. The basic conditions appear to be geography and socio-economic conditions. Children can only attend supplementary classes when they live within reasonable travelling distance of a suitable school. What is deemed a suitable school does depend not only on perceptions of the quality of the teaching but also, on its political, ideological or religions basis which is important when communities such as the Jews or Greeks and Greek Cypriots are divided by political ideology or religious doctrine and have separate supplementary school organizations reflecting these divisions. Ethnic communities which are geographically concentrated not only in certain cities but in particular areas of cities such as the Greeks/Greek Cypriots in areas of north and north east London have advantages in supplementary schools attendance over relatively dispersed groups such as the Chinese. However, the pattern of settlement itself is sometimes affected by a need to live close to supplementary school provision as with the Japanese in London who have remained mainly within short travelling distance of their supplementary schools, in Camden Town and St. John's Wood.

Socio-economic conditions have an important bearing since the ability to pay for supplementary schooling, or in some communities to incur the loss of child labour, appears to have a significant effect on attendance. This may not be necessarily the ability of the individual parents to pay for tuition, but that of the ethnic community as a whole. The most successful supplementary schools which have the highest participation rates are of those groups such as the Greeks and Greek Cypriots, Jews and Japanese who are, in differing degrees, relatively affluent, have community organizations which both administer and to some extent finance the schools and charge tuition fees. This allows for teachers to be paid an honorarium and for regular school buildings to be hired. The least successful in terms of participation rates and school survival are those of poorer groups such as West Indians which, though they may sometimes charge fees, are dependent upon volunteer teachers and somewhat unreliable public authority support.

These conditions have been modified by two developments. Firstly, governments of the country of origin have become involved in the supplementary school movement and, to a very variable degree, some local authorities have provided help for some supplementary schools. The governments of Greece, Turkey, Cyprus, Italy, Japan among others have helped supplementary schools in this country mainly through providing qualified teachers whose salaries they pay. This clearly has given greater organizational stability to the schools allowing for more consistent participation by children and parents. Yet this involvement can also be rejected by the minority community when, as has happened, governments attempt to give a particular political character and sometimes try to suppress private efforts within the community in Britain which are not deemed politically amenable.

Local authority intervention also has not been entirely beneficial to the supplementary school movement. Individual local authorities have given grants to supplementary schools or have allowed the free use of maintained school buildings. But these grants, which sometimes have had the effect of allowing schools to survive which would otherwise have closed, have been awarded on an irregular and patchy basis so, rather than aiding the development of the supplementary school movement, have tended to distort more natural patterns of growth.

The pattern of demand suggests that the state education system cannot easily fulfil the same functions as the supplementary schools. The use of supplementary schools to improve performance in mainstream education indicates a severe loss of confidence in state schooling by West Indian parents particularly. On the other hand, the function of

supplementary schools of transmitting the mother
culture to children whose parents wish them to
succeed in the economically valuable areas of state
education cannot be taken over easily by state
schools when the degree of demand for culture
maintenance varies so considerably within each
ethnic group, and when different members of the same
cultural group expect different kinds of mother
culture maintenance. This can be seen in the
variations in character and aims between
supplementary schools of the same cultural group.
Finally, the use of education as a means of return
to the country of origin is a sensitive issue where
hard, final and exclusive choices are avoided.
Here, too, there are great variations of intention
within groups. It would seem to be wiser for the
voluntary supplementary schools to have this
function rather than compulsory state schools.

<u>The character of the supplementary schools</u>
    There are two main issues concerning the
organization and the ethos of supplementary schools
as they affect co-operation or co-existence with the
state education system. Firstly there is the
question of whether the supplementary schools are
sufficiently well organized to survive and to become
an established part of the education system in
Britain. Secondly, there is the problem of
reconciliation of their teaching in bothstandards
and values with the aims of the state education
system.
    (a) Administration:
    The conventional stereotype of a supplementary
school is still often the one of one class for
pupils of different ages taught by an unqualified
zealot, or cynical entrepreneur, in unsuitable
premises and surviving only as long as the
enthusiasm of the organizer or the gullibility of
the consumers.
    The actual structure of supplementary schools
rarely conforms to this prejudice. A large number
of supplementary schools are run by representative
organizations of the community, especially religious
organizations (Muslim, Sikh, Hindu, Jewish, Greek
Orthodox and West Indian Seventh Day Adventist and
Pentacostal churches); which have their own
buildings in which classes can take place and full-
time clergy who act as teachers. There are secular
organizations such as the Japanese Nippon Club or
the Chinese Chamber of Commerce which can provide a
financial backing for the schools. There are parent

organizations, often running one school only as in the West Indian case or grouped into federation as with the Greek/Greek Cypriot OESEKA. The school set up o the initiative of an individual or small group does exist, especially for Afro-Caribean children, but the larger and representative organization is also common. Increasingly, where there is more than one school of a particular ethnic group in one geographical area, there is an umbrella organization to give them greater stability and continuity, for example, the Polish Ex-Combatants Association.

Yet an ideal supplementary school organization is still far from common and faces several obstacles. This ideal would be a representative organization of each cultural group in Britain which can raise the finance and resources to provide a range of classes in a number of schools, to hire and pay competent teachers and to make available accommodation and teaching materials. The obstacles to the achievement of this ideal have been: ideological, political or doctrinal divisions within the ethnic communities; the lack of a firm financial basis; and the intervention of the governments of the country of origin in ways that have undermined the autonomy of the British-based ethnic community. These constraints have affected different communities in varying degrees but have generally retarded efforts to create a stable and effective supplementary school movement.

Even so, ideological, political or doctrinal divisions within communities have not always had a deleterious effect. They have allowed parents to choose between alternatives - sometimes between relatively separatist and relatively accommodationist approaches to British society as in the case of the Jewish Liberal and Orthodox supplementary school organizations. [11] A similar division is found between the Greek/Greek Cypriot Church and Parent Association Organizations which reflects differences between political ideologies and affiliations as well as religious emphases. Some West Indian supplementary schools are run by churches while others are more secular and politically radical.

These divisions do not produce weakness when each organization is large. For instance Greek Orthodox church schools had over 5,000 pupils in 1980 while there were 3,000 students in Parent Association (OESEKA) schools. [12] They do weaken the supplementary school movement when there are a large number of small and ideologically conflicting bodies as has typified many West Indian organizations. Conflicts can be mutually destructive as when Greek conservative agencies tried to undermine the Greek Parent Association schools in the early 1970s. [13] These conflicts also make it difficult for supplementary school organizations to deal effectively with British public authorities.

Finance is a crucial issue in the effectiveness of supplementary schools. Ethnic communities whose supplementary school organizations are able to charge fees for tuition, are in a stronger position. Qualified teachers can be recruited and paid for their services, teaching materials can be bought and suitable accommodation rented. Yet the ability of parents to pay is dependent upon their economic circumstances. Few supplementary schools can emulate that of the Japanese in London which charged $pound450 per pupil in 1981 for fewer than forty Saturday morning sessions in a year. [14] Resources can be provided by sponsoring ethnic organizations or by governments of the country of origin such as those of Greece, Cyprus and Japan which recruit and pay teachers for supplementary schools. German, French or American schools are financed entirely by their governments. There is growing Polish involvement. When parents cannot afford realistic fees and when there is no sponsorship and no foreign government involvement, as in the case of many Asian and Caribbean schools, then the survival of the classes is dependent entirely on voluntary teachers' enthusiasm and the willingness of local authorities to make buildings and grants available.

The involvement of governments of the country of origin can be an organizational asset. They provide teachers and other resources over an extended period which gives greater stability and continuity to the supplementary schools. They allow for recognition of educational attendance and qualifications achieved at supplementary schools in the country of origin which facilitates the use of these schools as a means for pupils to return. But national politics also affect their involvement so that support can be withdrawn - as happened for a time with the government of Cyprus in the early 1970s. Furthermore the supplementary schools in Britain can be used to propagate the ideologies of militaristic regimes as has occurred in the cases of the governments of Greece and Turkey. Perhaps more significantly, a major contribution by foreign governments can distort the degree to which supplementary schools serve their major purpose as expressions of the cultural identity and aspirations of particular communities in Britain.

Clearly, most supplementary schools in Britain have become better organized and financed in the later 1970s and early 1980s. There are more schools which are larger and have a longer continuous history than in the 1960s and early 1970s. But a major division still exists between large, well resourced organizations and more unstable small scale schools which are dependent on voluntary effort and official support.

(b) Internal Organization:

There are two main aspects of the internal organization of the supplementary schools. Firstly there are questions about the quality of teaching and secondly issues of social values contained in it. Stereo-typical views of supplementary schools have held that the teaching is poor, ineffective and traditional and that the curriculum content, at best, is remote from the interests of the pupils and, at worst, contains wholly unacceptable values. Neither aspect of this stereotype holds good in most supplementary schools in Britain but there are still problems in both areas.

Questions about quality of teaching include the degree to which it is systematic, progressive and related to the capacities of the children; the skills and qualifications of teachers; and the teaching materials and methods used. Like most new school systems, the supplementary schools in Britain initially did teach together children of different ages whose attendance was irregular. However, most of the bigger ethnic school systems, such as the Greek or the Jewish, do provide age grading, progression of pupils through classes and systematic teaching of between two and four hours a week on one or two evenings, often on Saturdays. Many schools have a system of internal examinations, and the language based schools prepare a minority for 'O' level and 'A' level GCE examinations; a minority, since most language schools understandably concentrate on primary age range children. Where there is a clear intention that children will return to the country of origin, then classes prepare for examinations in that country, as in the Japanese case.

Schools which are not as large or well-established have attempted to compensate for the lack of systematic class progression by emphasizing individual tuition and teachers' support for

children, especially in West Indian schools. [15]
The claim that supplementary school teachers
are unqualified child-minders without any serious
pedagogic skills does not stand up in relation to
most schools which are currently operating.
However, there are difficulties regarding teachers
of several distinctly different kinds. In the
bigger and more centrally organized supplementary
school systems like those of the Greeks, Jews and
Japanese there are two kinds of teacher. There are
teachers who are fully qualified in the country of
origin (Israel, in the case of the Jews), who are
appointed and employed by that government where this
government is involved as the Greek, German or
Japanese case. There are part-time teachers from
the community who do not usually have teacher
training but, as students or professionals, have a
reasonably high educational level. Where there are
full-time qualified teachers they can set standards
of teaching for the whole school, especially when,
as in the case of Greece, Cyprus and Japan, there is
keen competition among qualified teachers to get
these jobs. Almost all teachers come from the
ethnic group and know it sufficiently well to
transmit the language, religion and culture
effectively.
However, there are complaints that teachers
appointed from the country of origin or from foreign
students with short-term residence in Britain do not
understand the British culture within which the
children live or the kind of educational experiences
they are likely to have, especially in British
primary schools. In effect they are appointed
because of their acquaintance with the mother
culture, but encounter classroom difficulties
because of their lack of familiarity with British
culture and the British education system which form
a major part of the experience of the children.
Supplementary school authorities have asked that
teachers should know more of British classroom
practice and be prepared in their teacher education
courses to deal with the kind of difficulties they
are likely to encounter more effectively.
In most West Indian and Asian schools teachers
are unpaid volunteers. Again there is a division
between qualified teachers – although in this
particular case they are qualified and work in the
British state system – and the unqualified. There
are clearly fewer problems of lack of understanding
of British culture and educational practice in the
former case though sometimes there is a lack of full

appreciation of the aspirations of the ethnic
community especially, but not exclusively, when the
teachers are British rather than from the ethnic
communities served by the school. But the central
problem is the dependence of the schools on unpaid
teachers who are working full-time in other jobs and
whose commitment is based on a self-sacrificial
enthusiasm.

Teaching methods tend to reflect the experience
and qualifications of teachers though deficiencies
in part are balanced by generally small teaching
groups, often 5 or 6 and rarely more than 15.
Teaching materials, where the government of the
country of origin is involved, tend to be the texts
used in primary schools in that country. Some
attempts have been made, especially involving Greek
and Bengali schools and the Schools Council, to
create teaching materials particularly suited to
ethnic community children born and raised in
Britain. However, the lack of permanent
accommodation, especially when classes take place in
the evenings in state schools, means that displays
and relatively stationary equipment are excluded
which inhibits the development of a richer range of
teaching methods. Nevertheless, these deficiencies
of teachers and methods are of the kind that can be
remedied by greater cooperation with public
education authorities without sacrificing the
autonomy of the supplementary schools.

(c) Curriculum:

The content of the curriculum of supplementary
schools - or more usually the mythology about it -
has been the basis of some hostility to these
institutions. There have been three kinds of
criticism. The curriculum has been criticised for
being very narrow especially in language studies,
but also sometimes in religious studies. Secondly,
the content has been felt to be remote from the
experience and interests of the pupils. Thirdly,
curriculum content and values transmitted encourage
ethnic separatism and intolerance at a time when
state schools have the aim of developing mutual
tolerance and understanding.

These criticisms, if they have any substance,
apply mainly to the schools which transmit the
ethnic culture. West Indian supplementary school
teaching focuses largely upon the subject and
content of the state school curriculum with the
express purpose of enhancing the performance of West
Indian pupils in the state school system. Some
attention has been given to an Afro-Caribbean

cultural heritage but this has been designed usually
to strengthen the cultural pride and identity of the
pupils   in   order   to   improve   their   academic
performance.   Attempts to make   it   central   to   the
work   of   the   West Indian supplementary schools has
been met by parental opposition. [16]
    The   criticisms   may   have   some   validity   for
relations   in   other   supplementary   schools.   But
clearly they have been overstated,   though   in   many
supplementary   schools   measures   have to be taken to
meet them.   The curriculum is narrow   in   the   sense
that   it   concentrates   on   the main elements of the
ethnic community identity.   This means that language
or religion form the core of   the   curriculum.   But
they   are   rarely   the   only   subjects.   Religious
schools usually also provide language teaching   such
as   Arabic   or   Urdu for Moslems or Hebrew for Jews,
with one subject   supporting   the   other.   Language
schools   often   teach   religious education as in the
Greek/Greek   Cypriot   or   Polish   classes.   Most
language   or   religious schools also have classes in
history   or   geography.   Many   include   music   and
dancing,   especially   the   Greek   schools.   Music and
dancing are central subjects in   the   curriculum   in
Greek   schools   in Cyprus.   Frequently supplementary
schools are also linked   to   youth   club   and   other
recreational   activities.   The   claim that they are
exclusively academic in character does   not   usually
stand   up to examination, except in some cases, such
as the Japanese, or in less developed   supplementary
classes.   Supplementary   schools   do   attempt   to
transmit   the   ethnic   group   culture but   usually
through a broad definition of this culture.
    The   claim   that   the   supplementary   school
curriculum is remote   from   the   experience   of   the
British   born   and British resident pupils does have
some validity, especially when   the   syllabuses   and
the textbooks of the school system of the country of
origin are used by teachers newly arrived from those
countries.   There   are   differences   between   the
experience and culture of diasporic groups   and   the
mother   country   of   which   the   curriculum does not
always take account.   But   the   work   of   producing
materials   exclusively for the supplementary schools
has been designed to overcome this problem.
    The question of   the   socially   and   culturally
divisive   effect   of   the   supplementary   school
curriculum   is   more   complex.   At   one   level
supplementary   schools in their fundamental aims are
inevitably culturally separatist.   But this does not
mean necessarily that an ethnic identity fostered by

the supplementary schools inevitably undermines the work of the state schools of encouraging mutual understanding and tolerance. The two activities can coexist providing that each is carried out in ways that are not antagonistic to the other.

Certainly there are variations between supplementary schools in the ways that a separate cultural identity is fostered. In some, the charges of an antagonistic separatism may be proven. In others there are deliberate attempts to emphasize that the children are not only part of an ethnic culture but live in a British multicultural society. This applies in many Greek schools and in all the Polish schools. In the Japanese schools, British teachers are employed to teach English and the British way of life to Japanese children. There is a recognition that the children have more than one cultural affiliation.

Analysis of supplementary schools in Britain does suggest considerable variations in aims and organization. Some are weak, fragile and probably ephemeral. Some are separatist. Some are strong and well organized. Some are culturally liberal and accomodationist. The overall trend, to the extent to which it is possible to detect one, is one of growth of numbers. There is improvement in organization and quality by the criteria used in the state system and of greater awareness of the need to reconcile the two cultures to which children belong. Yet the growth of supplementary schools, despite better organization and wider functions, still creates a threat of collision with the state education system based as much on the inflexibility and intransigence of state schooling as on similar traits in the supplementary schools.

Relations with public authorities and the state education system

There are a number of areas of existing or potential conflict between supplementary schools and the state school system. These conflicts may be examined through three main questions. First, can the supplementary schools and state schools coexist without each group changing its present character and without inflicting considerable damage on each other? Secondly, can they effectively cooperate? This cooperation may be between the communities rather than the supplementary schools and the state schools, since it might involve either the state schools taking over the functions of the supplementary schools completely or public authorities recognizing that some kinds of educational activities can only be undertaken by supplementary schools and not by the state system. Thirdly, what present policies and practices are pursued by public authorities in regard to supplementary schools and how are these likely to affect future relations between them?

Perhaps the last question is best considered first. At central government level there does not appear to have been recognition of the existence of supplementary schools, let alone any policy regarding them. Yet the British government is party to the 1977 EEC Directive which involves the provision of mother culture teaching for the children of immigrant workers. Clearly Britain has done less in this area than other European Community countries. So the supplementary schools carry out this function which few state schools undertake. It may be argued, however, that since ethnic minorities of immigrant origin (little more than 4 per cent of the population) are concentrated in a few urban areas, then the issue is one for affected Local Authorities rather than Central Government. However, some of the bases of the conflict between supplementary schools and the state system it will be seen, may require resolution at national level.

Local Authority responses have been varied. Generally they have given aid to some groups either in the form of rent-free use of state school buildings for supplementary classes, (though in other cases rents are charged), or small grants to help with the provision of resources or the transport of pupils. Yet the level of aid is small – never enough, for instance, to pay teachers – and it is unevenly distributed between ethnic groups. Though some Local Authorities have stated their support for supplementary schools in principle, [17] officials in other cases have expressed fears that supplementary schooling could undermine the achievement of the aims of state education. Local Authority support for supplementary schooling can be seen to be linked to political needs to meet the demands of ethnic group organizations at local level. The very restricted and partial nature of this support generally reflects fears about the effects of supplementary schooling on state education.

A similar pattern of response can be seen at school level. While some representatives of teacher organizations have condemned supplementary schools for being socially divisive and for placing

unreasonable pressures on children, [18] state
school headteachers in some instances have used
supplementary school teachers to give classes in
minority cultures in their schools. As with Local
Authorities there is both a recognition that the
supplementary schools are serving a role in meeting
a real demand from the community and a fear that
they could damage state education.

The main threat to the achievement of the aims
of state education in Britain posed by the
development of supplementary schools is to the ideal
of the common school and common socialization of
children. Educational policy since the 1960s, in
the main, has been directed to the reduction of
group differences within specific neighbourhoods.
Institutionally separate provision on the basis of
social class or income, sex or academic achievement
has been seen to be in conflict with the achievement
of this ideal. To the extent that the ideal of the
common school has been to help to achieve greater
equality of opportunity through education the
supplementary schools are not a threat. West Indian
classes which do aim to improve some pupils' chances
in mainstream examinations can be seen as positive
help for a particularly disadvantaged group and do
not threaten the overall aim of common schooling.

However, there has also been a secondary aim of
the comprehensive school movement of aiding contact
and social mixing between children of different
groups. This has been given another perspective
with the development of a multicultural society in
Britain. The socialization aim of the common school
has been to encourage children of different ethnic
backgrounds to learn to live together in tolerance
and in mutual appreciation. [19] It is this aim that
the supplementary schools are often believed to
threaten. This threat may not be real. The
teaching of a mother culture in supplementary
schools may not challenge the encouragement of
inter-cultural understanding among the same
children. The possibility of incompatibility does
arise, however, when the two activities do take
place in quite separate institutions.

The major conflict occurs in relation to the
broadest interpretation of the ideal of the common
school. This is that state schools should provide a
complete and common educational experience for all
children. Such an aim is clearly threatened by the
development of the supplementary schools. This
conflict could be resolved if the state education
system took over the functions of the supplementary

schools. There are obstacles to this process in the nature of the supplementary schools and in the aspirations that support them, particularly the desire of parents to have that kind of mother culture education for their children that they want and the lack of confidence of West Indian parents in state schooling. But there are also constraints related to the nature of British state education which do not allow easily for the teaching of ethnic group minority cultures.

These obstacles lie particularly in the present position of two of the major elements of mother culture identified by ethnic groups - language and religion - in state school organization and curriculum. State schools are still bound by the 1944 Education Act which states that schools must provide Christian religious education for all pupils of compulsory schooling age, albeit with the right of parents to withdraw their children from such classes. Introduction of the type of religious education provided in supplementary schools in the state system could not be accommodated easily within the terms of the 1944 Act. State schools would have ceased to remain undenominational Christian institutions.

Though a 1981 Government statement suggested that mother tongues could be taught to some pupils in secondary schools in place of the traditional European languages such as French and German, [20] foreign languages generally have experienced a decline in state comprehensive schools, related to perceptions that their teaching is over-academic and remote from pupils' experience. To incorporate the work of the supplementary schools, mother tongues would have to be taught in state primary schools where hostility to foreign language teaching - seen in the failure of French in the elementary school Teaching programmes - is even greater. [21]

There are great difficulties in the way of the incorporation of supplementary school activities in the state schools not only in the aims and practices of state schools but also the scattered and small scale of each minority culture group which creates obstacles to organizing classes for particular groups in most state schools. State schools could not accommodate easily the desire of parents in many ethnic groups to choose between the different kinds of mother culture teaching that are at present available. Attempts by state schools to supplant the supplementary schools would have many organizational difficulties and would restrict the

existing range of choice available to parents.
Public authority support for supplementary
schools is more feasible. But again there are
difficulties. The claims of different groups and
organizations have to be evaluated which involves
public arbitration between rival organizations
within the same ethnic group. Patterns of demand
have to be judged sensitively so that weakly
supported organizations are not kept alive only by
public support and popular schools are not
neglected. The major obstacle is the continuance of
official support for a monopoly of education for the
state school system when a variety of cultural
groups strongly challenge this monopoly. The trend
in the mid 1980s however is a slow move away from
the state comprehensive system.

Notes and References

1. Linguistic Minorities Project, Linguistic
Minorities in England. London University Institute
of Education, 1983.
2. Kamijo M. and McLean M., The Japanese
Community and Japanese Supplementary Schools. Paper
presented to the 11th Conference of the Comparative
Education Society in Europe, Wuerzburg, July 1983;
Chazan, B. Models of Ethnic Education: the case of
Jewish Education in Great Britain. British Journal
of Educational Studies 1978, 26.
3. Michael, M. and McLean, M., Greek and Greek
Cypriot Supplementary Schooling in England and
Wales. Paper presented to the 11th Conference of
Comparative Education Society in Europe, Wuerzburg,
July 1983;
Patterson, S. The Poles: an exile community in
Britain. In: Watson, J.L. ed., Between Two
Cultures, Blackwell, 1977.
4. Ballard, R. and C., The Sikhs, in ibid.
5. Furnivall, J.S., Colonial Policy and
Practice. Cambridge University Press, 1948.
6. Little, A. et al., The Education of
Immigrant Pupils in Inner London Primary Schools.
Race, 1968, 9;
Committee of Inquiry into the Education of Children
from Ethnic Minority Groups: Interim Report, West
Indian Children in Our Schools. (Rampton Report).
London: HMSO, 1981.
7. Ibid.
8. Wood, N., Blacks Start Out on a Par. Times
Educational Supplement, 3521, December 1983.
9. Kamijo, M. and McLean, M., op cit.

Multicultural Britain

10. Castles, S., The Social Time Bomb: Education of an Under-Class in West Germany. Race and Class. 1980, 21.
11. Chazan, B., op cit.
12. Michael, M. and McLean, M., op cit.
13. Erotikritou, M., The Cypriot Community in London and the Problem of Mother Tongue Teaching. Unpublished MA Dissertation. London University Institute of Education, 1982.
14. Kamijo, M. and McLean, M., op cit.
15. Stone, M., The Education of the Black Child in Britain. Fontana, 1981.
16. Sharron, H., Night School. Times Educational Supplement, 3523, January 1984.
17. Inner London Education Authority, Multi-Ethnic Education, 1983.
18. Spencer, D., Lessons and More Lessons for Muslims. Times Educational Supplement, 3413, November 1981.
19. Children and their Primary Schools. (Plowden Report). London: HMSO, 1967; Department of Education and Science, Education in Schools: a Consultative Document. London: HMSO, 1977.
20. Department of Education and Science, The School Curriculum. London: HMSO, 1981.
21. Department of Education and Science, Modern Languages and Comprehensive Schools. London: HMSO, 1977.

Index

Index

70, 220-6, 229, 244-
70, 287, 304-5, 307-
9, 311-12, 314-20
Stalin 146
Swahili 293
Switzerland 7
Sufism 197

Tanzania 84
Tasmania 271
teachers/teaching 12-14,
17-18, 23, 26, 45,
56, 76-7, 81, 83, 98,
99-100, 149, 151,
154, 162, 164-7, 208,
228, 231, 250, 253,
256-7, 260-1, 263-5,
279, 292-4, 299, 311,
316-17, 326, 329,
332-8, 340-3
teacher training 18, 23-
4, 53, 75, 77, 79,
81-2, 85, 98, 100-1,
124, 128-9, 147, 149,
165-6, 231, 244, 253,
261, 264-5, 279-80
Turkey 332, 335
Turkish Cypriot 330

UK 3, 9, 69-70, 75, 78,
87, 107, 123, 125,
274-5, 287, 304-5,
326-45
Ukrainian 328
unemployment 50, 53-5,
152, 262
university 16-21, 30,
40, 45, 54, 57, 79,
97-8, 103, 124, 147,
154-5, 165-8, 212-13,
221, 253-5, 257, 260,
264, 280, 294-5, 298,
312
USA 2, 4-5, 8-9, 69, 74,
78-9, 86-8, 92, 94-8,
100, 105-7, 224, 272,
286-325, 335

Vietnam 7-9, 11-39
vocational education 17,
43, 45, 52-3, 59, 64,

66, 84, 98, 100-3,
107, 123-4, 146, 152-
4, 156, 164-5, 168,
175, 212, 233, 251,
253, 258, 262

Zionism 205, 207, 209

350